industry and labor dynamics

the agent-based computational economics approach

edited by

Roberto Leombruni
Matteo Richiardi

LABORatorio R. Revelli, Italy

industry and labor dynamics

the agent-based computational economics approach

proceedings of the
wild@ace2003 workshop

Torino, Italy 3 – 4 October 2003

World Scientific

NEW JERSEY • LONDON • SINGAPORE • BEIJING • SHANGHAI • HONG KONG • TAIPEI • CHENNAI

Published by

World Scientific Publishing Co. Pte. Ltd.
5 Toh Tuck Link, Singapore 596224
USA office: 27 Warren Street, Suite 401-402, Hackensack, NJ 07601
UK office: 57 Shelton Street, Covent Garden, London WC2H 9HE

British Library Cataloguing-in-Publication Data
A catalogue record for this book is available from the British Library.

INDUSTRY AND LABOR DYNAMICS
The Agent-Based Computational Economics Approach
Proceedings of the Wild@Ace 2003 Conference

ISBN 981-256-100-5

Printed in Singapore by World Scientific Printers (S) Pte Ltd

Contents

THE WILD@ACE PROJECT*

BRUNO CONTINI
Università di Torino [†] *& LABORatorio Revelli* [‡]
bruno.contini@unito.it

ROBERTO LEOMBRUNI
LABORatorio Revelli
leombruni@labor-torino.it

MATTEO RICHIARDI
LABORatorio Revelli
m.richiardi@labor-torino.it

Keywords: Computational economics; agent-based simulation; economic methodology.

1. The Wild@Ace Project

From time to time, innovative methodologies are introduced to the modeling arena which produce a sense of great excitement in some researchers and a sense of great irritation in others. The latest of these self-proclaimed "revolutions" may very well be Computational Economics, among whose enthusiast non-practitioners stands Richard Freeman. In his well-known "War of the Models" article [5], Freeman expresses great faith in the potential of several techniques which lie at the intersection of Evolutionary Economics, Computer Science and Cognitive Science:

*the authors are grateful to the participants of the wild@ace 2003 conference for their valuable comments and suggestions. usual disclaims apply.
[†]università di torino, dipartimento di economia, via po 53, 10124 torino, italy
[‡]laboratorio revelli, via real collegio 30, 10024 moncalieri (torino), italy, http://www.labor-torino.it

> Our empirical tools are wonderful for *ceteris paribus* problems, but many issues regarding labor institutions are *mutatis mutandis* problems. Lots of interrelated changes with no empirical counterfactuals. This implies that if we are to make progress, we need something more in our tool bag. Game theory? A language and framework, but not sufficiently specific. General equilibrium? Too general and static. Then what? [...] There are a new set of theoretic and empirical tools that seem suited for the problem of analyzing labor systems and the War of the Models. The tools range from theoretical simulations of nonlinear dynamic systems to a theoretic data-mining. Complexity analysis. Neural networks. Data-mining for knowledge discovery. Landscape models. Artificial agent simulated societies. Chaos theory. Complex adaptive systems. Nonparametric statistical tools of diverse shapes and sizes. Cellular automata. The hills are alive with the sound of new tools and jargon.

True, simulations have been around in Economics for years, although they have been used mainly for predictive purposes. And, true, simulations have played an important role in only a limited number of relevant results, whether these be theoretical or empirical. In fact, one often has to draw on the classic work of Schelling [16], in order to defend the simulation approach against the arguments of skeptical economists. Yet despite all this, and perhaps unbeknownst to the general public, a vigorous strand of research is growing and developing in the field. The Wild@Ace project forms part of this movement. The acronym, which stands for "Workshop on Industrial and Labor Dynamics – The Agent-based Computational Approach", identifies the intersection between a specific area of interest, namely Labor Economics and Industrial Organization, and a methodology, the agent-based simulation approach. The project was inaugurated in 2003, with the first Wild@Ace conference held on October 3–4 at the LABORatorio Revelli Centre for Employment Studies in Turin, Italy. The workshop, which was jointly organised by the LABORatorio Revelli, the Department of Economics "S. Cognetti De Martiis" of the University of Turin, and the Social Interaction Economics and Computing group (SIEC) of Ancona (Italy), was the first event ever to have this particular focus. The workshop will be run annually.[a] This volume is a collection of the papers presented at the

[a]The next workshop is scheduled to be held again at the LABORatorio Revelli in December 2004.

Wild@Ace 2003 conference.

This introduction is structured as follows. In section 2 we briefly discuss the meaning of agent-based simulations and their potential for use in economic modeling. Then, in section 3 we elaborate on Freeman's hot list of topics for which traditional (algebraic) modeling has proved – to his and our judgment – insufficient, focusing in particular on the role of institutions. Then, we turn to the appropriateness of agent-based simulations for taking on these challenges (section 4). In particular, we respond to the skepticism that mainstream economists often express toward this novel methodology. We analyze the main objections that can be made against agent-based simulations, and show that appropriate solutions do exist. Finally, Section 5 summarizes the main contributions to this volume.

2. Why Write an Agent-based Simulation?

Agent-based models are computer models in which a multitude of agents - each embodied in a specific software code - interacts. These agents can represent individuals, households, firms, institutions, etc. Moreover, "special" agents can be added to observe and monitor individual and collective behavior.

Agent-based simulation models have two distinguishing features. One is that they are *agent-based*, *i.e.* they follow a micro approach; the other is that they are *simulation models*, *i.e.* they follow an inductive approach to the discovery of regularities. Neither feature is exclusive to the methodology. Many algebraic models have micro-foundations (e.g. Game Theory), and many simulation models adopt an aggregate perspective (e.g. System Dynamics). However, it is the intersection of the two approaches that defines the methodology and that permits the extreme flexibility in design of the model, while avoiding all the problems connected with merely aggregate representations of the world [9], [10]. Agent-based simulation models are a third way between fully flexible but not computable and hardly testable literary models (which provide no more than a verbal description of the causal relationships behind a given phenomenon) on one side, and more transparent but highly simplified algebraic models on the other side [6]. The biggest advantage of ACE models over the algebraic approach is their flexibility, since the results are computed and need not be solved analytically. With ACE, the researcher gains almost complete freedom over the specification of the interaction structure and individual behavior.[b]

---

[b]As is always the case, this freedom must be exercised with caution. With less of a need

Building on Robert Axtell [1], three distinct uses of agent-based computation in the social sciences can be identified and ranked according to their auxiliary nature in comparison with algebraic modeling.[c] The first use is *numerical computation of analytical models.* Note with Axtell that

> [t]here are a variety of ways in which formal models resist full analysis. Indeed, it is seemingly only in very restrictive circumstances that one ever has a model that is completely soluble, in the sense that everything of importance about it can be obtained solely from analytical manipulations.

Situations in which numerical computation may prove useful include cases where (a) a model is not analytically soluble for some relevant variable, (b) a model is stochastic, and the empirical distribution of some relevant variable needs to be compared with the theoretical one, of which often few moments are known, (c) a model is solved for equilibrium, but the out-of-equilibrium dynamics are not known. In particular, with reference to this last point, it may be that multiple equilibria exist, that the equilibrium or (at least some of) the equilibria are unstable or that they are realized only in the very long run. Conversely, it may be that equilibria exist but are not computable. Axtell provides references and examples for each case. Finally, it is often the case that the equilibrium is less important than the out-of-equilibrium fluctuations or extreme events. Clearly, agent-based simulations are not the only way to perform numerical computations of a given analytical model. However, they may prove effective and simple to implement, especially for models with micro-foundations.

The second use is *testing the robustness of analytical models* with respect to departures from some of the assumptions, which may relate to the behavior of the agents, or to the structure of the model. ACE models can easily include bounded rationality [15], [12], [4] and heterogeneity at an individual level, and investigate variations in the way agents interact with one another or with the institutional setting. One important feature of ACE is that in considering departures from the assumptions of the reference model, a number of different alternatives can be investigated, thus offering clues toward a generalization of the model itself.

---

to adopt standard modeling frameworks comes the risk of losing the comparability of models. Also, the greater variability in modeling choices can lead to greater variability in the quality of ACE works.

[c]The three categories identified below only partially correspond to Axtell's.

The first two uses of ACE models are *complementary* to algebraic analysis. The third use is a *substitute*, as it goes beyond the existence of an algebraic reference model. It provides *stand-alone simulation models* for (a) problems that are analytically intractable, or (b) problems for which an algebraic solution bears no advantage. The latter may occur when negative results are involved, for instance. A simulation may be all that is needed to show that some institution or norm is wrong, or that it does not work in the intended way. Algebraic intractability may arise when more complicated assumptions are needed, or when the researcher wants to investigate the overall effect of a number of mechanisms (each of which is possibly already understood analytically in simpler models) simultaneously at play.

3. Old and New Challenges: A Bulletin from the War of the Models

However, one may ask, *do we really need* to recur to agent-based simulations? Are the limitations of algebraic models described above really so important to the understanding of economic phenomena, and in particular of labor economics issues? Freeman, in the above quoted article, stresses that one of the most difficult challenges faced by the profession is understanding how institutions and markets interact. The few things we do know about this point remain mostly at a qualitative level. In Freeman's words:

(1) there is no law of one institution: capitalism allows variety;
(2) institutions affect work / non work decisions (institutions that pay people not to work will reduce work);
(3) institutions affect outcomes by affecting incentives (shadow economy, tax evasion, illegal immigration, wages below minimum, unsafe working conditions);
(4) human psychology matters; people's rationality is bounded;
(5) institutions do not affect macro-outcomes consistently;
(6) some institutional solutions don't work: training and active labor market policies have at best only modest effect on outcomes; work sharing didn't work in Germany and France, while it did in Holland (with substantial wage moderation and various welfare state reforms).

This is not much indeed. The crucial problem is that we lack systemic understanding of labor institutions (unions, employer associations, government agencies, *etc.*): we do not know how much other institutions matter in shaping the relationship between a particular institution and the observed outcome.

The multidimensional features of the institutional setting are well illustrated in a recent and very welcome paper by Botero *et al.* [3]. Their careful taxonomical study of labor regulation in 85 OECD countries reveals the existence of a great number of different typologies, as shown in table 1.

alternative employment contracts	9 typologies
conditions of employment	13 typologies
job security	18 typologies
industrial relations laws	12 typologies
collective disputes	16 typologies
social security laws	6 typologies
sickness and health benefits	6 typologies
unemployment benefits	6 typologies
political and economic constraints	6 typologies

It would be inaccurate to suggest here that the overall number of configurations characterizing labor market activities is equal to all the possible combinations of the above typologies (of the order of 9 to the 9th power). Nonetheless it is all too evident that the degree of complexity of the system is gigantic.

The authors compress the above typologies into 12 multidimensional indicators and 3 supercompressed aggregate indicators of employment laws, industrial relations laws and social security laws, and heroically produce some econometric estimation about the features of government regulation of labor. In their veiw, the reported evidence is inconsistent with efficiency theories since, contrary to predictions, poor countries regulate labor markets more than rich countries, social security is not a substitute for labor regulation, and such regulation has adverse consequences on unemployment, participation and official economic activity. The evidence is also inconsistent with a basic version of political theory, which sees heavier regulation of labor as a reflection of the political power of the left. The evidence is, instead, broadly consistent with legal theory, according to which patterns of regulation across countries are shaped largely by their legal structure, which came down to most countries through transplantation of four main legal systems: the English, Socialist, French and German ones.

While it is premature to draw conclusions from this important but very preliminary work on the impact of institutions on economic outcomes, it is evident that the underlying degree of "complexity" cannot be dealt with using standard econometric tools.

We thus return to the theme of the advantages offered by agent-based simulations. While they obviously will not be able to furnish answers to all open-ended questions, still

> the new tools can sharpen our thinking about competing models of capitalism and allow us to assess alternative theories or explanations about which we could previously only hand wave. Say, we have evidence that people care deeply about fairness in the market and are more willing to form a group or support state interventions when they see market outcomes as unfair. Say, we have evidence that firms oppose unions strongly unless the unions can organise enough competitors to take wages out of competition, and that workers are more likely to join unions when their neighbours are joining. Say, we have evidence that political parties respond to employee discontent by enacting redistributive legislation. We have all the elements for an artificial agent computer model in which inequalities that workers judge as unfair produce either spurts in unionisation or state interventions in the distribution of earnings, or maybe both. Perhaps most important, the new tools make demands on our knowledge that should spur us to greater efforts to measure key parameters and relations. If we believe that there are important synergies among institutions, and we are forced to simulate those interactions on a computer rather than simply talk about them, we will quickly find out which parameters or relations are critical to outcomes, and hopefully, try to figure out ways to gather that evidence. We may not be able to apply our normal empirical tools to entire models, but those tools should help us identify some of the key parts of the models. (Freeman, *ibidem*).

4. Rationalizing Criticism

However, many economists remain highly skeptical. Their battle horse is that simulations, as opposed to algebraic modeling, "do not prove anything". To a closer inspection, this general concern boils down to the belief that agent-based simulations are (i) *difficult to interpret*; (ii) *difficult to generalize* and (iii) *difficult to estimate.* In this section we briefly discuss each issue. With respect to the first problem, in order to understand the dynamics of a simulated system the aggregate law of motions must be recovered. These functions, which in algebraic models usually have an explicit and compact form, in an agent-based model can be explored locally and estimated in the artificial data resulting from a number of simulation runs. The second issue relates to the problem of making statements about the behavior of a model even for cases not included in the data on which the model is validated. While very little can be done to this respect when the model is nonlinear (but this is true regardless of the methodology of inspection adopted, *i.e.* both for algebraic and simulation models), the great number of simulation runs that can easily be performed on modern computers assures a good level of confidence in the characterization of the dynamics of the model. The last objection concerns the possibility of estimating the structural parameters of a simulation model. Since the law of motion of the aggregate variables, which can be considered as *reduced forms* of the system, are not explicitly derived, it is not possible to exploit the one-to-one relationship between the structural and the reduced form parameters, in identified models. But other econometric techniques, such as the method of simulated moments, can be successfully employed for structural estimation.

4.1. *Interpretation*

A rather common misunderstanding about simulations is that they are not as sound as mathematical models. In particular, they do not offer a compact set of equations – together with their inevitable algebraic solution – which can easily be interpreted and discussed.

Actually, simulations *do* consist of a well-defined (although not concise) set of functions. These functions, which may be either deterministic or stochastic, unambiguously define the macro dynamics of the system. Moreover, the eventual unique equilibrium of the macro dynamics is, in turn, a known function of the structural parameters and initial conditions of the simulation. We will show here that the only difference from a model consisting of an algebraically solved set of equations is in the degree of knowledge that we have about these functions.

Let us start from the following general characterization of dynamic micro models. Assume that at each time t an individual i, $i \in 1 \dots n$, is well described by a status variable $x_{i,t} \in \Re^k$. Let the evolution of her status variable be specified by the difference equation:

$$x_{i,t+1} = f_i(x_{i,t}, x_{-i,t}; \alpha_i). \tag{1}$$

where we assume that the behavioral rules[d] may be individual-specific both in the functional form of the phase line $f_i(.)$ and in the parameters α_i, and may also be based on the status x_{-i} of all individuals other than i.

Once we have specified the behavior of each individual, we will typically be interested in some macro feature of our economy, that we may represent as a statistic Y defined over the entire population:

$$Y_t = s(x_{1,t}, \ldots, x_{n,t}). \tag{2}$$

Is it always possible to solve equation (2) for each t, or does it depend on the functional form that we choose for $f_i(.)$? The answer is that it is always possible, no matter what specification is adopted. It is sufficient to solve iteratively each term $x_{i,t}$ in (2) using (1), to end up with:

$$\begin{aligned} Y_0 &= s(x_{1,0}, \ldots, x_{n,0}) \\ Y_1 &= s(x_{1,1}, \ldots, x_{n,1}) \\ &= s(f_1(x_{1,0}, x_{-1,0}; \alpha_1), \ldots, f_n(x_{n,0}, x_{-n,0}; \alpha_n)) \\ &\equiv g_1(x_{1,0}, \ldots, x_{n,0}; \alpha_1, \ldots, \alpha_n) \\ &\vdots \\ Y_t &= g_t(x_{1,0}, \ldots, x_{n,0}; \alpha_1, \ldots, \alpha_n) \end{aligned} \tag{3}$$

The law of motion (3) uniquely relates the value of Y at any time t to the initial conditions of the system and to the values of the parameters α_i. Sometimes[e], g_t may converge to a function not dependent on t[f], so that we also have an expression for the equilibrium value of Y, again as a function of the initial conditions and parameters:

$$Y^e = \lim_{t \to \infty} Y_t \equiv g(x_{1,0}, \ldots, x_{n,0}; \alpha_1, \ldots, \alpha_n), \tag{4}$$

Notice that this formalization describes both "traditional" dynamic micro models and agent-based simulations. The fact that a behavioral rule

[d]here and in the following we use "behavioral rules" and similar terms in a loose sense that encompasses the actual intentional behaviors of individuals as well as other factors such as technology *etc.*

[e]When the dynamic system has a unique, stable equilibrium and the initial conditions lie in its basin of attraction.

[f]or even not dependent on the initial conditions

is embedded within a piece of code in a simulation and may be full of "if...then..." clauses, does not mean that it is not a function. The only relevant difference between two very simple functions such as a Cobb Douglas and a rule of thumb is that the latter is a bit more unhandy to manipulate algebraically.

Indeed, given this common framework, it is easy to discuss the alleged differences in terms of "mathematical soundness". To explore this point, let us consider how the framework is implemented in the two approaches.

As an example of the "traditional approach" think of a model based on a representative agent. The behavioral rule (1), will be very simple in structure, since all subscripts i can be dropped, along with any reference to other individuals' behavior.

In turn, any "macro" statistic considered will collapse on a transformation of the status variable of just one individual, and the resulting law of motion (3) will also be very simple.

We thus end up with a simple formulation for all equations (1)-(3), and usually also for equation (4). By "simple formulations" we mean that they can be manipulated algebraically, and general propositions about our economy can be stated by computing derivatives, comparing different equilibrium solutions, and so on.

Let us turn to the agent-based simulation approach. The critical factor rests in the formula for the macro dynamics (3), the law of motion of Y. As t and n get higher, the expression for $g_t(.)$ can easily grow enormous, hindering any attempt at symbolic manipulation, *i.e.* any attempt to solve it algebraically.[g]

Nevertheless, the functions (3) are completely specified. It is thus possible to explore their local behavior, by computing the value of Y corresponding to different values of the parameters and the initial conditions. A way to extrapolate this point evidence, and thus to recover a local approximation of the shape of $g_t(.)$, is to specify a functional form $\hat{g}_t(x_{1,0}, \ldots, x_{n,0}, \alpha_1, \ldots, \alpha_n, \beta)$ to be fitted on the artificial data generated by the simulation runs, where β are the coefficients of $\hat{g}_t(.)$. For instance, if $\hat{g}_t(.)$ is assumed to be linear, there will be two coefficients β_0 and β_1 (the intercept and the slope) to be estimated in the artificial data.

The use of econometric techniques to approximate $g_t(.)$, starting from

[g]This difficulty is the same experienced in game theory models, where games typically become intractable if they involve more than a handful of players.

a number of - somehow designed - artificial experiments is indeed common practice in the computer science literature. The resulting regression model is also known as *metamodel, response surface, compact model, emulator, etc.* [11].

4.2. *Generalization*

A cause of concern with this procedure stems from the possibility that the artificial data may not be representative of all outcomes the model can produce. In other words, it is possible that as soon as we move to different values of the parameters, the behavior of $g_t(.)$ will change dramatically, for example exhibiting singularities. The metamodel $\hat{g}_t(.)$ will then become a poor description of the simulated world. While algebraic results are conditional only on the specific hypothesis made about the model, simulation results are conditional on the specific hypothesis of the model, the specific values of the parameters used in the simulation runs and the initial conditions. At a theoretical level, this issue can be answered with two observations. First, if it applies to what we know about the artificial world defined by the simulation model, it also applies to what we know about the real world. As the real data generating process is itself unknown, stylized facts could in principle go wrong at some point in time. From an epistemological point of view, our belief that the sun will rise tomorrow remains a probabilistic assessment. Second, we should not worry too much about the behavior of a model for particular "evil" combinations of the parameters, as long as these combinations remain extremely rare.[h] If the design of the experiments is sufficiently accurate (often particular combinations of the relevant parameter can be guessed, and oversampled in the artificial experiments), the problem of how "local" the estimated local data generating process is becomes marginal.

While the curse of dimensionality places a practical upper bound on the size of the parameter space that can be checked for robustness,

[h]The relevant exception is when rare events are themselves the focus of the investigation, for instance as in risk management. Here, simulations may prove extremely useful, by dispensing from making assumptions - such as the gaussian distribution of some relevant parameters - which may be necessary in order to derive algebraic results but have unpleasant properties - like excessively thin tails. In a simulation, the reproduction of such rare events is limited only by the computational burden imposed on the computer. However, techniques can be used in order to artificially increase the likelihood of their occurrence.

> it is also the case that vast performance increases in computer hardware are rapidly converting what was once perhaps a fatal difficulty into a manageable one [1].

A rather different problem stems from the application of agent-based simulations to the analysis of complex systems. ACE enthusiasts often link the future of the methodology to the claim that it is best suited for the analysis of such systems. Since the world is intrinsically non-linear and complex, the argument goes, ACE should take the center stage in the modeling arena (see [7] and Kirman, this volume). Now, it is true that non-linear models often resist algebraic analysis, while their implementation in an agent-based simulation setting brings little additional cost, with respect to linear models. But non-linear models of complex systems generally give rise to a number of issues, which may pose severe limits on the possibility of generalizing the results. The first one is *sensitive dependence on initial conditions*, *i.e.* the well-known "butterfly effect" (the possibility that a butterfly's wing in Brazil may set off a tornado in Texas, in Lorenz's original words). A second problem is *equifinality* [2], [14], *i.e.* the existence of many structural models characterized by the same fit with the real data, but having different out-of-sample properties. A third problem is *overfitting*, *i.e.* the risk of having a model that is too complex, and that may fit the noise in addition to the signal in the data. The "butterfly effect" challenges the possibility of fitting a reduced metamodel to the artificial data, and of estimating the parameters of the structural model. Equifinality on the other hand challenges the very possibility of choosing an appropriate specification for the structural model. Overfitting is a much narrower problem, as it merely increases the risk of making an incorrect specification choice. While we recognize the theoretical relevance of these problems, we would like to point out that they are equally an issue for algebraic models as well as for simulations. Moreover, as they have not prevented the development of many successful models of non-linear systems, either in Economics or in other fields, they will be discussed no further here.

4.3. *Estimation*

The approximation of the law of motion $g_t(.)$ of the aggregate variable Y cannot be used for further estimation on real data. It has no unknown coefficients. It simply describes how the simulation model behaves, for given values of the structural parameters and the initial conditions. As such, it can be used to assess whether the simulation model is able to mimic the phenomenon of interest, by imposing the same metamodel $\hat{g}_t(.)$ on the real data, and comparing the coefficient vector $\hat{\beta}$ estimated on the artificial data with the coefficient vector $\tilde{\beta}$ estimated on the real data. Now, different coefficient vectors $\hat{\beta}$ are obtained for different values of the structural parameters vectors α_i. Intuition may suggest that we are not far from being able to estimate the structural parameters themselves. For instance, we could compare the outcome of the simulation with the real data, and change the structural coefficients values until the distance between the simulation output and the real data is minimized. In the simulation literature, this is called *calibration*. In the econometrics literature, it is called *structural estimation*, and can also be performed by means of *simulation-based estimation* methods [8].

Another objection says that the richer specifications of simulation models often lead to underidentification, due to the lack of exclusion restrictions. This claim seems to suggest that algebraic models are characterized by lean specifications only to avoid the problem of underidentification, and not because of symbolic tractability.

Moreover, underidentification should not be the greatest fear in writing a model. Rather, the inability of a model to provide a good description of the underlying phenomenon is a much greater limit.

> Economic variables are considered by econometricians as mutually dependent, but the degree of simultaneity is recognized only to the extent that it does not prevent the structural coefficients from being identified. But is there any logical reason why the degree of simultaneity must always stop short of causing real troubles? The answer given in the literature is that economic theory or a priori information often requires us to exclude from a given structural relationship a sufficient number of variables so that it become overidentified. [...] [Q]uite to the contrary, economic theory requires the inclusion of a much larger number of variables than those included in the existing models of economic structures. The complexity of modern economic societies makes it much more likely that the true structural relationships are underidentified rather than overidentified. [13]

Simulation allows complex models. This must be considered as a positive rather than a negative feature, since it makes possible a more detailed description of the phenomena of interest. The risk of underidentification is often simply unavoidable, the structural coefficients being *really* indeterminate: algebraic models that claim to be immune are sometimes only poor models.

5. The Wild@Ace Contributions

The models presented in this volume provide worthy attempts at improving on the existing literature in several ways, although they obviously do not answer all of the still unresolved questions we discussed in section 3. Their specification is indeed generally richer than that of their traditional (algebraic) counterparts. This is in line with the logic of agent-based simulations described above.

The volume is structured as follows. Part 1 (**Methodology**) is devoted to methodological issues. The first contribution is by Kirman and can be considered a sort of second editorial. It deals with the opportunity of exploiting ACE models in order to gain intuitions about the two-way feedback between the microstructure and the macrostructure of a phenomenon of interest. How is it that simple aggregate regularities may arise from individual disorder? Or that a nice structure at an individual level may lead to a complete absence of regularity in the aggregate? How is it that the complex interaction of very simple individuals may lead to surprisingly complicated aggregate dynamics? Or that sophisticated agents may be unable to organize themselves in any interesting way? Kirman suggests, with examples, that the economy should indeed be conceived of as a complex system. Thus, its aggregate properties do not reflect and are not derived from the corresponding characteristics of individual behavior. The second contribution, by Leombruni, explores the methodological status of agent-based simulations. Then, we turn to an historical perspective with the chapter by Novarese. Sonnessa concludes this section with a presentation of JAS, a new set of libraries that greatly facilitate the design and implementation of agent-based models.

Part 2 of the volume (**Microsimulation of Labor Dynamics**) is devoted to the study of the labor market. In particular, we present a set of articles that deal with extensions of the search paradigm, which has captured center stage in Labor Economics in recent years. Dosi and coauthors, Neugart and Richiardi all focus on job search and matching between firms and workers. Dosi, Fagiolo and Gabriele present an innovative evolutionary model with endogenous formation of aggregate demand and price. They are able to recover aggregate regularities such as the Beveridge, Wage and Okun curve. Moreover, they show that an Okun coefficient > 1 can arise even if individual firms employ production functions exhibiting constant returns to labor. Neugart focus on the properties of a matching function emerging endogenously from the microstructure of the model. In his model, and contrary to what is normally acknowledged in the literature, the endogenous matching technology is subject to decreasing returns to scale. Moreover, the aggregate matching function is affected by labor market policies. This raises concerns about the validity of labor market policy evaluations conducted with flow models of the labor market employing exogenous matching functions. Richiardi innovates on the existing literature by introducing industrial dynamics issues such as the distribution of firm size and age and endogenous birth and death rates into a search theoretic framework. By comparing a benchmark equilibrium algebraic model with its bounded rationality, off-equilibrium agent-based implementation, he shows that the equilibrium model has very uninteresting out-of-equilibrium behavior, but that simple variations in its specifications may lead to more realistic dynamics.

The section is concluded by Pingle and Tesfation, who study the evolution of employer-employee networks under different payment structures, and by Bianchi *et al.*, who in an applied work present a microsimulation model of the Italian economy, considering heterogeneous workers who choose their retirement age based on expected lifetime incomes. The model is used to evaluate different reform proposals of the pension system.

Part 3 (**Understanding Firm Behaviour**)deals with the analysis of firms. In their chapter, Gallegati *et al.* look at the connection between firm size distribution and the business cycle. They develop an agent-based model of the financial fragility of firms that is able to reproduce Power Law distributions of firm size and shifts of this distribution over the business cycle. The chapter by Kaufmann focuses on the innovative capacities of the firms, while the one by Dal Forno and Merlone studies their hierarchical structure.

Part 4 (**Industrial Clusters and Firm Interaction**), with articles by Zhang, Ahrweiler *et al.*, Ciarli and Valente, Boero *et al.* and Khoshyaran, concerns the analysis of networks of firms. In particular, Zhang focus on the relationship between entrepreneurship and the local social context, in order to explain the emergence of clusters.

Part 5 (**Mathematical tools**), although different in the methodology used, is highly connected with part 4. It consists of only one paper, by Garibaldi, Costantini and Viarengo, who offer a mathematical tool (a finitary characterization of the Ewens Sampling formula) for the analysis of clustering.

Finally, Gilbert – based on the panel discussion at the end of the Wild@Ace conference – offers a concluding overview of the opportunities provided by ACE modeling and the still unresolved methodological issues. In particular, he focuses on the connection of agent-based models with other studies employing more traditional techniques, on their empirical validation, and on the criteria that should be used to evaluate their explanatory success. His main point, which can be stated as the need for more integration between real and artificial data, is the key topic of the Wild@Ace 2004 conference.

References

1. R. Axtell. Why agents? on the varied motivations for agent computing in the social sciences. In *Proceedings of the Workshop on Agent Simulation: Applications, Models and Tools.* Argonne National Laboratory, IL, 2000.
2. L. V. Bertalanffy. *General System Theory Foundations, Development, Applications.* George Braziller, New York, revised edition, 1969.
3. J. Botero, S. Djankov, R. L. Porta, F. L. de Silanes, and A. Shleifer. The regulation of labor. NBER WP 9756, 2003.
4. J. Conlisk. Why bounded rationality. *Journal of Economic Literature,* 34(2):669–700, June 1996.
5. R. Freeman. War of the models: Which labour market institutions for the 21st century? *Labour Economics,* 5:1–24, 1998.
6. N. Gilbert and P. Terna. How to build and use agent-based models in social science. *Mind & Society,* (1):57–72, 2000.
7. G. Goldspink. Methodological implications of complex systems approaches to sociality: Simulation as a foundation for knowledge. *Journal of Artificial Societies and Social Simulation,* 5(1), 2002.
8. C. Gourieroux and A. Monfort. *Simulation-Based Econometric Methods.* Oup/Core Lecture Series. Oxford University Press, Oxford, 1997.
9. A. P. Kirman and M. Gallegati. *Beyond the Representative Agent.* Edward Elgar, Oxford, 1999.
10. A. P. Kirman and J.-B. Zimmerman. *Economics with Interacting Agents.* Springer Verlag, Heidelberg, 2001.
11. J. Kleijnen. Experimental design for sensitivity analysis, optimization, and validation of simulation models. In J. Banks, editor, *Handbook of Simulation,* chapter 6, pages 173–223. Wiley, New York, 1998.
12. A. Leijonhufvud. Towards a not-too-rational macroeconomics. *Southern Economic Journal,* 50(1):1–13, 1993.
13. T. Liu. Underidentification, structural estimation, and forecasting. *Econometrica,* (28):855–865, 1960.
14. K. A. Richardson. On the limits of bottom-up computer simulation: Towards a nonlinear modeling culture. In *Proceedings of the 36th Hawaii International*

Conference on System Sciences, 2002.

15. T. J. Sargent. *Bounded Rationality in Macroeconomics.* Clarendon Press, Oxford, 1993.
16. T. Schelling. *Micromotives and Macrobehaviour.* W.W.Norton, New York, 1978.

Section 1
Methodology

ECONOMICS AND COMPLEXITY

ALAN KIRMAN
CGREQAM, EHESS, Universite d'Aix Marseille
2 Rue de la Charite, 13002 Marseille
kirman@ehess.vcharite.univ-mrs.fr

This paper presents a view of the economy as a complex system with heterogeneous interacting agents who collectively organise themselves to generate aggregate phenomena which cannot be regarded as the behaviour of some average or representative individual. There is an essential difference between the aggregate and the individual and such phenomena as bubbles and crashes, herd behaviour the transmission of information and the organisation of trade are better modelled in the sort of framework suggested here than in more standard economic models.

Keywords: Aggregation; interaction; self-organisation; herd behaviour; rationality.

1. Introduction

Complexity and complex systems are terms which are widely used but not always carefully defined. Few would argue that the economy is not a complex system, but without a clear specification of what we mean by this, we are not much further forward. What might be thought of as the characteristics of a complex system and how many of these characteristics are shared by economies? Three of the charateristics most frequently found in the literature on complex systems are the following: they are composed of interacting "agents", these agents may have simple behavioural rules, the interaction among the agents means that aggregate phenomena are intrinsically different from individual behaviour. The idea that a large collection of interacting objects can produce behaviour at the aggregate level which could not be thought of as corresponding to some blown up version of individual behaviour is far from new. What is newer is the idea that such systems may tend to organise themselves and, perhaps more, that there may be common features of that behaviour in many, apparently very different, types of system. Thus, features of the behaviour of collections of neurons may share properties with air masses and with social systems. It is the "emergence" of organisation and the associated aggregregate features that is emphasised by the founders of what has come to be known as the science of "complexity". Among the leading exponents of what might loosely be called complexity theory are Anderson, Gell-Mann, and Kauffman, all of whom are closely identified with the Santa Fe Institute. Several collections of papers applying these ideas to economics have appeared [1], [4]. [18] presents a simple and clear account of the basic notions.

How are these developments related to the standard view of economics? In economics, many of the features of interaction mentioned are what have been referred to as "externalities", the fact that the behaviour of some individuals has direct consequences for others. Such externalities are typically thought of as "market imperfections" whereas the main theme of this paper is that they should be considered as central and not marginal. Rather than regard externalities as an annoying distortion of the basic model the idea here is that our models should be built around the interactions and the externalities generated by those interactions. Hans Föellmer [10] in a path-breaking paper showed how important direct interactions were in determining whether or not an economy would have well determined aggregate behaviour as the number of agents becomes large. His important contribution was to show that this was not necessarily the case if the interactions between agents were strong enough.

In the more conventional economic literature, the first substantial plea for taking externalities more seriously was that of Schelling [23]. He argued that in the presence of externalities there might be many equilibria of the economic system some of which might be highly unsatisfactory from a collective point of view. The more recent work on complexity puts less emphasis on the notion of equilibrium in the classical sense and more weight on the idea of the economy as an evolving, open-ended system. Hayek's ideas of the emergence of order bear a resemblance to the sort of ideas considered here.

Another important related thread running through the economic literature is the "evolutionary approach". Here the interest is in the collective result of a situation in which myopic individuals with limited comprehension and rationality grope their way forward. This sort of idea discussed by Nelson and Winter [20] is clearly related to the view of the economy as having self organising properties. [9] presents a series of papers which might be thought of as in the Nelson Winter tradition.

One of the standard criticisms of this approach has been that the analysis was not rigorous, in the mathematical sense, but the strong recent interest in evolutionary game theory, (see [22], [28]) reveals that this sort of approach has now penetrated into areas which could hardly be accused of being less than analytically rigorous. I will not attempt to expound the basic ideas of complexity theory and self organisation since these are also dealt with at length elsewhere. My aim is to show that these ideas can play an important role in developing economic theory. There are two essential things to examine: how the organisation of the interaction between the individuals and the component parts of the system affects aggregate behaviour and how that organisation itself emerges. The purpose of this paper is to look at these two aspects of economic systems. The first question is of particular interest in the economic context since organisation is rarely considered directly in economic models. The basic model underlying most modern economic analysis remains the General Equilibrium model. This model seems to have the great merit of considering all markets as interdependent and having a well defined equilibrium notion. The essential feature of the model is, from the point of view of this project, that only one type of organisation is considered and, even that consideration is implicit. Yet more and more dissatisfaction is expressed with this model. Our aim is to show that by building rather different models we can explain economic phenomena which seem to be inconsistent with the standard model.

It should be said at the outset that the current benchmark model is not as its originators intended it to be. From Adam Smith and his "invisible hand" to Walras, economists had in mind a complicated interactive system in which individuals acting in their own interest came to organise themselves. Contrary to the purified form of the model they did not have in mind any centralised price determining system. Prices themselves are part of the organisation of the system and where those prices come from is a necessary part of the explanation of economic activity.

The standard view of the economy revolves around two themes, the rationality of the individuals and the specific view of the way in which agents interact. In that model agents are "rational" optimisers and are isolated. We suggest that both of these features should be modified and that once we allow for direct interaction between agents we can assume less about their rationality and still observe interesting aggregate behaviour which is no longer, however, the behaviour of an average economic agent. As Forni and Lippi [11] have emphasised, aggregate behaviour is not the behaviour of a representative individual and trying to test models based on this idea leads to erroneous conclusion. Such an idea is so familiar to physicists and biologists that it seems banal. Nevertheless it is still far from being generally accepted in economics. Why should we be dissatisfied with the General Equilibrium model as a benchmark? Simply because it has become clear that it fails to satisfy certain important criteria, even if one accepts the notion of equilibrium involved. As the results of Sonnenschein [27] and Debreu [8] show, there is no guarantee that the economy will converge to an equilibrium if it starts in an out of equilibrium situation, and furthermore, the equilibrium may not be unique. Put more briefly the equilibrium is not well determined.

A radical reaction to this situation was that of Hildenbrand [14], one of the leading scholars of General Equilibrium Theory who said,

> When I read in the seventies publications of Sonnenschein, Mantel and Debreu on the structure of the excess demand function of an exchange economy, I was deeply consternated [*sic*]. Up to that time I had the naïve illusion that the microeconomic foundation of the general equilibrium model, which I admired so much, does not only allow us to prove that the model and the concept of equilibrium are logically consistent, but also allows us to show that the equilibrium is well determined. This illusion, or should I say rather this hope, was destroyed, once and for all, at least for the traditional model of exchange economies. I was tempted to repress this insight and continue to find satisfaction in proving existence of equilibrium for more general models under still weaker assumptions. However, I did not succeed in repressing the newly gained insight because I believe that a theory of economic equilibrium is incomplete if the equilibrium is not well determined.

There are two ways out of this dilemma. Either one changes the foundations of the model, and this is what Hildenbrand has proposed, or one makes the heroic assumption that the average behaviour of the market or economy can be assimilated to that of an individual. This avoids both of the problems mentioned and reduces the aggregate behaviour to a problem that economists know how to solve. How appropriate is this, however, when we have no theoretical reason to believe that this can be done? Let me, at this point start out with an example.

2. Aggregate and individual behaviour: an example, the Marseille fish market.

What I wish to show is that, once one allows for direct interaction among agents, macro behaviour cannot be thought of as reflecting the behaviour of a "typical" or "average" individual. There is no simple direct correspondence between individual and aggregate regularity. As an illustration consider the following simple empirical example, the behaviour of agents on a market for a perishable product, fish. In [13] we showed that, although the transactions of individuals, on the wholesale market for fish, do not necessarily reveal any of the standard properties of a demand curve, nevertheless in aggregate there is a nice downward sloping relationship between prices and quantities transacted.

To understand this, assume for a moment that changes in the prices of fish do not result in a large amount of intertemporal substitution by consumers. This will lead fishmongers and other buyers on the wholesale market to behave in a relatively myopic way. This, in turn, justifies considering each day as a separate observation. This is particularly true since fish is evidently perishable. Indeed, this explains why, when considering particular markets, fish has been so widely used as an example, (for example by Marshall, Pareto, Hicks) since with no stocks, successive markets can be thought of as independent. In our case, when fitting our price quantity relations we are implicitly treating price changes as resulting from random shocks to the supply of fish although the amount available is, at least in part, a result of strategic choice.

If we fit a demand system in the usual way we are assuming that market behavior corresponds to that of an individual, or rather, that the aggregate relation has the same properties as the individual one. In our models we assume that individual relations have certain properties, yet, examination of individual data reveals none of the properties that can be derived for standard individual demand.

The main problem here, then becomes, can aggregation restore some of the properties that are lacking at the individual level? Individuals whose behaviour does not satisfy the criteria that can be derived from standard assumptions may indeed, in the aggregate, satisfy such criteria. Aggregation may add structure. This is one side of the problem of aggregation. The other is that even if individuals did happen to satisfy certain properties it is by no means necessary that these properties carry over to the aggregate level (see e.g. [27], [8]). Aggregation may destroy structure. The two taken together emphasize the basic theme of this paper: there is no direct connection between micro and macro behavior. This basic difficulty in the testing of aggregate models has been insisted upon in the past (see [15], [19]) when discussing representative individual macro models but as Lewbel observed, this has not, and is unlikely to, stop the profession from testing individually derived hypotheses at the aggregate level. Hence in our example, although some empirical properties of the aggregate relationships between prices charged and quantities purchased can be established, I would suggest that these should be viewed as independent of standard maximizing individual behavior.

If the market exhibits such features and one claims that they do not correspond to classical individual maximizing behavior then one has to try to explain how the market organizes itself so that this comes about. On the Marseille market no prices are posted. Thus, information is highly dispersed among agents. Yet, a particular feature that one does observe on the Marseille fish market, is that over the day markets do more or less clear in the sense that the surplus left unsold never exceeds 4%. Furthermore, since sellers become aware, from the reactions of buyers to their offers, of the amount available on the market and vice versa it would not be unreasonable to expect average prices to be lower on those days where the quantity is higher. However, the situation is not simple. For example, some buyers have to transact early, before such information becomes available, and others only make one transaction for a given fish on a given day. Thus to deduce such a property formally from a complete model of the individuals' behaviour and interactions on this market, would require very strong and unrealistic assumptions.

The important thing to re-emphasize here is that the "nice" monotonicity property of the aggregate price quantity curves does **not** reflect and is **not** derived from the corresponding characteristics of individual behaviour. Nor indeed, given the previous discussion, should we expect it to be. But what is the lesson here? As I said previously we are not looking at a standard demand curve but what we can say is that the market has organized itself in such a way that essentially all the fish is sold and, on those days where there is less supply, the prices are, on average, higher. These classic results arise from a complicated set of interactions in which agents know each other, price discriminate and attend the market with different frequencies. So the market replaces or reduces the capacity to calculate that agents need to use. This was the point of Gode and Sunder's [12] famous "zero intelligence" agents who finally arrived at the competitive price on a double auction market, even though they bid at random. The way in which the market was organized led unthinking agents to the result that would have been achieved by highly rational forward looking economic agents. Furthermore, in our case, this occurs on a market which is not organized according to the standard model. Prices are not posted and individuals have to infer their information from their own observations, since they cannot observe the prices at which other transactions are occurring. The basic idea that I am trying to convey should, by now, be clear. Aggregation across agents can add structure and in so doing, generate coherent aggregate behaviour from the interaction of agents who interact directly with each other.

A second question is as to how prices are distributed. Most economists, faced with a situation in which some 500 buyers are faced with some 50 sellers under the same roof, would suggest that a unique price would be established for each good and that there would be little variation around that price. This is far from being the case: price distributions for each day show considerable variations and they do not have the sort of unimodal characteristic that standard analysis would lead us to expect. The question then arises as to whether, over time, some sort of structure emerges. Is there, for example some sort of stability of the distributions if they are taken over a longer period of time? To answer this question we tested the hypothesis that for each individual fish the daily observed price distribution is stable over time. The statistical analysis could not reject it. Here then is a second message. Aggregation of a system with complicated patterns of interaction between agents may show little organisation in the very short run but aggregation over time of this behaviour may yield stability. Once again the behaviour of the aggregate evolves in a rather stable way, something which is not true for the individuals.

3. Trading relationships

One of the reasons for the separation of aggregate and individual behaviour in the previous discussion is that agents interact with only a subset of the others. Thus, information is being transmitted in an asymmetric way. Indeed, it is well known that in many markets individuals typically trade with very few partners. Thus markets are characterised by small trading groups. How the choice of trading partners is made is one of the fundamental problems in economics. Either those with whom one trades are given exogenously or one assumes some anonymous mechanism through which trade takes place. One of the major challenges is to show how agents can learn to choose their trading partners in a simple market framework.

Some models of economic network formation attribute a great deal of rationality to the agents concerned and permit very limited conclusions. Others use simpler learning structures such as a reinforcement learning rule which can be justified theoretically and which produces stronger conclusions. Another type of learning model uses Holland's "classifier system" approach and makes very limited demands on the agents. Both of the latter class of models produce striking results as to the type of groups that emerge. I will give an example from the work based on the Marseille wholesale fish market by Weisbuch *et al.* [29], who used methods from statistical physics. I will show how the sorts of group that emerge correspond to those found in the data concerning the trading relationships on the Marseille wholesale fish market used as an example in the previous discussion.

One of the important features of the market is that individuals establish different sorts of relationships with each other. On the one hand, there are those buyers who regularly buy from the same seller and are extremely loyal, and on the other hand, there are people who shift between their sellers all of the time. This, of itself, seems to be a feature that one should try to explain. If one tries to go back to the framework that I outlined earlier with a full game theoretic model this becomes extremely complicated because one has to develop now a dynamic game in which the experience of playing with each seller is taken into account or one has to think of a situation in which people have strategies which are so complicated that they can take into account of all the prices that they may face from different sellers. So the idea here is to develop a much simpler theoretical model in which people simply learn from their previous experience and they in consequence change their probability of visiting different sellers as a result of their experience. In [29] we consider a market in which buyers update their probability of visiting sellers on the basis of the profit that they obtained in the past from those sellers. If we denote by $J_{ij}(t)$ the cumulated profit, up to period t, that buyer i has obtained from trading with seller j then the probability p that i will visit j in that period is given by

$$P = \frac{exp(\beta J_{ij})}{\sum_j exp(\beta J_{ij})} \tag{1}$$

where β is a reinforcement parameter which describes how sensitive the individual is to past profits. The non-linear updating rule 1 will be familiar, for example, from the model developed by Blume [6], and, as the logit decision, or the quantal response rule, and is widely used in statistical physics. Given this rule one can envisage the case of 3 sellers and 30 buyers, for example, as corresponding to the simplex in figure 1 below. Each buyer has certain probabilities of visiting each of the sellers and thus can be thought of as a point in the simplex. If he is equally likely to visit each of the three sellers then he can be represented as a point in the centre of the triangle. If, on the other hand, he visits one of the sellers with probability 1 then he can be shown as a point at one of the apexes of the triangle.

Figure 1. Sellers' simplex.

Thus, at any one point in time, the market is described by a cloud of points in the triangle and the question is how will this cloud evolve? If buyers all become loyal to particular sellers then the result will be be that all the points, corresponding to the buyers will move rapidly over time to the apexes of the triangle as in figure 1. This might be thought of as a situation in which the market is "ordered". On the other hand, if buyers learn to search randomly amongst the sellers, then the result will be a cluster of points at the centre of the triangle, which will persist over time. What we show in [29], is that which of these situations will develop depends crucially on the parameter β in (1), the discount rate of the buyers, and the profit per transaction. The stronger the reinforcement, the slower the individual forgets and the higher the profit, the more likely is it that order will emerge. In particular the transition from disorder to order, as β changes, is very sharp. In our model this sort of "phase transition" is derived analytically using the "mean field" approach. The latter is open to the objection that random variables are replaced by their means and, in consequence, the process derived is only an approximation. The alternative is to consider the full stochastic process but this is often not tractable, and that is why we resorted to the simulations illustrated above. We wished to see whether the theoretical results from the approximation capture the features of the simulated stochastic process. [a]

A natural question is to ask what happens when there is a mixture of types in the market. The reason that the system consolidates itself on a network with highly loyal customers is that there is a co-evolution of the learning on both sides of the market. When buyers are loyal sellers learn exactly how much fish to provide, buyers are also sure to get what they want. Yet the presence of customers who are not loyal will interfere with this process since they may buy and prevent a loyal customer from getting what he wants. This could undermine the process by which loyalty develops. To see if this was the case, we simulated the process with two types of agents those with a low critical value of β and those with a high one. The result is shown in figure 2. There is a clear separation between the two types. Those who have a low critical value of β become loyal and are represented by the dots at the corner of the simplex and the others continue to shop around.

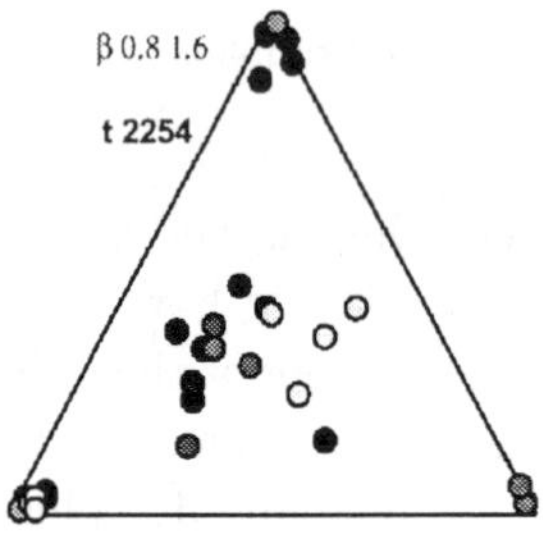

Figure 2. Sellers' simplex with different types of buyers.

This is precisely what happens on the actual fish market. There is a clear separation between very loyal customers and those who search. Furthermore loyal customers pay higher prices than casual shoppers but get what they want.

Even in a situation where the pay-offs from buying from the different sellers are the same and there seems to be no good *a priori* reason for loy-

[a]A detailed discussion of this sort of problem is given by Aoki [3], who thinks of the buyers in the markets as being partitioned between the sellers and each buyer as having a probability of transiting from one seller to another. He looks at the limit distributions of such a process.

alty to develop, the waste in a market with loyalty is much less than in one in which buyers search and the market learns to organise itself appropriately. Thus, organisation is an emergent property of the aggregate and not something directly intended by the agents.

4. Learning in public goods experiments

I will now turn to another example where we see clearly the difference between individual and aggregate behaviour. [b] The problem concerns that of people deciding how much of their money they should keep and how much they should contribute to a public good which everyone benefits from. In such games there are two reference points. There is a cooperative solution or collective optimum (CO), in which the average payoff of the agents is maximised. But there is also the non-cooperative solution in which everyone chooses his contribution as a best reply to the amounts chosen by the others. This involves individuals trying to "free-ride" and is the Nash equilibrium (NE) with a much lower level of contribution than in the social optimum.

There is a wealth of information from public goods experiments showing that, although people start out by contributing generously, with repetition, people contribute less to public goods. A typical explanation is that people "learn to play Nash" or something approaching it. Saijo and Yamaguchi [21], for example, classified people, from their behaviour, as Nash, and found that at the beginning of their experiments 50% of players were Nash and, at the end, 69% fell into this category. This makes it tempting to believe that the people who switched had "learned to play Nash". I will examine this idea by analysing average and individual behaviour in a series of public goods experiments.

In the basic game of private contribution to a public good, each subject $i, (i = 1, \ldots, N)$ has to split an initial endowment E into two parts: the first part $(E - C_i)$ represents his private share and the other part C_i represents his contribution to the public good. The payoff of each share depends on and vary with the experimental design, but in most experiments is taken to be linear [2]. If π_i is the total payoff of individual i, it can be represented by the following expression:

[b] This section is based on joint work with Walid Hichri, who ran the series of experiments described here.

$$\pi_i = E - C_i + \theta \sum_{j=1}^{N} C_j \tag{2}$$

This linear case gives rise to a corner solution. In fact, assuming that it is common knowledge that players are rational payoff maximisers, such a function gives a Nash equilibrium (NE) at zero and full contribution as a collective optimum (CO). Nevertheless, experimental studies show that there is generally overcontribution (30 to 70% of the initial endowments) in comparison to the NE.

The theoretical model and design used for the experiments, I discuss here, concerns a public goods game modified slightly so that the NE and CO solutions are interior. This allows us to see if individuals can contribute below the non-cooperative level or above the cooperative level. The individual payoff function is

$$\pi_i = E - C_i + \theta \left(\sum_{j=1}^{N} C_j \right)^{1/2} \tag{3}$$

It is easy to show that for a group of N subjects, at the CO the total contribution is given by the following expression:

$$\bar{Y} = \sum_{i=1}^{N} y_i = N^2 \frac{\theta^2}{4} \tag{4}$$

and at the NE is equal to:

$$Y^* = Ny^* = \frac{\theta^2}{4} \tag{5}$$

where y^* is the symmetric individual Nash equilibrium.

There were 6 groups of 4 players who played 25 rounds of the game and after each round they were told the total contribution to the public good of the group. The average contribution over all the groups is illustrated in figure 3.

As it is easily seen from figure 3 the contributions start out just below the social optimum and decline towards the Nash Equilibrium without actually attaining it. This is the sort of evidence that has been used to test the idea that there is learning of a certain type going on. This learning could be

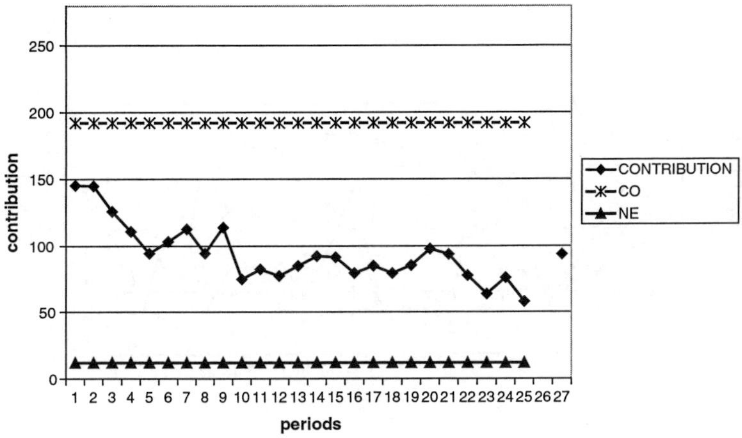

Figure 3. Total contribution.

of a reinforcement type in which individuals simply update their choices on the basis of their experience with those choices in the past. Alternatively, it could be one in which agents learn to anticipate the contributions of the other agents. These two types of learning are incorporated in Camererer and Ho's Expected Weighted Attraction (EWA) learning model [7] and this cannot be rejected on the average data.

Yet, the EWA model is a model of individual learning and it does not seem appropriate to apply it to average data. If we now look at the contributions of the groups in figure 4 we see that the picture is very different than in the aggregate.

Here, for certain groups, we rejected even the simple hypothesis that contributions declined during the experiments. Rather complicated behaviour is going on in the different groups and it is clear that agents in different groups behave differently and that the monotonic declining behaviour of the average is an artifact of the aggregation process and does not reflect the actual behaviour of groups. This is emphasised when we look at individuals within the groups (figure 5 gives the contributions of the individuals in two groups). We can clearly see the differences between the individuals and there is a clear indication that certain individuals try to signal in order to achieve a certain coordination. The overall message could not be simpler, the average behaviour is the result of very different individual behaviour and the apparent aggregate regularity does not reflect the variability of the individuals' behaviour.

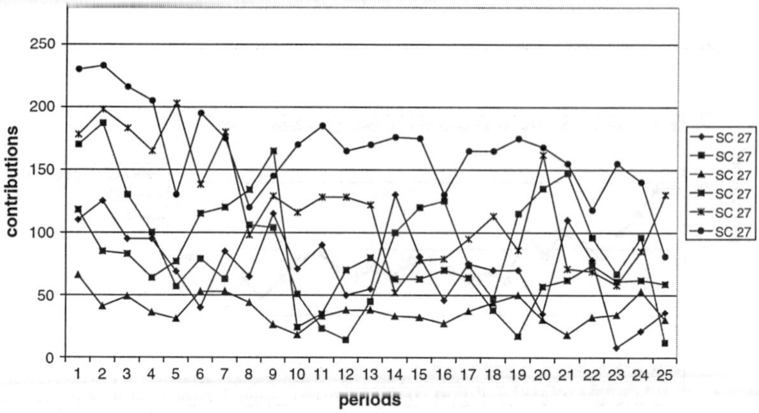

Figure 4. Group contributions without communication.

5. Information cascades

To this point, the examples I have given reflect the idea that there is more structure at the aggregate level than at the individual level, but it can also lead to a loss of information and thus a worse collective outcome may occur than would have happened had the individuals not interacted directly. To see this, remember that an important consequence of interaction is the sort of "herd behaviour" that may arise as agents are influenced by what other agents do, and, indeed, a number of phenomena corresponding to Keynes' "beauty queen" contest can arise. [c] To see how this can happen, recall that one of the most important features of markets is that the actions taken by individuals reveal something about the information they possess. This feature of markets is poorly incorporated in most economic models and yet is an important feature of many financial markets. Within the efficient-markets framework, this idea has no importance because the private information of individuals is immediately transmitted into the central price signal. However, there are many situations in which this does not happen. Indeed one of the main problems in analysing financial markets has been to explain why the movement of stock prices is so much more volatile than that of the dividend process on which those prices are supposed, according to the standard theory, to be based, (see e.g. [25]). In

[c]See, for example, [5], [16], [24].

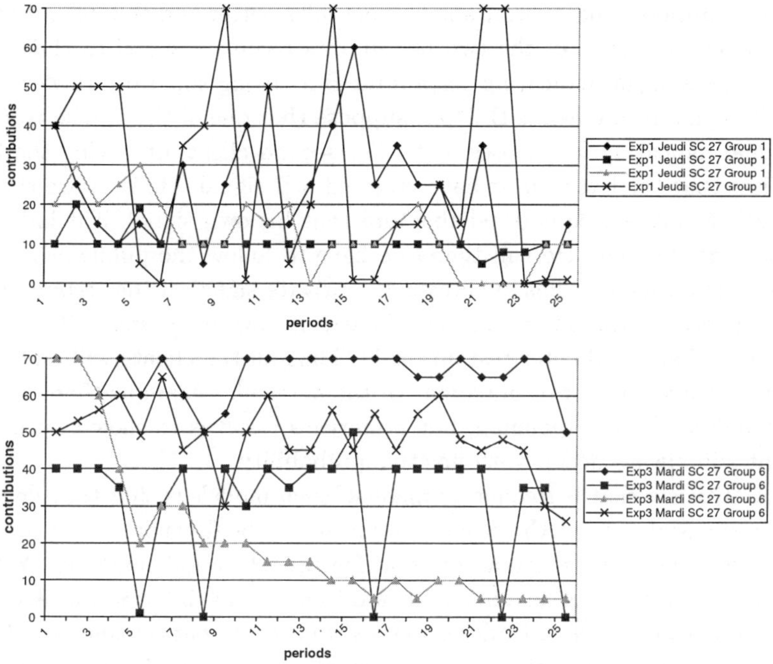

Figure 5. Individual contributions for two groups.

seeking to explain this "excess volatility", economists have been led to the idea that individuals are influenced by each others' behaviour, (see e.g. [26], and may, for example, be led to modify their choices in the light of the choices or experience of others. This may lead to self fulfilling situations in which agents all "herd" on some particular choice or forecast which may not reflect any underlying "fundamental". A series of such events might explain the volatility of stock prices.

In an example, due to Banerjee [5], agents receive private signals, but also observe the choices made by others. There are two restaurants, A and B and one is, in fact "better" than the other. Individuals receive two sorts of signals as to which of the two is better. They receive a public signal which is not very reliable and which, say, has 55% probability of being right and a private, independently drawn, signal which has 95% probability of being correct. Suppose that restaurant A is actually better and that 95 out of the 100 potential clients of the two restaurants receive a signal to that effect and 5 get a signal indicating restaurant B as being superior. However the public signal recommends B. Now, suppose that one of the 5, who received a signal indicating B, chooses first. The second client, observing the first, realises that the latter must have received a B signal. He is aware that all private signals are equally reliable and that his own signal, if it indicated A, is cancelled out. He will therefore have to follow the public signal and enter restaurant B. Thus, whatever the private signal of the second agent, he will enter restaurant B. The third client is now in the same situation as the second and will enter restaurant B. Thus all the clients will end up in B, and this is an inferior outcome. In the particular example there is a 5% probability of this happening, but Banerjee's result is to show that such a result will always occur, with positive probability.

A criticism that is frequently made of such models is that they depend, in an essential way, on the sequential nature of the decision taking process. This, it is argued, is not a common feature of actual markets. Yet, in financial markets, for example, in addition to any information acquired from a private source, a trader observes what other participants are doing, or at least, proposing to do. Consider the market for foreign exchange, for example. Traders try to anticipate the direction of the move of market prices and they gain a great deal of information by listening to brokers, watching the bids and asks on the screens, and by telephoning other traders to ask for a quote. Each such piece of information modifies their individual information set. However, since there is no central equilibrium price, this information cannot be incorporated and become public through the price. It can only be inferred from the observable actions of the individuals. Thus, the action of one individual, based on some private piece of information may give rise to a whole sequence of actions by others and may, as a result, lead to significant moves in exchange rates.

Again, on the stock exchange we do not observe "equilibrium prices", we see the price of each successive transaction. Thus each price change reflects an action by some individual. Thus any change of opinion by an agent in the light of observed price changes corresponds to observing the actions of others. When agents change their actions, in the light of the information they obtain from observing others, a so-called "information cascade" may arise just as in the restaurant example. In such a situation individuals progressively attach more importance to the information they infer from the actions of others. They gradually abandon their private information.

Thus, as the number of people involved grows, the cascade reinforces itself. Whilst quite fragile to start with, cascades later become almost immune to relevant, private, information. Hence, as more and more individuals act in this way, a trader would have to have almost unbounded confidence in his own information not to conform, particularly if such cascades lead to self-fulfilling outcomes. There is a significant loss of efficiency here. The private information, acquired by all the early agents, would be of use to their later counterparts, but, if they choose to follow what others do, this information is not made available. In this way, possibly relevant information about fundamentals, for example, could never be used and prices could get detached from these fundamentals. Thus the conclusion to be drawn from this work is that the information obtained by observing the actions of others can outweigh the information obtained by the individuals themselves and lead to inefficient outcomes. Thus interaction generates a result other than that which would have obtained had individuals acted on their own signals and not on the behaviour of the others. In this case again the aggregate result does not directly reflect what happens at the individual level. Furthermore, the aggregate result can be inefficient from a social point of view.

6. Bubbles and fluctuations in financial markets

Bubbles and crashes are phenomena typically associated with mass or herd behaviour and not with the aggregation of isolated individual optimisers. This is fertile territory for the view of the economy that I have been advancing. A number of us have been building models based on rather simple characterisations of individual behaviour but where the individuals change their expectations as a result of the influence of other agents. An important feature is that agents change their forecasts as a function of their experience with these rules. Furthermore the success of rules depends on how many people follow it. Such models are capable of reproducing some of the features found in the empirical data from financial markets. Fat tails, long memory, and the periodic emergence of bubbles for example. There are a number of such models which reproduce these features when simulated, (for references to this literature and for examples, see [17] for example). All of this can be seen in the following simple example based on the market for foreign exchange.

7. Conclusions

In this paper I have suggested, with examples, that the economy should be conceived of as a complex system. Such systems are characterised by having interacting agents who may have rather limited powers of reasoning and it is the aggregation of these interacting agents that generates a number of macroeconomic phenomenal which are difficult to explain with standard models. The key distinction that I have emphasised is the difference between micro and macroeconomic behaviour. Complex systems such as the economy are characterised by the fact that aggregates cannot be treated as individuals. It is a fundamental mistake to reduce the behaviour of the system to the behaviour of an individual and efforts to do so prevent us from getting at the heart of many economic phenomena.

References

1. P. W. Anderson, K. J. Arrow, and D. Pines, editors. *The Economy as an Evolving Complex System.* Addison-Wesley, Redwood City, CA, 1988.
2. J. Andreoni. Warm-glow versus cold-prickle: The effects of positive and negative framing on cooperation in experiments. *Quarterly Journal of Economics*, 110:1–22, 1995.
3. M. Aoki. *New approaches to macroeconomic modeling: evolutionary stochastic dynamics, multiple equilibria, and externalities as field effects.* Cambridge University Press, Cambridge, 1996.
4. W. B. Arthur. Asset pricing under endogenous expectations in an artificial stock market. In W. B. Arthur, S. N. Durlauf, and D. Lane, editors, *The Economy as an Evolving Complex System II*, volume XXVII of *Santa Fe Institute Studies in the Sciences of Complexity Proc.* Addison Wesley, Reading, MA, 1997.
5. A. Banerjee. A simple model of herd behavior. *Quarterly Journal of Economics*, 107:797–817, 1992.
6. L. Blume. The statistical mechanics of strategic interaction. *Games and Economic Behaviour*, 5:387–424, 1993.
7. C. Camererer and T. H. Ho. Experienced weighted attraction in normal form games. *Econometrica*, 67:827–873, 1999.
8. G. Debreu. Excess demand functions. *Journal of MathematicalEconomics*, 1:15–23, 1974.
9. G. Dosi. *Innovation, Organization and Economic Dynamics: Selected Essays.* Edward Elgar, Cheltenham, 2000.
10. H. Föllmer. Random economies with many interacting agents. *Journal of MathematicalEconomics*, 1(1):51–62, March 1974.
11. M. Forni and M. Lippi. *Aggregation and the Micro-foundations of Microeconomics.* Oxford University Press, Oxford, 1997.
12. D. K. Gode and S. Sunder. Allocative efficiency of markets with zero-

intelligence traders: Markets as a partial substitute for individual rationality. *Journal of Political Economy*, 101:119–137, 1993.
13. W. Härdle and A. Kirman. Non classical demand: a model-free examination of price quantity relations in the marseille fish market. *Journal of Econometrics*, 67:227–257, 1995.
14. W. Hildenbrand. *Market demand : theory and empirical evidence.* Princeton University Press, Princeton, NJ, 1994.
15. A. P. Kirman. Whom or what does the representative individual represent. *Journal of Economic Perspectives*, 6(2):117–136, Spring 1992.
16. A. P. Kirman. Ants, rationality and recruitment. *Quarterly Journal of Economics*, 108:137–156, February 1993.
17. A. P. Kirman and G. Teyssiere. Micro-economic models for long memory in the volatility of financial time series. In P. J. J. Herings, G. V. der Laan, and A. J. J. Talman, editors, *TheTtheory of Markets.* North Holland, Amsterdam, 2002.
18. P. Krugman. *The Self-Organizing Economy.* Blackwell, Cambridge, MA, 1996.
19. A. Lewbel. Exact aggregation and a representative consumer. *Quarterly Journal of Economics*, 104:622–633, August 1989.
20. R. Nelson and S. Winter. *An Evolutionary Theory of Economic Change.* Harvard University Press, Cambridge, MA, 1982.
21. T. Saijo and T. Yamaguchi. The spite dilemma in voluntary contribution mechanism experiments. Paper presented at the New Orleans Public Choice Meetings, March 1992.
22. L. Samuelson. *Evolutionary Games and Equilibrium Selection.* MIT Press, Cambridge, MA, 1997.
23. T. Schelling. *Micromotives and Macrobehaviour.* W.W.Norton, New York, 1978.
24. D. S. Sharfstein and J. C. Stein. Herd behaviour and investment. *American Economic Review*, 80:465–479, 1990.
25. R. J. Shiller. Do stock prices move too much to be justified by subsequent changes in dividends? *American Economic Review*, 71(3):421–436, June 1981.
26. R. J. Shiller. Comovements in stock prices and comovements in dividends. *NBER Working Papers*, (2846), 1989.
27. H. Sonnenschein. Market excess demand functions. *Econometrica*, 40:549–563, 1972.
28. J. W. Weibull. *Evoutionary Game Theory.* MIT Press, Cambridge, MA & London, 1996.
29. G. Weisbuch, A. P. Kirman, and D. Herreiner. Market organisation and trading relationships. *Economic Journal*, 110:411–436, 2000.

SIMULATIONS, THEORY AND EXPERIMENTS. NOTES FROM AN HISTORICAL PERSPECTIVE

MARCO NOVARESE
Centre for Cognitive Economics; Università del Piemonte Orientale
Alessandria. Italy
E-mail: marco@novarese.org

This paper aims at presenting the methodological approach to simulations, proposed at the beginning of the sixties by a group of scholars of the Carnegie Mellon University. This approach can be defined cognitive and behavioural, because of the attention to real perception and decision-making and to the role assigned to learning processes. One of the main points of departure is constituted by the wish to relay on more realistic assumptions, as a condition for better an understanding and forecast of the reality. Simulations are seen as the most important, even if not unique, way to model the resulting complexity.

1. Introduction

This paper aims at presenting the methodological approach to simulations, proposed at the beginning of the sixties by a group of scholars of the Carnegie Mellon University who, in those years, started to work on computer programs as a way to model human and economics behaviour.

This paper shows the main features of their approach and its link with the relative general methodology proposed for Economics, which is based on the need for more realistic hypothesis as a way to get better explanations and previsions of the social phenomena. There is so, also a link between simulations and empirical analysis (seen as the point of departure to build models and not only as the way to test them).

These works seem to have been neglected in the following development of Economics (for example the synthesis proposed by Clarkson–Simon, [2], it is quoted just two times in all article available in Jstor and is never quoted in a specialized journal as Jass).

The same Herbert Simon [14], in a paper written some years later, notes that, while in normative microeconomics simulations have made large contributions, in positive microeconomics, their contribution has been modest, especially in dealing with the theory of organization (see also Simon, [17]).

Nevertheless the works under exam can be useful in the actual debate on simulations, as many of the problems still to solve has just emerged and faced at that time. The solutions proposed are maybe not general, as based on a behavioural and cognitive approach, but are anyway worth of being considered.

2. The different typologies of simulations

In the paper titled "Simulation of Individual and Group Behaviour", published in the 1960 in the American Economic Review, Herbert Simon and Geoffrey Clarkson [2] clarify many general aspects related to simulations, theory and econometric analysis, and of their reciprocal relations. In the same period, other authors published also papers dealing with the same issue.

Most of these scholars come from the same University as Simon. The papers were all published in important journals.

Clarkson–Simon [2] individuate three kinds of simulation analysis. Among the three typologies of models there are, as usual when dealing with classifications, some possible intersections, beyond many obvious points of contact.

1.A. Dynamic macroeconomic

The main examples of this group are the models used in the analysis of the business cycle and market behaviour. This situation can be handled also with differential and difference equations or with the method of comparative static.

In this realm, simulations are so seen as an additional technique for numerical analysis that can be useful because of computer speed and computational power. They can be used to manage more complexity and non-linearity.

For this reason, the use of simulations represents here a development in mathematical and econometric techniques and is just a different way to handle a given situation.

The requirements for building such simulations are the following: (1) hypothesize a functional form of a function, (2) estimated it with any of the available instruments; (3) to define all initial values necessary to run the model.

The simulations will then generate a series of observations. Their output is, in fact, a numerical series and not a mathematical general relation. This series of numbers (even if does not allow general conclusions; as known this is one of the main criticism to the simulation procedures) can be directly compared with real data. So empirical tests are easier.

In many cases it's possible that traditional econometric procedures give best results. In fact the in the simulations, a part from the starting values, all the numbers of the series are generated by the program and then the input variables will probably be different from the real values, used in the traditional econometric analysis.

As observed by Cohen and Cyert (in Cyert–March, [5]), these differences reflect the fact that traditional models are "one period change models" while simulations are "process models", i.e. models characterized by an internal evolution.

When a model contains a feedback mechanism, simulations could, yet, allow more accurate forecasting (an example is the analysis proposed by Cohen [4]).

1.B. Normative Models Developed In The Management Science

In this realm the complexity of the environment can be managed more easily and with greater flexibility by simulations than by the traditional mathematical techniques as linear programming.

The difference with the other two kinds of simulations is clear, as these models have a normative dimension and not a positive one.

This kind of simulations was very relevant and frequent in the period under exam. Shubick [13] states that simulations born in this realm (with military and management purposes).

Also Simon [14], looking back at the development of these techniques in economics and management, stress the relevance of such procedures for American business firms, in dealing with their inventory, cash-holdings and investment decisions.

It's so not surprising that the first authors to propose this procedure in Economics were scholars with a high tendency to interdisciplinary and with interest in management.

The same reason could also explain the low interest solicited among traditional economists.

The decisions procedures of these organizations are, so, much different from the previous years ones1. These techniques allow, sometimes, firms to take almost rational decision, or, at least, to apply more powerful heuristics.

1 That's an important notes to remember also for modelling (American big) firm's behaviour.

1.C. Economic Decision-Making

Almost all economics models are based on some decision making process of economic actors.

Also macroeconomic models can be read in this way. A demand curve, for example, can be seen as a representation of a series of decisions. So this group is interrelated with the first one.

When we move from macro to micro models, and from normative to positive analysis, the behavioural elements became, yet, even more relevant.

Again the usefulness of simulations is related to the degree of complexity they allow to handle.

There is also another important aspect, according to the authors. Computer allows, in fact, building agents that manipulate symbols and information different from numbers (like words or sentences). This characteristic would permit to model situations in which the important factors cannot be represented as real numbers. Simon proposes two example of the limits imposed by the need to model all economics aspects with number: the risk is represented with a probability distribution and utility is analyzed with a cardinal function.

Important aspects related to decision-making, cannot be represented using numbers. Computers can be programmed to allow different kinds of model.

The next two paragraphs propose two examples of simulations developed by the authors under exam, and falling into this third category.

1.C.I. The analysis and modelling of perception and memory storage of individual chess players

Simon–Barenfeld [18] and Simon–Gilmartin [19] build a computer program to model perception and memory of chess players.

The analysis is based on a detailed reconstruction of the real mechanisms working in this situation. It is useful to recall it here and to relate to the characteristics of the simulation.

During the first moments in which a skilled player is faced with a new game position, he does not appear to engage in a search of possible moves. In fact, he seems to be gathering information on the problem. This finding results from a series of empirical investigations, based on different procedures, like protocol analysis and experiment on perception (de Groot, [6] and [7].

Another empirical finding is then considered: the way in which individuals look at the new position they are exposed to. This aspect can be analysed using the record of eye movement (a procedure used also in other experiments, see for example Rumiati, [12]). Such procedure (that can show the succession of fixations but not what information is being processed at each time) allows to observe that at each point of fixation the subject is acquiring information about the location of a piece at or near the point observed, and also information on the pieces around that bearing a significant relation to the fixed one.

A first general aspect should be noticed: also the software designed to play chess by "selective search" (as the one used by Simon) contain processes that can be labelled "perceptual" and it's then a possible way to model situations of this kind. Some kind of perception is, in fact, necessary to allow a selective search.

Simon and Barenfeld simulate the initial sequence of the eye movements of human subjects using a program called perceiver.

A part from the empirical analysis, the program requires a series of other hypothesis, for example: for each of the pieces near to the one fixed, four aspects are detected: (a) if they defend the piece in exam, (b) if they attack it, (c) if they are defended by it, (d) if they are attacked by it. The order in which these items are noticed is relevant, as when a piece is noticed for one of the reason seen, the fixation is moved on it. It is also necessary to define the starting point of fixation (a piece near to the centre of the board)2.

Figures 1b and 1c, taken, from the paper under exam, show a comparison among the path of fixations of respectively an expert real player and a simulated artificial player in the game position of Figure 1a.

Six of the human's player fixations fall in unoccupied squares (these can be related to problems of calibration in the analysis of eye movement, or can have other unknown explanations), while the artificial player always look at occupied squares.

Nevertheless, Simon and Barenfel notice a considerable concordance between the objects of attention in the two cases (the same pieces and the same relations with their neighbours; these aspects can be seen better looking also at the output of the program reporting in detail the aspects analyzed, see figure 2).

---

2 The author don't discuss the origins of these hypothesis and their relevance on the results. We'll come back on the problem of assumptions in simulations.

Figure 1a. A game position studied by Simon–Barenfeld [18]

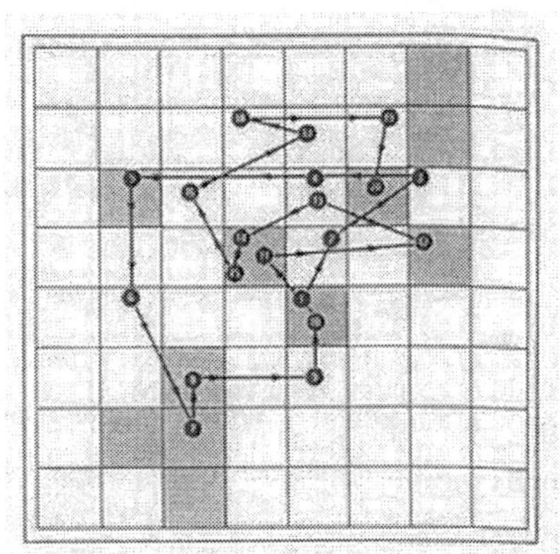

Figure 1b. The path of fixation on the game position in figure 1a of a real expert player

It should be evidenced that perceiver's focuses of attention don't rest on particular evaluation of the possible moves and development of the game, but just on a series of simple search rules. At the end of the series of fixations, perceiver identifies the Black pawn as under defended. Then it starts a new exploration to find moves that could protect it (using the same perceptual processes as before). In this way it discovers three possible moves. One of this is discovered in the same way by the human expert used as a benchmark.

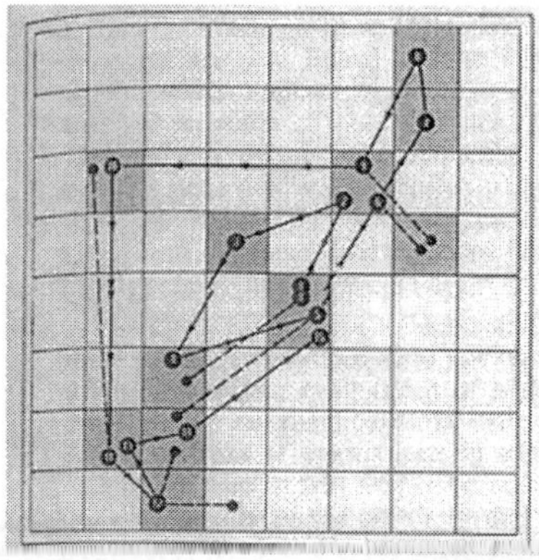

Figure 1c. The path of fixation on the game position in figure 1a of an artificial player

Table 1. Sequence of Fixations and Noticing Acts; PERCEIVER Program.

1. Black pawn (K4)	attacked by	White Knight
	defended by	Black Knight
2. Black Knight	attacks	White pawn (Q5)
3. White pawn (Q5)	defended by	White Knight
4. White Knight	attacks	Black pawn (K4)
5. Black pawn (K4)	attacked by	White Queen
	defended by	Black Knight
6. Black Knight	attacked by	White Bishop
	defended by	Black Bishop
7. Black Bishop	defended by	Black King
8. Black King	defended by	Black Knight
9. Black Knight	attacked by	White Bishop
	defended by	Black Queen
10. Black Queen	attacks	White pawn (N2)
11. White pawn (N2)	defended by	White King
12. White King	defended by	White Rook
	defended by	White Queen
	defends	White pawn (N2)
13. White pawn (N2)	attacked by	Black Queen
	defended by	White Queen
14. White Queen	attacks	Black pawn (K4)
15. Black pawn (K4)		

Figure 2. Sequences of fixation of PERCEIVER; source Simon–Barenfeld [18]

The main aim of this example is to show that a computer can use perceptual processes resembling those used by human subjects. perceiver is, in fact, able to extract from the board almost the same information of a skilled human player.

The detail of the processes should yet be best understood also because, there are important aspects unknown that should be hypothesized. The program can consequently be improved.

There is a second aspects that define the human performance in chess game perception: the capacity to retain the information gathered and to reproduce it in the memory. This aspect is reproduced with another program.

Again, the analysis starts from experimental results showing that the ability of real players to reproduce a chess position after a few seconds' exposure to it depends sensitively on:

a) his chess proficiency and

b) on the meaningfulness of the position.

This is again a central aspect in the work under exam, as Simon and Barenfel (p. 369) state that "an explanation of chess perception must be consistent with this data if it is to be regarded as satisfactory".

The explanation should also be consistent with the known characteristics of human short and long term memory. Simon's analysis of this aspects is based on the idea of chunck3. Here it is defined as any configuration that is familiar to the subject and can therefore be recognized by him. Chunks differs among individuals, in the case of chess, according to their experience and level of skills.

If a configuration of relations is recognized as familiar it can be represented in memory by a single chunk. In this way the short term memory can retain many more relations than if they must be held independently. Then expert players can retain in their short term memory much information, given an exposition of the same time.

Subjects can usually held in their short term memory only about seven chunks (and in such a short term they can probably transfer to long term memory only one chunk).

This part of the perception process is simulated using a program called epam, that was originally developed in a different setting, where it was able to make correct predictions on the effects of familiarity in rote verbal learning.

The new complete program concatenate perceiver and epam and aim to simulate the memory for chess position of both a weak and a master chess player (Simon–Gilmartin, [19]).

---

3 "Chunk is a technical term; in Psychology it means any unit of knowledge that has become familiarized and has a place in the memory index. As it has a place in the index, a chunk is anything you can recognize in your field of expertise" (Simon, [16])

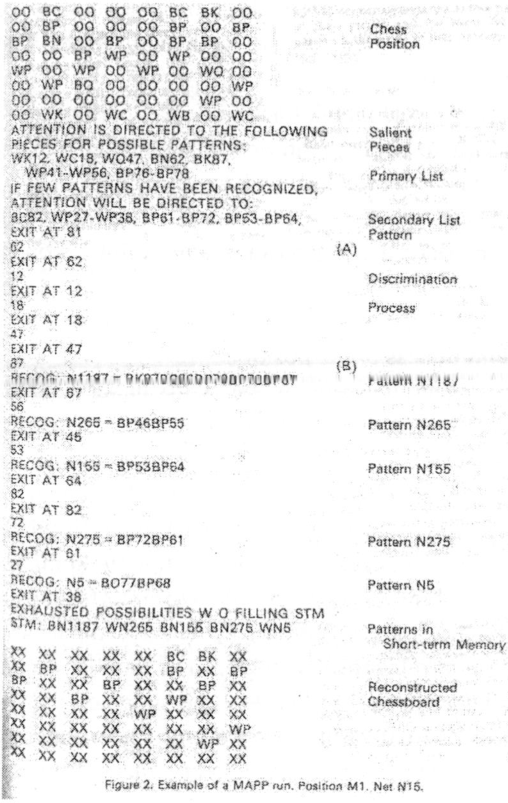

Figure 3. The output of EPAM, source Simon–Gilmartin [19]

It is composed by two main parts:

(1) a learning component that stores in the long-term memory a varying amounts of information about simple recurring patterns of pieces on a chess board, proposed in a training session;

(2) a performance component that: (2a) detects the pieces on the board; (2b) recognizes patterns (the recognition depend on the chunks —i.e. on the patterns — that have previously been stored in the long term memory; only these sequences can be recognized) and stores them in the short term memory (that is limited in capacity and than contain a maximum of seven names); (2c) decodes the information in the short term memory and reproduces as much of the original board position as possible.

Figure 3 shows the output of the second part of the program.

To test the model, different nets of patterns were build by proposing to the program a series of usual chess positions (drawn from games in the published literature).

Two kinds of net were build, with different dimension, standing for different level of ability of a player (Chase–Simon [1] showed that chess skills depends in large part upon a vast and organized long term memory of chunks; see also Simon, [14]).

The performance of MAPP in recognizing patterns was then compared (in different direction and in quantitative and qualitative terms) to that of an experimental sample of master and class A chess players. It resulted again a qualitative resemblance between real and simulated behaviour (a similar percentage of pattern recognised, the same pattern recognized more frequently). The program is then again able to account for the main features of the human performance.

A neoclassical representation of this situation would probably have lead to a model to generate the best moves. This program, on the contrary, try to account for real human decisions.

As seen, the simulation just described are, in fact, based on a detailed reconstruction of the real human processes, in relation to the different steps of the perception mechanism of chess board positions. The main distinctive features of such mechanisms are empirically individuated and extrapolated from the reality, using many different methodologies: experiments, protocol analysis, eye movement analysis ..., and looking at analysis from different domain (not only from studies on chess, but also on memory; perception in other situations ...).

These empirical practices are generally used in psychology. In economics they are widely not seen as useful or even "scientific", also because the interest is generally focused, at maximum, on testing models predictions, and not in finding real hypothesis on behaviour. Neoclassical Economics, in fact, don't take care of the realism of its hypothesis.

Experiments, so, should just reproduce the simple theoretical environment and are built to test theories. Different instruments, and different kind of experiments and of analysis are necessary, on the contrary, when the interest is also directed to understanding real behaviour and not only in testing model (this is a second step in the empirical analysis and it requires different kind of data from the previous one) as I have noted in Novarese [9]. In this paper I individuated, yet, a new stream of experimental research (experimental cognitive economics) whose aim is also that of entering the black box of human reasoning and than resembling the empirical methodologies recalled here (Simon is, in fact, one of the main reference of this new stream).

As seen in the previous paragraph, is obvious that this way of modelling reality requires naturally a simulation approach.

Another important aspect is related to the generality of the proposed analysis. Chess is taken as an example, of a more generalized kinds of situations.

The same elementary processes that have been employed to simulate problem solving and learning in chess, operating in essentially the same way, produce the same known features of the human perceptual performances in other perceptive tasks. Therefore, similar programs revealed able to describe perception in different environment.

This generality can be read in another direction too. Recalling also Simon [14] we can say that chess behaviour analysis stress the relevance of the information stored in long term memory. Direct retrieval of possible action as a result of familiar pattern, provides a basis for professional performance in many other areas. Where familiar situation are faced4, we can expect more sophisticated behaviours and levels of performance, than in new areas. We should also expect that this model do not imply history-free path of action. On the contrary learning becomes more and more relevant.

In chess, players differ in their skills, and the differences are related to their experience, both in term of number of board position seen, and of their characteristics. Two players with the same training (in term of number of position faced) can perform differently, if their chunks differ, because of the different positions faced in the past. So, individual knowledge of an individual is based on his own experience. This idea is coherent with a path dependent analysis of learning mechanism and decision-making (see Rizzello, [11]).

This model could then represent a general reference for other models of learning, based on simulations, to be developed.

In the same period, a similar methodological approach (with more problems because of the more complicated situations faced) was proposed also by Cyert and March, to describe and model the behaviour of another economic agents: the firm5.

1.C.II. The simulation of oligopolistic firm's behaviour

The analysis proposed by Cyert–March [5] represents a big effort to build a realistic theory of the firm, empirically founded and going beyond the traditional

4 As pointed by Egidi [8], it's also possible that some pattern of action can be extended to new situations, showing some elements of similarity with those in which a given strategy has been learned.

5 Similar approach can be found in other of the applications developed in that period and surveyed in many of the paper recalled.

economic vision (when the analysis was realized, the main theory of the firm was that proposed by the general equilibrium model; the theory of transaction cost was still not well know and studied).

Methodology of the empirical analysis

The first part of the contribution in exam is, in fact, again based on an empirical analysis realized on the field, looking at several real organizations' behaviour.

The firm studied operate in oligopolistic markets.

The empirical effort is based on the analysis of

a) different kind of internal documentations (receipts, letters, memoranda ...),

b) interviews with the members of the firms,

c) direct observations of decision making processes (a member of the research group participated to the main meeting of some of the firms, eventually verbalizing it).

Two experiments on organizational communication complete the empirical evidence available.

For example the authors describe four problems of decision, in which expectations, available information and their interpretation play a crucial role.

Main empirical results

These last aspects are central, because firm's decisions rely on estimations of alternatives costs and payoffs, and on a vision of the world that are generally partial and different from the reality, also because only a subset of the possible available choices is generally taken into account.

Firm's organization and characteristic influence both perception and exploration of the alternatives. There are, besides, always conflicts of interests among the different internal sub-groups.

There is also a strong inertia in the decision processes (alternative more similar to those taken in the near past have an higher chance of being accepted).

It's also relevant the order in which the different possibilities are found and then evaluated. If alternatives are generated sequentially, the first that allow a satisficing payoff is, in fact, chosen.

These general findings are used to propose a general theory of the decisions making into a complex organization.

The general model is not formalized. It's based on a series of general ideas.

The authors develop in detail some specific formalized models, as simplified examples of the possible applications of the general ideas. All these applications are realized using computer simulations that for the authors represent the natural theoretical language to model this theory. Even if the examples proposed are simplified in respect to the general model, in fact, simulations (and flow charts) are the only way to manage such complexity.

The main problems related to simulations are also presented and discussed during the presentation of the examples. The book has also two methodological appendixes, on simulations and on explanation and forecast in economics. We'll recall them in the next paragraph.

In synthesis the model proposed as examples are the following.

1) The first one is a particular model of duopoly, in which an ex-monopolist faces a "new firm". The main decision is related to the level of the production.

An important feature of all these models, is that firms have a goal that represent both the variable(s) to take care (the variable to maximize in the neoclassical model) and a criteria to take the main decision (the level that the variable should reach, i.e. a level of aspiration). The goal is here the profit.

The decisions are based on an estimation of the market price. The real price can be different from the estimated one.

For both agents, the process start with a forecast of demand, costs, and of the reaction of the other firm and with the definition of the desired profit (based on a mean of the past profits; the ex-monopolist compute the mean on a longer number of years; the new firms take also in exam its relative productive capacity).

In the second phase, given the results of the previous step, each actors look for the best available choice. If such alternative don't allow to reach the desired profit, there is a new step in which the function of costs (according to the empirical analysis performed, Cyert and March think that, because of the "inertia" of each organization, there are always costs that can be reduced, given appropriate conditions forcing to do that; this process or re-examination stimulate the firm to reduce its cost; in the model under exam, costs are reduce of a 10% percentage) and demand are estimated again.

The Figure 4 proposes a comparison between the markets shares of the two firms in the model and that of two real firms, in a duopoly similar to that under exam (the two firms are: the American Can Company and the new entrant is the

Continental Can Company; the vertical axis reports the ratio between the market shares of the ex-monopolist and of the other firm; the horizontal axis shows the years; the dashed line represents the true data.).

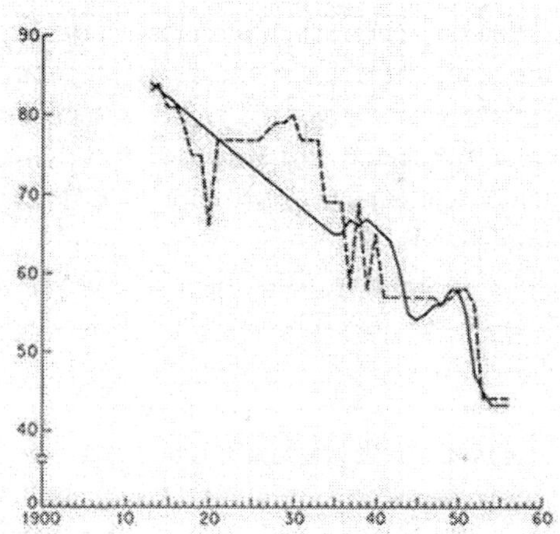

Figure 4. The market shares of the two firms in the real and simulated duopoly of Cyert–March [5]

This comparison is not supposed to prove for itself the validity of the model, even if the fit is very good. According to the authors, in fact, the model proves that given a series of conditions, it is possible to fit the real data. The problems are related to such assumptions. As in the model there are many degree of freedom (many parameters), it possible that a set of its series could be able to fit the real data. Even if in this particular case, such parameters are few, and most of them were defined a priori, the difficulty remains.

This is one of the main problems related to simulations, on which Cyert and March insist in the book and on which we'll come back later.

2) Another example is that of a department of a discount. In this case the oligopolistic market is composed by the three discounts of a city.

According to the authors the model could be extended, with few differences, to the other departments of the same firm or to other discounts, as the decision processes are very similar.

The general goals of this organization are related to the sales and to the mark-up on the costs.

These decisions are taken accordingly to a general model (again based on empirical observations of the real functioning of the department under exam), based on four principles:

a) the firm is seen as a coalition of individuals characterized by different personal goals; the conflict that born from this situation is solved (or at least the solution is searched, even if not necessarily successfully) thanks to: (i) the use of a "local rationality" (division of the problems in sub-problems assigned to sub-units for the solutions, and then specialization in the decisions: for example sales department is the main responsible for sales, the production department is the main responsible for production ...); (ii) the fact that the coherence of the rules is weak (so allowing to keep together different goals); (iii) a sequential attention at the problems (with the consequent possibility of different an not coherent solutions in different moments);

b) firms try to avoid, uncertainty, using rules of reaction in the short period and making the environment more known through negotiation (standard procedures, industrial traditions ...);

c) "problematic research": the search of new solutions is driven by the problems faced (a mechanism of search different from more systematic kinds ones, as the search aimed to understand: technical approach vs. science). Then search is oriented by one problem, and motivated by that problem. It's also distorted by the characteristics of the organization;

d) organization learns and then evolves, modifying its goals and its rules.

This general model is specified (and partly simplified) for the department under exam.

Where possible, the previsions of this model are compared to the reality. The data available (i.e. the data gathered by the firm) doesn't allow testing all parts of the model.

There are good data on the prices and on the mark-up. Using as input the data on real costs and on the classifications of each goods, the program produces as output a price for each item. These prices can be compared to the real ones decided by the department. In the 95% of the cases, the model gives a perfect prevision. The model has a good capacity to forecast also the liquidation prices of some items and the special offers (it is designed to individuate when a liquidation price or a special promotion will be proposed)

3) The last example proposed is a general model on price and production for oligopolistic firms.

The program represents a first attempt to build a general model and should be further developed.

In respect to the traditional models is yet much more complicated, as it takes into account several aspects.

The choices that a firm should take are: the price, the level of production and the marketing strategy. Each of them can be related to a sub-division of the firm that operate with a relative independence from the other departments.

An agent-based model of the oligopoly market results from the interaction of many firms, represented by a similar model but with different starting conditions and parameters.

Firms interact both trough market price and demand, and with a reciprocal attention when a price should be defined.

The model generates a detailed series of decisions, related to the internal results and aims, for each of the firms and a market price and quantity.

The analysis of this general model is just a first step, and allows authors to discuss an important question: the relevance of the parameters on the general results of a simulation.

They try to individuate the parameters that have a significant influence on the output. This analysis is based on a regression of the main output variable of the model on a selection of parameters.

Some of them, show in fact, a strong influence, while others seems to be less relevant.

As the authors say, this problem is related to the lack of empirical observations on some aspects (when the research on the field started, the model and the parameters were, obviously, still to be planned, and so not all the empirical aspects relevant for it were gathered; besides, there are aspects that cannot be seen).

To solve this problem, some of the parameters should probably be modelled and get as results of learning mechanism of higher level.

3. Simulations and the Methodology of Economics

As seen in the examples, simulations are introduced by the authors under exam, as a necessary tool for managing complex models, based on realistic hypothesis founded on empirical findings of different types. The need for realism is a central point in the methodological program of this school, from which the other aspects follow in a related way and it is seen as a necessary condition to allow a better comprehension of the reality, and maybe also a better prevision, thanks to the fact that more complicated models can be performed using computers. The complication in models is strongly related to the search for more realism (Cohen [3]).

Unrealistic hypothesis are, yet, not refused a priori (also in the models seen here there are many aspects not empirically tested) but cannot be accepted if they are proved to be false and if a more realistic one can be found (and should be found), independently from the performance of the model.

Even traditional models are not refused for itself.

Computer programs just allow expressing theories in a new language (beyond verbal language, graphics and maths) with different characteristics.

When possible, simulations should be performed in parallel to traditional mathematical models, has both of them has limits and advantages.

Simulations are less general, as they need more information than traditional models and their results are a series of number. That's not necessary a limit, it's just a different characteristics, that has many positive implications.

In fact, for example, these series of number make it possible to test immediately the theory more easily than traditional models.

That's particularly important because using simulations it is possible, not only to handle very complex situations, but also to build theory that are intrinsically dynamic, and not only based on one period movements.

As real data are dynamics, in this way it's easier to compare theory and reality (but again, empirical verification is not so relevant for some of the traditional economist).

Cohen [3] proposes other positive elements related to simulations.

- In respect to aggregate economic modelling, a micro approach has many advantages. Markets, for example, become emergent phenomena, arising from the interaction of a series of firm (whose heterogeneity can also be modelled, while this characteristic is more difficult to be accounted for it in traditional micro models and it's excluded in aggregate theorization6). It's possible that factors that differ among agents and that are excluded by aggregate models (or that are not explainable by them) could compensate each other in aggregate set. But that's not necessarily true. In other cases these individual factors can also have a strong effect on the general result. A micro founded model is then a better way to proceed.

Even firms can be modelled as emerging from the individual characteristics of their members (see Novarese 2003, where the relevance of this aspects is empirically analysed). Cyert–March [5] include, more or less directly, these aspects in their models, taking into account the conflict of interests and the role played by the different departments in an organization.

In simulations, heterogeneity can be related to some differences posed by the researches but can also results from different learning processes, given the same general model (as, for example, in Simon analysis of different chess players, that differs in relation to the length of the training and can differ also in relation to the positions faced).

6 But that has the disadvantage to increase the costs of the analysis, as it make necessary also a wider study to individuate all possible kinds of agents and to model them

- The assumptions are easy to modify and change than in traditional analysis7.

Econometrics is not refused by the scholars under exam. They think that the two approaches should interact.

Simulations pose new statistical problems and need new tools and analysis (this point is signalled by Cohen [3] as another critical factor for the development of simulations; Cohen–March [5] gives some preliminary ideas of the possible direction in which find a solution), as econometrics developed in strict relation with traditional one-period models8.

The novelty of the approach under exam and its attention to empirical analysis is reflected also in the variety of empirical data and analysis used. Consider the following examples.

- Chase–Simon [1] proposes an experiment with a detailed analysis of the behaviour of just three chess players. Their aim is that of understanding how they play, not to test a model.

Experimental economics is generally used to test theory and there is generally no attention in understanding why players behave in that given way (see Novarese [9]).

- Cyert–March [5] proposes a series of case studies, as a way to understand how firm takes decisions.

Case studies are another tool that economics tend to avoid, for many reasons. There is still no methodological agreement on how to conduct them and present their data9. The main problems are related to the way decisions are analyzed. The researcher can, also unconsciously, be influenced by his persona ideas and interest in gathering information. His presence can influence the

---

7 Simulations allows to work with formal models also to non mathematical economists. They should, yet, be able to manage computer simulations. In the last years more and more economics courses are starting to include such skill, but in the 60s it was probably not so, and this can be another factors able to explain the low interest in this approach.

The suitability of easy programming language were posed by the same Cohen as one of the crucial factors for the development of this approach. It's possible that the development of object oriented programming helped to increase the role of simulations in economics (Prietula et al [10]).

Clarkson-Simon [2] and Simon [14] pose also the attention on the relevance of the development of "heuristic programmation" allowing to simulate system that manage non numerical values.

8 It's not possible to analyse here this aspect, that are just mentioned in the studies under exam. In short, the problems recalled are related to:

-criteria to postulate and estimate more complicate functional forms have to be developed,

- the estimations of the parameters (to be done before the simulation is run and representing one of the possible way to solve the problem seen) poses other problems as most of them can be generated by simultaneous equations of a model;

- it is necessary to devise test allowing to define the goodness of fit of simulated and real data (considering also that real data can have measure problems)

9 Also because of privacy problems of the firms under exam.

behaviour of the subjects under exam. There is also an obvious problem of generality of the results found10.

Simon ([15], p. 20) has yet an answer to such criticism: "If you are trying to understand what firms are and how they operate, you will learn a lot from this kind of very detailed study of the processes of decision … Of course, we should not stop with five firms. Biologists have described millions of species of plants and animals in the world, and they think they've hardly started the job. Now, I'm not suggesting that we should go out and describe decision making in a million firm; but we might at least get on with the task and see if we can describe the first thousand. That doesn't immediately solve the aggregation problem, but surely, and in spite of the question of sampling, it is better to form an aggregate from detailed empirical knowledge of a thousand firms, or five, than from direct knowledge of none. But the latter is what we have been doing in economics for too many years".

The authors in exam don't discuss in detail the specific problems of the empirical analysis (probably also because at that time there were a different status among economist for the empirical research; for example the contemporary, more rigorous, way to present experimental results developed later) but stress the need of getting better data and observations on real behaviour, as a condition for the development of simulation techniques and of the more general (behavioural) economic methodology.

March and Grunberg (in Cyert–March, [5], p. 366) put the empirical analysis as the starting point of their methodology. They think, in fact, that economics should be seen as part of the study of human behaviour and than it need true empirical hypothesis that can be used in all contests and models.

Cohen [3] states that simulations are especially adapted to the development of a behavioural model of the firm at a micro economic level. This statement can be extended to the models of all areas.

To take full advantage of simulations, it is then necessary to obtain a great body of empirical materials11 (Cohen [3]). Computer programs can represent a framework around which organize the collection of data.

This is a positive elements, but again also a possible bound, as to develop a behavioural approach, a lot of data are necessary and they should be very

10 The fitness of the specific model proposed by Cyert and March [5] can be also attributed to its peculiarity and lack of generality.

11 Simulations requires also a detailed analysis of working principles and institutions (in that there is a parallel with experimental economics).

detailed and so complicated and costly to collect (this can be another factors able to explain the low success of this approach)12.

This view of the economic requires, obviously, a dialogue with other disciplines (psychology first of all).

4. Conclusion

This paper proposed an analysis of the methodological approach to economics developed and proposed by a series of authors in the sixties. This approach can be defined cognitive and behavioural, because of the attention to real perception and decision-making and to the role assigned to learning processes.

One of the main points of departure is constituted by the wish to relay on more realistic assumptions, as a condition for better understanding and forecast of the reality. This idea leads to the need of more data and of different empirical methodologies (see also Simon [17]).

Simulations are seen as the most important, even if not unique, way to model the resulting complexity.

The papers discussed individuate a series of problems and need, that are related to the kind of general approach pursued, but that have, in some cases, also a more general validity and seems then useful for the contemporaneously debate on simulations (that is not necessarily linked to a behavioural approach and based on realistic assumptions), as many of the problems seems to be again present, as testified by Testfatsion [20].

References

1. Chase W.G. and Simon H.A., Perception in chess, *Cognitive Psychology*, 4, 55-81 (1973)
2. Clarkson G.P.A. and Simon H.A., *Simulation of Individual and Group Behaviour*, The American Economic Review, Vol. 50, Issue 5, Dec, 920-932 (1960)
3. Cohen K.J., *Simulation of the Firm*, The American Economic Review, Vol. 50, Issue 2, Papers and Proceedings of the Seventy-second Annual Meeting of the American Economic Association, May, 534-540 (1960)

12 The costs comprises also the "mental" difficulties of a more interdisciplinary approach by the economist that should be, in fact, less specialized to perform it (in the recalled papers, empirical analysis, theoretical modelling and computer programs were all present together), losing the advantage of division of the labour.

4. Cohen K.J., *Computer Models of the Shoe*, Leather, Hide Sequence. Englewood Cliffs, New York (1960)

5. Cyert R.M. e March J.G., *A Behavioural Theory of the Firm*, Englewood Cliffs, New York, Prentice-Hall, also published as *Teoria del Comportamento dell'Impresa*, F. Angeli, Milano, (1963)

6. de Groot A.D., Perception and memory versus thought: Some old ideas and recent findings. In B. Kleinmuntz (ed), *Problem Solving*, Wiley, New York, 19-50 (1966)

7. de Groot A.D., *Thought and choice in chess*, The Hague, Mouton (1965)

8. Egidi M, "Biases in Organizational Behavior", in M Augier and J.J. March (eds), *The Economics of Choice, Change and Organization: Essays in Memory of Richard M. Cyert*, Aldershot, Edward Elgar (2002)

9. Novarese M., *Toward a Cognitive Experimental Economics*, in Rizzello Salvatore (ed) *Cognitive Paradigms in Economics*, Routledge, London (2003)

10. Prietula, M. J., Carley K.M, and Gasser L., *Simulating organizations: Computational models of institutions and groups*. Cambridge, MA: The MIT Press (1998)

11. Rizzello, S., *The Economics of the Mind*, Edward Elgar, Aldershot (1999)

12. Rumiati R., Giudizio e decisione. Teoria e applicazioni della psicologia delle decisioni, Il Mulino, Bologna (1990)

13. Shubick M., *Economics, Management Science, and Operation Research*, The Review of Economics and Statistics, Vol. 40, Issue 3, Aug, 214-220 (1958)

14. Simon H.A., On How to Decide What to do, *The Bell Journal of Economics*, Volume 9, Issue 2, Autumn, 494-507 (1978)

15. Simon H.A., Colloquium with H. A. Simon, in Egidi M., Marris R., (eds.), *Economics, Bounded Rationality and the Cognitive Revolution*. Elgar, Aldershot (1992)

16. Simon H.A., *What We Know about Learning, speech at the 1997 Frontiers in Education conference*, Pittsburgh < http://fie.engrng.pitt.edu/fie97/papers/1501.pdf> (downloaded on September, 1, 2003) (1997)

17. Simon H.A., *Bounded Rationality in Social Science: Today and Tomorrow*, Mind & Society, Vol 1, n. 1, 25-40 (2000)

18. Simon H.A. and Barenfeld M., *Information-processing analysis of perceptual processes in problem solving*, Psychological Review, 76, 473-83 (1969)

19. Simon H.A. and Gilmartin K., *A simulation of Memory for chess positions*, Cognitive Psychology, 5, 29-46 (1973)

20. Tesfatsion, L., *Agent-Based Computational Economics*, ISU Economics Working Paper No. 1, Department of Economics, Iowa State University (2002)

JAS: JAVA AGENT-BASED SIMULATION LIBRARY, AN OPEN FRAMEWORK FOR ALGORITHM-INTENSIVE SIMULATIONS

MICHELE SONNESSA[1]

Department of Computer Science, University of Torino,

C.so Svizzera 185, Torino, Italia

This paper shows how agent-based modelling technique is a suitable approach for social scientists to model complex adaptive systems, using computer as experimental environment. Unfortunately advanced tools are lacking as well as an unified language supporting its development. We present JAS, a new agent-based simulation tool, developed with the aim to improve AB models designing. We give a brief methodological introduction to its use and a short description of its architecture.

Keywords: complex adaptive systems, agent-based simulation, open source software

1. Introduction

Since the birth of the quantum physics, the science of the twentieth century has been characterized by the explorations of alternative modelling languages.
Ilya Prigogine [14] suggested the use of probability within the traditional mathematical models:

> In recent years, a radical changes of perspective has been witnessed in science following the realization that large classes of systems may exhibit abrupt transitions, a multiplicity of states, coherent structures or a seemingly erratic motion characterized by unpredictability often referred to as *deterministic chaos*.
>
> [...]
>
> Non-linearity and instability force us to adopt a different point of view concerning the formulation of the laws of nature. They now express possibilities instead of certainties.

The successes in the studies of the fractal mathematics [12] is the basis for one of these new alternative perspectives: the experimental mathematics, in which

[1] (sonnessa@di.unito.it)

the computer becomes the favourite instrument of research [3]. Particularly in the field of complexity, the massive presence of non-linear phenomena, the adaptive topological interactions and the evolving behaviours of system elements, makes the formal mathematics harder and harder to be managed.
It is shown from Gilbert *et al.* [7] how scientific modelling could be carried out using different kind of languages and their effectiveness deeply depends on the choice of the most appropriate one.
A complex adaptive system (CAS) may be defined as an open system, made of several elements which interact, driven by non-linear behaviours, forming a unique organized and dynamic entity, able to evolve and adapt to the environment [6].
Such kind of systems seems to be well studied with the ABM formalism. They are modelled as a collection of rules and algorithms, which can be numerically simulated. The attention is concentrated on the single agents' behaviour. It is represented in terms of reactive system, often determined by IF..THEN..ELSE conditions, typical computer language construction. So, with no doubt, the computer language becomes an alternative way to design dynamic systems.

ABMs and classical dynamic linear models are also different from a purpose point of view. According to Tikhonov *et al.* [17], scientific modeling can be carried out with two different perspectives: the direct and inverse problem. The attempt to reproduce empirical phenomena, starting from a given model, is considered a direct problem, while the observation of the empirical data in order to infer the cause-effect laws, which are subsequently used to forecast the future behaviour of the system, is called inverse problem. The ABMs are mostly used to represent CAS with the direct problem perspective, differently from linear dynamic modelling which is used to "compress" knowledge about a system in equation based laws.
Agent-based simulation models are experiments of minds, with the aim of understanding the internal adaptive processes of a system [10]. The forecast of its future dynamics is not a real objective for this models, also because in presence of chaotic laws the long term forecasts are mathematically uncertain.

2. Swarm

Building a computer simulation model requires a good skill in computer programming. In addition, the code plays the role of the modelling language and it must be also used for model validation, because revolutionary outcomes might be caused by code bugs rather than by emerging properties of the model.

The programming languages are to generic to describe a scientific model and they are full of technicalities due to computers' architecture[2], so it is necessary to define a language subset and a description formalism with a specific semantic for agent-based models. In other words, we need a common language for ABM. The most known toolkit for building ABM simulation is Swarm[3], developed by Minar *et al.* [13] at the Santa Fe Institute[4].
Through the experiences of the Swarm user community, we have today a clearer idea of the potentialities and the limits of agent-based simulation models.
The advantages of this methodology have been shown in different subjects like the game theory (the Prisoner's Dilemma [1]), the biology [9], the epidemiology [2], the financial applications [16] [11].

The Swarm Development Group (SDG) gave the community three main contributions.

2.1. *A simplified approach to the ABM development*

Simulations always need a piece of software driving the time evolution, random number generators, statistical tools, plotters. They are common to every simulation model. A library of tools simplifies its designing, reduces the programming time and improves the code reliability.

2.2. *A definition of a schema in model designing*

Much important is a definition of a methodology for writing models. The SDG suggested, for instance, to keep a strong separation between the model (a piece of software which simulates the system) and the observer (a set of routines looking into the model, collecting statistics and showing them to the user). This approach is very much elegant and it has a similitude with the real world, where things happen and the researchers look at them from the outside, without participating to the system evolution.
The separation between model and observer may have also a relation with the ontological distinction between the *design complexity* and *control complexity* made by John Casti *et al.* [5]. The *design complexity* expresses the idea of complexity perceived by the observer of a system, while the *control complexity* is complexity of the observer perceived by the system itself. In other words, the

[2] For instance, let's think about the complex notation used to manage reference pointers to the memory...
[3] http://www.swarm.org
[4] http://www.santafe.edu

complexity may be not an absolute property of the system, but something emerging by the interaction between observer and observed.

2.3. *The creation of a community of users*

The aggregation of many people using Swarm, through mailing lists and web site (collecting their works), represents a sort of *agora* for the "ABM people" and gives an important contribute to the community.

Many useful features were not implemented in Swarm although, thanks to the open source world, powerful libraries may be included into the model implementation. However, we think this is an unpromising approach, because it increases the difficulty of writing and sharing AB models. In fact, Swarm is not only a simulation library but also a methodology, a reference framework to build models in such a way that anyone, knowing its interface, can easily understand the source code and check any model detail.
In learning to use a tool, the community of modellers also learns to "speak the same language". On the contrary, when a modeller imports an external tool, he or she introduces a new dialect, reducing the communication possibilities.

3. JAS[5]

JAS, Java Agent-based Simulation library is:

- an environment for simulation experiments,
- a framework for building agent based models,
- a Java library, rich of simulation-oriented tools.

It is an open source project, hosted by the SourceForge open source portal and consists of a collection of Java utilities composing a framework for building agent based simulation models.
The library has been developed adopting the same Swarm philosophy of model-observer frame, because with no doubts it has become a standard.

In order to let models to be further standardised, it is necessary to enrich the basic tool with further features. The use of external libraries is welcome, but they have to be homogenized with the features of the tool. JAS includes well tested and standard libraries[6], but they appear as a part of JAS through some

[5] http://jaslibrary.sourceforge.net
[6] See JAS web site or JAS about box for a complete list of the libraries included in the package.

specific wrapper classes. For instance, we used the ptPlot[7] library as standard plotter, but its rich and complex interface has been filtered and now it is able to natively plot the statistical probes contained in the *jas.stats* package.
This way, the final user is not required to know their implementation, this remaining a problem of the developers. We think this is a fruitful way to work with open source code, that facilitates continuous improvements of the tool.

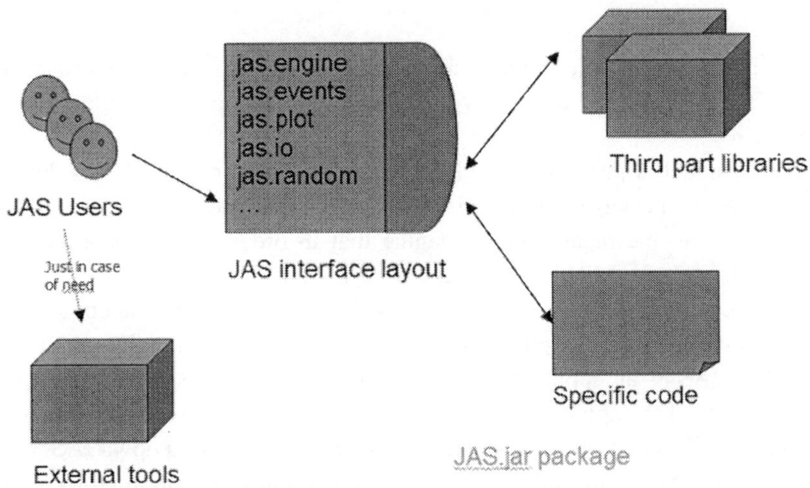

Figure 1. The architecture of JAS

The following list represents the main new features of JAS in comparison with Swarm.

- A pure Java code implementation, so it is easy to be installed and configured. No operating system dependent libraries have been used.
- The possibility to execute in parallel agents' actions.
- A network protocol (Sim2Web[8]) to publish simulations on the web and to allow humans interactions with the simulation through a web page.
- A reduced set of turtle's movement instructions taken from Starlogo[9] [15].
- XML file format support.
- A powerful random number generator and statistical functions taken from COLT library[10].

[7] http://ptolemy.eecs.berkeley.edu/java/ptplot
[8] http://wf.econ.unito.it/sim2web
[9] http://education.mit.edu/starlogo

- AI library supporting GA, ANN and CS to implement agent's intelligence.
- A discrete event time management, with real time emulation and different time unit representation.
- A dynamic class loader, to reduce the problems in configuring CLASSPATH variable for models execution.
- A multi-run protocol to perform automatic parameter calibration.

JAS is not only a library but an application. After the installation procedure, in fact, it can be started like every other Java application. This could seem to be hazy.
A JAS model is just a Java application mostly based on the classes defined in the *JAS.jar* package, compiled with a standard Java compiler (JDK, for instance). So the reader could imagine that in order to execute a model it is necessary to start it like every other Java application.
JAS is equipped with a custom Java class loader, which can load compiled class "on-the-fly", without a previous CLASSPATH specification. Thanks to it, we can run JAS as an application and start simulation models as they were simple documents of the application (with the File/Open menu command). Moreover, it is possible to stop a simulation and restart it without shutting down JAS.
Thanks to this feature, we were able to define a multi execution protocol, useful to automate the parameter calibration.
The *Control Panel* (Figure 2) is the main JAS window, through which is possible to:

- create a model project specifying the paths, libraries and parameters for the simulation enginee, thanks to the project editor;
- load and run a compiled model (through the XML project file);
- edit seed random number, windows position and so on;
- open a console output window (useful when JAS is started with the javaw command)
- control the simulation engine status (event list, models currently running, windows, ..).

---

[10] http://hoschek.home.cern.ch/hoschek/colt

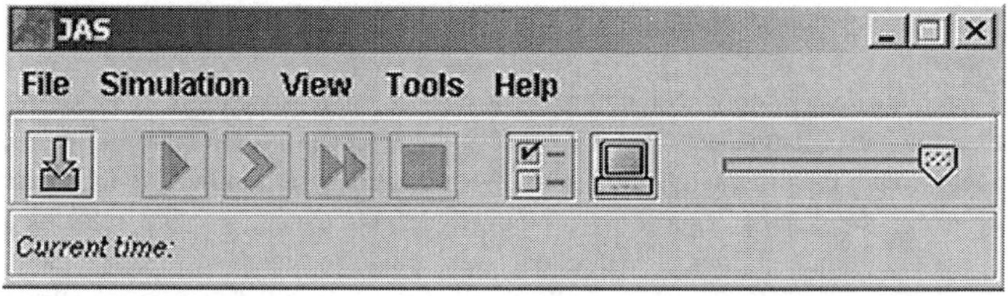

Figure 2. JAS Control Panel

4. Why Java

It has been asserted above that the choice of modelling language is crucial. At the same time the choice of the programming language determines the characteristics of the simulation tool.

Although programming languages are only formal collections of rules to express the same concept: the algorithms, which are always translated by compiler in the same machine code, they implies different styles of expression.

JAS is written in Java language, because we want it to be open source and platform independent. Java is with no doubt the most diffused and appreciated multi-platform language. The open source java community offers a very large set of ready-to-use libraries. It is suited for scientific applications since its arithmetic is based on 64-bit words, the best numeric precision nowadays available [8].

In addition, Java has two interesting features: the executable are never linked and it natively supports reflection.

Traditional compilers link each part of the compilation process into a unique executable file. This mechanism creates a shielded code which can be accessed only by the executable itself. On the contrary, every Java application is not linked by compilers (jar files are simple extractable archives). This means that each package may be at the same time a library of functions and an executable program. Thanks to this feature JAS is both a library to write AB models and an application able to control simulation run.

The reflection mechanism is a technical, but very relevant, issue. It allows to take off "the lid" of object instances and look inside them. Doing it with other languages requires to access directly the computer memory[11] with the high risk to cause a system crash. Java has native methods to do it in a safe and easy way.

[11] The memory zone where compiled code is loaded. Accessing the code segment is a dangerous operation.

The implementation of the probes has been much easier in JAS rather than in Swarm.

These advantages notwithstanding, Java has an unpleasant limit. It is slower than the native languages. This is a problem when code execution has to be fast, as it is often the case with simulations. With this concern in mind, we took care of using the fastest algorithms in looped actions execution, like scheduled operations, and particular attention was paid to memory management, developing customized garbage collectors[12]. Swarm is still faster, especially in graphics, but the difference is acceptable considering Java pros.

5. Simulation Environment

This paragraph shows the skeleton of any simulation model developed with JAS. A JAS simulation model is a Java application with some specific constraints. A JAS-compliant simulation model must have a main class, inheriting from the *jas.engine.SimModel* template. The *SimModel* class represents a bridge between the user's model and the simulation engine.

The *SimModel* interface provides a reference to the JAS' centralized timer, the *eventList* variable, and a set of standard methods which are invoked by the JAS when particular events happen.

The *SimModel* class is abstract and force the model designer to override two methods:

- setParameters()
- buildModel()

and optionally *simuationEnd()*.

The first method is called by JAS just when the model is loaded into memory. At this time the model set (collection of agents and widgets) has not been instanced yet and the user can still modify the parameters of the simulation experiment. The *setParameters()* method allows the modeller both to set directly some constant parameters, loading them from a file, and to open a probe (or other kind of visual interface) to let the choice to the user.

Only when the user presses the "Build model" button, JAS calls the *buildModel()* method, which plays a key role: it represents the point when the simulation model is finally set into memory.

Usually the *buildModel()* method performs two tasks:

- creates instances of the agents and all the model stuff ;
- defines the event structure: which events will happen and when.

This implementation is left to the model designer.

[12] The garbage collector is a software component which stores objects that are no more used, in order to recycle them when a new object of the same type is needed by the application.

If, for instance, at the end of the simulation data are to be written into an output file, the modeller might also override the *simuationEnd()* method, defining which operations are to be executed when an *EVENT_SIMULATION_END* event is raised or when the user clicks the "Simulation\End" menu item.

In the Swarm protocol two special objects are defined with the aim of coordinating the experiment: the *ModelSwarm* and the *ObserverSwarm* classes. JAS generalizes this structure introducing only the *SimModel* interface as controller. So, an observer and any other kind of model controller must always override the *SimModel* class.

The reason for this choice is due to the fact that, from a technical point of view, an observer is not different from a model: it creates some objects (typically statistical and graphical widgets) and schedules their updating frequencies.

In Swarm they are nested. So when the observer is started, it creates an instance of the model it wants to observe. In JAS, observer and model are executed independently (we can run in parallel as many model as we want) and the observer is put in the condition to look into the model retrieving its reference from the JAS engine. In other words, an observer class looking at the model is implemented simply like another model, running in parallel and observing its state variables.

One of the advantages of this architecture consists in the possibility to run a model silently, simply deactivating the observer in the project definition file.

Through an XML project file, in fact, we can define a simulation experiment, specifying one or more models which are executed all together (the swarm of swarms). The action sequence of each sub-model is coordinated by the JAS engine, with a unique timer.

The following XML code is used to start an example model. It has been visually designed with the JAS project editor.

```
    <?xml version="1.0" encoding="UTF-8" ?>
    <JAS projectName="SimpleBug">
    <ProjectParameters>
         <TimeUnit>7</TimeUnit>
         <MajorVersion>0</MajorVersion>
         <Seed randomSeed="true">1024304619192</Seed>
         <ProjectDescription>The simplest agent based
example.
    </ProjectDescription>
         </ProjectParameters>
    <Model className="SimpleBugModel">
          <Window title="Simple bug
model">9,128,414,403</Window>
         </Model>
    <Model className="SimpleBugObserver">
           <Window title="Space
viewer">432,8,400,400</Window>
```

```
        </Model>
<ClassPath>
            <Path>.\examples\SimpleBug</Path>
        </ClassPath>
    </JAS>
```

It is interesting to notice that if the *SimpleBugObserver* element (<Model> XML tag) is present in the XML document tree, the observer will be executed, otherwise the model will run in a non-graphical mode.

6. The Package Overview

Java allows the programmer to organize his or her code into packages. The package system is primarily used to avoid namespace conflicts so that two Java classes with the same name will not be confused.
JAS consists of 11 packages, which are shortly described below.

6.1. *jas.ai*

The artificial intelligence package contains a simulation oriented implementation for the main evolving algorithms: artificial neural networks are based on the original implementation of the *bp-ct* package by Pietro Terna; genetic algorithms and classifier systems are based on the work by Gianluigi Ferraris[13].

6.2. *jas.engine*

The engine classes are responsible for setting up and driving the simulation event-based engine. The simulation engine (SimEngine) is a typical discrete-event engine, particularly optimized to speed up the execution of looped schedules. In fact, ABM are often executed with a repeated sequence of events.
The SimModel is the template class for all models managed by JAS. The ControlPanel is responsible for handling user interaction with a simulation through a GUI. The engine package contains a custom java class loader, which is able to dynamically manage the java CLASSPATH.

6.3. *jas.events*

The events are the core of the scheduling and message dispatching mechanism. The events package contains a rich collection of event, which might be scheduled for single agents (unicast), for entire collections (broadcast) and for

[13] http://www.swarm.org/community-contrib.html

restricted group (multicast) of them. In addition they are defined particular system events, understood by the JAS SimEngine.
It is implemented a garbage collector for reducing memory occupancy and the EventList and RealtTimeEventList are the threads managed by the SimEngine to schedule events and raise them in time. In particular, the real time implementation of the event list is able to fire event using a real timer for emulation purposes.

6.4. *jas.io*

The input/output operations are very important for a simulation model. They are responsible for the input/output communications with the user and for reading from disk and writing to it.
The io package supports the comma separated values (CSV), the Microsoft Excel spreadsheet and the eXtensible Markup Language (XML) formats for disk I/O operations.

6.5. *jas.net*

The net package is the repository for each network service of JAS. Particularly, all the interfaces for the XML-RPC communications are contained by this package. They have been used to realise the Sim2Web architecture, which allows to publish simulation models on the web, via Zope web server. In addition, they might receive commands from the remote users. See the website http://wf.econ.unito.it/sim2web for more details.

6.6. *jas.plot*

All the graphic widgets are available in the plot package. There is a raster class, which is able to draw bi-dimensional overlapped surfaces. The TimePlot and the BarPlot are the standard plotters of JAS. They are based on the ptPlot library from the Berkely University.

6.7. *jas.probe*

The probes are particular graphic objects, which inspects an object instance and shows the user current values for its state variables, allowing him or her to change some values or to invoke object methods.
The probes are very important to let the observer to watch inside the simulation model, checking the internal dynamic of a particular element of the system.
The probe is based on the java reflection library.

6.8. *jas.random*

The pseudo random number generation is an essential tool for computer simulations. It represents a critical activity, because the algorithm generating pseudo random number could be affected by loops, when the generation algorithm is not complex enough. At the same time, this operation requires a lot of CPU resources. It is a difficult compromise and this is the reason why we used a well known and hi-level speed library: the COLT library, developed at CERN, Geneve. It is probably the best Java implementation for random and statistical functions.

6.9. *jas.space*

The space package contain 2D grid surfaces for mapping topological spaces, particularly useful in model based on cellular automata. They are logical representation of space, while their graphical rendering is left to the classes of the jas.plot package.

6.10. *jas.stats*

A simulation model does not give only graphic results, but many numerical series, which represent the basis of the latter statistical analysis. They are useful to understand both the overall behaviour of the system and of the single agents.
The stats package contains probes able to inspect agents' state and to collect statistics. While data are collected a rich set of statistical indicators is available. They are able to write data to disk, too.
They are based on the same COLT library used in the random package.

7. Conclusions

Many researchers are upset when they discover that the only way to build an agent based model is to learn a programming language. Their first idea is to search for a visual application that allows them to build models in a couple of minutes. The reason for the absence of such applications or environments in the world of ABM is due to the difficulty in defining reusable building blocks for these kind of models. In fact, they are distributed, parallel and their relations are loosely coupled. Rarely they present a stable network of relations.
We said that an ABM is an algorithm-intensive formalism, because the classes representing agents have to drive their behaviour, using a rich set of algorithms. They are characterized by a list of things to do, with many conditions testing the external inputs in order to decide the right action to be taken.

These models are rich in behaviour routines and the visual editing of such complex algorithms may result in a very complicated graphical representation.
A proof of this comes observing the structure of available ABM tools: Starlogo uses its own language; Ascape, Repast, JAS are based on Java; Swarm is based on Objective-C.
A probably good way to resolve this impasse is the definition of a specific subset of instruction, a specific semantic and use the UML formalism to represent such kind of models. The model-observer paradigm introduced by Swarm authors could be a starting point.

In comparison with Swarm, JAS has some improvements and it is easier to use. The modeller has still to type code, but we tried to hide as many technicalities as we could. This was possible thanks to Java. The Swarm original source code was written in Objective-C, and this means that implementation of the probes and the Selector class has been very hard. Using the Java Reflection and other Java features, JAS code is much lighter and requires the user to write down fewer technical instructions than Swarm.

References

1. R. Axelrod, *The Evolution of Cooperation*, Basic Books, New York (1984).
2. R. Bagni, R. Berchi, P. Cariello, *A Comparison of Simulation Models Applied to Epidemics*, Journal of Artificial Societies and Social Simulation vol. **5**, no. 3 (2002).
3. J. D. Barrow, *Pit in the Sky. Counting, Thinking and Being,* Oxford University Press, London (1992).
4. A. Beltratti, S. Margarita, P. Terna, *Neural Networks for Economic and Financial Modelling*, ITCP, London (1996).
5. J. L. Casti and A. Karlqvist, *Complexity, Language and Life*, Mathematical approaches, Springer, Berlin pp.146-73 (1986).
6. A. Gandolfi, *Formicai, Imperi, Cervelli*, Bollati Boringhieri, Torino (1999).
7. N. Gilbert and P. Terna, How to Build and Use Agent-based Models in Social Science, Mind & Society 1 (2000).
8. C. Horstmann and G. Cornell, *Java 2*, vol. 1 & 2, Sun Microsystems press (2001).
9. S. A. Kauffman, *The Origins of Order: Self-Organization and Selection in Evolution*, Oxford University Press, New York (1993).
10. D. Lavoie, H. Baetier, W. Tulloh, *High-tech Hayekians : some possible research topics in the economics of comuptation*, Market Process, **8**, Spring, pp.120-147 (1990).
11. B. LeBaron, *Asset Pricing Under Endogenous Expectation in an Artificial Stock Market*, Santa Fe Institute Working Paper **96-12-093** (1996).
12. B. Mandelbrot, *Les objets fractals*, Flammarion, Paris (1975).

13. N. Minar, R. Burkhart, C. Langton, M. Askenazi, *The Swarm Simulation System: A Toolkit for Building Multi-agent Simulations*, Santa Fe Institute Working Paper **96-06-042** (1996).
14. I. Prigogine, *Non-linear Sciences and the Laws of Nature*, *Journal of The Franklin Institute* Volume: 334, Issue: **5-6**, September 11, 1997, pp. 745-758 (1997).
15. M. Resnick, *Turtles, Termites and Traffic Jams: Explorations in Massively Parallel Microworlds*, MIT Press (1994).
16. P. Terna, *SUM: a Surprising (Un)realistic Market: Building a Simple Stock Market Structure with Swarm*, presented at CEF 2000, Barcelona, June 5-8 (2000).
17. A. N. Tikhonov and A. V. Goncharsky, *Ill-Posed Problems in the Natural Sciences*, Mir, Moskva (1987).

Section 2
Microsimulation of Labor Dynamics

MATCHING, BARGAINING, AND WAGE SETTING IN AN EVOLUTIONARY MODEL OF LABOR MARKET AND OUTPUT DYNAMICS *

G. FAGIOLO AND G. DOSI
Sant'Anna School of Advanced Studies
Laboratory of Economics and Management

R. GABRIELE
Sant'Anna School of Advanced Studies
Laboratory of Economics and Management
and
D.I.S.A., University of Trento

In this paper, we present an agent-based, evolutionary, model of output- and labor-market dynamics. Firms produce a homogeneous, perishable, good under constant returns to scale using labor only. Labor productivities are firm-specific and change stochastically due to technical progress. The key feature of the model resides in an explicit microfoundation of the processes of: (i) matching between firms and workers; (ii) workers search; (iii) wage setting; (iv) endogenous formation of aggregate demand; (v) endogenous price formation. Moreover, we allow for a competitive process entailing selection of firms on the basis of their revealed competitiveness. Simulations show that the model is able to robustly reproduce Beveridge, Wage and Okun's curves under quite broad behavioral and institutional settings. The system generates endogenously an Okun's coefficient greater than one even if individual firms employ production functions exhibiting constant returns to labor. Montecarlo simulations also indicate that statistically detectable shifts in Okun's and Beveridge curves emerge as the result of changes in institutional, behavioral, and technological parameters. Finally, the model generates sharp predictions about how system parameters affect aggregate performance (i.e. average GDP growth) and its volatility.

*Thanks to Uwe Cantner, Herbert Dawid, Peter Flaschel, Alan Kirman, Willi Semmler, Mauro Sylos Labini, Leigh Tesfatsion, two anonymous referees, and the participants to the conference "Wild@Ace: Workshop on Industry and Labor Dynamics. an Agent-based Computational Economics approach", Laboratorio Revelli, Turin, October 3-4, 2003, for valuable comments and suggestions.

1. Introduction

In the last decades, the issue of microfoundations of macroeconomic dynamics has played a central role in the economic profession (cf. Dosi and Orsenigo (1994) for a discussion). Theoretical explanations of observed aggregate regularities have at least begun to employ formal frameworks where macroeconomic outcomes are interpreted as the result of the interactions of individual firms, workers, consumers, etc..

Traditionally, efforts of microfounding macroeconomic dynamics have been grounded upon a hyper-rational, maximizing, "representative agent", thus avoiding by construction the challenges posed by aggregation of heterogeneous agents (Kirman, 1992).

Despite their high formal sophistication, the degrees of success of these models is, at best, mixed. In particular, they turn out to be unable to *jointly* account for multiple empirically observed "stylized facts". For example, as far as labor market dynamics is concerned, existing literature seems to completely lack a joint explanation of the most important aggregate regularities concerning: (i) the process through which firms and workers meet in the labor market; (ii) how this matching process affects wage setting and (un)employment dynamics; and (iii) the extent to which unemployment and output interact over the business cycle[a].

More specifically, existing (standard) microfoundations of labor market dynamics seem to have failed in jointly explaining three crucial stylized facts that one can typically observe in the data, namely: (a) the Beveridge curve, which predicts a negative relationship between rates of vacancies and rates of unemployment; (b) the Phillips (respectively, Wage) curve, suggesting that changes in wage rates (respectively, levels of wage rates) are negatively related to unemployment rates; (c) the Okun's curve, which posits a more than proportional increase in real GDP for every one percentage point reduction in the unemployment rate.

In this paper, we propose an alternative, evolutionary-based, approach to the microfoundation of labor-market and output dynamics[b]. In the

---

[a]For a quite exhaustive overview of the state-of-the-art of both theoretical and empirical labor market literature, cf. Ashenfelter and Layard (1986), Ashenfelter and Card (1999) and Petrongolo and Pissarides (2001).

[b]More on the general *Weltanschauung* of the evolutionary approach is in Dosi and Nelson (1994) and Dosi and Winter (2002). The model we present has large overlappings with the "Agent-Based Computational Economics" (ACE) approach (Tesfatsion, 1997; Epstein and Axtell, 1996; Aoki, 2003), as well as with self-organization models of labor markets pioneered by Lesourne (1992).

model we present in the following, the economy is populated by boundedly-rational firms and workers. Firms produce a homogeneous, perishable, good under constant returns to scale using labor as the sole input of production. Workers are skill-homogeneous and buy the good spending all their wage. Labor productivities are firm-specific and change stochastically due to technical progress. Both firms and workers hold expectations about desired wages they want to offer and get, and they are able to adaptively revise their expectations on the base of observed market dynamics.

A key feature of the model resides in an explicit microfoundation of the processes of: (i) matching between firms and workers; (ii) worker search; (iii) wage setting; (iv) endogenous formation of aggregate demand; (v) endogenous price formation. Moreover, in the spirit of evolutionary-based approaches, we allow for selection (e.g. exit) of firms on the basis of their revealed competitiveness (as measured by last-period profits). Since firms interact both in the labor market and in the product market, their revealed competitiveness is affected not only by their production decisions, but also by their hiring and wage-setting behaviors.

Macroeconomic dynamics is generated in the model via aggregation of individual behaviors. Statistical properties exhibited by aggregate variables might then be interpreted as emergent properties grounded on persistent micro disequilibria. Consequently, even when some equilibrium relationship exists between aggregate variables (e.g. inflows and outflows from unemployment), the economy might persistently depart from it and follow some disequilibrium path. The observed stable relations amongst those same aggregate variables might emerge out of turbulent, disequilibrium, microeconomic interactions.

Computer simulations show that the model is able to robustly and jointly reproduce Beveridge, Wage and Okun's curves over sufficiently large regions of the parameter space. Moreover, the system endogenously generates (absolute values of) Okun's coefficients larger than one even if production at the individual level does not enjoy increasing returns to labor. Montecarlo simulations also indicate that statistically detectable shifts in Okun's and Beveridge curves emerge as the result of changes in institutional, behavioral, and technological parameters. Finally, the model generates quite sharp predictions about how system parameters affect aggregate performance (i.e. average GDP growth) and its volatility.

Our results lend support to a disequilibrium foundation of aggregate regularities: despite the economy always departs from equilibrium (if any), aggregate regularities emerge as the outcome of decentralized interactions, adaptive behavioral adjustments, and imperfect coordination.

The paper is organized as follows. In Section 2 we briefly survey empirical findings about aggregate regularities in labor market dynamics and we discuss how mainstream economic theory has been trying to provide explanations of such stylized facts. In Section 3, we introduce the model. Sections 4 and 5 present the results of simulation exercises. Finally, in Section 6 we draw some concluding remarks.

2. Labor Market Dynamics: Empirical Findings and Theoretical Explanations

When dealing with the interplay between labor market and output dynamics, three aggregate stylized facts stand out.

First, the Beveridge curve (BC) postulates a negative relationship (over time) between the rate of unemployment u and the rate of vacancies v, where rates are defined in terms of total employment[c]. The intuition is simple: if an economy experiments higher level of vacancies - in turn plausibly corresponding to a higher level of aggregate demand - it is easier for workers to find a job. Thus, one should also observe a lower level of unemployment. Movements along the curve should be typically induced by the business cycle, while the position of the BC in the (u, v) space is typically related to the degree of "frictions" in the market and, more generally, to its institutional setting. The closer the curve to the axes, the lower - *ceteris paribus* - market "frictions", cf. Nickell, Nunziata, Ochell, and Quintini (2001).

As far as co-movements between unemployment and wages are concerned, a *second* and complementary empirical regularity is the famous Phillips curve (i.e. negative relationship between *changes* of wage rate and unemployment rate); or the alternative Wage curve (Blanchflower and Oswald, 1994), which characterizes economies with a negative relationship between *levels* of wage rate and unemployment rates (Blanchard and Katz, 1997; Card and Hyslop, 1996; Flaschel, Kauermann, and Semmler, 2003). Empirical studies (Blanchflower and Oswald, 1994; Card, 1995) show that in homogeneous areas WC is in general valid, while PC is not[d]. This

[c]Observation of reliable proxies for actual vacancies entails many empirical problems, especially in Europe, see Solow (1998). For instance, one is typically bounded to observe only *ex-ante* vacancies (i.e. job openings). *Ex-post* vacancies (i.e. unfilled job openings) are much more affected by frictions than *ex-ante* ones and thus should be in principle preferred as object of analysis.

[d]As the WC pertains to homogeneous data cells, one cannot "see it" in rough data.

empirical evidence seems to robustly hold across regions, countries, etc. but also among different institutional setups (Borsch-Supan, 1991; Bleakley and Fuhrer, 1997). The interpretation of a WC is quite controversial and bears some important theoretical implications. For instance, the competitive equilibrium framework cannot be invoked to account for WC emergence. In fact, a competitive labor market with all its canonical features would lead to a *positive* correlation between unemployment and wage rate. Climbing up a downward demand for labor schedule - i.e. raising wage - would indeed induce higher levels of unemployment, as the unmet supply of labor would grow.

A *third* fundamental aggregate regularity is the Okun's curve (OC), which characterizes the interplay between labor markets and economic activity (Okun, 1962, 1970). Inspection of aggregate data typically shows that a decrease of one percentage point in the unemployment rate - *ceteris paribus* - is associated with a growth rate of GDP of about two-to-three percentage points (according to original Okun's estimations). The standard interpretation runs in terms of under-utilization of labor resources with respect to full employment, carrying a more-than-proportional effect on economic activity (Prachowny, 1993; Attfield and Silverstone, 1997).

Mainstream economic theory has been trying to explain the foregoing aggregate regularities in the familiar *equilibrium-cum-rationality* framework, building the explanation on the shoulder of hyper-rational, maximizing, representative worker and firm. Hence, any aggregate regularity is interpreted as the equilibrium outcome of some maximizing exercises carried out by such agents.

A paradigmatic example of such modeling strategy can be found within the theoretical literature aimed at micro-founding and explaining the BC (Pissarides, 2000; Blanchard and Diamond, 1989). In these models, all search and matching, which in reality is an inherently dynamic process, is thus described in a static setting by means of a deterministic (aggregate) matching function, whose functional form and parametric assumptions tautologically imply a BC. The latter is treated as a static (long-run) equilibrium locus in the unemployment-vacancy space. Furthermore, one typically requires that all flows in and out of unemployment must always compensate[e]. Needless to say, this is at odds with any empirical observation.

Panel data estimation must be performed in order to control for variables such as personal characteristics of workers, labor market institutions, "fixed" effects allowing to discriminate among sectors or regions, etc. .

[e]On the contrary, the model we present below allows the economy to evolve on a

Moreover, in order to get the desired results, many over-simplifying assumptions are required. *First*, the environment must be strictly stationary, ruling out any form of technological and organizational change, as well as any type of endogenous selection amongst firms and workers. *Second*, the presence of a hyper-rational, representative individual rules out the possibility of accounting for any form of heterogeneity across firms and workers. More than that: it excludes the very possibility of analyzing any *interaction* process among agents (cf. Kirman (1997) for a discussion). *Third*, as a consequence, one is prevented from studying the dynamic outcomes of multiple (reversible) decisions of hiring, firing, quitting, and searching which unfold over time.

Similar critiques also apply to the purported micro foundations of Wage and Okun curves[f]. Therefore, despite the existence of some competing, although not entirely persuasive, interpretations of each of the three aggregate regularities *taken in isolation*, the economic literature witnesses a dramatic lack of theories attempting to *jointly explain* Beveridge, Okun and Wage curves.

In the following, we begin to explore a radically different path and study the properties of a model where the most stringent assumptions of standard formalizations are abandoned and we explicitly account for the processes of out-of-equilibrium interactions among heterogeneous agents. We will try to provide an explicit microfoundation - within an evolutionary framework - of labor market dynamics regarding the processes governing e.g. job opening, job search, matching, bargaining, and wage setting.

Notice that the bottom line of the exercises belonging to the "pure equilibrium" *genre* is that they turn out to be unable, almost by construction, to account for involuntary unemployment or even endogenous changes in the "equilibrium" rates of unemployment.

It must be noticed that important advances, incrementally departing from the standard model, have nevertheless tried to incorporate agents' informational limitations, in order to account for phenomena such as endogenous fluctuations in aggregate activity and persistent involuntary unemployment (see e.g. the seminal work by Phelps and Winter (1970) and Phelps (1994)).

In addition, some contributions have attempted to introduce "endoge-

---

permanent disequilibrium path.

[f]Cf. Hahn and Solow (1997) and Fagiolo, Dosi, and Gabriele (2004) for a thorough discussion on this and related points.

nous matching" mechanisms to describe the (Walrasian) decentralized process governing the meetings between firms and workers in the labor market[g]. This is certainly a point our model takes on board in its full importance, and it does so through an explicit account of the (disequilibrium) unfolding of the interaction process.

In this respect, our model has three important antecedents in the labor market literature. *First*, the out-of-equilibrium, interaction-based, perspective that we pursue is a distinctive feature of "self-organization" labor market models[h]. *Second*, the ACE model in Tesfatsion (2001) also assumes many heterogenous, interacting agents, characterized by "internal states" and behavioral rules, who exchange information in the market. *Third*, Aoki (2003) extends the ACE model of fluctuations and growth proposed in Aoki and Yoshikawa (2003) to allow for unemployment dynamics[i].

Notwithstanding many overlappings with "self-organization" and ACE formalizations, our model proposes advances, *vis-à-vis* the state of the art in this area, at least at four levels. *First*, it accounts for the co-evolutionary dynamics between the labor market and the product market. More specifically, we try to nest labor market interactions in what one could call a "general disequilibrium" framework with endogenous aggregate demand. This feature allows us to study also market properties associated with an endogenous business cycle. *Second*, we explicitly model (as endogenous processes) job opening, matching, wage bargaining, and wage setting. *Third*, we allow for technical progress and the ensuing macroeconomic growth. *Fourth*, in the analysis of the results we go beyond an "exercise in plausibility" and we explicitly compare the statistical properties of the simulated environments with empirically observed ones, specifically with respect to the emergence of Beveridge, Wage, and Okun's curves.

---

[g]See Lagos (2000), Peters (1991), Cao and Shi (2000), Burdett, Shi, and Wright (2001), Smith and Zenou (2003) and Julien, Kennes, and King (2000).

[h]Cf. Lesourne (1992) and Laffond and Lesourne (2000). Self-organizing processes are discussed in Witt (1985).

[i]Similarly to our model, co-evolution between product and labor market dynamics is explicitly taken into account and simulations allow to reproduce (albeit in some benchmark parameterizations) Okun's curves. However, matching and wage bargaining are not incorporated in the model as endogenous processes. Therefore, no implications about wage and Phillips curves can be derived from simulation exercises.

3. The Model

Consider an economy composed of F firms and N workers[j]. Time is discrete: $t = 0, 1, 2, ...$ and there is a homogeneous, perishable, good g whose price is $p_t > 0$. In each period, a firm $i \in \{1, ..., F\}$ produces q_{it} units of good g using labor as the sole input under a constant returns to scale (CRTS) regime:

$$q_{it} = \alpha_{it} n_{it}, \tag{1}$$

where α_{it} is the current labor productivity of firm i and n_{it} is the number of workers hired at t by firm i. Workers are homogeneous as far as their skills are concerned. If the firm offers a contractual wage w_{it} to each worker, current profits are computed as:

$$\pi_{it} = p_t q_{it} - w_{it} n_{it} = (p_t \alpha_{it} - w_{it}) n_{it}. \tag{2}$$

Contractual wages offered by firms to workers are the result of both a matching and bargaining process. We assume that any firm i has at time t a "satisficing" wage w_{it}^s she wants to offer to any worker. Similarly, any worker $j \in \{1, ..., N\}$ has at time t a "satisficing" wage w_{jt}^s which she wants to get from firms. Moreover, any worker j can only accept contractual wages if they are greater or equal to their *reservation wage* w_j^R, which we assume to be constant over time for simplicity.

We start by studying an economy where jobs last only one period. Hence, workers must search for a new job in any period. Job openings are equal to labor demand and, at the same time, to "ex-ante" vacancies. However, workers can be unemployed and firms might not satisfy their labor demand.

Let us turn now to a brief description of the flow of events in a generic time-period. We then move to a detailed account of each event separately.

Dynamics

Given the state of the system at the end of any time period $t-1$, the timing of events occurring in any time period t runs as follows.

(1) Firms decide how many jobs they want to open in period t.
(2) Workers search for a firm posting at least one job opening and queue up.

[j]The ratio between the number of workers and the number of firms (N/F) can be interpreted as a measure of concentration of economic activity.

(3) Job matching and bargaining occur: firms look in their queues and start bargaining with workers who have queued up (if any) to decide whether to hire them or not.

(4) After hiring, production takes place according to eq. (1). Aggregate supply and demand are then formed simply by aggregating individual supplies and demands. Subsequently, a "pseudo-Walrasian" price setting occurs. We assume that the price of good g at t is given by:

$$p_t Q_t = W_t, \tag{3}$$

where $Q_t = \sum_{i=1}^{F} q_{it}$ is aggregate (real) output and $W_t = \sum_{j=1}^{N} w_{jt}$ is total wage. Thus, total wage equals aggregate demand, as we assume that workers spend all their income to eat good g in any time period. Then, firms make profits:

$$\pi_{it} = (p_t \alpha_{it-1} - w_{it}) n_{it}.$$

(5) Given profits, firms undergo a selection process: those making negative profits ($\pi_{it} < 0$) exit and are replaced by entrants, which, as a first approximation, are simply "average" firms (see below).

(6) Firms and workers update their satisficing wages (w^s_{it-1} and w^s_{jt-1}).

(7) Finally, technological progress (if any) takes place. We assume that in each period labor productivity may increase at rates which are exogenous but firm-specific (see below).

Job Opening

At the beginning of period t, each firm creates a queue of job openings. Since in reality only *ex-ante* vacancies (i.e. new job positions) can be empirically observed, we will employ throughout the term job openings as a synonym of (ex-ante) vacancies. "Ex-post" vacancies will be computed as the number of unfilled job-openings.

Let us then call v_{it} the number of new positions opened by firm i at time t. As far as firm's decision about how many vacancies to open is concerned, we experiment with two alternative "behavioral" scenarios.

In the first one, a firm simply observes current (i.e. time $t-1$) price, quantity produced and contractual wage offered, and sets vacancies v_{it} as:

$$v_{it} = \overline{v}_{it-1} = \left\lceil \frac{p_{t-1} q_{it-1}}{w_{it-1}} \right\rceil, \tag{4}$$

that is she creates a queue with a number of open slots equal to the "ceiling" of (i.e. the smallest integer larger than) the ratio between revenues and contractual wage offered in the last period. We call this job opening scenario the "**Wild Market Archetype**", in that no history-inherited institution or behavioral feature is built into the model.

In the second "behavioral" scenario (which we shall call the "**Weak Path-Dependence**" scenario), we introduce some rather mild path-dependence in vacancy setting. We suppose that: (a) jobs opened by any firm at time t are a non-decreasing function of last-experienced profits growth rate; and (b) cannot exceed $\overline{v}_{it-1}$. More formally:

$$v_{it} = \min\{\overline{v}_{it-1}, v^*_{it}\}, \tag{5}$$

and:

$$v^*_{it} = \begin{cases} \lceil v_{it-1}(1+|X|) \rceil, \text{ if } \frac{\Delta\pi_{it-1}}{\pi_{it-1}} \geq 0 \\ \lceil v_{it-1}(1-|X|) \rceil, \text{ if } \frac{\Delta\pi_{it-1}}{\pi_{it-1}} < 0 \end{cases}, \tag{6}$$

where X is an i.i.d. random variable, normally distributed with mean zero and variance $\sigma_v^2 > 0$, and $\lceil x \rceil$ denotes the ceiling of x. Notice that the higher σ_v, the more firms react to any given profits growth rate by enlarging or shrinking their current queue size. Hence a *higher* σ_v implies *higher* sensitivity to market signals. Notice that in both scenarios firms always open at least one vacancy in each period.

Job Search

In our model, workers can visit in any time period only one firm. Similarly to job opening, we consider two "behavioral" scenarios also for the job search procedure employed by workers to find a firm who has just opened new job positions. In the first one, called "**No Search Inertia**", each worker j simply visits any firm i in the market with a probability proportional to the last contractual wage w_{it-1} she offered. If the selected firm has places still available in her queue, the worker gets in and demands a wage equal to her "satisficing" one, i.e. w^s_{jt-1}.

In the second scenario, which we label "**Search Inertia**", we introduce some stickiness (loyalty) in firm visiting. If worker j was employed by firm i in period $t-1$, she visits first firm i. If i still has places available in her queue, the worker gets in and demands w^s_{jt-1}. Otherwise, the worker employs the random rule above ("No Search Inertia") to select among the remaining $F-1$ firms.

In both scenarios, a worker becomes unemployed if she chooses a firm who has already filled all available slots in her queue.

Job Matching and Bargaining

After workers have queued up, firms start exploring workers wage demands to possibly match them with their *desiderata.* Suppose that at time t firm i observes $0 < m_{it} \leq N$ workers in her queue. Then, she will compute the average wage demanded by those workers:

$$\overline{w}_{it} = \frac{1}{m_{it}} \sum_{h=1}^{m_{it}} w^{s}_{j_h t-1}, \tag{7}$$

where j_h are the labels of workers in i's queue. Next, she sets her contractual wage for period t as a linear combination of $\overline{w}_{it}$ and her satisficing wage w^s_{it-1}. Thus:

$$w_{it} = \beta w^s_{it-1} + (1-\beta)\overline{w}_{it}, \tag{8}$$

where $\beta \in [0,1]$ is an institutional parameter governing firms' strength in wage bargaining. A higher β implies a higher strength on the side of the firm in wage setting. If $\beta = 0$, firms just set contractual wage as the average of wages demanded by workers in the queue. If $\beta = 1$, firms do not take into account at all workers' *desiderata.*

Once the firm has set the contractual wage at which she is willing to hire workers in her queue, any worker j in the queue will accept the job only if w_{it} exceeds her reservation wage w^R_j.

As soon as a worker j accepts the job, she temporarily changes her satisficing wage to keep up with the new (actual) wage earned, i.e. $w^s_{jt-1} = w_{it}$. Similarly, a firm who has filled at least a job opening will replace w^s_{it-1} with w_{it}[k].

Given the number of workers n_{it} hired by each firm, production, as well as price setting and profits determination occur as explained above. *Ex-post* firm i's vacancies are defined as $\widetilde{v}_{it} = m_{it} - n_{it}$.

Selection, Exit, and Entry

Suppose that - given the new contractual wage, price p_t, and current pro-

[k]These new values of satisfying wages will then be employed in the updating process. Since satisfying wage can be interpreted as (myopic) expectations, satisfying wage updating plays in the model the role of expectation formation process.

ductivity α_{it-1} - firm j faces negative profits, i.e. $p_t\alpha_{it-1} < w_{it}$. Then selection pressure makes firm j exit the market.

Each exiting firm is replaced by a new firm which starts out with the average "characteristics" of those firms still in the market at t (i.e. those making non-negative profits)[1]. Notice that this entry-exit process allows to keep an invariant number of F firms in the economy at each t.

Satisficing Wages Updating

Surviving firms, as well as the N workers, will then have the opportunity to revise their satisficing wage according to their perceptions about the outcome of market dynamics.

- **Firms**: We assume that each firm has an invariant desired ratio of filled to opened jobs $\rho_i \in (0,1]$ which she compares to the current ratio:

$$r_{it} = \frac{n_{it}}{v_{it}}.$$

If firm i hired too few workers (as compared to the number of job positions she decided to open), then she might want to increase the wage she is willing to offer to workers. Otherwise, she might want to decrease it. We capture this simple rule by positing that:

$$w^s_{it} = \begin{cases} w^s_{it-1}(1+|Y|) \text{ if } r_{it} < \rho_i \\ w^s_{it-1}(1-|Y|) \text{ if } r_{it} \geq \rho_i \end{cases}, \tag{9}$$

where Y is an i.i.d. random variable distributed as a standard normal. Notice that w^s_{it-1} is equal to w_{it} (i.e. contractual wage just offered) if the firm has hired at least a worker.

- **Workers**: If worker j remains unemployed after matching and bargaining, she might want to reduce her satisficing wage (without violating the reservation wage threshold). Otherwise, she might want to demand a higher wage during the next bargaining session. We then assume that:

$$w^s_{jt} = \begin{cases} \max\{w^R_j, w^s_{jt-1}(1-|Y|)\} \text{ if } j \text{ unemployed} \\ w^s_{jt-1}(1+|Y|) \qquad\qquad \text{if } j \text{ employed} \end{cases},$$

[1]All results we present in the next Section are robust to alternative assumptions concerning entry and exit.

where Y is an i.i.d. random variable distributed as a standard normal. Again, $w^s_{jt-1} = w_{jt}$ if j has been just hired.

Technological Progress

The last major ingredient of the model regards labor productivity dynamics. Here, we experiment with two "technological scenarios". In the first one ("**No Technological Progress**"), we study a system where labor productivity does not change through time (i.e. $\alpha_{it} = \alpha_i$, $\forall i$)[m]. In the second scenario ("**Technological Progress**"), we allow for an exogenous, albeit firm-specific, dynamics of labor productivities. We start with initially homogeneous labor coefficients ($\alpha_{i0} = \alpha$) and we let them grow stochastically over time according to the following multiplicative process:

$$\alpha_{it} = \alpha_{it-1}(1 + Z), \tag{10}$$

where Z, conditionally on $Z > 0$, is an i.i.d. normally distributed random variable with mean 0 and variance $\sigma^2_Z \geq 0$[n]. The latter governs the opportunity setting in the economy. The larger σ_Z, the more likely firms draw large productivity improvements. Notice that if we let $\sigma^2_Z = 0$ we recover the "**No Technological Progress**" scenario.

Initial Conditions, Micro- and Macro-Dynamics

The foregoing model, as mentioned, genuinely belongs to an evolutionary/ACE approach. Given its behavioral, bottom-up, perspective, one must resort to computer simulations to explore the behavior of the system[o].

The dynamics of the system depends on four sets of factors. *First*, we distinguish behavioral (e.g. concerning job opening and job search) and technological scenarios. We call such discrete institutional and technological regimes "system setups". *Second*, a choice of system parameters (F/N, σ_v, β, σ_Z) is required (see Table 1). *Third*, one should explore the would-be importance of different initial conditions[p]. Since simulations show that

[m]Labor productivity may in turn be either homogeneous across firms ($\alpha_i = \alpha$) or not.

[n]Hence, there is a probability 0.5 to draw a neutral labor productivity shock ($Z = 0$), while positive shocks are distributed as the positive half of a $N(0, 1)$.

[o]Simulation code is written in C++ and is available from the Authors upon request.

[p]In the model this implies defining initial values $(n_{i0}, \alpha_{i0}, w^s_{i0}, w_{i0})_{i=1}^F$ for firms and $(w^s_{j0})_{j=1}^N$ for workers. Moreover, an initial price p_0, and some distributions for desired ratios $(\rho_i)_{i=1}^F$ and reservation wages $(w^R_j)_{j=1}^N$ have to be chosen.

the latter do not dramatically affect the long run properties of aggregate variables, we typically define a "canonical" set of initial conditions. All results presented below refer to this benchmark choice. Finally, individual updating by firms and workers' induces a stochastic dynamics on micro-variables (e.g. contractual wages, desired production, desired employment, etc.). By aggregating these individual variables over firms and workers, one can study the properties of macro-dynamics for the variables of interest.

We will focus on unemployment:

$$U_t = N - \sum_{i=1}^{F} n_{it}, \tag{11}$$

total wages:

$$W_t = \sum_{j=1}^{N} w_{jt}, \tag{12}$$

and (real) GDP:

$$Q_t = \sum_{i=1}^{F} q_{it}, \tag{13}$$

as well as its growth rate:

$$h_t = \Delta \log(Q_t). \tag{14}$$

4. Simulation Results: Some Qualitative Evidence

In this section, we firstly run simulation experiments in order to identify general setups and parameters choices under which the model is able to *jointly* replicate the three aggregate regularities characterizing labor markets dynamics and economic activity discussed in Section 2. In the following Section, we shall perform Montecarlo exercises aimed at understanding how statistical properties of labor-market dynamics and economic activity change across different parameterizations and setups.

All simulation exercises we present in the paper refer to (and compare) four basic "system setup". Each "system setup" is characterized by a choice for behavioral/institutional assumptions (i.e. job opening and workers' job search) and a choice for the technological scenario (with or without technological change).

We experiment with the following two combinations of behavioral/institutional assumptions: (i) Walrasian Archetype (WA): We employ the "Wild Market Archetype" scenario as far as job opening is concerned and the "No Search Inertia" scenario for workers' job search; (ii) Institutionally-Shaped Environment (ISE): Firms open new job positions within a "Weak Path-Dependence" scenario, while workers search for a firm under the "Search Inertia" scenario.

Note that in the WA world, there is no path-dependence in job openings, nor in job search. Workers visit firms at random, while the latter open a number of new positions in each period without being influenced by past experienced profits. Conversely, in the ISE workers and firms face some path-dependence in job opening and job searching, as firms adjust job openings according to last profits growth and workers visit first the last firm where they were employed.

Each of the two foregoing behavioral choices is then associated to a technological scenario (with or without technological change) to get the four basic "system setups" under analysis[q].

We start by qualitatively investigating the emergence of Beveridge, Wage, and Okun's curves in an economy characterized by the "Walrasian Archetype", i.e. a world where agents decide myopically and do not carry over past information. The system does not allow to recover any aggregate, statistically significant, negative relationship between vacancy and unemployment rates. Simulations show that the Beveridge curve fails emerge for a quite large regions of the system parameters (F/N, β, σ_Z) space, cf. Figs. 1 and 2 for an example.

Conversely, both Wage and Okun's curve robustly emerge no matter whether technological progress is shut down or not. Notice that if $\sigma_Z = 0$, the economy works as a dynamic allocation device trying to match in a decentralized and imperfect way individual labor demand and supply *for given resources*. It is then easy to see that both Okun's and Wage relationships are a consequence (and not an emergent property) of the joint assumptions of quasi-Walrasian price-setting and constant returns to scale. Indeed, from (1) and (3), one gets: $W_t = -p_t U_t + p_t(N - N_t + \sum_i \alpha_i n_{it})$ and $Q_t = -U_t + (N - N_t + \sum_i \alpha_i n_{it})$. Thus, both curves are somewhat implied by the assumptions.

[q]In all exercises that follow, we set the econometric sample size $T = 1000$. This time span is sufficient to allow for convergence of the recursive moments for all variables under study.

If on the contrary technological progress occurs in a WA scenario, there is no apparent reasons to expect both OC and WC to robustly emerge. Yet, as simulations show, they both characterize system dynamics for a large region of the parameter space, even if no path-dependent behavior drives the economy (cf. Figs. 3 and 4).

Consider now an "Institutionally-Shaped Environment". Then, irrespective of the technological regime, the model is able to robustly generate Beveridge curves with statistically significant (negative) slopes: see for illustration Figs. 5 and 6. Furthermore, when technological progress is present, both Wage and Okun's curves still characterize macro-dynamics as robust, emergent, properties of the system, cf. Figs. 7 and 8.

5. Montecarlo Experiments

The set of qualitative results presented in the last Section suggest that some path-dependence seems to be a necessary condition for a Beveridge relationship. Moreover, a standard Okun's curve seems to be in place even when technological progress persistently boosts available production capacity. Finally, despite persistent heterogeneity arising endogenously from labor productivity dynamics, Phillips-curve type of regularities are typically rejected by the simulated data in favor of a Wage curve relationship.

To check whether these qualitative results are robust to changes in system parameters, we turn now to a more detailed Montecarlo analysis. We discuss two sets of exercises. First, we ask whether the three regularities we are interested in, robustly emerge in each of the four main "setups" under study. To this end, we generate M independent (Montecarlo) simulations for each choice of relevant parameters over a sufficiently fine grid. We then study the moments of the distributions of the statistics of interest. We focus in particular on test statistics for the significance of coefficients in Beveridge and Okun regressions, the magnitude of Okun's coefficient, as well as test statistics discriminating between Wage and Phillips curves.

Second, we will perform some simple "comparative dynamics" exercises to investigate what happens to emergent regularities when one tunes system parameters within each "setup". We are in particular interested in detecting shifts (if any) in the Beveridge curve and changes in Okun's coefficients. Once again, we will discuss the outcome of Montecarlo statistics coming from independent time-series simulation runs for any given parametrization[r].

---

[r]All Montecarlo experiments are undertaken using a Montecarlo sample size $M =$

Emergence of Aggregate Regularities: Robustness Tests

To begin with, consider the emergence of Beveridge curves. Consider, for any setup under analysis, a given parametrization. Following existing empirical literature, we computed, for each of M independent simulated time-series, estimates (and R^2) for the simple time-series regression:

$$u_t = b_0 + b_1 v_t + \epsilon_t, \tag{15}$$

where ϵ_t is white-noise, u_t is unemployment rate and v_t is vacancy rates (both defined as activity rates). We then computed Montecarlo statistics (e.g. average) of estimates $\widehat{b_1}$ and goodness-of-fit R^2, together with the percentage of rejections for the test $b_1 = 0$ (i.e. a proxy for the likelihood of BC emergence, in case of a negative estimate). By repeating this exercise as parameters change within a given system setup (WA vs. ISE), one is able to investigate Beveridge curves emergence, how large are their slopes, and how good is the correspondent linear fit on average[s].

Notice first that, in a WA, the likelihood of emergence of a BC is quite low. As Fig. 9 shows, the percentage of rejections of $H_0 : b_1 = 0$ is almost always below 50% as we tune firms' strength in wage bargaining (β) and technological opportunities (σ_Z). Accordingly, the estimated slope does not dramatically change across the parameter space, ranging from -0.938 and -0.263 (not shown). In particular, technological progress seems to favor BC emergence: the higher σ_Z, the larger the percentage of rejections and the larger the goodness of fit of the correspondent regression (cf. Fig. 10). To see why this happens, recall that a stronger technological boost induces firms to open more vacancies, which the system seems to be able to more easily fill. When technology is strong enough, a lower β also appears to favor the emergence of a BC, even if this effect turns out to be milder than the technological one.

If on the contrary the economy is characterized by an "institutionally-shaped environment", the percentage of rejections is almost always close to 100% across the entire $(\sigma_v, \sigma_Z, \beta)$ space and the average estimated slope is negative (not shown). Thus, unlike in a WA economy, the presence of some frictions and path-dependence in the institutional and behavioral settings allows a BC to robustly emerge. Here, firms' bargaining strength

100. Initial conditions are always kept fixed (see above).

[s]Standard errors of estimates, as well as Montecarlo (across simulations) standard deviations of all statistics of interest appear to be very small. Therefore, we do not report here confidence intervals.

(β) appears to have a strong impact on the goodness of fit. In fact, when β is low ($\beta = 0.1$), the linear fit turns out to better describe the vacancy-unemployment relationship (cf. Fig. 11) than in the case when firms' bargaining strength is high ($\beta = 1.0$), see Fig. 12. In this latter case, however, a higher sensitivity to market signals (σ_v) favors the emergence of well-shaped BC. Indeed, in presence of technical progress, a larger σ_v allows firms to turn higher profits in a higher number of vacancies, which are more easily filled when firms are stronger in the wage-bargaining process.

While the Beveridge curve tends to robustly emerge only in an "institutionally-shaped" economy, simulations show that a Wage curve always characterizes our system in all four setups. In particular, statistical tests aimed at discriminating between a Phillips and a Wage world, show that the latter is almost always preferred. Following Card (1995), we perform the lagged regression:

$$\Delta \log \widetilde{W}_t = g_t + a_1 \log u_t + a_2 \log u_{t-1} + \Delta e_t, \tag{16}$$

where $\widetilde{W}_t$ is the wage rate, u_t is unemployment rate, g_t is a time trend, and first-differencing is taken to avoid serial correlation in e_t. As Card (1995) shows, the Wage curve hypothesis implies $a_1 = -a_2$ (together with $a_1 < 0$), while the Phillips curve hypothesis requires $a_2 = 0$. Table 2 reports Monte-carlo testing exercises in our four setups for a benchmark parametrization[t]. Notice that the percentage of rejections of a Phillips world is quite high, while we tend not to reject the hypothesis that wage levels are negatively correlated with unemployment rates in almost all simulations.

The R^2 is very high in all setups. This might be an expected result when $\sigma_Z = 0$, because without technological progress a Wage curve follows from price-setting and constant returns. However, when $\sigma_Z > 0$ the goodness-of-fit remains high (and standard errors very low). Our model seems to allow for well-behaved Wage curves also when technological progress induces persistent heterogeneity in labor productivity dynamics. Furthermore, a quite general and robust result (see also below) concerns the effect of technological progress upon the slope of the curve. As discussed above, the latter is expected to be around -1.0 when $\sigma_Z = 0$, but nothing can in principle be said about the expected slope when $\sigma_Z > 0$. Our results suggest that, even when technological progress is present, the Wage curve robustly emerges.

[t]As far as emergence of Okun's and Wage curves are concerned, one does not detect any statistically significant differences in percentage of rejections when parameters change across different system setups. See below for some considerations on shifts of Beveridge and Okun's curves across different parameterizations.

Indeed, wage rates become even more responsive to unemployment than in the $\sigma_Z = 0$ case.

Alike the Wage curve, the Okun's curve, too, turns out to be a robust outcome of our labor market dynamics. Evidence of this effect simply appears by linearly regressing GDP growth rates against changes in the rates of unemployment:

$$\Delta \log(Q_t) = c_0 + c_1 \Delta \log(u_t) + \epsilon_t. \tag{17}$$

We computed Montecarlo estimates of the Okun's coefficient c_1 and we tested for $H_0 : c_1 = 0$ (i.e. emergence of an Okun's curve - as long as $c_1 < 0$), see Table 3 for an example. Our economy allows for an Okun's relationship in all settings, especially when technological progress is present. Again, this might be considered as a not-too-surprising result when $\sigma_Z = 0$, but it becomes a truly emergent property when $\sigma_Z > 0$.

The absolute value of the Okun's coefficient is larger than one (and indeed close to Attfield and Silverstone (1997) empirical estimates), implying some emergent aggregate dynamic increasing returns to labor. The effect becomes stronger when an ISE is assumed: Montecarlo averages of the Okun's coefficient range from -2.196 to -3.072.

Notice that one did not assume any increasing returns regime at the individual firm level. In fact, firms produce using constant returns production functions, see (1). Moreover, no Phillips curve relationships is in place: our economy typically displays a negative relationship between unemployment rates and wage *levels*. This suggests that aggregation of imperfect and persistently heterogeneous behaviors leads to macro-economic dynamic properties that were not present at the individual level. Therefore, aggregate dynamic increasing returns emerge as the outcome of aggregation of dynamic, interdependent, microeconomic patterns (Forni and Lippi, 1997).

Some Comparative Dynamics Montecarlo Exercises

We turn now to a comparative dynamics Montecarlo investigation of the effect of system parameters on emergent aggregate regularities. We focus on the "institutionally-shaped" setup, wherein the economy robustly exhibits well-behaved Beveridge, Wage, and Okun's curves, and we study what happens under alternative parameter settings. In particular we compare parameter setups characterized by:

(1) low vs. high N/F ratio (i.e. degrees of concentration of economic activity);

(2) low vs. high σ_v (i.e. sensitivity to market signals in the way firms set their vacancies);
(3) low vs. high β (i.e. firms' bargaining strength in wage setting);
(4) low vs. high σ_Z (technological opportunities).

We *first* ask whether a higher sensitivity to market signals in vacancy setting induce detectable shifts in aggregate regularities. As Table 4 shows, the smaller σ_v, the stronger the revealed increasing dynamic returns: GDP growth becomes more responsive to unemployment growth and the Okun's curve becomes steeper. Notice that σ_v can also be interpreted as an inverse measure of path-dependence in firms' vacancy setting. The smaller σ_v, the more firms tend to stick to last-period job openings. Therefore, a *smaller* path-dependence implies a steeper Okun's relation.

Analogously, we investigate the impact on the BC of simultaneously increasing N/F (i.e. increasing N for a given F) and σ_v (i.e. firms' "sensitivity to market signals"). Notice that a higher concentration allows firms - *ceteris paribus* - to more easily fill their vacancies. Similarly, the higher σ_v, the more firms are able to react to aggregate conditions and correspondingly adjust vacancies. Therefore, one might be tempted to interpret economies characterized by high values for both N/F and σ_v as "low friction" worlds, and expect the BC curve to lie closer to the axes. Notice, however, that in our model an "indirect" effect is also present. If labor demand is very low (e.g. because the economy is in a recession), then the unemployment rate might be high irrespective of the value of N/F. Moreover, if σ_v is high, firms will fire more workers during downswings, thus inducing a sort of "accelerator" effect on the recession. Thus, the consequences on the BC of assuming a larger market concentration and a higher sensitivity to market signals are *ex-ante* ambiguous: if "indirect" effects dominate, we should observe various combinations between shifts to the right and "business-cycle" movements along the curve.

Notwithstanding all that, Montecarlo simulations show that the model is able to reproduce the predicted shifts in the BC. We observe (cf. Table 5) that as N/F and σ_v both increase in a ISE economy, Montecarlo averages of estimated intercepts stay constant, while the BC becomes, on average, steeper (and thus closer to the origin). A steeper BC implies that firms adaptively learn to open less vacancies and to adjust their filled-to-open vacancy ratios in response to market signals.

Second, we explore what happens to (within-simulation) average and standard deviation of GDP growth time-series[u] when both σ_v and firms' bargaining strength β are allowed to vary. Recall that the higher β, the less firms take into account workers satisficing wages when they decide their contractual wage. Figs. 13 and 14 show Montecarlo means of average and standard deviation of GDP growth rates. We find that the *higher* firms' bargaining strength, the *smaller* both average growth rates and their variability. Thus, allowing for some bargaining power on the workers' side implies better aggregate performance, but also more fluctuations. Furthermore, if firms are *less* responsive to market signals (e.g. they employ a path-dependent vacancy setting rule) the economy enjoys persistently higher average growth rates and persistently smaller fluctuations.

Finally, we assess the consequences of "fueling" the economy with higher technological opportunities (i.e. higher σ_Z) for different levels of β (and setting σ_v to an intermediate level). While a higher σ_Z implies higher average growth rates in all parameter settings (Fig. 15), a stronger bargaining power for workers still implies better aggregate performances. Together, more technological opportunities also entail a higher volatility in the growth process (see Fig. 16). Volatility can be weakened if one increases firms strength in wage bargaining.

6. Conclusions

In this paper, we have presented an evolutionary model of output and labor market dynamics describing from the bottom-up individual behaviors of multiple firms and workers and their interactions. In particular, we have explicitly modeled from an agent-based perspective the processes of vacancy setting, as well as matching, wage bargaining, and wage setting.

We assume that firms produce a homogeneous, perishable, good under constant returns to labor, enjoy labor productivity improvements thanks to technological progress, and undergo a selection process shaped by their revealed competitiveness (which is also affected by their hiring and wage-setting behaviors). Both demand and price formation are modeled as endogenous processes.

The interplay between labor and output markets allows also to appreciate the relationships between business cycle and unemployment. Such an interplay provides a joint, evolutionary, interpretation of some of the most

[u]That is, we compute average and standard deviation of GDP growth rates within a simulation $\{h_t, t = 1, ..., T\}$, $h_t = \Delta \log Q_t$.

important aggregate stylized facts in labor market dynamics and business cycle, such as the Beveridge curve, the Wage curve, and the Okun's curve.

Simulations show that Beveridge, Wage and Okun's curves can be jointly generated by our model as emergent properties under quite broad behavioral and institutional settings. Moreover, the emergent Okun's curves exhibit aggregate dynamic increasing returns notwithstanding firms employ linear production functions.

Montecarlo simulations also indicate that statistically detectable shifts in Okun's and Beveridge curves emerge as the result of changes in institutional, behavioral, and technological parameters. For example, a higher concentration of market activity (i.e. a higher number of workers per firm) and a higher sensitivity to market signals in firms' vacancy setting rules imply Beveridge curves which lie closer to the axes.

Finally, the model generates quite sharp predictions about how the average aggregate performance (and volatility) of the system changes in alternative behavioral, institutional, and technological setups. For example, we find that the *higher* firms' bargaining strength, the *smaller* both average growth rates and their variability. Furthermore, if firms are *less* responsive to market signals, the economy enjoys persistently higher average growth rates and persistently smaller fluctuations. Similarly, higher technological opportunities imply higher average growth rates but more volatile growth rate time-series. Volatility can be however weakened if one increases firms strength in wage bargaining.

Table 1. System Parameters

Parameter	Range	Meaning
N/F	R_{++}	Concentration of economic activity (Number of Workers / Number of Firms)
σ_v	R_{++}	Sensitivity to market signals in vacancy settings (only in a Weak Path-Dependence Scenario)
β	$[0,1]$	Labor-market institutional parameter governing the strength of firms in wage-setting
σ_Z	R_{+}	Technological parameter tuning the availability of opportunities in the system ($= 0$ means no technological progress)

Table 2. Emergence of the Wage curve in alternative setups. WA = "Walrasian Archetype". ISE= "Institutionally- Shaped Environment". Functional form tested: $\Delta \log \widetilde{W}_t = g_t + a_1 \log u_t + a_2 \log u_{t-1} + \Delta e_t$. Rejecting Phillips curve hypothesis means rejecting $H'_o : a_2 = 0$. Rejecting Wage curve hypothesis means rejecting $H'_o : a_1 = -a_2$. Montecarlo Standard Errors in parentheses. Montecarlo sample size $M = 100$. Benchmark parametrization: $N/F = 5$, $\beta = 0.5$, $\sigma_Z = 0.1$ (when >0), $\sigma_v = 0.1$ (under ISE).

	Setups			
	WA		ISE	
	$\sigma_Z = 0$	$\sigma_Z > 0$	$\sigma_Z = 0$	$\sigma_Z > 0$
MC Average of $\widehat{a_1}$	−0.814 (0.025)	−1.643 (0.093)	−1.019 (0.072)	−2.329 (0.225)
MC Average of $\widehat{a_2}$	0.781 (0.019)	1.520 (0.083)	0.977 (0.020)	2.134 (0.169)
R^2	0.985 (0.003)	0.906 (0.023)	0.978 (0.017)	0.914 (0.026)
% of rejections ($H_0 : a_2=0$) at 5%	100%	99%	99%	100%
% of rejections ($H_0 : a_1=-a_2$) at 5%	10%	5%	5%	1%

Table 3. Emergence of the Okun's curve in alternative setups. WA = "Walrasian Archetype". ISE= "Institutionally- Shaped Environment". Estimation of $\Delta \log(Q_t) = c_0 + c_1 \Delta \log(u_t) + \epsilon_t$. Montecarlo Standard Errors in parentheses. Montecarlo sample size $M = 100$. Benchmark parametrization: $N/F = 5$, $\beta = 0.5$, $\sigma_Z = 0.1$ (when >0), $\sigma_v = 0.1$ (under ISE).

	Setups			
	WA		ISE	
	$\sigma_Z = 0$	$\sigma_Z > 0$	$\sigma_Z = 0$	$\sigma_Z > 0$
MC Average of $\widehat{c_1}$	−2.064 (0.042)	−2.196 (0.047)	−2.635 (0.068)	−3.072 (0.063)
R^2	0.939 (0.026)	0.925 (0.060)	0.928 (0.064)	0.936 (0.025)
Max of Tail Prob. Distrib. for $H_0 : c_1=0$	0.000	0.001	0.000	0.001
% of rejections ($H_0 : c_1=0$) at 5%	100%	99%	100%	99%

Table 4. Shifts in the Okun's coefficient in an "Institutionally- Shaped Environment" under alternative parameter settings. HSMS: High Sensitivity to Market Signals. LSMS: Low Sensitivity to Market Signals. Estimation of $\Delta \log(Q_t) = c_0 + c_1 \Delta \log(u_t) + \epsilon_t$. Montecarlo Standard Errors in parentheses. Montecarlo sample size $M = 100$. Benchmark parametrization: $N/F = 5$, $\beta = 0.5$, $\sigma_Z = 0.1$.

	ISE Setup			
	$\sigma_v = 1.0$ (HSMS)		$\sigma_v = 0.2$ (LSMS)	
	$\sigma_Z = 0$	$\sigma_Z > 0$	$\sigma_Z = 0$	$\sigma_Z > 0$
MC Average of $\widehat{c_1}$	−2.700 (0.082)	−2.960 (0.085)	−2.900 (0.064)	−3.270 (0.060)
R^2	0.928 (0.064)	0.936 (0.025)	0.939 (0.026)	0.925 (0.060)
Max of Tail Prob. Distrib. for $H_0 : c_1=0$	0.001	0.001	0.000	0.001
% of rejections ($H_0 : c_1=0$) at 5%	100%	99%	100%	99%

Table 5. Shifts in the Beveridge curve in an "Institutionally- Shaped Environment" under alternative parameter settings for: (i) concentration of economic activity N/F; (ii) sensitivity to market signals σ_v. Estimation of $u_t = b_0 + b_1 v_t + \epsilon_t$. Montecarlo Standard Errors in parentheses. Montecarlo sample size $M = 100$. Benchmark parametrization: $\beta = 0.5$. No technical progress is assumed to focus on BC shifts for given resources.

	Parameter Settings			
N/F	50	20	10	5
σ_v	1.0	0.6	0.2	0.1
MC Mean of $\widehat{b_0}$	0.684 (0.018)	0.689 (0.024)	0.691 (0.043)	0.692 (0.043)
MC Mean of $\sigma(\widehat{b_0})$	0.020 (0.002)	0.027 (0.002)	0.040 (0.004)	0.033 (0.004)
Max of MC Tail Prob. Distr. for H_0: $b_0 = 0$	0.001	0.000	0.001	0.001
% of Rejections for H_0: $b_0 = 0$	99%	100%	98%	99%
MC Mean of $\widehat{b_1}$	−0.679 (0.030)	−0.631 (0.043)	−0.535 (0.071)	−0.413 (0.077)
MC Mean of $\sigma(\widehat{b_1})$	0.031 (0.003)	0.044 (0.004)	0.065 (0.006)	0.056 (0.007)
Max of MC Tail Prob.Distr. for H_0: $b_1 = 0$	0.000	0.001	0.002	0.001
% of Rejections for H_0: $b_1 = 0$	100%	99%	98%	99%
MC Mean of R^2	0.816 (0.038)	0.677 (0.045)	0.408 (0.064)	0.410 (0.062)

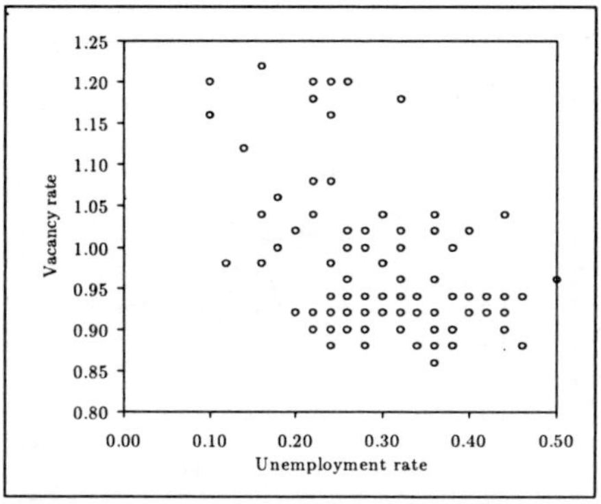

Figure 1. Vacancy vs. Unemployment Rate in a "Walrasian Archetype" Economy **without** Technological Progress. Parameters: $N/F = 5$, $\beta = 0.5$.

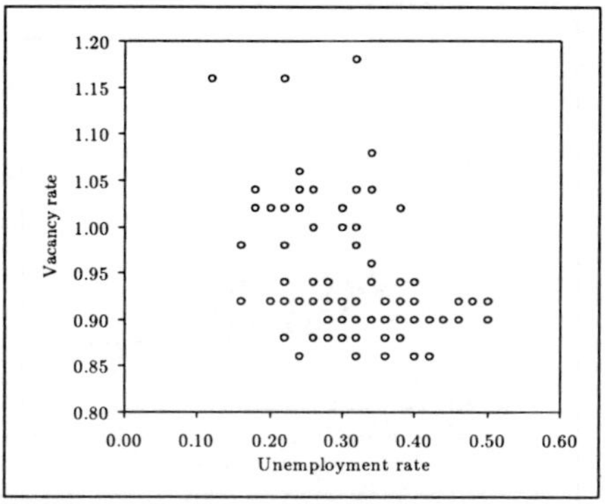

Figure 2. Vacancy vs. Unemployment Rate in a "Walrasian Archetype" Economy **with** Technological Progress. Parameters: $N/F = 5$, $\beta = 0.5$, $\sigma_Z = 0.1$.

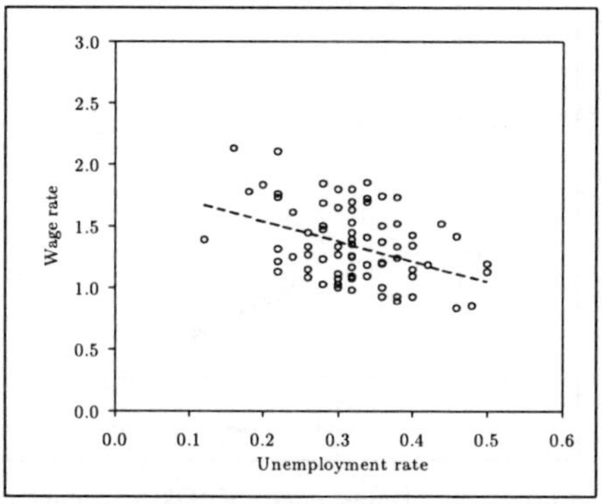

Figure 3. Emergence of Wage curve in a "Walrasian Archetype" Economy **with** Technological Progress. Parameters: $N/F = 5$, $\beta = 0.5$, $\sigma_Z = 0.1$.

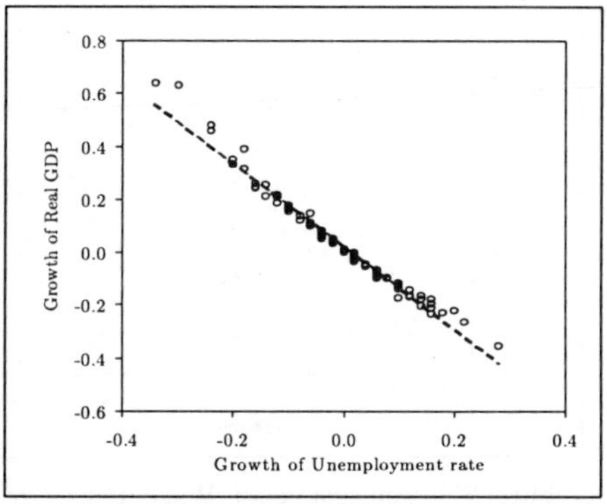

Figure 4. Emergence of Okun's curve in a "Walrasian Archetype" Economy **with** Technological Progress. Parameters: $N/F = 5$, $\beta = 0.5$, $\sigma_Z = 0.1$.

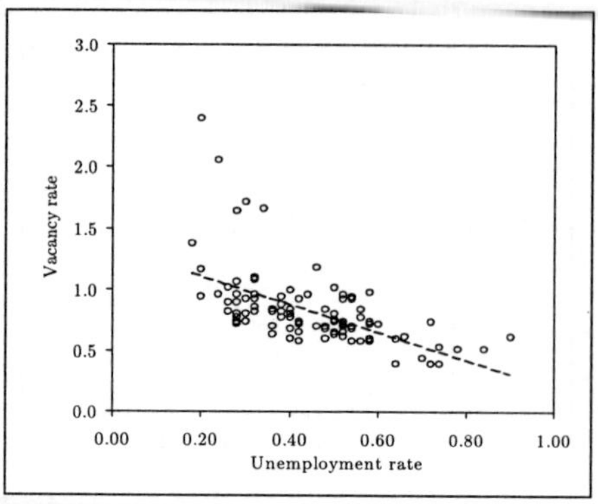

Figure 5. Emergence of Beveridge curve in a "Institutionally-Shaped" Environment **without** Technological Progress. Parameters: $N/F = 5$, $\beta = 0.5$.

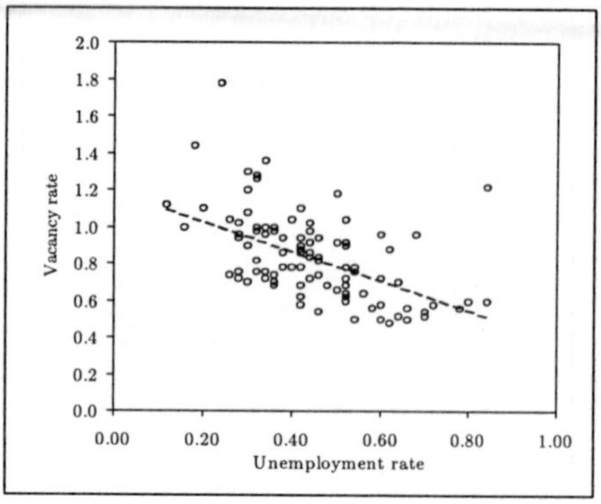

Figure 6. Emergence of Beveridge curve in a "Institutionally-Shaped" Environment **with** Technological Progress. Parameters: $N/F = 5$, $\beta = 0.5$, $\sigma_Z = 0.1$.

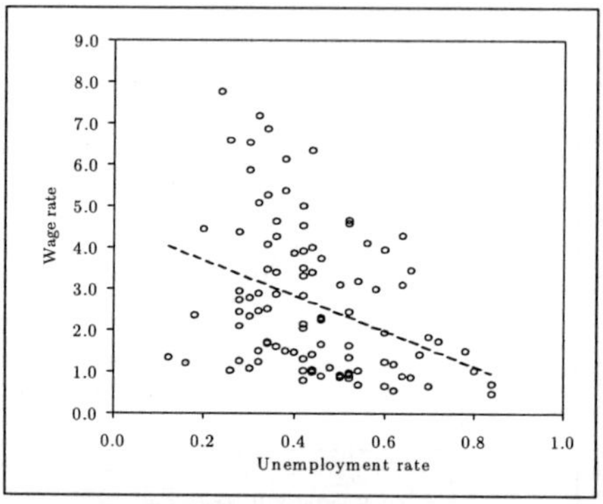

Figure 7. Emergence of Wage curve in a "Institutionally-Shaped" Environment **with** Technological Progress. Parameters: $N/F = 5$, $\beta = 0.5$, $\sigma_Z = 0.1$.

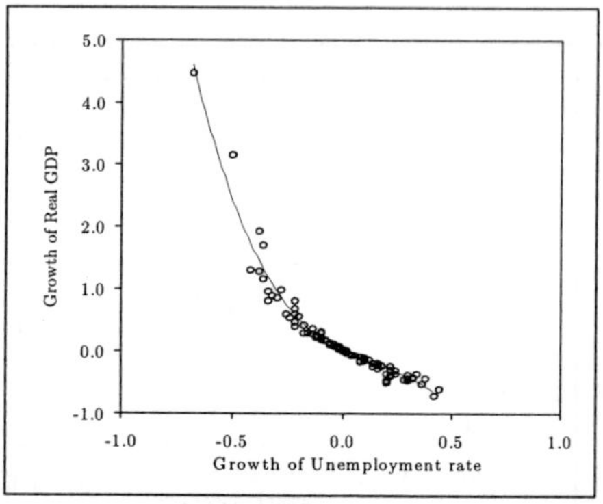

Figure 8. Emergence of Okun's curve in a "Institutionally-Shaped" Environment **with** Technological Progress. Parameters: $N/F = 5$, $\beta = 0.5$, $\sigma_Z = 0.1$.

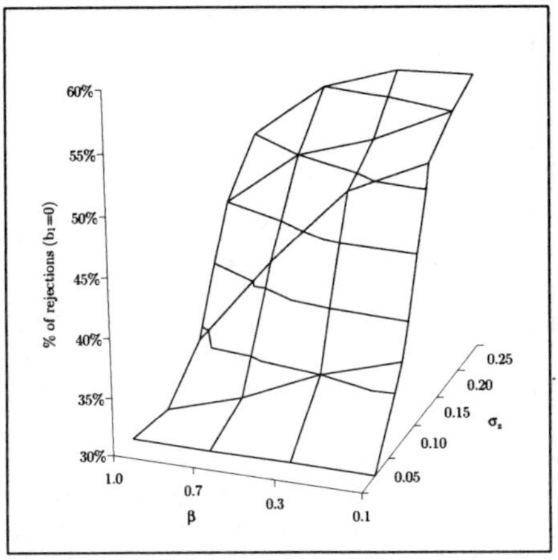

Figure 9. Percentage of rejections of $H_0 : b_1 = 0$ for the Beveridge Regression $u_t = b_0 + b_1 v_t + \epsilon_t$ in a "Walrasian Archetype" as firms' strength in wage-setting (β) and technological opportunities (σ_Z) change ($N/F = 5$).

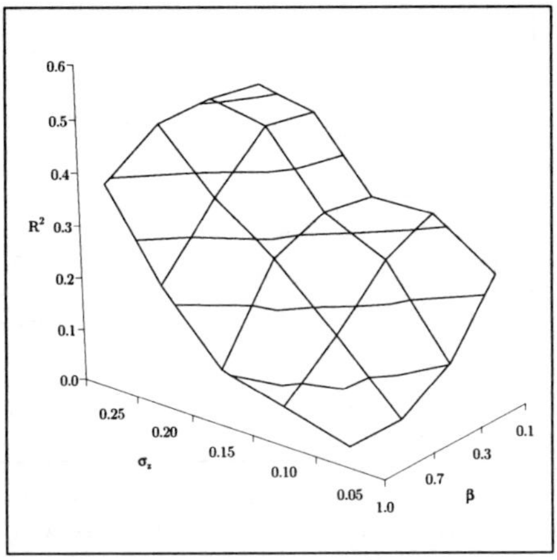

Figure 10. Goodness of fit (R^2) of Beveridge Regression $u_t = b_0 + b_1 v_t + \epsilon_t$ in a "Walrasian Archetype" as firms' strength in wage-setting (β) and technological opportunities (σ_Z) change ($N/F = 5$).

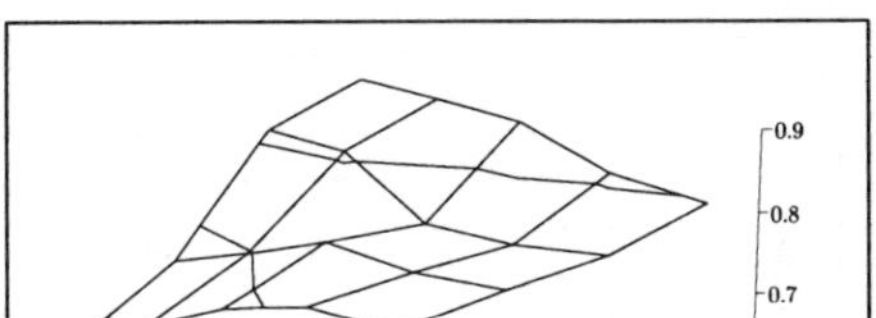

Figure 11. Goodness of fit (R^2) of Beveridge Regression $u_t = b_0 + b_1 v_t + \epsilon_t$ in a "Institutionally-shaped Environment" characterized by a low firms' strength in wage-setting ($\beta = 0.1$) as firms' sensitivity to market signals (σ_v) and technological opportunities (σ_Z) change ($N/F = 5$).

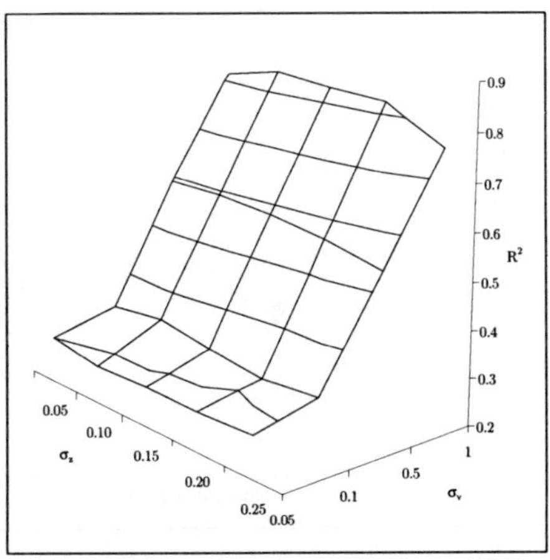

Figure 12. Goodness of fit (R^2) of Beveridge Regression $u_t = b_0 + b_1 v_t + \epsilon_t$ in a "Institutionally-shaped Environment" characterized by a high firms' strength in wage-setting ($\beta = 1.0$) as firms' sensitivity to market signals (σ_v) and technological opportunities (σ_Z) change ($N/F = 5$).

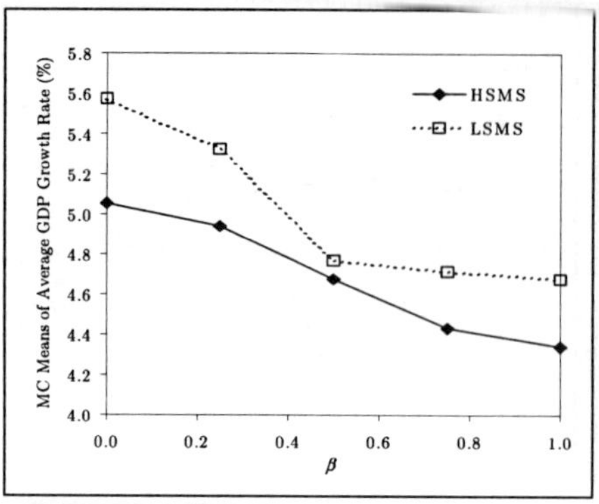

Figure 13. Montecarlo Means of (within-simulation) Average Real GDP Growth Rates as a function of firms strength in wage bargaining (β). LSMS vs. HSMS: Low ($\sigma_v = 0.1$) vs. High ($\sigma_v = 1.0$) sensitivity to market signals in vacancy setting. "Institutionally-Shaped" Environment. Parameters: $N/F = 5$, $\sigma_Z = 0.1$.

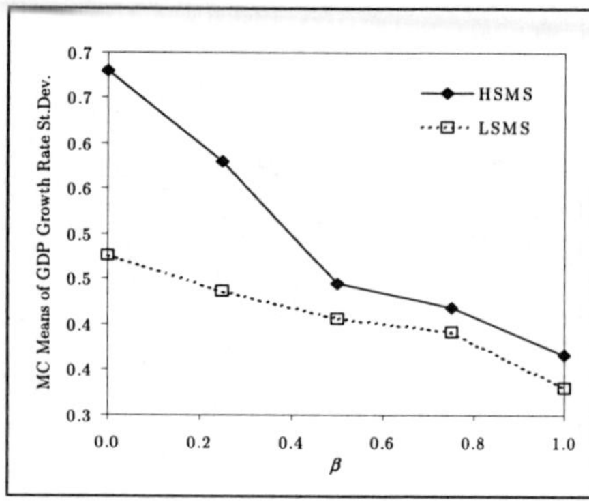

Figure 14. Montecarlo Means of (within-simulation) Standard Deviation of Real GDP Growth Rates as a function of firms strength in wage bargaining (β). LSMS vs. HSMS: Low ($\sigma_v = 0.1$) vs. High ($\sigma_v = 1.0$) sensitivity to market signals in vacancy setting. "Institutionally-Shaped" Environment. Parameters: $N/F = 5$, $\sigma_Z = 0.1$.

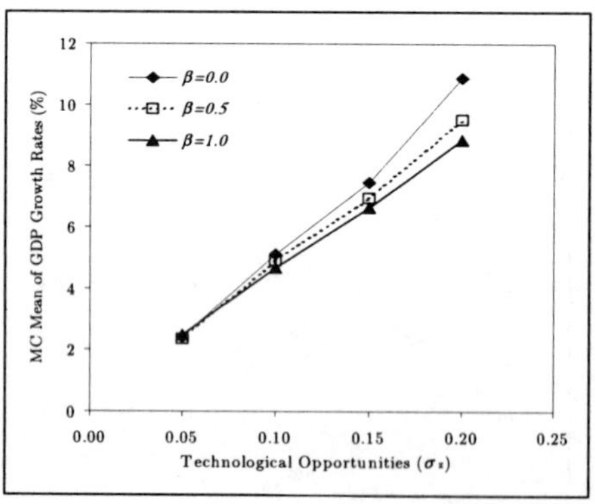

Figure 15. Montecarlo Means of (within-simulation) Average Real GDP Growth Rates as a function of technological opportunities (σ_Z) and firms strength in wage bargaining (β). "Institutionally-Shaped" Environment. Parameters: $N/F = 5$, $\sigma_v = 0.1$.

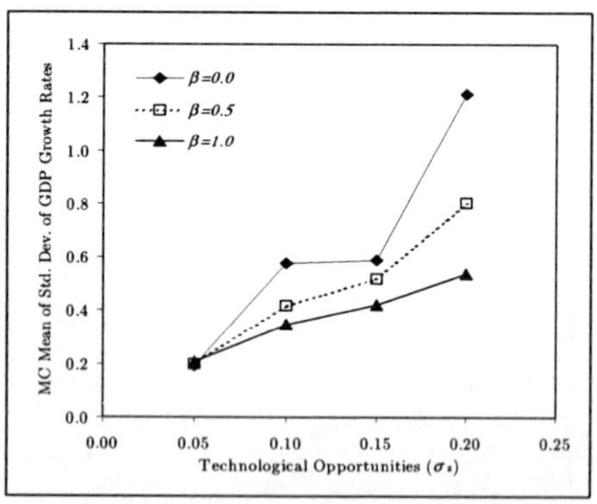

Figure 16. Montecarlo Means of (within-simulation) Standard Deviation of Real GDP Growth Rates as a function of technological opportunities (σ_Z) and firms strength in wage bargaining (β). "Institutionally-Shaped" Environment. Parameters: $N/F = 5$, $\sigma_v = 0.1$.

References

Aoki, M. (2003), "A New Model of Output Fluctuation: Ultrametrics, Beveridge Curve and Okun's Law", Economics online papers, no. 234, UCLA.

Aoki, M. and H. Yoshikawa (2003), "A Simple Quantity Adjustment Model of Economic Fluctuations and Growth", in Cowan, R. and N. Jonard (eds.), *Heterogeneous Agents, Interaction and Economic Performance.* Berlin, Springer.

Ashenfelter, O. and D. Card (eds.) (1999), *Handbook of Labor Economics. Volume 3.* Elsevier Science, Amsterdam.

Ashenfelter, O. and R. Layard (eds.) (1986), *Handbook of Labor Economics. Volume 2.* Elsevier Science, Amsterdam.

Attfield, C. and B. Silverstone (1997), "Okun´s coefficient: A comment", *The Review of Economics and Statistics*, 79: 326–329.

Blanchard, O. and P. Diamond (1989), "The Beveridge curve", *Brooking Papers on Economic Activities*, 1: 1–76.

Blanchard, O. and L. Katz (1997), "What We Know and Do Not Know about the Natural Rate of Unemployment", *Journal of Economic Perspectives*, 11: 57–72.

Blanchflower, D. and A. Oswald (1994), *The Wage Curve.* Cambridge, Massachussetts, The MIT Press.

Bleakley, H. and J. Fuhrer (1997), "Shifts in the Beveridge Curve, Job Matching, and Labor Market Dynamics", *New England Economic Review*, pp. 3–19.

Borsch-Supan, A. (1991), "Panel Data Analysis of the Beveridge Curve: Is There a Macroeconomic Relation between the Rate of Unemployment and Vacancy Rate?", *Economica*, 58: 279–297.

Burdett, K., S. Shi and R. Wright (2001), "Pricing and Matching with Frictions", *Journal of Political Economy*, 109: 1060–1085.

Cao, M. and S. Shi (2000), "Coordination, matching and wages", *Canadian Journal of Economics*, 33: 1009–1033.

Card, D. (1995), "The Wage Curve: A Review", *Journal of Economic Literature*, 33: 785–799.

Card, D. and D. Hyslop (1996), "Does Inflation Grease the Wheels of the Labor Market", Working paper 5538, NBER.

Dosi, G. and R. Nelson (1994), "An introduction to evolutionary theories in economics", *Journal of Evolutionary Economics*, 4: 153–172.

Dosi, G. and L. Orsenigo (1994), "Macrodynamics and microfoundations: an evolutionary perspective", in Granstrand, O. (ed.), *The economics of technology.* Amsterdam, North Holland.

Dosi, G. and S. Winter (2002), "Interpreting Economic Change: Evolution, Structures and Games", in Augier, M. and J. March (eds.), *The*

Economics of Choice, Change, and Organizations. Cheltenham, Edward Elgar Publishers.

Epstein, J. and R. Axtell (1996), *Growing Artificial Societies: Social Science from the Bottom-Up.* Washington D.C., MIT Press.

Fagiolo, G., G. Dosi and R. Gabriele (2004), "Towards an Evolutionary Interpretation of Aggregate Labor Market Regularities", Working paper, LEM-WP 2004-02, Sant'Anna School of Advanced Studies, Laboratory of Economics and Management.

Flaschel, P., G. Kauermann and W. Semmler (2003), "Testing Wage and Price Phillips Curves for the United States", Unpublished manuscript, Bielefeld University, Faculty of Economics.

Forni, M. and M. Lippi (1997), *Aggregation and the Microfoundations of Dynamic Macroeconomics.* Oxford, Clarendon Press.

Hahn, F. and R. Solow (1997), *A Critical Essay on Modern Macroeconomic Theory.* Cambridge, MA, The MIT Press.

Julien, B., J. Kennes and I. King (2000), "Bidding for Labor", *Review of Economic Dynamics*, 3: 619–649.

Kirman, A. (1992), "Whom or what does the representative individual represent ?", *Journal of Economic Perspectives*, 6: 117–136.

Kirman, A. (1997), "The Economy as an Interactive System", in Arthur, W., S. Durlauf and D. Lane (eds.), *The Economy as an Evolving Complex System II.* Santa Fe Institute, Santa Fe and Reading, MA, Addison-Wesley.

Laffond, G. and J. Lesourne (2000), "The genesis of expectations and of sunspot equilibria", *Journal of Evolutionary Economics*, 2: 211–231.

Lagos, R. (2000), "An Alternative Approach to Search Frictions", *Journal of Political Economy*, 108: 851–872.

Lesourne, J. (1992), *The Economics of Order and Disorder.* Oxford, Clarendon Press.

Nickell, S., L. Nunziata, W. Ochell and G. Quintini (2001), "The Beveridge curve, Unemployment and wages in the OECD from 1960s to 1990s", Working paper no. 502, CEPR, London, U.K.

Okun, A. (1962), "Potential GDP: Its Measurement and Significance", *Proceedings of the Busisness and Economics Statistics*, pp. 98–103.

Okun, A. (1970), *The political economy of prosperity.* The Brookings Institution, Washington D.C.

Peters, M. (1991), "Ex ante price offers in matching games non-steady states", *Econometrica*, 59: 1425–1454.

Petrongolo, B. and C. Pissarides (2001), "Looking into the Black Box: A Survey on the Matching Function", *Journal of Economic Literature*, 39: 390–431.

Phelps, E. (1994), *Structural Slumps.* Cambridge, Harvard University Press.

Phelps, E. and S. Winter (1970), "Optimal Price Policy Under Atomistic Competition", in Phelps, E., G. Archibald and A. Alchian (eds.), *Microeconomic Foundations of Employment and Inflation Theory.* New York, Norton.

Pissarides, C. (2000), *Equilibrium Unemployment Theory.* Oxford, Blackwell.

Prachowny, M. (1993), "Okun´s Law: Theoretical Foundations and Revised Estimates", *The Review of Economics and Statistics*, 75: 331–336.

Smith, T. and Y. Zenou (2003), "A Discrete-Time Stochastic Model of Job Matching", *Economic Dynamics*, 6: 54–79.

Solow, R. (1998), "What is Labour-Market Flexibility? What is it Good for?", *Proceedings of the British Academy*, 97: 189–211.

Tesfatsion, L. (1997), "How Economists Can Get ALife", in Arthur, W., S. Durlauf and D. Lane (eds.), *The Economy as an Evolving Complex System II.* Santa Fe Institute, Santa Fe and Reading, MA, Addison-Wesley.

Tesfatsion, L. (2001), "Structure, Behavior, and Market Power in an Evolutionary Labor Market with Adaptive Search", *Journal of Economic Dynamics and Control*, 25: 419–457.

Witt, U. (1985), "Coordination of Individual Economic Activities as an Evolving Process of Self-Organization", *Economie appliquée*, 37: 569–595.

ENDOGENOUS MATCHING FUNCTIONS: AN AGENT-BASED COMPUTATIONAL APPROACH

M. NEUGART
Chemnitz University of Technology
Department of Economics
Reichenhainer Strasse 40,
09107 Chemnitz, Germany
E-mail: michael.neugart@wirtschaft.tu-chemnitz.de

The matching function has become a popular tool in labor economics. It relates job creation (a flow variable) to two stock variables: vacancies and job searchers. In most studies the matching function is considered to be exogenous and assumed to fulfill certain properties. The present study, instead, looks at the properties of an endogenous matching function. For this purpose we have programmed an agent-based computational labor market model with endogenous job creation and endogenous job search behavior. Our simulations suggest that the endogenous matching technology is subject to decreasing returns to scale. The Beveridge curve reveals substitutability of job searchers and vacancies for a small range of inputs, but is flat for relatively high numbers of job searchers and vertical for relatively high numbers of vacancies. Moreover, the matching technology changes with labor market policies. This raises concerns about the validity of labor market policy evaluations conducted with flow models of the labor market that employ exogenous matching functions.

1. Introduction

The key feature of the matching function is that it neatly summarizes the behavior of firms trying to fill vacancies and of workers looking for jobs, and then relates this behavior to job creation. The matching function plays a central role in flow models of the labor market explaining equilibrium unemployment (see [1] or [2]), and has also undergone extensive testing (see [3]).

One aim of this paper is to study the properties of an endogenous matching function and to compare them to assumptions usually imposed on exogenous matching functions in the theoretical and empirical labor economics literature. Rather than assuming a holistic function we are interested in determining whether properties like job creation being an increasing function of vacancies and job searchers, concavity, or constant returns to scale can be generated by a model that takes into consideration the micro-behavior of firms and workers.

The second topic addressed in the current work is endogeneity of the matching function in relation to labor market policies. Policy experiments exploiting a labor market model with an exogenous matching function may give misleading results if the policies prove to influence the properties of the matching function. Such a concern is not farfetched, as the properties usually imposed on exogenous matching functions are justified on the basis of the agents' micro-behavior. As the policies aim to change agents' choices, for example through firm subsidies or mobility vouchers to job searchers, they may very well also affect the properties of the matching technology.

Agent-based computational research is gaining interest among scholars in economics (see for example [4], [5] or [6]) and in other social sciences.[a] The appeal of agent-based computational economics (ACE) stems from its flexibility of modelling. For example, the heterogeneity and the interaction of agents can be explicitly treated. After programming the characteristics of the agents and of the rules governing their interaction, the emerging macro-behavior can be studied.

We employ an agent-based computational setting as it allows the heterogeneity of the firms and workers to be captured to a larger extent than possible with analytical models, without becoming unwieldly. Our study also departs from the existing literature on endogenous matching functions in another respect. While agents are usually modelled as optimizers with rational expectations, the agents in this study maintain the strategies with which they were born. Thus, workers always send the same number of applications and firms always post the same number of vacancies for the duration of their life-cycle. However, workers and firms are obliged to exit the market if their behavior fails to yield positive payoffs. In that case they are replaced by new agents who adopt a strategy of the surviving workers and firms, respectively. Thus, over time the market will be populated with agents exhibiting 'survival' behavior.

In labor economics agent-based computational modeling has been attributed great potential (see [8]). Especially in the study of market outcomes in a world where labor market institutions, such as unemployment benefit or employment protection systems, are set by policy makers, and where the outcomes may lead the policy makers to reconsider their institu-

[a] [7] surveys, for example, agent-based modeling in the political sciences.

tional choices, thereby altering labor demand and supply.

The institutions considered in our paper are exogenous, in order to be able to isolate the labor market outcomes when firms and workers make their choices in a stable institutional setting. However, we simulate changes in labor market policies in order to study their impact on the properties of the matching function.

Endogenous matching functions are an intriguing research issue that has thus far only been dealt with on the basis of analytical models.[b] The following section surveys this literature. Section 3 describes our model. Section 4 reports on the simulation results. The last section concludes and reports on some of the implications of our findings on the suitability of exogenous matching functions as a modelling tool.

2. A review of the literature

The urn ball model[c] has been widely used to study coordination failures as one source of frictional unemployment. Within this framework, balls (workers) have to be placed in urns (vacancies) so that a vacancy becomes productive. As workers simultaneously apply for jobs without knowing where the other workers are sending their applications, some urns may remain empty while others receive multiple applications. As a result, some workers may not find a job, despite remaining vacancies on the market. More recent approaches studying the endogenous matching function are rooted in the urn ball model but attempt to develop a richer labor market context. Here, we will briefly sketch out the ideas and results of some of those papers, pointing out to where our work contributes to the existing analytical work on endogenous matching functions.

If, rather than using the standard urn ball model, multiple applications are allowed, a new coordination failure will arise (c.f. [12]). In the standard model, coordination failure may lead to a situation where some vacancies receive no applications and are thus forced to remain unproductive. Instead, if workers can send more than one application, every vacancy will very likely receive at least one application. Nevertheless, coordination failure may arise from competition among firms for individual candidates. A firm may offer a position to an applicant who has in the meantime been hired

[b]To the best of our knowledge the paper by [9] in the present volume is the only other work which also looks at matching functions from an ACE perspective.

[c]Among the first to analyze these models were [10] and [11]. See [3] for a brief summary of the problem of coordination failure.

by a competing firm. The position at the first firm thus goes unfilled. As a result, providing for more applications per worker may not increase the matching efficiency of labor markets. The authors also show that for high but finite numbers of market participants the matching functions exhibits constant returns to scale.

[13] differ from the urn ball model in that firms post wages and are heterogenous in the number of vacancies they post. In the first version of the model, the number of vacancies each firm offers differs exogenously, while in the other it is made endogenous. Firms post wages simultaneously, and all vacancies and wages posted are known to workers who simultaneously choose a vacancy for application. If there is more than one application, firms randomly choose one applicant to get the job at the posted wage. The authors find a matching function with decreasing returns to scale that converges to constant returns to scale as the number of market participants increases. They also find an outward shift of the Beveridge curve as more firms offer fewer jobs. This leads the authors to conclude that empirically observable shifts in the Beveridge curve could be explained by shifts in job distribution over firms.

Skill mismatch with jobs having different skill requirements and workers having different skills is allowed for in [14]. With a finite and an infinite number of agents they find that the matching function is concave and that matches are increasing in both arguments. But only for infinite inputs does the matching function have constant returns to scale.

Addressing only homogenous labor supply and demand, [15] emphasize the role of wages. An endogenous matching function arises from a labor market in which firms post wages to attract workers. A relatively high wage is not considered merely as a cost factor. Firms also take into account that higher wages will lead to more applications and therefore make it more likely that the vacancy will be filled. On the other hand, however, workers may also expect that jobs offering relatively high wages to be crowded with applications, reducing the chances of receiving an offer. The trade-offs for the workers and firms drive their wage posting and application strategies. [15] are interested in the effect of coordination failure on welfare. They find that welfare loss is highest when there are equal numbers of traders on both sides of the market, no matter how large the market is.

The auction model for wage determination presented in [16] sets this paper apart from the others. Whereas the assumption in wage posting models is that firms offer a binding wage and are then approached by applicants among whom they choose, auction models reverse this. Here, workers announce a reservation wage for which they are willing to work before being approached by firms. If more than one firm contacts a worker, the worker can bid up the wage. The authors show that this results in wage dispersion, even under the assumption of homogenous firms and workers. As in the other models, friction is introduced by coordination problems, capacity constraints, and – in a version where vacancy creation is endogenous – , externalities associated with new vacancies entering the market. The endogenous matching function is characterized by constant returns to scale and matches increasing in vacancies and job searchers.

As already noted in the discussion of the various urn ball models, it is usually assumed that either a single worker does not know what other workers do, or that firms make offers not knowing what their competitors' choices are. These assumptions are present in matching models in the form of the random behavior of agents. The contribution by [17] is to show that even when the assumption of 'nobody knows what the others do' is dropped, frictions – firms and workers do not come together even though both sides are willing to trade – nevertheless occur. To grasp this result it may be helpful to briefly sketch out the model. [17] considers a grid where cabs can be located. Passengers stochastically want to move from one location to another but can only do so by taking a cab. It is shown that cabs may optimally locate on the grid such that some passengers do not get served. The properties of the endogenous matching function are constant returns to scale and a right angle shape of the iso-matching curve (or Beveridge curve). While non-substitutability between cabs and passengers is not an empirical characteristic of matching functions it may nonetheless vanish with the introduction of non-administered prices in the market. The upshot of the argument is that policy analysis on the basis of exogenous matching functions may be misleading when friction results from the optimal choices of agents, as the agents' new choices may also affect the matching technology of the market.

Like [17], we are interested in the endogeneity of the matching function in relation to labor market policies which has until now attracted very little attention. In addition, our work relates to the existing literature in that we also analyze the properties of the endogenous matching function. Contrary to the existing studies on endogenous matching functions, we model an agent-based computational labor market. This allows for more structure on both sides of the market. For example, vacancy creation and job search is endogenous in our model. We also depart from other studies by not assuming agents with rational expectations (see also e.g. [18]). Our agents simply stick to the strategies with which they were born. However, those that do not come up with positive payoffs have to leave the market. They are replaced by newly born agents who adopt a strategy of the surviving firms and workers, respectively.

3. The model

There are $m > 0$ workers and $n > 0$ firms. Firms can create vacancies at a cost $costVac$. Those costs can be interpreted as costs for advertising a vacancy but also as some fixed capital cost such as buying a computer required by the job. The initial number of vacancies $numVac_i$ that each firm i posts is randomly drawn from the interval $[0, numFirms]$ where $numFirms$ is the number of firms in the market.

Workers, indexed with j, are born with different reservation wages r_j reflecting different tastes for leisure. Each worker is initially assigned an application strategy $numAppli_j$ out of the interval $[0, numWorkers]$ with $numWorkers$ being the number of workers in the labor market.[d]

A worker j sends applications, given the behavior of all the other workers. Technically, workers send applications randomly. Applications are sent to firms that have at least one vacancy. No worker applies to the same firm twice. The assumption of random applications captures the idea of coordination failures on the labor supply side of the market giving rise to frictional unemployment in the model.

Firms may receive no application or at least one. If no application arrives, the vacancy cannot be filled, and the job does not become productive. If there is more than one applicant for a vacancy at a firm, the firm makes a binding offer to the worker with the lowest reservation wage. Reservation wages are known to the firms, as the posting asks applicants to state their wage requests. (In fact, such requests can often be found in newspaper or online adds.) The order in which firms are allowed to make a job offer is random, approximating simultaneous choices made by firms. The worker who gets a job offer accepts it, and is then paid his reservation wage. Hence, all the 'bargaining power' is with the firms. As a consequence, there is wage dispersion within firms. Workers in the same firm may earn different wages.[e]

---

[d] In general, having no upper bound for the assignment of strategies would be easiest to justify but would slow down the code. However, given the logic of the market selection mechanism the only requirement is that strategies with the potential to yield a positive payoff are not ruled out at the initial stage.

[e] We are aware of extremely few studies on wage dispersion within firms that would allow

The payoff function of the firm i writes:

$$payOff_i = \begin{cases} y * numJobs_i - wageSum_i - costVac * numVac_i & \text{if at least one vacancy is filled,} \\ -costVac * numVac_i & \text{otherwise.} \end{cases} \tag{1}$$

A filled job creates output y from which the firm has to deduct the costs of wages and for creating vacancies. If no vacancy is filled, the payoff is equal to the vacancy posting costs. We normalize the price at which homogenous goods are sold to one so that all variables are in real terms.

A worker who finds a job receives the reservation wage requested. Whether employed or unemployed, the worker has to carry the application costs.

$$payOff_j = \begin{cases} wage_j - costAppli * numAppli_j & \text{if employed,} \\ -costAppli * numAppli_j & \text{otherwise.} \end{cases} \tag{2}$$

The market selection mechanism is such that workers and firms lacking positive payoffs are eliminated from the market and replaced by new agents. The new agents are randomly assigned strategies of the surviving firms and workers, respectively. Thus, the newly-born agents profit from the 'knowledge of the market' concerning which strategies are helpful for achieving positive payoffs.

After each period, all jobs are dissolved and a new application and hiring process starts. Note, however, that all (surviving) agents stick to their strategies over the life-cycle. Figure 1 illustrates the pseudocode for our model, summarizing the sequence of actions taken by the agents.

4. Simulations

For the simulations we normalize per period labor productivity y to one. Thus, workers' reservation wages are assigned from the interval $[0, 1]$. Our baseline simulation refers to the case where the application costs are

---

us to judge such an outcome against real labor market features. One exception is [19] who analyze wages for care assistants and find, as they claim, surprisingly little wage dispersion within firms. Nonetheless they start speculating on how wage dispersion might be explained. Their favored hypothesis is based on a frictional labor market, which also lies behind our result.

```
Create n firms each posting numVac_i vacancies
Create m workers with reservation wages r_j sending applications numAppli_j
for k periods
      Applying
      for each worker j
            selects all firms i with numVac_i>0
            applies randomly at firms i
      end for each worker
      Hiring
      for each vacancy of n firms
            randomly draw vacancy to be filled
            if workers applied and at least one is still available
                  firm selects worker j with lowest reservation wage r_j
            else
                  vacancy is not filled
      end each vacancy of n firms
      Market selection
      for each firm i
            if payoff of firm i smaller or equal 0
                  firm i exits
                  new firm is born with strategy numVac randomly adopted from
                  surviving firm
      end each firm
      for each worker j
            if payoff of worker j smaller or equal 0
                  worker j exits
                  new worker is born with strategy numAppli randomly adopted
                  from surviving worker
      end each worker
      All jobs are dissolved
end k periods
```

Figure 1. Pseudocode

Table 1. Parameters

Parameter	Value
Labor productivity	$y = 1$
Application cost for workers	$appliCost = 0.1$
Costs for posting a vacancy	$vacCost = 0.4$
Number of Workers	$m = 10, 11, .., 50$
Number of Firms	$n = 10, 11, .., 50$

$costAppli = 0.1$ and the costs for opening up a vacancy $costVac = 0.4$, see table 1. We run simulations for different combinations of firms and workers. Starting with 10 workers and 10 firms the numbers are increased by one up to 50. That makes for a total of 1,681 cases. Each case is replicated 10 times so that we arrive at 16,810 runs. Finally, each run consists of 20 periods from which we only report the market outcome of the last period in all runs.

4.1. *Properties of the matching function*

Figure 2 plots one such run for a labor market with 30 workers and firms for 40 periods. The left-hand scale refers to the average number of vacancies posted by firms and the average number of applications sent by workers. Both variables start off at relatively high values, driven by the random assignment of strategies from the uniform distribution. As the firms and workers with negative payoffs are eliminated, these numbers drop quickly to one for the average number of vacancies posted and six for the average number of applications. The employment rate is around 0.95 and the average wage (wage sum divided by employed workers) is slightly less than 0.5. It appears that adjustment processes have worked themselves out at period 20. This is also the outcome that we report in subsequent simulations.

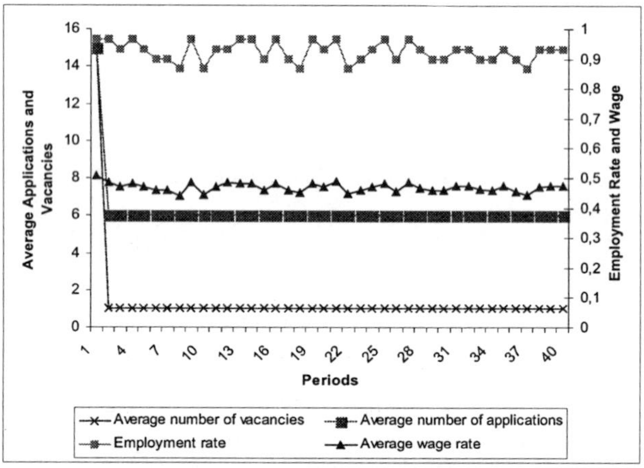

Figure 2. Average applications and vacancies (left hand scale), and employment rate and average wage rate (right hand scale), $numWorkers = 30$, $numFirms = 30$, $costAppli = 0.1$, $costVac = 0.4$

Figure 3 shows job creation in our labor market as the number of vacancies posted increases while holding job searchers fixed at 30. It can be seen that more jobs are created as more vacancies are posted by firms. There is an upper bound to job creation. For relatively large numbers of vacancies, labor supply restricts job creation. No more than 30 jobs are created as the number of job searchers was fixed at 30. However, the replications of the experiment show that the market does not always reach the labor supply constraint, even when vacancies exceed labor supply by a factor of two or more. For the regime where labor supply exceeds labor demand, the latter is the binding constraint for job creation. Job creation cannot be higher than the number of vacancies posted. But in this regime too, market outcomes may not be equal to the labor demand constraint. In fact, there is a cluster of points below the labor demand and supply constraints, indicating a frictional labor market. Coordination failure by workers when sending applications and by firms when hiring workers generates unemployment.

Job creation is also an increasing function of job searchers when labor demand is held constant (see figure 4). Once again, labor demand and supply restrictions become important. For relatively high numbers of job searchers the labor demand constraint, which was imposed at 30 vacancies is binding. Job creation becomes a flat function of job searchers. For the case where labor supply falls short of labor demand, the supply constraint is binding, as indicated by the upward-sloping portion of the graph. There is also a cluster of points below the restrictions due to coordination failures. Even though there are more job searchers than vacancies on the labor market in the flat part of the graph not every position is filled. Also in the upward sloping portion of the graph, not every replication yields full employment, in spite of the fact that there are more vacancies than job searchers.

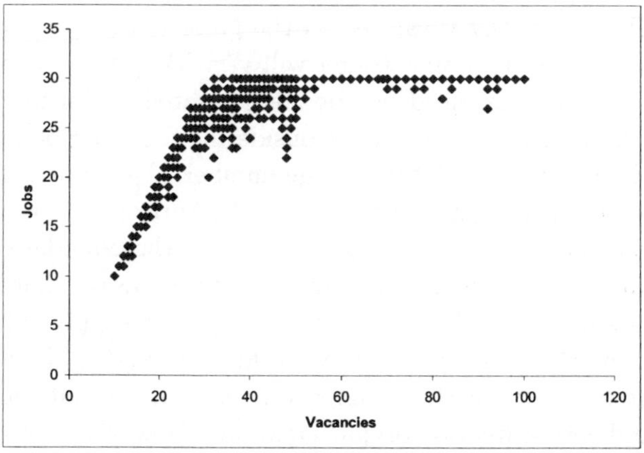

Figure 3. Jobs as a function of vacancies in the market, holding the number of workers fixed at 30.

The Beveridge curve (iso-matching curve) consists of combinations of workers and vacancies in the labor market that yield the same number

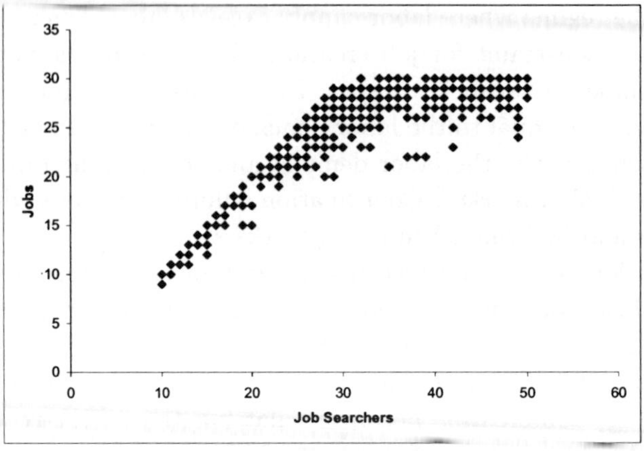

Figure 4. Jobs as a function of workers in the market, holding the number of vacancies fixed at 30

of jobs. Figure 5 shows the simulation results for 20 jobs. Once again, we plotted the market outcomes for all 10 runs. The boundaries of the Beveridge curve in figure 5 indicate that it is parallel to the vertical axis for relatively higher numbers of vacancies, and parallel to the horizontal axis for relatively higher numbers of job searchers. The reason is that if there are relatively many vacancies on the labor market but only a small number of job searchers, every worker will very likely find a job. Reducing the number of vacancies need not be compensated by an increase in job searchers to keep matches constant. Considering the other boundary, every vacancy will be filled if a relatively large number of job searchers apply for it. Thus, we find a straight line parallel to the horizontal axis at vacancies equal to job creation. Above and to the right of the boundaries there is a cloud of points. Hence, the market outcome is not always characterized by its constraints on either the labor demand or labor supply side – another way to illustrate the results of the previous figures 3 and 4. Not all vacancies and job searchers get matched. Moreover, one can see substitutability of vacancies and job searchers for job creation. However, the distribution of market outcomes does not imply a strong version of substitutability of inputs. In this example, almost anything can happen. Combinations of vacancies and job searchers that yield the same number of jobs are almost equally distributed in the interval where relatively low numbers of searchers and vacancies are combined.

Returns to scale play a prominent role in the matching function litera-

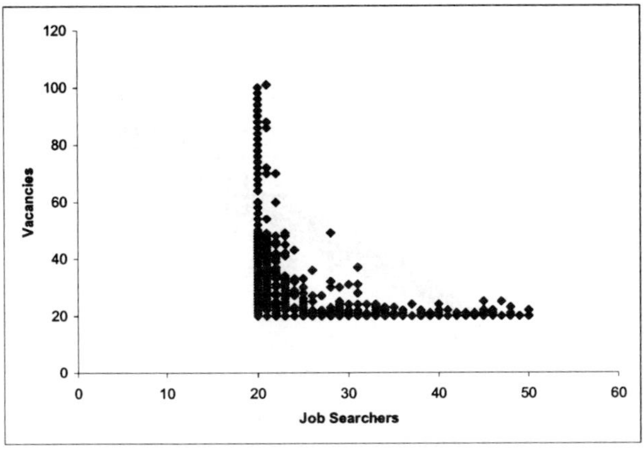

Figure 5. Beveridge Curve, 20 Jobs

ture. One reason for this is that a labor market with an increasing-returns-to-scale matching technology may have multiple equilibria.[f] In order to determine the returns to scale of our endogenous matching function, we plotted jobs over pairs of equal numbers of vacancies and workers in the market (see figure 6). The regression line with a slope of 0.86 reveals a decreasing returns to scale technology. This is in contrast to the widely accepted result of constant returns to scale or mildly increasing returns from the empirical literature on matching functions.[g]

4.2. *Impact of labor market policies*

In addition to investigating the properties of endogenous matching functions, we are also interested in measuring the degree of change of those properties if institutions governing the behavior of agents in the labor mar-

[f] For multiple equilibria in search models see e.g. [20] or [1].

[g] Note, however, that the returns-to-scale parameter depends on the ray chosen. In figure 6 we plotted jobs over job searchers for job searchers equal to the number of vacancies, describing a ray, defined as the ratio of vacancies over job searchers, equal to one. Inspection of the Beveridge curve shows that at the borders (!) the matching process can possibly be described by the function $Jobs = min(JobSearchers, Vacancies)$. Thus, had we chosen a ray that intersects the Beveridge curve at the borders, we would have gotten constant returns to scale. This is because if the ray is small or large enough, increasing inputs by a factor λ raises jobs by the same factor. However, these two extreme cases where the supply and demand constraints rule the job creation process do not apply to the case of a frictional labor market, which is in the center of our interest.

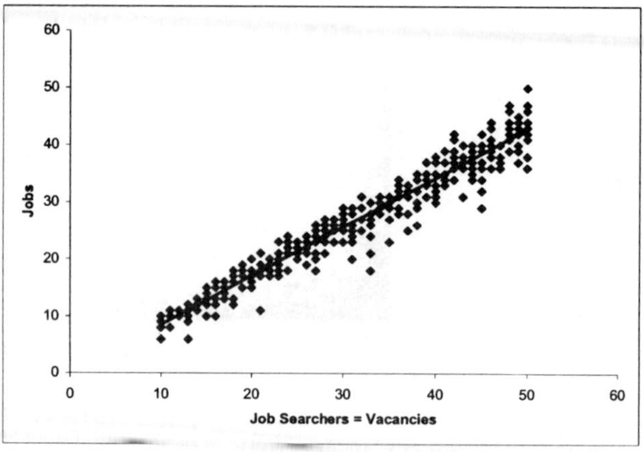

Figure 6. Returns to scale in baseline model

ket are altered. We therefore conducted two policy experiments. The first can be thought of as a subsidy to firms in order to increase labor demand. Firms are paid a lump-sum transfer by a third, external party. The transfer makes it less costly to open up a vacancy. The other policy is a transfer to the workers, thereby lowering their search costs. For example, this could be a mobility voucher giving workers the incentive to send applications even to firms that are not within commuting distance. To simulate the impact of the subsidy to the firm, we lowered the cost of opening up a vacancy to 0.2 and 0.3, respectively (as compared to 0.4 in the baseline model), leaving everything else constant (see table 2). Returns to scale hardly change with the vacancy costs. However, with respect to the application costs which we decreased from 0.1 to 0.05 in increments of 0.01 we observe a considerable change in the returns-to-scale parameter. It increases from 0.86 to 0.92 if the voucher lowers the costs for applying from 0.1 to 0.05 at vacancy costs of 0.4. This result is replicated at lower levels of vacancy costs with changes from 0.88 to 0.93 and 0.94, respectively. Clearly, this lends support to the idea that one has to be aware that policies may also change the matching technology of labor markets. It is the change in the number of applications sent out by workers that leads to these results. Reducing application costs by one half almost doubles the average number of applications (keeping *costVac* at 0.2). Changing the costs for opening a vacancy while leaving the application costs constant has hardly any impact on the behavior of the firms measured by the average number of vacancies posted.

Table 2. Returns to scale parameters

	appliCost					
	0.05	0.06	0.07	0.08	0.09	0.1
vacCost						
0.2	0.94	0.93	0.92	0.90	0.89	0.88
0.3	0.93	0.91	0.92	0.89	0.88	0.88
0.4	0.92	0.89	0.89	0.87	0.87	0.86

Table 3. Employment rates

	appliCost					
	0.05	0.06	0.07	0.08	0.09	0.1
vacCost						
0.2	0.96	0.93	0.92	0.90	0.89	0.89
0.3	0.95	0.92	0.91	0.90	0.88	0.85
0.4	0.97	0.92	0.90	0.89	0.87	0.86

It is clear that a more systematic investigation is needed before making stronger conclusions. Nevertheless our results indicate that assuming exogenous matching technologies may generate misleading results in policy experiments conducted within flow models of the labor market.

Table 3 shows how the policy measures translate into employment. To calculate the employment rates we took all those market outcomes that already entered the calculation of the returns to scale parameter. That is, we increased the level of inputs, job searchers and vacancies, but kept their ratio constant at one. Plotting the employment rates over job searchers revealed a regression line with an almost zero coefficient on the job searchers variable. In other words, the employment rate seems to be independent from the scale of inputs. Table 3 shows the intercept of the regression. While lowering application costs pushes up employment, lower vacancy costs have no impact on employment.

A further implication of the two main results presented here (decreasing returns to scale and independence of the employment rate from the scale of inputs with respect to the matching technology), is that the matching technology cannot be Cobb-Douglas, the pet assumption in empirical estimates of matching parameters and also in flow models of the labor market.[h]

[h]To see this, assume a Cobb-Douglas matching technology $E = AS^{\alpha}V^{\beta}$, where A, α and β are parameters satisfying $A > 0$ and $\alpha, \beta > 0$, and S shall be job searchers or workers, and V the number of vacancies. Then, the employment rate becomes $E/S =$

5. Conclusions

We programmed an agent-based computational labor market model with the following features: endogenous vacancy creation, endogenous job search, random applications, firms that pay workers their reservation wages, and a market selection process that eliminates agents that do not exhibit positive payoffs. One purpose of the exercise was to study the properties of the endogenous matching technology and to compare them to generally assumed characteristics of exogenous matching functions. We found that job creation is increasing in its arguments: vacancies and job searchers. Contrary to the results reported in most of the empirical literature, our endogenous matching technology has decreasing returns to scale. The simulated Beveridge curve is flat and vertical at the boundaries, and there is substitutability of inputs.

We were also interested in exploring the endogeneity of the matching function with respect to labor market policies. The matching technology proves to be affected by policies, thus indicating that exogenous matching functions may be an inappropriate tool for policy evaluations. Simulating the effects of a transfer to job searchers revealed that the matching technology changed – as indicated by an increase in the estimated returns to scale parameter. While no such effect is observable when subsidies are paid to the firms in our model, it nevertheless raises an important point concerning policy evaluations. The results from labor market policy evaluations based on models with exogenous matching functions may be biased if modelers do not take into account that the matching technology itself may also change with the policy. If one takes the interpretation which usually comes with the use of a holistic matching technology seriously, namely that it neatly captures the micro-behavior of agents, this is a serious claim.

Empirical work on the matching function usually starts with the assumption of a Cobb-Douglas technology which can easily be log-linearized for estimating the returns to scale coefficient. It is also popular to assume such a technology in flow models of the labor market. Our model does not lend support to a Cobb-Douglas technology. This raises concerns about the

$A/(S^{1-(\alpha+\beta)})$. As it is assumed that all jobs are dissolved after every period and every worker is looking for a job, the labor force is equal to the number of job searchers. Keep in mind that the simulation leading to the independence of the employment rate from the scale of inputs was conducted by imposing $S = V$. Clearly, an employment rate that is independent from the number of workers can only be achieved in the framework of a Cobb-Douglas function, if returns to scale are to be constant. This, however, proves not to be the case in our computational model as table 3 shows.

validity of empirical estimates of the parameters of the matching function. It also questions the macroeconomic effects of labor market policies found in flow models of the labor market. Whether our results are robust against different specifications of agent-based computational labor markets remains to be seen.

Acknowledgements

I would like to thank Richard Freeman whose encouraging discussions motivated me to do research with agent-based computational models, and Lars-Eric Cederman for his efforts helping me learn RePast. My thanks also go to my colleagues at Chemnitz University of Technology and to two referees for their comments. The responsibility for the content of the paper is mine alone. Financial support from the "Gesellschaft der Freunde der Technischen Universität Chemnitz" is gratefully acknowledged.

Appendix A.

The model is programmed in RePast. The code is available from the author (*michael.neugart@wirtschaft.tu-chemnitz.de*).

References

1. Pissarides, C., *Equilibrium unemployment theory*, (The MIT Press, 1990).
2. Mortensen, D., The matching process as a noncooperative bargaining game, in *The economics of information and uncertainty, ed. by J.McCall* , (University of Chicago Press, 1982).
3. Petrongolo, B. and Pissarides, C., Looking into the black box: a survey of the matching function, *Journal of Economic Literature* **XXXIX**, 390 (2001).
4. Roth, A. and Peranson, E., The redesign for the matching market for American physicians: some engineering aspects of economic design, *American Economic Review* **89**, 748 (1999).
5. Tesfatsion, L., Introduction to the special issue on agent-based computational economics, *Journal of Economic Dynamics and Control* **25**, 281 (2001).

6. Tesfatsion, L., Agent-based computational economics: growing economies from the bottom up, *Artificial Life* **8**, 55 (2002).
7. Cederman, L.-E., Agent-based modelling in political sciences, in *The Political Methodologist* **10**, 16 (2001).
8. Freeman, R., War of the models: which labour market institutions for the 21st century?, *Labour Economics* **5**, 1 (1998).
9. Richiardi, M., A search model of unemloyment and firm dynamics, *in this volume*, (2004).
10. Butters, G., Equilibrium distribution of sale and advertising prices, *The Review of Economic Studies* **44**, 465 (1977).
11. Hall, R., A theory of the natural unemployment rate and the duration of employment, *Journal of Monetary Economics* **5**, 153 (1979).
12. Albrecht, J.P., Gautier, J.P. and Vroman, S., Matching with multiple applications, *Economics Letters* **78**, 67 (2003).
13. Burdett, K., Shi, S. and Wright, R., Pricing and matching with frictions, *Journal of Political Economy* **109**, 1060 (2001).
14. Smith, T. and Zenou, Y., A discrete-time stochastic model of job matching, *Review of Economic Dynamics* **6**, 54 (2003).
15. Cao, M. and Shi, S., Coordination, matching, and wages, *Canadian Journal of Economics* **33**, 1009 (2000).
16. Julien, B., Kennes, J. and King, I., Bidding for labor, *Review of Economic Dynamics* **3**, 619 (2000).
17. Lagos, R., An alternative approach to search frictions, *Journal of Political Economy* **108**, 851 (2000).
18. Conlisk, J., A note on convergence of adaptive satisficing to optimal stopping, *Journal of Political Economy* **111**, 1353 (2003).
19. Machin, S. and Manning, A., The structure of wages in what should be a competitive labour market, *London School of Economics, Centre for Economic Performance Discussion Paper 532*, (2002).
20. Diamond, P., Aggregate demand management in search equilibrium, *Journal of Political Economy* **90**, 881 (1982).

A SEARCH MODEL OF UNEMPLOYMENT AND FIRM DYNAMICS

MATTEO RICHIARDI

LABORatorio Riccardo Revelli Centre for Employment Studies
via Real Collegio 30, 10024 Moncalieri (Torino), Italy
m.richiardi@labor-torino.it

An urn-ball probabilistic model of the labor market is developed. Agents can be employed, (voluntary or involuntary) unemployed or entrepreneurs. The analytical long run equilibrium probabilities for each state and the matching function are derived. In equilibrium, a higher reservation wage increases the number of start-ups, but has an overall negative impact on the unemployment rate. A more buoyant economy (higher average growth rate and higher average wages) is shown to be associated with a lower unemployment rate. Higher start-up costs discourage entrepreneurship and increase unemployment. More active search behavior leads first to a decrease in the unemployment rate, and then to a small increase, due to increased coordination failure induced by the higher number of applications sent by job seekers. The out-of-equilibrium dynamics are investigated through an agent-based simulation, which also provides results on firm demography. Important empirical regularities such as the Beveridge and the Okun curve are recovered. Finally, the simulation model is used to investigate departures from maximizing individual behavior and the effects of more realistic assumptions about profits and the business cycle.

Keywords: Unemployment; start-up; search; simulation.

1. Introduction

The purpose of this paper is to incorporate the analysis of entrepreneurship and firm dynamics within a search-theoretic framework.

Search models have become the standard reference in the economic literature for the analysis of unemployment.[a] However, they still fail to take into account many features of real labor markets. In particular, firms are

[a] Reference 13, 15 and 16 provide extensive reviews of search models for the labor market.

hardly considered, and are replaced by vacancies, i.e. by single-job entities. Old firms never die; new firms are never born: instead, jobs appear and disappear. Job creation is endogenous, but job destruction is generally exogenously given. A first attempt to provide a more realistic description of layoffs is found in Ref. 4, where each job offer is characterized by two variables — a wage and a constant probability of the position being closed down. Clearly, this is still a rather simplistic way of treating job destruction. In order to improve the model, two mechanisms have been introduced. The first considers (stochastic) shocks to the productivity of each job. The job is then closed down if its productivity falls below a minimum threshold [12]. The alternative is to consider job obsolescence over time. Old jobs offer smaller wages. Thus, they will become increasingly less attractive to workers, and will eventually be closed down [1,5]. Note that in neither case does job destruction depend on unemployment. Because of their oversimplified description of firms, these models never allow job creation and job destruction to depend on variables such as the number of firms in the market, or the size of the firm. Moreover, job destruction is generally not modeled separately from firing decisions, making it impossible to distinguish between worker and job turnover. The only other way to provide for such a distinction without modeling layoffs is through consideration of on-the-job searches. The number of vacancies must then be updated accordingly, and should increase with a greater number of job-to-job changes. Reference 3 provides the first attempt to model on-the-job search. However, in this model there is no determination of the number of vacancies. Thus, job quits may be indifferently interpreted as job destruction. On-the-job search intensity may depend on experienced wage shocks, or on learning about the utility deriving from that work [10]. In particular, since learning increases with tenure, models like Jovanovic's imply that workers with longer tenures are less likely to quit, and are more likely to be gaining higher wages.

Job creation is obviously linked to entrepreneurship. In particular, the decision to create a new business rather than look for an existing vacancy plays a central role. Entrepreneurship, i.e. the option of creating one's own firm, has been added to a standard search model in Ref. 9. The authors show that higher start-up costs discourage entrepreneurs (who seek employment instead) and increase the unemployment rate. However, this result depends on the assumption of constant return to scale in an aggregate matching function.

Moreover, the realism of optimizing behavior could be called into question. Strong empirical evidence in the literature shows that labor market choices are often made on the basis of rules of thumb [11 18]. Only when learning is allowed can such rules lead to near-optimal choices [6]. However, the systemic (dynamical) consequences of their out-of-equilibrium properties are generally unknown.

In order to remain more closely related to the existing literature, we provide a simple reference analytical model in which individuals can be employees, employers or unemployed. The matching function is not exogenously assumed, but recovered from the searching behavior of individual workers. An agent-based simulation of the model is then developed, in order to explore the out-of-equilibrium dynamics and the effects of some variations in the main assumptions. In particular, a more behaviorist version of the model, with agents following rules of thumb, will be presented. Finally, more structured hypotheses on the value of some relevant parameters about the profitability of firms will be introduced. The model is set up in Sec. 2. State transition probabilities are derived in Sec. 3. Section 4 characterizes the long-run equilibrium of the system. Section 5 presents an agent-based implementation of the model, and investigates firm dynamics. Section 6 shows that the model is capable of reproducing some well-known aggregate labor market regularities, namely the Beveridge and the Okun curve. Section 7 deals with the above mentioned extensions of the model, while Sec. 8 concludes.

2. The Model

The model belongs to the class of urn-ball search models, with private information and single offer. However, the modeling approach considered is rather different from the typical search literature. Optimal individual choice rules are outlined, given a two-step decision process where workers are characterized by inertia and change job only when their satisfaction level falls below a threshold, no matter what the utility deriving from other choices is. Next, the *a priori* probability of each choice being made, in equilibrium, is computed. This allows filling a transition matrix, for each state of the system (unemployment, employment, self-employment), defining a regular Markov chain. The long-run probabilities for each state are then computed, using the global balance equations implied by the Markov chain. The approach is similar to that of Ref. 7.

2.1. *Labor supply*

Individuals can be self-employed, employed or unemployed, and in each period they face the choices described in Table 1.

Table 1. Individual choices.

Stay*	Remain in the present organization (firm)
Join	Apply for another job
Start	Found a new start-up
Quit	Withdraw from the labor market

Note: *Only if currently employed

Table 2. State transition matrix.

	Ending state		
Starting state	Unemployed	Employed	Self-employed
Unemployed	Unsuccessful Join Quit	Successful Join	Quit
Employed	Unsuccessful Stay	Successful Stay	
Self-employed	Unsuccessful Join Quit	Successful Join	Start

Considering that actions may not lead to the desired intentions (and thus can be either successful or unsuccessful), the state transition matrix looks like Table 2.

Let $P_{\text{stay}}, P_{\text{join}}, P_{\text{start}}$ and P_{quit} be the equilibrium probabilities of making either a Stay decision or, when having decided not to Stay, of making a Join, Start or Quit decision. Each individual has a reservation wage, r. Individuals are risk neutral. They first compute their expected wage in their present state, and compare it with their reservation wage. They only try to change their status if their expected wage falls below r. Thus, like many real people, they are characterized by inertia, and prefer not to change unless they are forced to. When they *are* forced to, their decision either to look for a new job, or to become entrepreneurs, or to remain idle, is based on a comparison of the expected payoffs of the different choices. On-the-job searching is not allowed. Therefore, employed individuals must quit their present job if they decide to apply for other jobs. Should all applications fail, they thus fall into unemployment.

There is a fixed number of N individuals. Let e and $u = 1 - e$ be the equilibrium employment and unemployment rate. The expected number of workers willing to stay in equilibrium is $N_{\text{stay}} = NeP_{\text{stay}}$ and the expected number of applicants is $N_{\text{join}} = N(u + e(1 - P_{\text{stay}}))P_{\text{join}} = N(1 - eP_{\text{stay}})P_{\text{join}}$. Finally, the expected number of new start-ups is $N_{\text{start}} = Ne(1 - P_{\text{stay}})P_{\text{start}} + NuP_{\text{start}} = N(1 - eP_{\text{stay}})P_{\text{start}}$. In addition, there is a (variable) number of F_t firms. Individuals and firms are not located in space: every worker can contact any firm.

2.2. *Labor demand*

In every period, each individual has a business idea, whose exploitation requires a new start-up that can employ up to J_i units of labor, with J_i randomly extracted from a distribution D_J with mean $\bar{J}$. These business opportunities are valid only for one period. Once a firm is set up, job opportunities grow at the rate g_t, with g_t randomly extracted each period for all firms from a distribution D_g. g_t can be interpreted as a business cycle parameter, and is thought to be purely stochastic.[b] This means that a W_f employee firm at time t will try to become a $W_f(1+g_t)$ employee firm at time $t+1$, thus opening (or destroying) $g_t W_f$ positions. The number of available vacancies will be equal to the number of new positions, plus the number of old positions left vacant by employees who have decided to leave the firm. Workers make their decisions before the rate g_t is revealed. Note that a positive value of g_t does not automatically imply the expansion of a particular firm or the economy as a whole, since jobs could remain vacant.

2.3. *Wages*

All firms in the market in each period receive a market return of $W_f(1+s_{f,t})$, where $(1+s_{f,t})$ is an *a priori* unknown firm- and time-specific multiplier, with $s_{f,t}$ randomly extracted from a distribution D_s, with mean $\bar{s}$. All employees receive equal pay. Wages are thus equal to $(1+s_{f,t})$. The wage shock $s_{f,t+1}$ is made known to employees before they make any decisions about whether to leave the firm, but it is unknown to applicants. The intuition behind this hypothesis is that this payoff accounts both for monetary and non-monetary rewards, which could well be assumed to be an experience good. Of course it would be reasonable to consider $s_{f,t}$ as being correlated over time, or across firms, or as being related to the business cycle parameter g_t in some way. Section 7 will discuss this parameter in more detail. Here, for the sake of simplicity, it is considered to be purely idiosyncratic.

Start-ups cause an additional cost of αJ_i for the entrepreneur, which is proportional to the size of the business opportunity, and accounts for all

[b]An autocorrelation of g was introduced in the simulation experiments, but failed to result in significant or interesting changes to the dynamics of the system.

the set-up costs. After the first period, all the differences between employer and employees disappear.

Thus, each employee receives $w_{f,t} = (1+s_{f,t})$, while the founder receives $(1+s_{f,t})-\alpha J_i$. Workers are aware of the uncertainty over s in the aggregate. Consequently, their expectations are

$$\begin{aligned} w^e_{\text{stay},f} &= (1+s_{f,t+1})P^{\text{succ}}_{\text{stay}}, \\ w^e_{\text{join}} &= (1+\bar{s})P^{\text{succ}}_{\text{join}}, \\ w^e_{\text{start}} &= (1+\bar{s}) - \alpha J_i, \end{aligned} \tag{1}$$

where P^{succ} is the probability of being confirmed in the present firm or being hired by another firm, once a Stay or Join decision is made.

2.4. *Stay*

As explained above, firms decide how many jobs they can sustain during each period. Jobs are first given to old employees, by means of a tournament. Only when the number of jobs exceeds the number of employees willing to stay are new vacancies opened. In the simplest case with no heterogeneity among workers (i.e. $r_i = r$), all the workers in the same firm make the same decision regarding whether to stay or to leave. If they all decide to stay, the probability of being confirmed depends on the business cycle parameter g_t. For positive realizations of g_t this probability is 1, while for negative realizations it is $1 + E[g_t | g_t < 0]$. Suppose g is uniformly distributed between $g_L > -1$ and $g_H > g_L$, then:

$$P^{\text{succ}}_{\text{stay}} = \frac{g_H}{g_H - g_L} - \frac{g_L}{g_H\, g_L}\left(1 + \frac{g_L}{2}\right) = 1 - \frac{g_L^2}{2(g_H - g_L)}. \tag{2}$$

2.5. *Join*

As in standard search models, workers apply for vacancies rather than to firms. When looking for a new job, each worker has a fixed number of applications A to send. Vacancies select randomly a prospective worker from all the applications received (if any). The worker accepts the first offer received. As already mentioned, the firm specific wage is revealed only after the employee has been hired. With homogeneous workers, all W employees in the same firm f make the same decision regarding whether to stay or to leave. Thus, the expected number of vacancies in any one existing firm, given that no information about $s_{f,t+1}$ is publicly available,[c]

[c]Although it is, as explained, privately available to individual employees.

is given by

$$
\begin{aligned}
g_{t+1} \leq 0: \quad V_{f,t+1}^e &= \begin{cases} W_{f,t}(1+g_{t+1}) & \text{with prob. } 1 - P_{\text{stay}}, \\ 0 & \text{with prob. } P_{\text{stay}}, \end{cases} \\
g_{t+1} \geq 0: \quad V_{f,t+1}^e &= \begin{cases} W_{f,t}(1+g_{t+1}) & \text{with prob. } 1 - P_{\text{stay}}, \\ W_{f,t}g_{t+1} & \text{with prob. } P_{\text{stay}}. \end{cases}
\end{aligned}
\tag{3}
$$

The expected number of vacancies in new start-ups is

$$V_s^e = N(1 - eP_{\text{stay}})P_{\text{start}}\bar{J} \tag{4}$$

and the total expected number of vacancies is $V^e = V_f^e + V_s^e$.

As in Ref. 2, the probability that any one applicant has applied to a particular vacancy is A/V^e, so the number of applications for a particular vacancy is $N_v = \text{bin}\,(N_{\text{join}}, A/V^e)$. The probability that the vacancy has at least one application to consider, assuming $V^e \geq A$, is

$$p = 1 - (1 - A/V^e)^{N_{\text{join}}}. \tag{5}$$

From the individual's perspective, the probability of selection of any single application sent out is 1 over the number of applications received for that vacancy. On average, this number is equal to the number of applications sent out (AN_{join}) over the number of vacancies that receive applications (pV^e). Consequently, the probability for an application to be selected for a vacancy, given $r_i = r$, is $q = \frac{pV^e}{AN_{\text{join}}}$. Note that in considering what happens to a particular vacancy we are considering the case $N_{\text{join}} \geq 1$. The probability of being selected for at least one vacancy is $1 - (1-q)^A$. Therefore, the *a priori* probability of a successful Join, given a Join decision, is

$$P_{\text{join}}^{\text{succ}} = 1 - \left(1 - \frac{pV^e}{AN_{\text{join}}}\right)^A. \tag{6}$$

At this point, the matching function can also be specified:

$$M(u, e, V, A) = N_{\text{join}}P_{\text{join}}P_{\text{join}}^{\text{succ}} = N(1 - eP_{\text{stay}})P_{\text{join}}P_{\text{join}}^{\text{succ}}. \tag{7}$$

Note that, unlike the exogenous matching function literature [14], all u, e and V are endogenous here.

2.6. *Start*

To successfully form a start-up, no particular requirements are necessary, and at least one vacancy is automatically filled (the founder). The recruiting mechanism involves first choosing an applicant and then asking if he is still on the market. The probability therefore that the selected applicant has not been recruited yet for other vacancies is proportional to the number of the selected worker's applications receiving positive answers, $(A-1)q+1$. The probability of filling any one vacancy is thus

$$z = \frac{p}{(A-1)q+1}. \tag{8}$$

Hence, the average number of vacancies a J_i start-up will be able to fill is

$$W_i^e = (J_i - 1)z + 1. \tag{9}$$

3. Choices

Suppose s is uniformly distributed between $s_L > -1$ and $s_H > s_L$. Substituting into Eq. (1) yields:

$$\begin{aligned} P_{\text{stay}} &= \Pr(w^e_{\text{stay}} \geq r) = \Pr\left(s_f \geq \frac{2(g_H - g_L)(r-1) + g_L^2}{2(g_H - g_L) - g_L^2}\right) \\ &= \begin{cases} 0 & \text{for } a > s_H, \\ \dfrac{s_H - a}{s_H - s_L} & \text{for } a \in [s_L, s_H], \\ 1 & \text{for } a < s_L, \end{cases} \end{aligned} \tag{10}$$

$$a = \frac{2(g_H - g_L)(r-1) + g_L^2}{2(g_H - g_L) - g_L^2}.$$

Note that the lower threshold for a, when $r = 0$, is $a = -1$.

Now, suppose J is uniformly distributed between $J_L > 0$ and $J_H > J_L$. In order to obtain P_{join}, P_{start} and P_{quit}, we must distinguish between the following cases:

$$\begin{aligned} &\text{(i)}\ \frac{1 + \bar{s} - r}{\alpha} \leq J_L \quad \text{and} \quad P^{\text{succ}}_{\text{join}} \leq \frac{r}{1+\bar{s}}, \\ &\text{(ii)}\ P^{\text{succ}}_{\text{join}} \geq \max(1 + \bar{s} - \alpha J_L, r), \\ &\text{(iii)}\ \text{otherwise}. \end{aligned} \tag{11}$$

We then obtain the results in Table 3.

Table 3. Choice probabilities.

Case	P_{join}	P_{start}	P_{quit}	Sum
(i)	0	0	1	1
(ii)	1	0	0	1
(iii)	$\dfrac{\alpha J_H - (1+\bar{s})(1-P_{\text{join}}^{\text{succ}})}{\alpha(J_H - J_L)}$	$\dfrac{(1+\bar{s})(1-P_{\text{join}}^{\text{succ}}) - \alpha J_L}{\alpha(J_H - J_L)}$	0	1

Note that when $J_L = 0$, $\frac{1+\bar{s}-\alpha J_L}{1+\bar{s}} = 1$ and case (ii) becomes very unlikely. Note also that the reservation wage does not directly affect individual choices, once a leave decision is made.

4. Long-Run Equilibrium

It is straightforward to see that in case (i) unemployment is the absorbing state. More generally, the transition matrix of Table 2 defines a regular Markov chain with stationary transition probabilities. Its limiting distribution, i.e. the long-run probability of finding the process in each state, regardless of the initial state (which is also the long-run mean fraction of time that the process is in each state) is given by

$$\begin{aligned}
\pi_e &= \frac{P_{\text{join}}P_{\text{join}}^{\text{succ}} + P_{\text{stay}}P_{\text{stay}}^{\text{succ}}P_{\text{start}}}{1 + P_{\text{stay}}\left(P_{\text{start}} + P_{\text{join}}P_{\text{join}}^{\text{succ}}\right) - P_{\text{stay}}P_{\text{stay}}^{\text{succ}}},\\
\pi_s &= \frac{P_{\text{start}}\left(1 - P_{\text{stay}}P_{\text{stay}}^{\text{succ}}\right)}{1 + P_{\text{stay}}\left(P_{\text{start}} + P_{\text{join}}P_{\text{join}}^{\text{succ}}\right) - P_{\text{stay}}P_{\text{stay}}^{\text{succ}}},\\
\pi_u &= 1 - \frac{P_{\text{start}} + P_{\text{join}}P_{\text{join}}^{\text{succ}}}{1 + P_{\text{stay}}\left(P_{\text{start}} + P_{\text{join}}P_{\text{join}}^{\text{succ}}\right) - P_{\text{stay}}P_{\text{stay}}^{\text{succ}}},
\end{aligned} \tag{12}$$

where π_e, π_s, π_u are the long-run probabilities of being employed, self-employed and unemployed, and thus $e = \pi_e + \pi_s, u = \pi_u$. The system is solved numerically. The figures below report the effects of the various parameters on individual choices, starting from a reference case with

$$\begin{array}{lllll}
g_L = -0.5, & g_H = 0.5, & s_L = -0.5, & s_H = 0.5 & A = 10,\\
J_L = 0, & J_H = 20, & r = 0.75, & \alpha = 0.01, & N = 1000.
\end{array} \tag{13}$$

The effect of the reservation wage is linear (Fig. 1(a)). Above a certain threshold, it starts lowering the probability of making a Stay decision; then, as it approaches 1 it decreases the probability of starting a new business to

0. An increasing average growth rate (Fig. 1(b)) increases the probability of making a Stay decision ($P_{\text{stay}}^{\text{succ}}$ gets higher, i.e. there are more chances of being confirmed, once this decision is made), and also — once the worker has left — the probability of applying for a new job (there are more vacancies: hence the probability of getting a new job $P_{\text{join}}^{\text{succ}}$ is higher). Higher average wages (Fig. 1(c)) increase the chances of staying, but — above a certain threshold — do not influence the other probabilities. A greater value of start-up sunk costs α (Fig. 1((d) has a positive effect on the probability of making a Stay decision and, of course, it has a negative effect on the probability of making a Start decision. The number of applications that can be simultaneously sent out by workers has very little impact on their choices (Fig. 1(e)).

The effects of the parameters on the final outcome, i.e. on (a) π_u, (b) π_s and (c) the number of matches M, are shown in Figs. 2–6, with reference to the benchmark case outlined above.

4.1. *Reservation wage*

Unemployment is affected by the reservation wage when it is above a certain threshold, but the relationship may appear counterintuitive: a greater reservation wage lowers the unemployment rate. In explanation, note first that the values of the parameters do not allow for case (i) situations, i.e. the probability of staying out of the labor market (making a Quit decision) is null. Hence, only two ways of becoming unemployed remain: the first is by making a Stay decision, and not being reconfirmed in the same job due to adverse business conditions; the second by making a Join decision, and not being selected for any of the A applications sent out. However, $P_{\text{stay}}^{\text{succ}}$ does not depend on r, while $P_{\text{join}}^{\text{succ}}$ is decreasing in r, as the number of vacancies increases (the number of matches also increases, as depicted in Fig. 2(c)). Since the probability of making a Stay decision is also decreasing in r, the resulting relationship between the reservation wage and the unemployment rate must be negative. By allowing all the parameters to change randomly, it becomes clear that the probability of having a case (i) situation is increasing in r (Table 4), thus leading to the expected positive correlation between unemployment and the reservation wage.

4.2. *Average growth rate*

Higher expected growth rates increase the probability of being confirmed in the present job, thus increasing the probability of making a Stay decision.

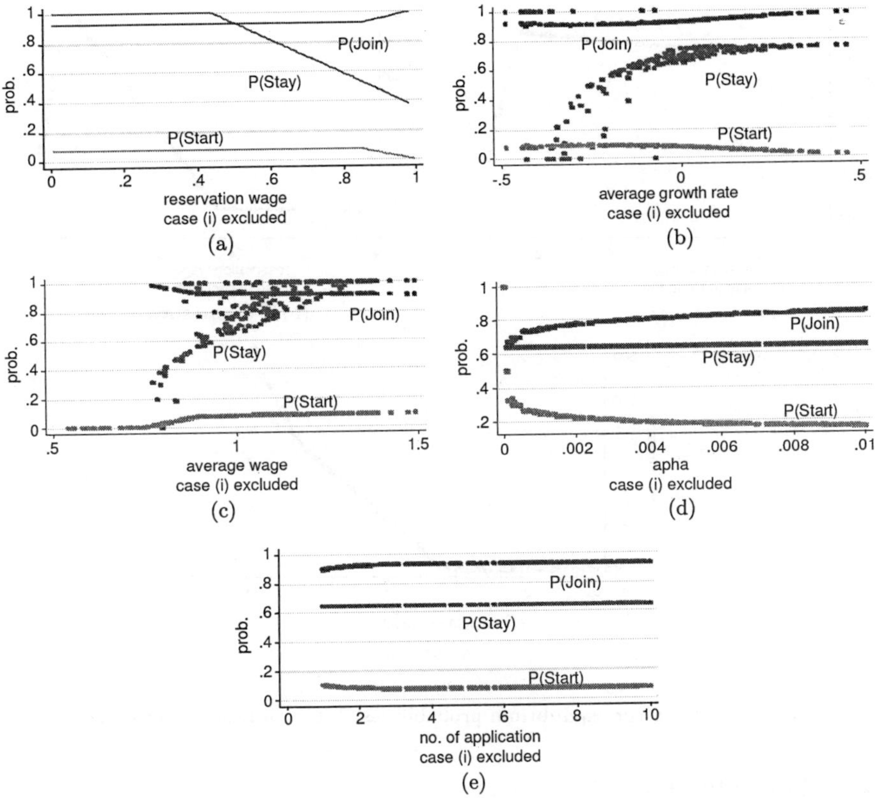

Figure 1. Choice probabilities.

This simultaneously lowers the unemployment rate, the number of matches and the number of new start-ups (Figs. 3(a)–(c)).

4.3. *Average wage*

A similar story holds for average wage (Figs. 4(a)–(c)). Here, however, the correlation between the start-up rate and the average wage is somehow tent-shaped. High average wages increase the probability of workers' satisfaction with their present job, and thus reduce the incentive for starting their own business. However, low average wages increase the significance of the α_J sunk cost, and thus also reduce the likelihood of starting a new business.

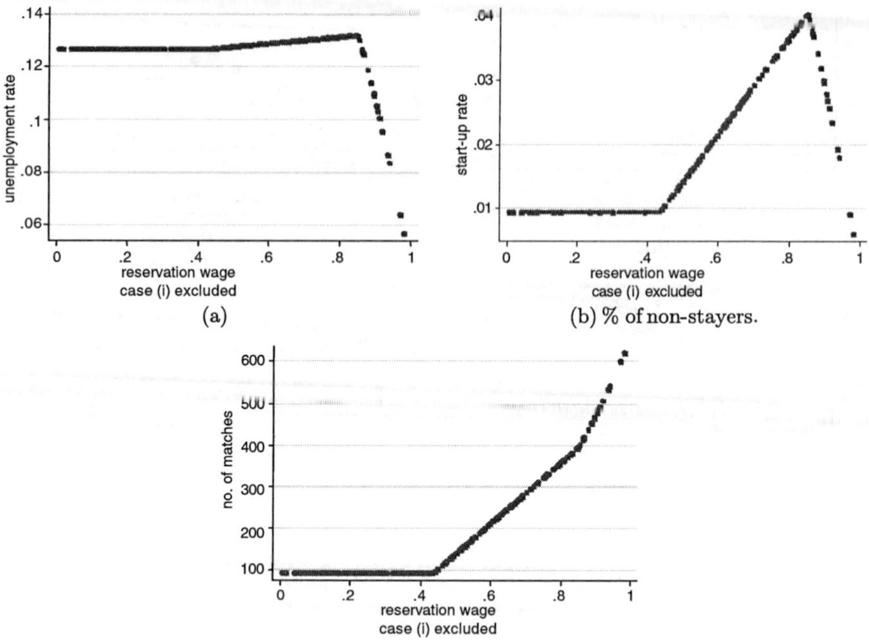

(a) (b) % of non-stayers. (c)

Figure 2. Long-run equilibrium probabilities. Effect of reservation wage.

4.4. *Start-up sunk costs*

An increase in sunk costs reduces incentives to start a new business, increasing the probability of applying for other jobs. Since the probability of making a Stay decision is unaffected, the total number of vacancies decreases. Hence the positive correlation with the unemployment rate (Figs. 5(a)–(c)). This is in line with the predictions of Ref. 9.

4.5. *Number of contemporary applications*

The effect of the number of applications A on the number of matches (Fig. 6(c)) is the same as in Ref. 2. The model presented here, however, also allows its effects on total unemployment and new businesses to be studied. A higher A increases the probability of making a Join decision (by increasing the probability that at least one application is selected), while decreasing the probability of making a Start decision. The overall effect

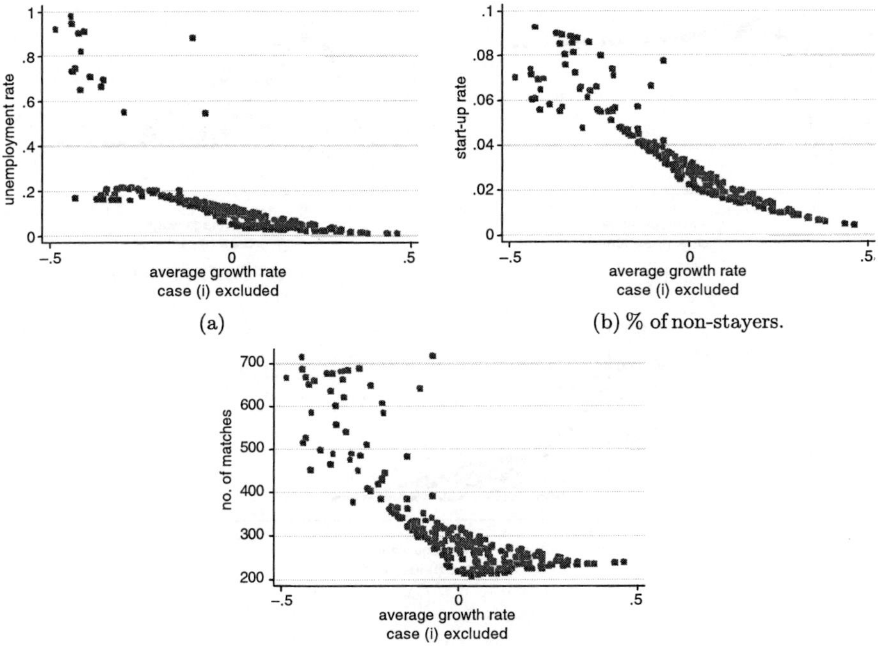

(a) (b) % of non-stayers. (c)

Figure 3. Long-run equilibrium probabilities. Effect of average growth rate.

Table 4. Case occurrences.

	Case		
r	(i) %	(ii) %	(iii) %
0–0.1	—	0.88	99.12
0.1–0.2	—	1.56	98.44
0.2–0.3	—	—	100.00
0.3–0.4	—	—	100.00
0.4–0.5	—	—	100.00
0.5–0.6	0.76	—	99.24
0.6–0.7	5.15	0.74	94.12
0.7–0.8	11.48	2.46	86.07
0.8–0.9	26.13	—	73.87
0.9–1.0	40.15	—	59.85

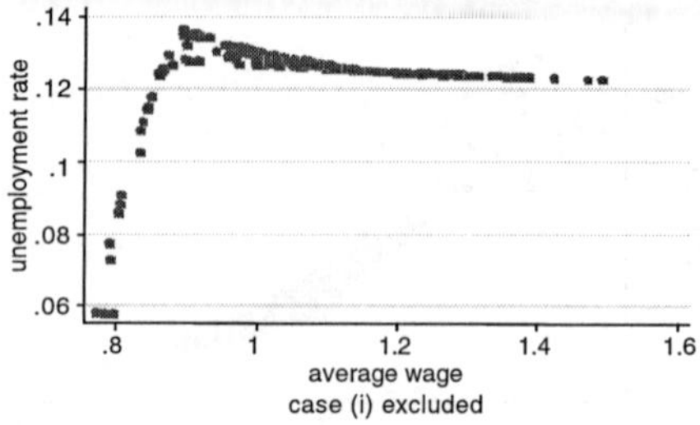

(a)

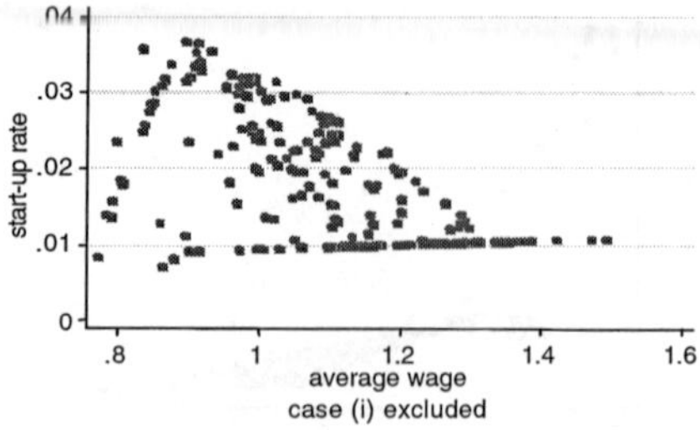

(b) % of non-stayers.

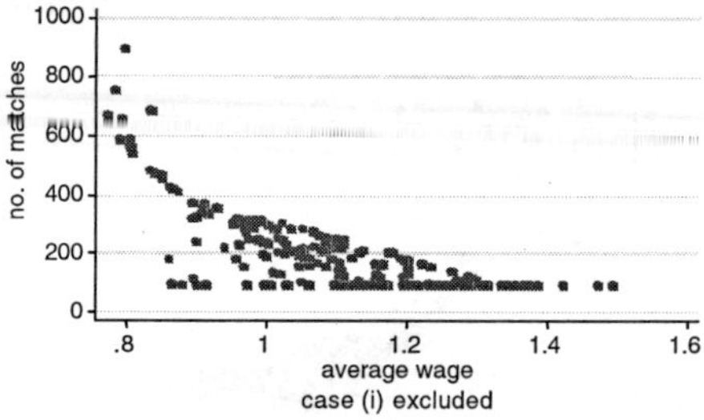

(c)

Figure 4. Long-run equilibrium probabilities. Effect of average wage.

on the total number of vacancies is decreasing in A, although this effect is slightly reversed above a certain threshold. The unemployment rate follows this trend (since the number of people holding their jobs remains constant), while the figure for the number of vacancies is reversed (Figs. 6(a) and (b)).

5. Firm Demography

In contrast to standard search models, here vacancies are linked to firms, thus allowing for the analysis of firm demography. While the birth rate of new firms is given by the start-up probability derived above, firm size distribution and firm number (which is obviously given by the interaction of the birth and death rates) are explored by means of an agent-based simulation. Agent-based models are computer programs that simulate the behavior of the basic entities in the system (i.e. workers, vacancies and firms), given specific interaction rules. Aggregate behavior is thus

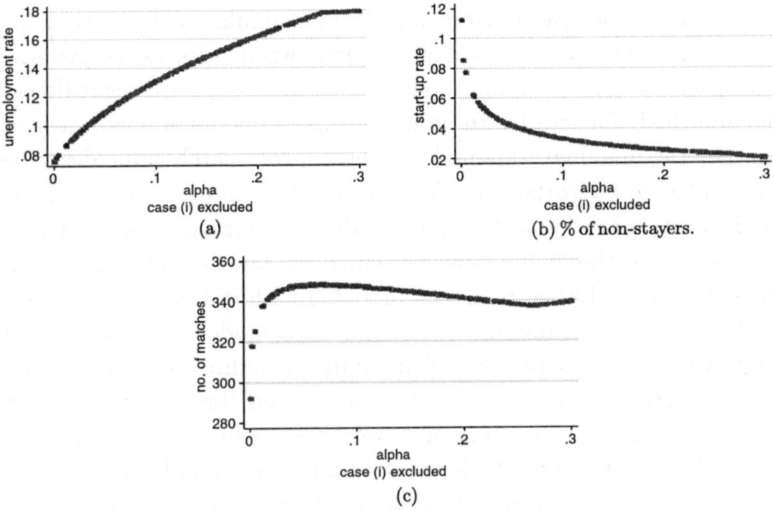

Figure 5. Long-run equilibrium probabilities. Effect of start-up costs.

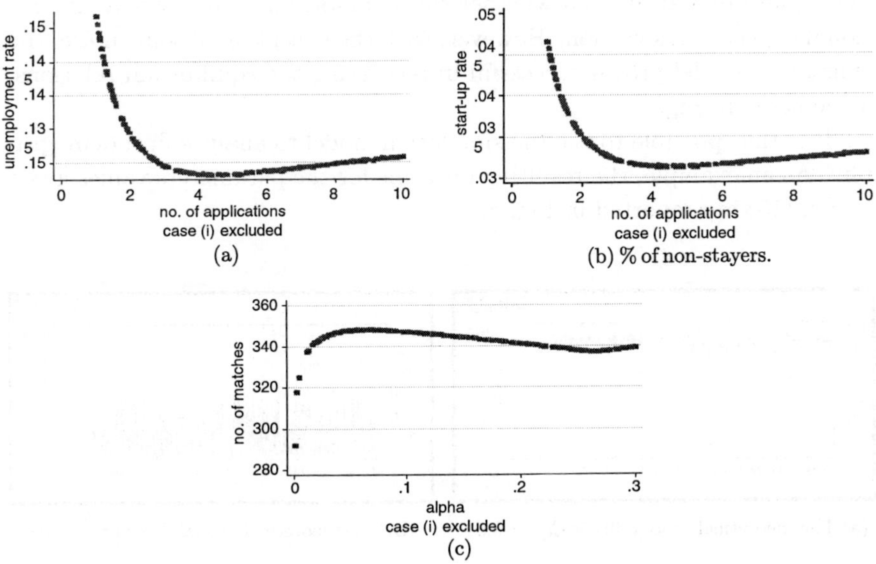

Figure 6. Long-run equilibrium probabilities. Effect of number of applications.

reconstructed "from the bottom up."[d] The simulation is written in Java code, using JAS libraries (http://sourceforge.net/projects/jaslibrary/). The decision to write a simulation has some consequences, regardless of the model specified. Generally, an analytical model is not immediately operational, i.e. the imaginary manual for playing the search game described by the model has to be worked out. This may induce some change in the model itself. In particular, due to the non-parallel discrete processing characteristics of most PCs, the model must be sequential and cast in discrete time, in contrast to the analytical reference model. In addition to time, some other variables that are continuous in the analytical model (such as the number of employees) have to be treated in units. Equilibrium relations cannot be used directly; rather, they have to be derived through non-equilibrium steps. For instance, the number of people expected to make a Join decision, which in the analytical model is the solution of an equilibrium equation involving rational expectations, is considered to be the same as the number of people making a Join decision in the last period (adaptive expectations). Similarly, the expected number of vacancies is the number of vacancies observed in the last period. Therefore, the question naturally arises as to whether this adaptive expectations version of the model converges toward any equilibrium at all, and whether this equilibrium is the same as the rational expectations version. However, with the exception of some noise, the simulation model proves successful in recovering the equilibrium relations, as depicted in Fig. 7.

It is thus possible to use the simulation model to analyze firm demography. As an example, the resulting outcome for the parameters values given in Eq. (13) are reported in Fig. 8.

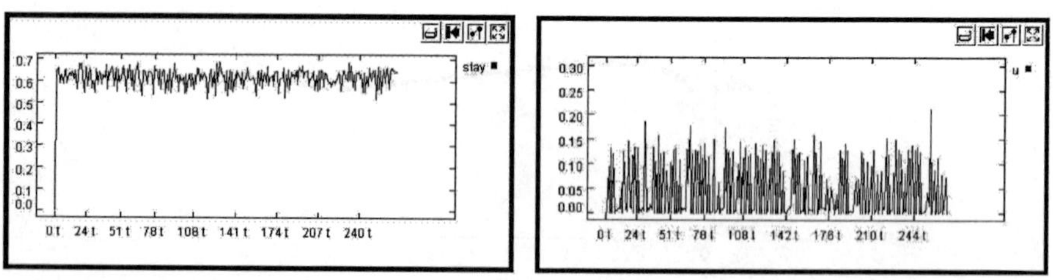

(a) The theoretical probability is $P_{\text{stay}} = 0.64$.

(b) The theoretical probability is $\pi_u = 0.08$.

Figure 7. Analytical versus simulation results. Parameter values given in Eq. (13).

[d]For a methodological discussion on agent-based computational models, see Ref. 17.

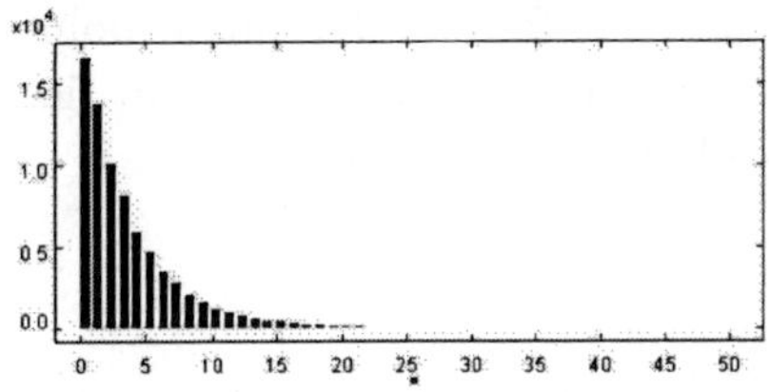

(a) Firm age distribution.

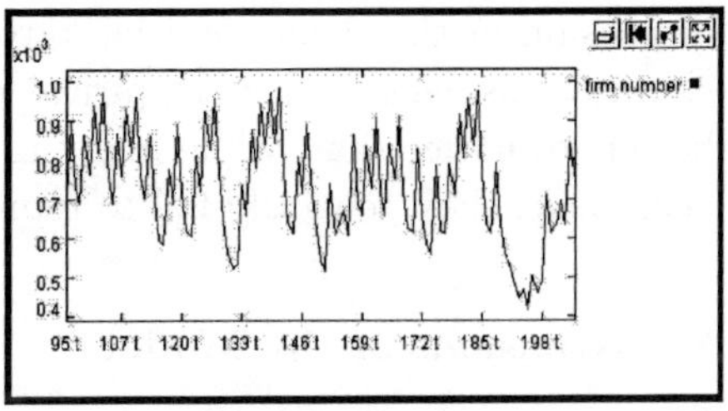

(b) Firm number.

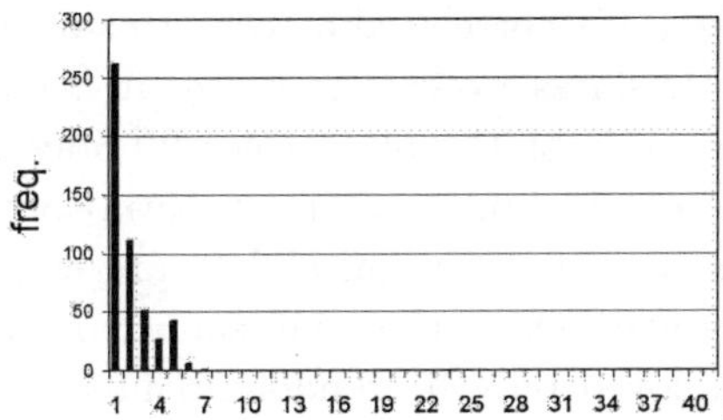

(c) Firm size distribution.

Figure 8. Firm demography. Parameter values given in Eq. (13).

6. Aggregate Labor Market Regularities

The model reproduces some aggregate regularities of actual labor markets, namely the Beveridge curve (BC) and the Okun curve (OC). This is shown in Fig. 9. The BC postulates a negative relationship between unemployment and vacancy rate, while the OC describes a negative, linear relationship between changes in the unemployment rate and GDP growth rates. For a

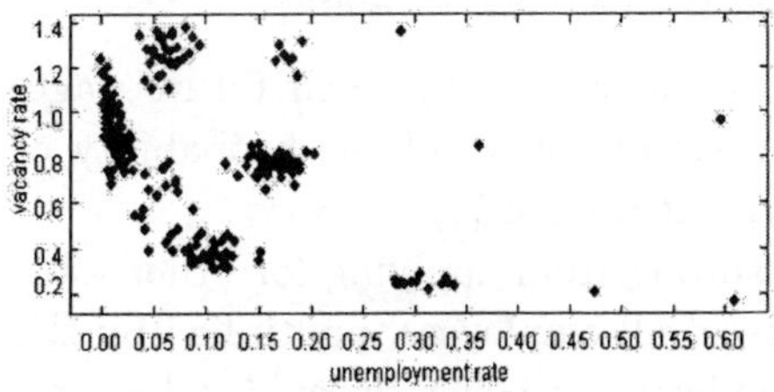

(a) Beveridge curve.

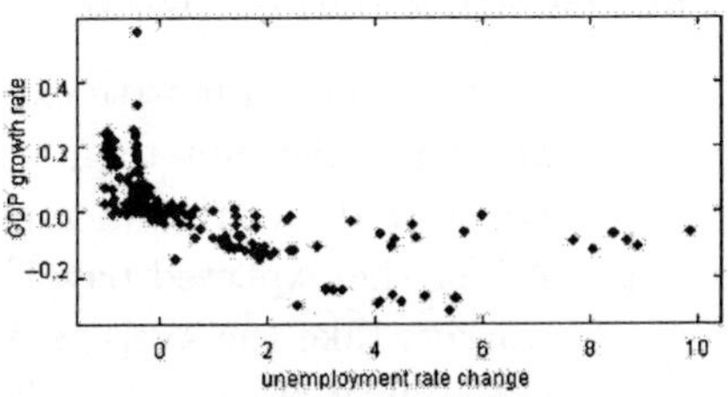

(b) Okun curve.

Figure 9. Beveridge and Okun curves. Parameter values given in Eq. (13).

discussion of the theoretical backgrounds of the BC and the OC, as well as an assessment of their empirical evidence, see Ref. 8. The main point here is to notice that, while many models reproduce these two regularities *separately*, they generally fail to reproduce both of them *jointly*.

7. Extensions of the Model

This section deals with the relaxation of some assumptions of the model. In particular, variations in the structure of the stochastic wage multiplier $s_{f,t}$ are considered. When s is correlated across firms or in time, or when it is dependent on the business cycle variable g, it becomes difficult to analytically solve for the probabilities of a successful Stay or Join decision, except in simple cases. For instance, when s is firm-specific, i.e. $s_{f,t} = s_f$, workers will always want to stay, once they are employed in a firm offering a high enough wage (which they will sooner or later find). They will then become unemployed only if (randomly) fired, when the firm is experiencing negative growth. The fact that the probability of a successful choice becomes difficult to compute in more complicated cases has more than analytical consequences. One could question whether real individuals could be thought of acting *as if* they were able to make such complex computations, in order to make the best choice. The realism of the model is thus challenged. When complex feedback is involved, it becomes more sensible to consider simpler individual choice rules, thus abandoning the realm of maximization in favor of a bounded rationality model of individual behavior.

7.1. *Bounded rationality*

The first step is thus to slightly change the rules of the game:

(i) Workers have adaptive expectations concerning their future wage, and they discount them for a simple proxy of the probability of being fired, i.e. the unemployment rate: $w^e_{\text{stay}} = w_{f,t}\pi_e$.

(ii) As for the expected payoff resulting from applying for other jobs, workers take the average wage of all employees, multiplied by the probability of one of their applications being selected, which remains unvaried: $w^e_{\text{join}} = \bar{w}_t P^{\text{succ}}_{\text{join}}$. Note that the average wage of all employees may differ from $(1+\bar{s})$, since workers with a low s are more willing to change job. The expected number of vacancies is again thought to be the same as in the last period.

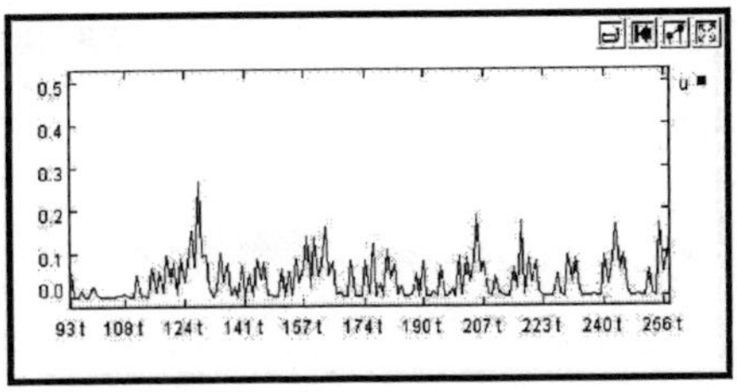

(a) Unemployment rate.

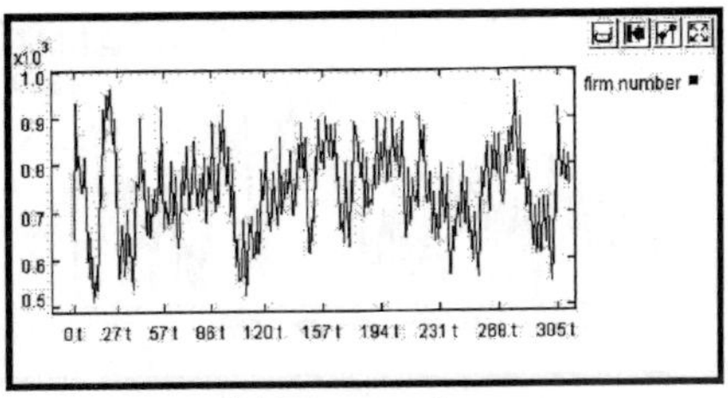

(b) Firm number.

Figure 10. Outcome of non-optimizing model. Parameter values given in Eq. (13).

(iii) When considering the option to start a new business, workers expect a payoff equivalent to the average wage of all entrepreneurs, net of the start-up costs: $w^e_{\text{start}} = \bar{w}_{\text{start}}, t - \alpha J_i$.

These rules are simple variations of those of the analytical model, which trade off optimality for computability and simplicity. When combined with firm- and time-specific wage shocks $s_{f,t}$ they typically produce cycles. These cycles are characterized both by periods of sharp decline in the number of active firms and consequent steep rise of the unemployment rate, and by periods in which the number of firms and the unemployment rate "breathe" in and out more regularly (Fig. 10).

Overall, these results do not differ substantially from those of the optimizing model, although the dynamics bear somewhat more resemblance to what happens in the real world. The analytical model is thus shown to be robust to its operationalization, and to small departures from optimizing behavior. Having a robust model of individual behavior makes it possible to add some structure to the stochastic wage multiplier $s_{f,t}$. Among the many possible variations, one simple extension of the benchmark model is presented here.

7.2. *Auto-correlation of start-up profits*

Suppose start-ups do not get their $s_{f,t}$ from the D_s distribution, but rather from the actual distribution of other start-ups. This may cause a self-sustaining process: following some particularly high extraction of the $s_{f,t}$ among the first start-ups, expectations of start-up profits will rise, hence producing more start-ups, which will also enjoy high profits. However, this will slowly raise the average s, thus leading, in conjunction with a decreased unemployment rate, to a higher probability of Stay decisions. Eventually,

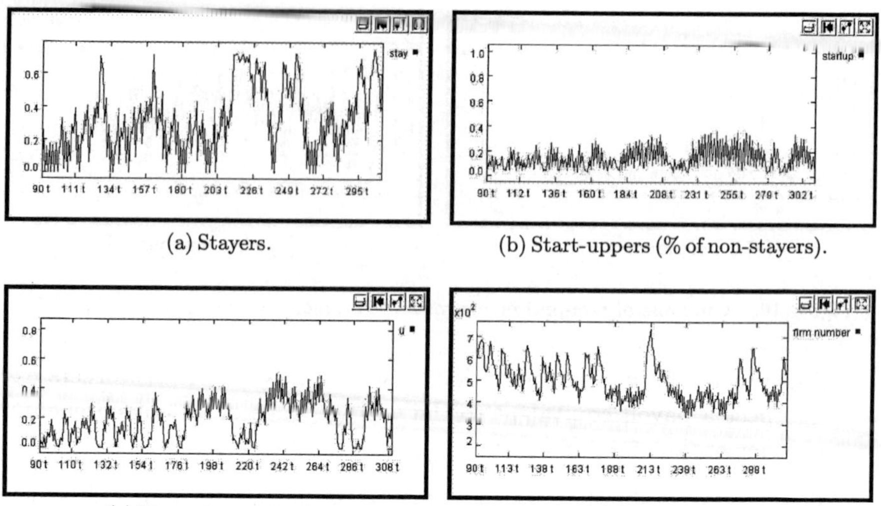

(a) Stayers. (b) Start-uppers (% of non-stayers).

(c) Unemployment rate. (d) Firm number.

Figure 11. Outcome of model in Sec. 7.2. Parameter values given in Eq. (13).

the number of start-uppers will decrease, thus making it easier for unlucky low-profit start-ups to impact the average start-up profits. A new period characterized by few low-wage start-ups can begin, and will last until a new generation of lucky new businesses appear. Typical results for this model are reported in Fig. 11. The dynamics now look more complex, with periods of high unemployment alternating with periods of almost full employment. Moreover, many combinations of the parameter values give rise either to full employment or to full unemployment, which becomes very stable, once established.

8. Conclusions

This paper provides an analytical model of (two-sided) search in the labor market, with optimizing individuals. Building on the previous literature on the topic, this model allows the joint investigation of unemployment and firm dynamics by explicitly considering the vacancy generation process of firms. The model is capable of reproducing a number of stylized facts about industry structure and labor market regularities (such as the Beveridge and the Okun curve). The convergence of the model to the equilibrium is tested through an agent-based simulation, which also shows that a non-optimizing but more realistic version of the model leads to similar results. This bounded rationality version of the model is then used to investigate the effects of different (and more realistic) assumptions about the relevant parameters.

A general consideration drawn from the result of this work is that the equilibrium model shows very uninteresting out-of-equilibrium behavior. While small changes toward more realistic models of individual behavior do not significantly alter the outcome, thus showing the robustness of the benchmark model, small changes in its structure may lead to more complex dynamics, which cannot be investigated analytically but bear a closer resemblance to that happening in the real world. More detailed investigation of these modified versions of the model, and of how they depart from the analytical benchmark, are left for future research.

Acknowledgments

The author would like to thank Howard Rosenthal for having introduced him to the Diermeier and Mieghem modeling strategy; Sergio Destefanis, who provided valuable comments and suggestions on an earlier version of this paper; and two anonymous referees.

References

1. P. Aghion and P. Howitt. Growth and unemployment. *Review of Economic Studies*, 61(3):477–494, 1994.
2. J. W. Albrecht, P. A. Gautier, and S. B. Vroman. Matching with multiple applications. *Economic Letters*, 78:67–70, 2003.
3. K. Burdett. A theory of employee job search and quit rates. *American Economic Review*, 68:212–220, 1978.
4. K. Burdett and D. T. Mortensen. Search, layoffs, and labor market equilibrium. *Journal of Political Economy*, 88(4):652–672, 1980.
5. R. J. Caballero and M. L. Hammour. The cleansing effect of recessions. *American Economic Review*, 84:1350–1368, 1994.
6. J. Conlisk. A note on convergence of adaptive satisficing to optimal stopping. *Journal of Political Economy*, 111(6):1353–1360, 2003.
7. D. Diermeier and J. A. V. Mieghem. Spontaneous collective action. Northwestern University, Center for Mathematical Studies in Economics and Management Science Discussion Papers Series No. 1302, 2001.
8. G. Dosi, G. Fagiolo, and R. Gabriele. Towards an evolutionary interpretation of aggregate labor markets regularities. In R. Leombruni and M. Richiardi, editors, *Labor and Industry Dynamics: the Agent-based Computational Approach. Proceedings of the Wild@Ace 2003 conference*, Singapore, 2004. World Scientific Press.

9. R. Fonseca, P. Lopez Garcia, and C. A. Pissarides. Entrepreneurship, start-up costs and unemployment. *European Economic Review*, 45:692–705, 2001.
10. B. Jovanovic. Job matching and the theory of turnover. *Journal of Political Economy*, 87:973–990, 1979.
11. A. Leijonhufvud. Towards a not-too-rational macroeconomics. *Southern Economic Journal*, 50(1):1–13, 1993.
12. D. T. Mortensen and C. A. Pissarides. Job creation and job destruction in the theory of unemployment. *Review of Economic Studies*, 61:397–415, 1994.
13. D. T. Mortensen and C. A. Pissarides. *Handbook of Labor Economics*, chapter New Developments in Models of Search in the Labor Market. North-Holland, Amsterdam, 1999.
14. B. Petrongolo and C. A. Pissarides. Looking into the black box: A survey of the matching function. *Journal of Economic Literature*, 39:390–432, 2000.
15. C. A. Pissarides. *Encyclopaedia of the Social and Behavioural Sciences*, chapter The Economics of Search. Elsevier, 2000. forthcoming.
16. C. A. Pissarides. *Equilibrium Unemployment Theory.* MIT Press, Cambridge, MA, 2 edition, 2000.
17. M. G. Richiardi. The promises and perils of agent-based computational economics. LABORatorio Revelli Workin Paper No. 29, 2003.
18. T. J. Sargent. *Bounded Rationality in Macroeconomics.* Clarendon Press, Oxford, 1993.

EVOLUTION OF WORKER-EMPLOYER NETWORKS AND BEHAVIORS UNDER ALTERNATIVE NON-EMPLOYMENT BENEFITS: AN AGENT-BASED COMPUTATIONAL STUDY*

MARK PINGLE
Department of Economics, University of Nevada, Reno
Reno, Nevada 89557-0016, USA

LEIGH TESFATSION
Department of Economics, Iowa State University
Ames, Iowa, 50011-1070, USA

This study experimentally tests the effects of a non-employment payment on work-site behaviors and market efficiency in the context of an agent-based computational labor market model with autonomous strategically-interacting workers and employers. On average, we find that a low but positive non-employment payment is most efficient, especially over the short and intermediate run. A high non-employment payment encourages those who enter employment relationships to be cooperative, but the cost of the non-employment payment program significantly reduces efficiency. Having no non-employment payment encourages the formation of employment relationships, but non-cooperation is common and this reduces efficiency. These "average" results should be viewed with caution, however. Because of strong network and learning effects, quite different paths and ultimate outcomes can result from the same initial structural conditions.

1. Introduction

Determining the effects of labor institutions on macroeconomic performance is a central concern of economic policymakers. Differences in labor institutions have been conjectured to be a key explanation for observed cross-country differences in the level and persistence of unemployment, in the distribution of income and wealth, and in growth rates for labor productivity and GDP.

For example, as discussed by Blau and Kahn [2], Ljungqvist and Sargent [6], and Nickell and Layard [10], European OECD countries over the past twenty years have tended to rely on administered wages and legislated job protection and have experienced sluggish job growth and persistently high unemployment. In contrast, the United States has had a relatively more flexible, less regulated labor market and has achieved much greater job growth and

* The authors thank Edward Elgar Publishers for permission to reprint this article here. The original article can be found as indicated in reference [14].

relatively lower unemployment rates. This has led many European policymakers to argue the need for reforms in their labor institutions.

Unfortunately, as discussed by Acemoglu and Shimer [1], Blau and Kahn [2], and Freeman [3], it is difficult to obtain conclusive empirical results regarding how labor institutions affect economic performance. Regression methods relating changes in labor institutions to economic outcomes quickly tax degrees of freedom. This problem is compounded if one institution's impact depends on the presence or absence of other institutions. Also, labor institutions are inherently endogenous. For example, governments continually revise labor institutions in response to economic and political pressures. This endogeneity makes it difficult to interpret the validity of empirical investigations.

In recognition of these difficulties, Freeman [3, pp. 19–20] suggests that agent-based computational modeling might offer a promising additional way to study the impact of labor institutions, particularly from a market design perspective. Tesfatsion [19, 20, 21] reports some preliminary work along these lines. An *agent-based computational economics (ACE)* framework is used to study path dependence, market power, and market efficiency outcomes for a labor market under systematically varied concentration and capacity conditions. ACE is the computational study of economies modeled as evolving systems of autonomous interacting agents (Tesfatsion [22], [23]).[1]

In this study we conduct an ACE labor market experiment to test the sensitivity of labor market outcomes to changes in the level of a non-employment payment. Our ultimate objective is to understand how the basic features of real-world unemployment benefit programs affect labor market performance.[2] However, as will be clarified below, a human subject experiment was run in parallel to this computational experiment as a check on the reliability of our findings and the adequacy of the learning representations for our computational workers and employers. To facilitate this initial benchmark check, a deliberately simplified experimental design is used. Specifically, we

---

[1] See http://www.econ.iastate.edu/tesfatsi/ace.htm for extensive resources related to ACE, including surveys, an annotated syllabus of readings, research area sites, software, teaching materials, and pointers to individual researchers and research groups.

[2] For example, in the U.S., unemployment benefits are *financed by taxes on employers* and are intended to provide *temporary* financial assistance to workers who become unemployed *through no fault of their own* and who *continue to seek work*. Understanding the separate and combined impacts of these and other unemployment benefit program features on labor market performance over time is an extremely challenging problem. A detailed discussion of theoretical and empirical labor market studies focusing on unemployment benefits and related issues can be found in Pingle and Tesfatsion [12].

consider a balanced labor market with equal numbers of workers and employers. In each trade cycle (work period), every worker has one work offer to make and every employer has one job opening to fill. An employer can reject a work offer received from a worker on two possible grounds: unacceptable past work history; or capacity limitations.

The workers repeatedly submit their work offers to preferred employers until either they succeed in being hired or they become discouraged by rejections and exit the job market. A worker must pay a small transaction cost each time he submits a work offer to an employer. As in MacLeod and Malcomson [7], each matched worker and employer individually chooses to shirk or cooperate on the work-site, and these choices are made simultaneously so that neither has a strategic informational advantage. Any worker or employer who does not enter an employment relationship during the trade cycle in question receives an exogenously specified non-employment payment. Workers and employers evolve their work-site behaviors over time on the basis of past experiences in an attempt to increase their earnings.

In this labor market, then, full employment with no job vacancies is possible. Nevertheless, the unemployment rate and the particular set of workers and employers in employment relationships endogenously evolve over the course of successive trade cycles. Two interdependent choices made repeatedly by the workers and the employers shape this evolutionary process: namely, their choices of work-site partners; and their behavioral choices in interactions with these partners.

Three non-employment payment (NEP) treatments are experimentally studied: a zero NEP; a low NEP; and a high NEP. As reported in Table 1, one main finding is that the average utility levels attained by workers and employers do not substantially change as the NEP is increased from zero to high. As will be clarified in Section 4, although the increase in the NEP increases the worker unemployment rate and the employer vacancy rate, this greater loss of productive activity is offset in part by the higher NEP and in part by the increased levels of mutual cooperation exhibited by the workers and employers who manage to match.

Another main finding reported in Table 1 is that a slightly higher average utility level for workers and employers is attained with a low NEP than with either a zero or a high NEP in the short and intermediate runs (generations1 through 50). As will be explained more carefully in Section 4, a zero NEP encourages shirking on the work-site (low risk of quits or firings in response to defections) while a high NEP results in a high risk of lost earnings due to coordination failure (high risk of quits or firings in response to defections). Interestingly, however, average utility tends to increase over time under each NEP treatment as the workers and employers become better at sustaining mutual cooperation on the work-site. Moreover, this movement towards higher average utility is strongest under the high NEP treatment. Thus, in the long run (generation 1000), the average utility level attained by workers and employers with a high NEP slightly exceeds the average utility levels attained with a zero or low NEP.

Table 1. Summary of Aggregate Outcomes: Average agent utility level (with standard deviation), worker unemployment rate, employer vacancy rate, and efficiency level for each non-employment payment (NEP) treatment.

Treatment	Generation 12		Generation 50		Generation 1000	
ZeroT	Utility	33.8 (5.9)	Utility	35.2 (2.8)	Utility	35.8 (3.6)
NEP=0	Unemp	0%	Unemp	0%	Unemp	0%
	Vacancy	0%	Vacancy	0%	Vacancy	0%
	Efficiency	85%	Efficiency	88%	Efficiency	90%
LowT	Utility	35.4 (3.6)	Utility	37.2 (2.0)	Utility	35.7 (1.8)
NEP=15	Unemp	1%	Unemp	0%	Unemp	2%
	Vacancy	2%	Vacancy	1%	Vacancy	3%
	Efficiency	88%	Efficiency	93%	Efficiency	88%
HighT	Utility	34.6 (1.0)	Utility	35.7 (0.5)	Utility	36.4 (0.6)
NEP=30	Unemp	48%	Unemp	36%	Unemp	32%
	Vacancy	50%	Vacancy	36%	Vacancy	33%
	Efficiency	50%	Efficiency	62%	Efficiency	67%

On the other hand, program costs should be taken into account as well as utility benefits in order to obtain a more accurate measure of economic efficiency. Let net earnings be measured by the average (per agent) utility level attained by workers and employers minus the average NEP paid to these workers and employers. Define efficiency to be the ratio of actual net earnings to maximum possible net earnings. As indicated in Table 1, although a high NEP results in a high average utility level, it also results in a significantly lower efficiency level than either the zero or low NEP due to high program costs. In the short and intermediate run low NEP delivers the highest overall efficiency level, while zero NEP is slightly more efficient that low NEP in the long run. Consequently, evaluated in terms of efficiency, our findings indicate that a low NEP is preferable overall to either a zero or a high NEP.

The aggregate outcomes reported in Table 1, while interesting, are only the tip of the iceberg. A careful study of individual experimental runs indicates that the response of the ACE labor market to changes in the NEP is much more intricately structured than this table suggests. As reported in Figures 1 through 3, the 20 runs generated for each NEP treatment tend to gravitate towards one of two "attractor states." The configuration of these two attractor states is similar under the zero and low NEP treatments: the first attractor state is characterized by latched pairs of mutually cooperative workers and employers, while the second attractor state is characterized by latched pairs of workers and employers who intermittently defect and cooperate. In contrast, under the high NEP treatment, one attractor state is characterized by latched pairs of mutually cooperative workers and employers while the other attractor state is a state of economic collapse in which each worker and employer ultimately becomes inactive. This apparent existence of multiple attractor states suggests caution in interpreting the aggregate outcomes reported in Table 1, since these outcomes could be based on inappropriately pooled data.

The existence of multiple attractor states for each NEP treatment is due to strong network and learning effects. Starting from the same initial structural conditions, chance differences in the initial interaction patterns among the workers and employers can cause the labor market to evolve towards persistent interaction networks supporting sharply distinct types of expressed behaviors.

For example, with a high NEP, the labor market evolves either towards a highly efficient economy in which all workers and employers are in long-run mutually cooperative relationships or towards economic collapse with 100% unemployment. Thus, while a change in the level of the NEP can be expected to have substantial systematic effects on key labor market outcomes such as efficiency and unemployment, our findings suggest that these effects will be in the form of spectral (multiple peaked) distributions with large standard deviations.

These computational experiment findings can be compared to findings reported in Pingle and Tesfatsion [13] for a human-subject experiment using a similarly structured labor market but with a smaller number of workers and employers participating in a much smaller number of trade cycles per experimental session. In the human-subject experiment, as in the computational experiment, a higher NEP resulted in higher average unemployment and vacancy rates as well as higher average utility levels among those who successfully matched. In the human-subject experiment, however, most relationships that formed between workers and employers were either short-lived or intermittent, with only modest amounts of behavioral coordination in

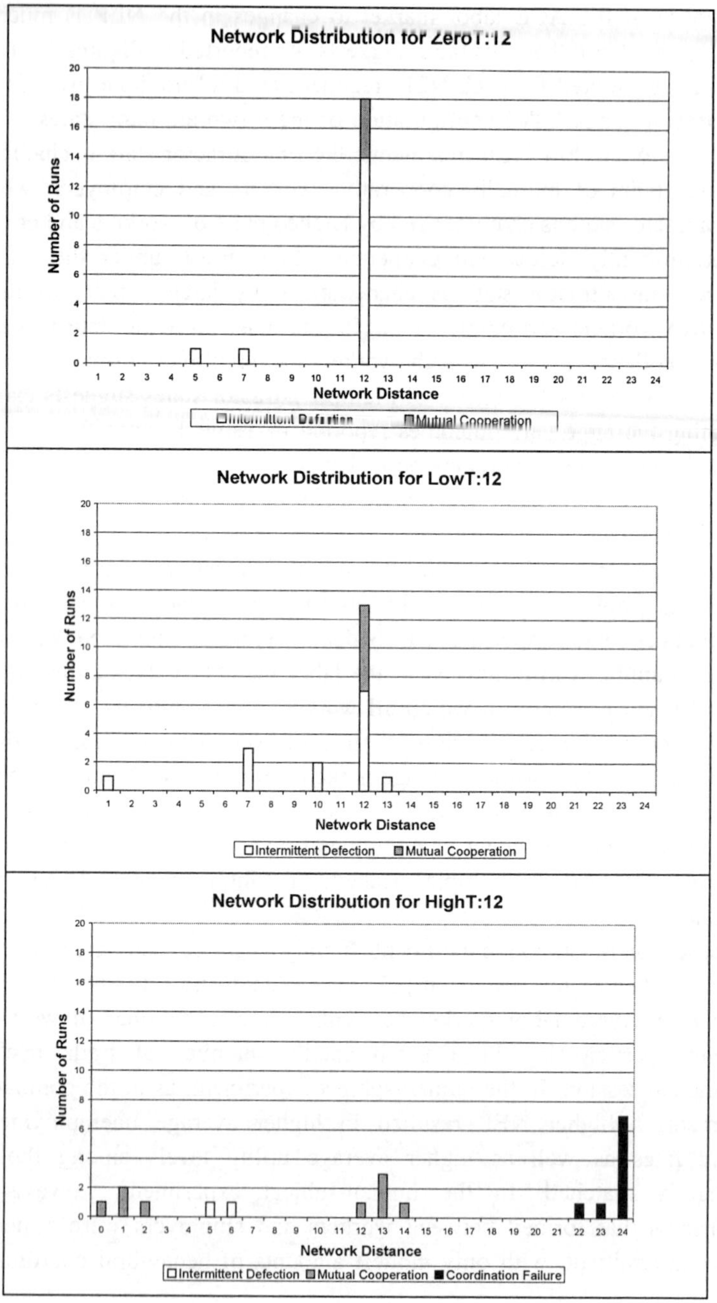

Figure 1: Network Distribution by Treatment (Generation 12)

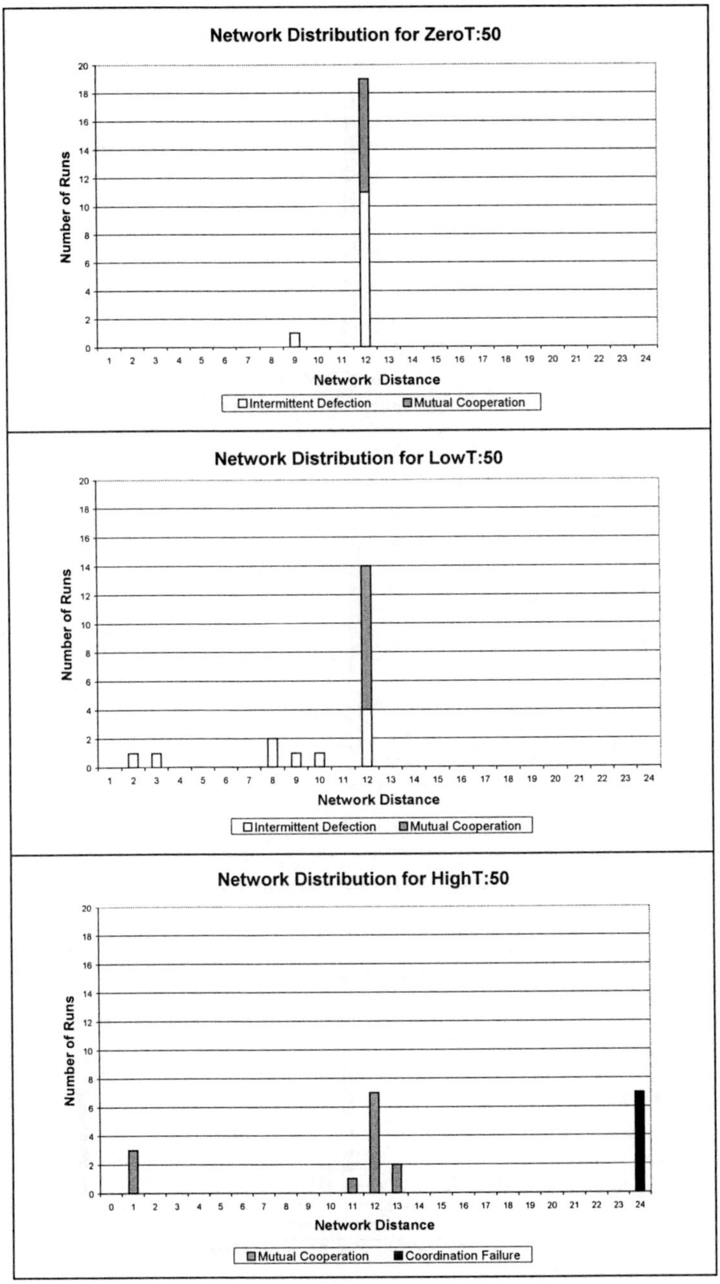

Figure 2: Network Distribution by Treatment (Generation 50)

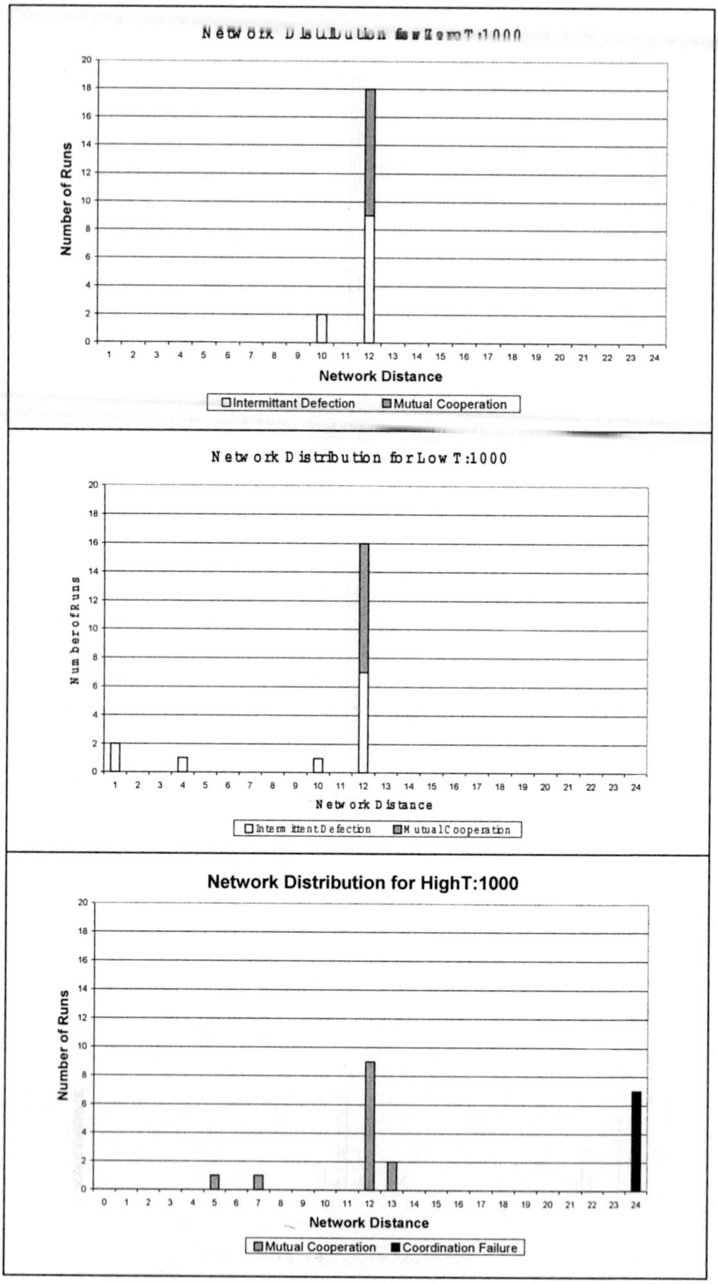

Figure 3: Network Distribution by Treatment (Generation 1000)

evidence. In contrast, in the computational experiment almost all workers and employers who succeeded in matching ended up in long-run relationships with one partner in which the behaviors of the partners were highly coordinated.

As detailed more carefully in Pingle and Tesfatsion [13], this difference in findings raises interesting questions. To what extent are the human-subject and computational experiments capturing the same economic structure but reporting over different time scales, short run versus long run? In particular, could it be that the "shadow of the past" weighs heavily on human subjects over the necessarily shorter human-subject trials, biasing behaviors towards unknown past points of reference? If so, the computational experiment might be providing the more accurate prediction of what would happen in actual labor markets over a longer span of time. Alternatively, the two experiments might differ structurally in some fundamental way so that differences in outcomes would be observed regardless of time scale. In particular, is the representation of agent learning in the computational experiment too inaccurate to permit valid comparisons with human-subject labor market experiments? Are the observed differences in types of network formations due to the different frequencies with which transaction costs are incurred due to scale effects? Careful additional studies, both empirical and experimental, will be needed to resolve these questions.

2. The ACE Labor Market Model

2.1. *Overview*

The ACE labor market consists of 12 workers and 12 employers. Each worker can work for at most one employer at any given time, and each employer can employ at most one worker at any given time. The workers and employers repeatedly seek preferred work-site partners using a modified form of a matching mechanism (Gale-Shapley [4]) that has been observed to evolve in various real-world labor market settings (Roth and Sotomayor [16]). The workers and employers who successfully match then engage in risky work-site interactions modeled as prisoner's dilemma games. At regular intervals the workers and employers separately update their work-site rules of behavior on the basis of the past earnings obtained with these rules.

The computational experiment is implemented by means of the *Trade Network Game Laboratory (TNG Lab)*, an agent-based computational laboratory developed by McFadzean, Stewart, and Tesfatsion [8] for studying the evolution of trade networks via real-time animations, tables, and graphical displays. [3] The specific TNG parameter settings used for the experiment at hand are described below. All other TNG parameter settings are the same as in Tesfatsion [20].

2.2. *Implementation Details*

As depicted in Table 2, ACE labor market activities are divided into a sequence of 1000 generations. Each generation in turn is divided into three parts: (a) a trade cycle loop consisting of successive trade cycles during which work-site interactions take place; (b) an environment step in which each worker and employer assesses their current utility (fitness) level as a function of their accumulated earnings to date; and (c) an evolution step in which the workers and employers separately evolve their work-site rules of behavior on the basis of the past earnings attained with these rules.

Each worker and employer in the initial generation is assigned a work-site rule in the form of a randomly specified pure strategy for playing an iterated prisoner's dilemma game with an arbitrary partner an indefinite number of times.

This work-site rule governs the behavior of the agent in his work-site interactions throughout the entire trade cycle loop for the initial generation. Each work-site rule is represented by means of a "finite state automaton"[4] with 16 internal states. Thus, the set of feasible work-site rules for each worker and employer, while extremely large, is nevertheless finite. Each worker and employer in the initial generation also assigns an initial expected utility assessment U^o to each of his possible work-site partners, where U^o is equal to the mutual cooperation payoff.[5]

The workers and employers in the initial generation then participate in a trade cycle loop consisting of 150 successive trade cycles. In each trade cycle they engage in two main activities: (1) a matching process during which they

---

[3] See http://www.econ.iastate.edu/tesfatsi/tnghome.htm for source code, executables, user instructions, tutorials, and research related to the TNG Lab.

[4] A *finite state automaton* is a system comprising a finite collection of internal states together with a state transition function that gives the next state of the system as a function of the current state and other current system inputs. For the application at hand, the latter inputs are the actions selected by a worker and employer engaged in a work-site interaction.

[5] This is not an innocuous specification, since it strongly affects the extent to which the workers and employers engage in experimentation with new partners. This issue is further considered in Section 3.

Table 2. Flow of Activities in the ACE Labor Market

```
int main () {

  InitiateEconomy();          // CONSTRUCT initial subpopulations of
                              // workers and employers with random
                              // work-site rules of behavior.

  For (G = 1,...,1000) {      // ENTER THE GENERATION CYCLE LOOP

                              // GENERATION CYCLE:

    InitiateGen();            // Configure workers and employers
                              //   with user-supplied parameter values
                              //   (initial expected utility assessments,
                              //   minimum tolerance levels,...)

    For (TC = 1,...,150) {    // ENTER THE TRADE CYCLE LOOP
                              // TRADE CYCLE:
      MatchTraders();         // Workers and employers determine
                              //   their work-site partners, given
                              //   their expected utility assessments,
                              //   and record job search and
                              //   inactivity costs.
      Trade();                // Workers and employers engage
                              //   in work-site interactions and
                              //   record their work-site payoffs.
      UpdateExp();            // Workers and employers update their
                              //   expected utility assessments, using
                              //   newly recorded costs and work-site
                              //   payoffs, and begin a new trade cycle.
  }

                              // ENVIRONMENT STEP:
  AssessFitness();            //   Each worker and employer assesses
                              //   his utility (fitness) level.

                              // EVOLUTION STEP:
  EvolveGen();                // Workers and employers separately
                              //   evolve their work-site rules,
                              //   and a new generation cycle begins.
  }
  Return 0;

}
```

search for preferred work-site partners on the basis of their current expected utility assessments for these partners; and (2) an employment process during which each matched worker-employer pair engages in one work-site interaction. Throughout these processes the workers and employers update their current expected utility assessments for each other every time they obtain a payoff from an interaction with each other.

Each worker and employer also has an exogenously specified minimum tolerance level, assigned as part of the initial generation configuration process. In the current experiment, these minimum tolerance levels are set equal to the non-employment payment. Thus, entering into a risky work-site interaction is viewed as a tolerable gamble if and only if it is expected to yield at least as high a payoff as would be earned through inactivity. If the expected utility assessment assigned to an employer by a worker ever falls below the minimum tolerance level, the worker will stop directing work offers to this employer. Similarly, if the expected utility assessment assigned to a worker by an employer ever drops below the minimum tolerance level, the employer will stop accepting work offers from this worker.

The manner in which workers direct work offers to employers during the matching process for each trade cycle proceeds as follows. Each worker and employer has a preference ranking over possible partners, determined by his current expected utility assessments. Each worker starts by directing a work offer to a most preferred tolerable employer. Each employer receiving at least one tolerable work offer places his most preferred tolerable work offer on his work offer list and refuses all the rest. Each worker having a work offer refused then redirects this work offer to a next most preferred tolerable employer who has not yet refused him in the current matching process, if any such employer exists. Once employers stop receiving new work offers, they accept the work offers currently on their work offer lists and the matching process comes to a close. Throughout this process, ties are broken by random selection.

Once a worker and employer are matched, they enter into a work-site interaction. This interaction is modeled as a prisoner's dilemma game with cooperation interpreted as meeting all work-site obligations and defection interpreted as shirking with regard to these obligations. As depicted in Table 3, one of four possible payoffs can be earned in each work-site interaction: a low payoff L=10, earned by an agent who cooperates against a defecting partner; a mutual defection payoff D=20; a mutual cooperation payoff C=40; or a high payoff H=60 earned by an agent who defects against a cooperating partner. Also, a worker incurs an offer cost OC=1.0 each time he directs a work offer to an employer, whether or not the work offer is accepted. A worker or employer who is not matched earns a non-employment payment (NEP) for the trade cycle.

Each worker and employer records all payoffs he receives during the course of each trade cycle, including work-site payoffs, negative payoffs due to offer costs, and non-employment payments.

Each worker and employer uses a simple reinforcement learning algorithm to update his expected utility assessments for possible partners in response to new payoffs. Recall that each agent (worker or employer) initially assigns an initial expected utility assessment U^o=C to each possible work-site partner. Subsequently, each time an agent v interacts with an agent z, agent v forms an updated expected utility assessment for z by summing U^o together with all payoffs received to date from interactions with z and dividing this sum by one plus the total number of these interactions. The payoffs included in this summation include work-site payoffs and negative payoffs due to offer costs. Consequently, an updated expected utility assessment for any agent z is the average of all payments received to date in interactions with z, augmented to include U^o as a virtual additional payoff. Under this method, if an agent interacts repeatedly with another agent for a sufficient length of time, his expected utility assessment for z will eventually approach his true average payoff level from interactions with z.[6]

At the end of the initial generation, the workers and employers enter into an environment step in which each agent calculates his utility (fitness) level. This utility level is taken to be the average total net payoffs per trade cycle that the agent earned during the course of the preceding trade cycle loop, i.e., the agent's total net payoffs divided by 150 (the number of trade cycles per loop). The workers and employers then enter into an evolution step in which they use their attained utility levels to evolve (structurally update) their work-site rules via both inductive and social learning. Inductive learning takes the form of experimentation; agents perturb their work-site rules by introducing random modifications. Social learning takes the form of mimicry; agents deliberately modify their work-site rules to more closely resemble the work-site rules used by more successful (higher utility) agents of their own type. Thus, workers imitate other more successful workers, and employers imitate other more successful employers.

---

[6] See McFadzean and Tesfatsion [9] for more details. Briefly, this long-run consistency property follows from the finite state automaton representation for work-site rules which ensures that the action pattern between any two agents who repeatedly interact must eventually enter into a cycle as the number of their interactions becomes sufficiently large.

Experimentation and mimicry are separately implemented for workers and for employers by means of genetic algorithms involving commonly used elitism, mutation, and recombination operations. Elitism ensures that the most successful work-site rules are retained unchanged from one generation to the next. Mutation ensures that workers and employers continually experiment with new work-site rules (inductive learning). Recombination ensures that workers and employers continually engage in mimicry (social learning).[7]

At the end of the evolution step, each worker and employer has a potentially new work-site rule. The memory of each worker and employer is then wiped clean of all past work-site experiences. In particular, initial expected utility assessments for possible partners are re-set to the mutual cooperation payoff level without regard for past work-site experiences. The workers and employers then enter into a new generation and the whole process repeats, for a total of 1000 generations in all.[8]

3. The Computational Experiment

The computational experiment focuses on only one treatment variable, the non-employment payment (NEP). The three tested treatments for NEP are NEP=0, NEP=15, and NEP=30. These three treatments are referred to as ZeroT, LowT, and HighT, respectively.

---

[7] See McFadzean and Tesfatsion [9] and Tesfatsion [20] for detailed discussions of this use of genetic algorithms to implement the evolution of work-site rules.

[8] A final technical remark about implementation should also be noted, in case others wish to replicate or extend this experiment. The minimum tolerance level is hardwired to zero in the TNG Lab, the software used to implement the computational experiment. Thus, to retain the non-employment payment NEP equal to the minimum tolerance level, experiments were actually run with each work-site payoff normalized by subtraction of NEP. In addition, for better TNG Lab visualization, the work-site payoffs were further normalized by multiplication by 0.10. For example, C* = 0.10[C-NEP] was used in place of the mutual cooperation payoff C, and similarly for the other work-site payoffs. The corresponding normalized non-employment payment then equaled NEP* = 0.10[NEP-NEP] = 0. Finally, to maintain consistency with this normalization, the offer cost OC was normalized to OC*=0.10. Note that it would *not* be consistent to subtract NEP from OC, since OC is a cost per work offer. For example, a worker who is refused k times and never hired during a trade cycle receives a total payoff NEP-kOC at the end of the trade cycle, and this is the payoff from which NEP must then be subtracted to implement the payoff normalization. This subtraction occurs automatically when NE*=0 is used in place of NEP. In all data tables presented below, utility levels and market power levels are translated back into non-normalized form prior to reporting, for easier comparison with the human-subject experimental findings reported in Pingle and Tesfatsion [13].

The interest in these three alternative treatments is seen by comparing them with the work-site payoffs depicted in Table 3. In treatment ZeroT, non-employment during a trade cycle results in the payment NEP=0. This is the worst possible trade cycle payoff, worse even than the sucker payoff L=10 that results from cooperating with a defecting work-site partner. In treatment ZeroT, then, unemployment or vacancy is never an attractive alternative to employment or hiring, and the workers and employers will be willing to put up with defections to avoid unemployment or vacancy.

Table 3. Payoff Matrix for the Work-Site Prisoner's Dilemma Game.

		Employer	
		C	D
Worker	C	(40,40)	(10,60)
	D	(60,10)	(20,20)

In contrast, in treatment LowT non-employment during a trade cycle results in the payment NEP=15. This payment is strictly higher than the sucker payoff L=10, meaning agents will prefer non-employment to being suckered. Thus, each agent who defects against a cooperative partner to attain a high payoff now faces a risk of future non-employment if this current partner chooses not to interact with him in the future. Finally, in treatment HighT non-employment results in the payment NEP=30. This payment dominates both the sucker payoff L=10 and the mutual defection payoff D=20. Consequently, agents will tend to be much more sensitive to defections, preferring unemployment or vacancy in preference to defecting back against a defecting partner.

For each NEP treatment, 20 runs were generated using 20 different seeds for the TNG Lab pseudo-random number generator: namely, {0,5,10,...,95}. In the data tables reported in Section 4, each run is identified by its corresponding seed value. Each run consists of 1000 generations in total. To investigate evolutionary change, the twenty runs for each treatment are sampled at three different points in time: generation 12, generation 50, and generation 1000. For each sampled generation, data is collected regarding network formation, market non-participation rates, work-site behaviors, welfare (utility and market power) outcomes, and persistent relationship type counts.

Before reporting our experimental findings in detail, it is important to explain carefully the descriptive statistics that have been constructed to help characterize the one-to-many mapping between treatment and outcomes.

3.1. *Measurement of Persistent Relationships*

As previously noted (see footnote 4), work-site rules are represented as finite state automata, implying that the actions undertaken by any one agent in repeated work-site interactions with another agent must eventually cycle. Consequently, the actions of any one agent in interactions with another agent during a trade cycle loop can be summarized in the form of a work-site history H:P. The "handshake" H is a (possibly null) string of work-site actions that form a non-repeated pattern, while the "persistent portion" P is a (possibly null) string of work-site actions that are cyclically repeated. For example, letting c denote cooperation and d denote defection, the work-site history ddd:dc for an agent v in interactions with another agent z indicates that v defected against z in his first three work-site interactions with z and thereafter alternated between defection and cooperation.

A worker and employer are said to exhibit a *persistent relationship* during a given trade cycle loop if two conditions hold. First, their work-site histories with each other during the course of this loop each have non-null persistent portions. Second, accepted work offers between the worker and employer do not permanently cease during this loop either by choice (a permanent switch away to a strictly preferred partner) or by refusal (one agent becomes intolerable to the other because of too many defections).

A persistent relationship between a worker and employer in a given trade cycle loop is said to be *latched* if the worker works continually for the employer (i.e., in every successive trade cycle) during the persistent portions of their work-site histories. Otherwise, the persistent relationship is said to be *recurrent.*

3.2. *Measurement of Market Non-Participation Rates*

A worker or employer who fails to form any persistent relationship during a given trade cycle loop is classified as *persistently non-employed* for that trade cycle loop. The percentage of workers who are persistently non-employed constitutes the *persistent unemployment rate* for that trade cycle loop. Similarly, the percentage of employers who are persistently non-employed constitutes the *persistent vacancy rate* for that trade cycle loop.

3.3. *Classification of Networks by Competitive Distance*

We will next construct a distance measure that permits the classification of experimentally observed "interaction networks" into alternative types. This distance measure will calculate the distance between an experimentally observed interaction network and an idealized interaction network capable of supporting a competitive (full employment) market outcome.

Recall from Table 2 that each generation G of the ACE labor market model consists of a single trade cycle loop plus an environment step and an evolution step. The *interaction network* N(G,R) for a particular generation G in a particular experimental run R refers to the observed pattern of interactions occurring among workers and employers in the trade cycle loop for that generation and run.

Each interaction network N(G,R) is represented in the form of a directed graph. The vertices V of the graph represent the workers and employers. The edges of the graph (directed arrows) represent work offers directed from workers to employers. Finally, the edge weight on any edge denotes the number of accepted work offers between the worker and employer connected by the edge. The reduced-form network PN(G,R) derived from N(G,R) by eliminating all edges of N(G,R) that correspond to non-persistent relationships is referred to as the *persistent network* corresponding to N(G,R).

In a standard competitive equilibrium situation, workers are indifferent among employers offering the same working conditions and employers are indifferent among workers offering identical labor services. Moreover, workers offering the same labor services have the same ex ante expected employment rate and employers offering the same working conditions have the same ex ante expected vacancy rate.

In the current labor market model, these same market characteristics would tend to prevail if all workers and employers always cooperated. In the latter case, due to indifference, workers would randomly distribute their work offers across all employers and employers would randomly select work offers from among all work offers received. The resulting interaction pattern would therefore tend to be fully recurrent (no latching and no persistent non-employment) with equal ex ante expected employment rates and vacancy rates for workers and employers, respectively. For these reasons, the following interaction pattern among workers and employers is referred to below as a *competitive interaction pattern.* Each worker is recurrently directing work offers to employers, and every worker and employer has at least one persistent relationship.

The *network distance* for any persistent network PN(G,R) is then defined to be the number of vertices (agents) in PN(G,R) whose edges (persistent relationships) fail to conform to the competitive interaction pattern. By construction, then, a distance measure of 0 indicates zero deviation and a distance measure of 24 (the total number of workers and employers) indicates maximum deviation. In particular, a perfectly recurrent persistent network has a network distance of 0, a perfectly latched persistent network has a network distance of 12, and a perfectly disconnected persistent network (no persistent relationships) has a network distance of 24.

3.4. *Classification of Work-Site Behaviors*

A worker or employer in generation G of a run R is called a *never-provoked defector (NPD)* if he ever defects against another agent that has not previously defected against him. The percentages of workers and employers who are NPDs measure the extent to which these agents behave opportunistically in work-site interactions with partners who are strangers or who so far have been consistently cooperative.

A worker or employer in generation G of a run R is referred to as a *persistent intermittent defector (IntD)* if he establishes at least one persistent relationship for which his persistent portion consists of a non-trivial mix of defections and cooperations. The agent is referred to as a *persistent defector (AllD)* if he establishes at least one persistent relationship and if the persistent portion of each of his persistent relationships consists entirely of defections. Finally, the agent is referred to as a *persistent cooperator (AllC)* if he establishes at least one persistent relationship and if the persistent portion of each of his persistent relationships consists entirely of cooperations. By construction, an agent in generation G of a run R satisfies one and only one of the following four agent-type classifications: persistently non-employed; a persistent intermittent defector; a persistent defector; or a persistent cooperator.

Two important points can be made about this classification of agent types. First, in contrast to standard game theory, the agents co-evolve their types over time. This co-evolution is in response to past experiences, starting from initially random behavioral specifications. Thus, agent typing is endogenous. Second, agent typing is measured in terms of persistently expressed behaviors, not in terms of work-site rules. An agent may have coevolved into an AllC in terms of expressed behaviors with current work-site partners, based on past work-site experiences with these partners, while still retaining the capability of defecting against a new untried partner. Indeed, work-site rules continually co-evolve in the evolution step through mutation and recombination operations even if expressed behaviors appear to have largely stabilized. This ceaseless change in work-site rules makes any apparent stabilization in the distribution of agent types all the more surprising and interesting.

3.5. *Measurement of Utility and Market Power Outcomes*

The utility level of a worker or employer at the end of generation G in a run R is measured by the average total net payoffs per trade cycle that the agent earns during the course of the trade cycle loop for generation G.

With regard to market power, we adopt the standard industrial organization approach: namely, market power is measured by the degree to which the actual utility levels attained by workers and employers compare against an idealized competitive yardstick. We take as this yardstick a situation in which there is absence of strategic behavior, symmetric treatment of equals, and full employment. Specifically, we define *competitive market conditions* for the ACE labor market to be a situation in which each worker is recurrently directing work offers to employers, and each worker and employer is a persistent cooperator (AllC).

Ignoring offer costs, the utility level that each worker and employer would attain under these competitive market conditions is simply the mutual cooperation payoff level, C. Therefore, as in Pingle and Tesfatsion [12,13], we define the *market power (MPow)* of each worker or employer in generation G of a run R to be the extent to which their attained utility level, U, differs from C: that is, MPow = (U-C)/C.

3.6. *Classification of Persistent Relationship Types*

A persistent relationship between a worker and employer in generation G of a run R is classified in accordance with the persistent behaviors expressed by the two participants in this particular relationship.

If both participants are persistent intermittent defectors (IntDs), the relationship is classified as *mutual intermittent defection (M-IntD).* If both participants are persistent defectors (AllDs), the relationship is classified as *mutual defection (M-AllD).* If both participants are persistent cooperators (AllCs), the relationship is classified as *mutual cooperation (M-AllC).* Note that the relative shirking rates for an M-IntD relationship can be deduced for the participant worker and employer by examining their relative market power levels.

A persistent relationship in which the worker and employer express distinct types of behaviors is indicated in hyphenated form, with the worker's behavior indicated first. For example, a persistent relationship involving a worker who is an IntD and an employer who is an AllC is indicated by the expression IntD-AllC.

4. Experimental Findings

4.1. *Overview*

The results for the computational experiment display a startling degree of regularity. This regularity is visible as early as the twelfth generation and persists through generation 1000.

For each of the three NEP treatments ZeroT, LowT, and HighT, the twenty trial runs tend to cluster into two distinct attractor states. Each attractor state supports a distinct configuration of market non-participation rates, work-site behaviors, utility levels, market power outcomes, and persistent relationship types. These attractor states can be Pareto-ranked, in the sense that the average utility levels attained by workers and by employers are both markedly higher in one of the two attractor states. The exact form of the attractor states varies systematically across the three NEP treatments.

4.2. *Network Formation*

For each of the twenty runs corresponding to each treatment ZeroT, LowT, and HighT, the form of the persistent network was determined at three sampling points: generation 12; generation 50; and generation 1000. Using the network distance measure defined in Section 3, the distribution of these persistent networks across runs was then plotted, conditional on treatment and sampled generation. Thus, a total of nine network distributions were plotted, three for each of the three treatments.

These nine network distributions are depicted in Figures 1-3. Network distance is measured along the horizontal axes and the number of runs clustered at this network distance is indicated on the vertical axes. Recall that a network distance of 0 corresponds to a perfectly recurrent ("competitive") persistent network, a network distance of 12 corresponds to a perfectly latched persistent network, and a network distance of 24 corresponds to a perfectly disconnected persistent network (no persistent relationships).

In treatment ZeroT, perfectly latched networks are strongly dominant even by generation 12. For each sampled generation, all but one or two of the twenty runs exhibit persistent networks consisting of perfectly latched worker-employer pairs. This is indicated by the sharp peak in the network distribution at network distance 12.

In treatment LowT, perfectly latched networks are again dominant. Nevertheless, at each sampled generation, the network distribution is less sharply peaked at network distance 12 than it was for treatment ZeroT.

In treatment HighT, a new phenomenon arises. For each sampled generation, seven runs out of twenty lie at network distance 24, indicating that the workers and employers in these runs have failed to form any persistent relationships. At generation 12, the remaining 13 runs are scattered over network distances from 0 to 23. By generation 1000, however, the network distribution displays two sharp peaks, one at network distance 12 (latching) and one at network distance 24 (complete coordination failure).

Figures 1-3 also indicate the behavioral modes supported by each network distribution. For example, consider the 19 runs clustered at network distance 12 for the ZeroT treatment sampled at generation 50. Figure 2 indicates that workers and employers generally attained M-IntD (mutual intermittent defection) relationships in 11 of the runs and M-AllC (mutual cooperation) relationships in the remaining 8 runs.

4.3. *Overall Utility and Efficiency Levels*

As indicated in Table 1, the following results are obtained for the average (per agent) utility achieved by workers and employers across treatments. For generations 12 and 50, average utility is highest in treatment LowT. By generation 1000, however, average utility is actually highest in treatment HighT. The latter finding results from the high NEP for inactive agents as well as the previously noted observation that workers and employers who do manage to match under treatment HighT become increasingly more successful over time at coordinating on persistent mutual cooperation (the first attractor state) rather than persistent non-employment (the second attractor state). Although this evolution over time of increased cooperative behavior between matched workers and employers is observed under all three NEP treatments, it is observed most strongly for treatment HighT.

On the other hand, consider the overall level of economic efficiency attained under each NEP treatment, where efficiency takes into account both utility benefits and program costs. Specifically, for each NEP treatment, let net earnings be measured as the average utility level attained by workers and employers minus the average NEP paid to workers and employers. Ignoring offer costs, the maximum possible net earnings under each NEP treatment is the mutual cooperation payoff 40, attained by mutually cooperative workers and employers in latched pairings. For each NEP treatment, let *efficiency* be measured by actual net earnings as a percentage of 40. As indicated in Table 1, efficiency is substantially lower under treatment HighT than under treatments ZeroT or LowT. In particular, the relatively higher average utility level attained under treatment HighT at generation 1000 is more than offset by the higher average NEP to unemployed workers and vacant employers. In contrast, program costs are minimal at all sampled generations under treatments ZeroT and LowT since unemployment and vacancy rates remain close to zero. As Table 1 indicates, evaluated in terms of efficiency, the best program option overall turns out to be the low NEP.

Table 4 provides a breakdown of the average utility levels reported in Table 1 by agent type (workers and employers) and by attractor state for each of the three NEP treatments. The generally higher average utility levels attained by employers reflects in part the structural asymmetry that workers shoulder all of the offer (transaction) costs associated with network formation and maintenance. As detailed below, in some cases this structural asymmetry also appears to provide employers a strategic advantage in their work-site interactions.

Table 4. Utility and Efficiency Outcomes: Average utility levels (with standard deviations) attained by workers and by employers in the two attractors and overall, together with the general efficiency level, for each non-employment payment (NEP) treatment

		Generation 12 w	Generation 12 e	Generation 50 w	Generation 50 e	Generation 1000 w	Generation 1000 e
ZeroT NEP=0	CoopAtt	35.4 (6.6)	40.1 (5.5)	39.1 (1.5)	40.7 (1.4)	36.4 (2.7)	39.9 (3.6)
	IntDAtt	32.2 (5.9)	33.1 (6.0)	31.8 (2.7)	32.8 (2.8)	33.2 (4.1)	34.2 (3.2)
	Overall	32.5 (5.9)	35.1 (5.8)	34.0 (2.3)	36.3 (2.5)	34.7 (3.6)	36.8 (3.6)
		Efficiency=85%		Efficiency=88%		Efficiency=90%	
LowT NEP=15	CoopAtt	38.3 (2.3)	40.1 (2.3)	38.9 (1.4)	40.8 (1.4)	38.5 (0.8)	38.8 (1.5)
	IntDAtt	33.6 (4.3)	36.7 (4.4)	28.0 (2.3)	40.5 (3.1)	34.2 (2.1)	33.9 (2.2)
	Overall	34.0 (3.6)	36.8 (3.6)	35.7 (2.0)	38.6 (2.0)	36.0 (1.5)	35.3 (2.0)
		Efficiency=88%		Efficiency=93%		Efficiency=88%	
HighT NEP=30	CoopAtt	38.1 (2.0)	40.2 (1.6)	38.9 (0.7)	40.2 (0.5)	38.9 (0.5)	41.3 (0.5)
	IntDAtt	30.2 (0.4)	30.3 (0.3)	30.0 (0.0)	30.1 (0.0)	30.0 (0.0)	30.1 (0.0)
	Overall	33.5 (0.9)	35.7 (1.1)	35.5 (0.5)	35.9 (0.4)	35.5 (0.6)	37.2 (0.5)
		Efficiency=50%		Efficiency=62%		Efficiency=67%	

4.4. *Market Non-Participation Rates, Work-Site Behaviors, Utility Levels, and Market Power Levels*

Table 5 reports market non-participation rates, work-site behaviors, utility levels, and market power outcomes for the twenty runs constituting treatment ZeroT, each sampled at generation 12. These descriptive statistics are reported separately for each of the twenty individual runs comprising this treatment. More precisely, for each run, the following descriptive statistics are given: Persistent unemployment rate for workers (UnE-w); Persistent vacancy rate for employers (Vac-e); A count of never-provoked defectors for workers

Table 5: Non-Participation Rates, Work-Site Behaviors, and Welfare Outcomes---ZeroT Treatment for Generation 12

NetID	Run	NON-PARTICIPATION RATES AND WORK-SITE BEHAVIORS										WELFARE OUTCOMES						NETWORK
		UnE-w	Vac-e	NPD-w	NPD-e	IntD-w	IntD-e	AllD-w	AllD-e	AllC-w	AllC-e	Util-w	Util-w SD	Util-e	Util-e SD	M Pov-w	M Pov-e	PATTERNS
5	40	0	0	0	8	9	7	0	2	3	3	32.5	3.5	37.6	4.1	-0.19	-0.06	Mix of latched pairs and recurrent relations
7	45	0	0	0	12	10	6	0	2	2	4	25.6	6.5	40.9	6.2	-0.36	0.02	
Average		0.00	0.00	0.00	10.00	9.50	6.50	0.00	2.00	2.50	3.50	29.1	5.0	39.3	5.2	-0.27	-0.02	
%		0%	0%	0%	83%	79%	54%	0%	17%	21%	29%							
12	30	0	0	0	11	2	1	0	4	10	7	28.2	9.4	45.1	6.1	-0.29	0.13	Perfect latched pairs with high percentage of AllC Cooperators
12	50	0	0	2	3	5	6	0	0	7	6	34.2	5.9	42.0	2.3	-0.15	0.05	
12	90	0	0	12	4	2	3	0	0	10	9	36.2	4.5	37.2	3.7	-0.10	-0.07	
12	65	0	0	2	0	0	0	2	0	10	12	42.8	6.6	36.2	9.9	0.07	-0.10	
Average		0.00	0.00	4.00	4.50	2.25	2.50	0.50	1.00	9.25	8.50	35.4	6.6	40.1	5.5	-0.12	0.00	
%		0%	0%	33%	38%	19%	21%	4%	8%	77%	71%							
12	60	0	0	7	12	11	11	0	1	1	0	28.1	5.7	39.6	5.3	-0.28	-0.01	Perfect latched pairs with high percentag of Int-Defectors
12	35	0	0	1	12	9	9	1	1	2	2	30.9	5.6	36.3	4.7	-0.23	-0.09	
12	95	0	0	5	12	10	9	0	1	2	2	30.4	5.3	35.6	2.8	-0.24	-0.11	
12	75	0	0	12	12	11	9	0	2	1	1	28.0	7.6	35.1	8.3	-0.30	-0.12	
12	15	0	0	6	11	10	9	1	2	1	1	30.9	6.6	35.1	6.5	-0.23	-0.12	
12	55	0	0	7	6	12	12	0	0	0	0	31.6	3.3	34.8	3.7	-0.21	-0.13	
12	85	0	0	6	8	11	12	0	0	1	0	31.5	3.6	34.7	4.6	-0.21	-0.13	
12	5	0	0	5	12	11	11	1	1	0	0	29.7	5.2	33.9	5.1	-0.26	-0.15	
12	10	0	0	1	10	7	8	2	0	3	4	36.6	7.0	33.0	8.2	-0.09	-0.18	
12	20	0	0	11	8	9	10	2	0	1	2	35.9	5.4	30.7	6.4	-0.10	-0.23	
12	80	0	0	5	8	10	10	1	0	1	2	37.4	7.2	30.5	6.5	-0.07	-0.24	
12	25	0	0	8	5	9	11	2	0	1	1	36.0	6.1	29.3	8.6	-0.10	-0.27	
12	0	0	0	2	11	8	8	4	3	0	1	31.5	8.2	29.0	6.4	-0.21	-0.28	
12	70	0	0	11	12	9	10	3	2	0	0	32.2	5.7	25.1	6.3	-0.20	-0.37	
Average		0.00	0.00	6.21	9.93	9.79	9.93	1.21	0.93	1.00	1.14	32.2	5.9	33.1	6.0	-0.20	-0.17	
%		0%	0%	52%	83%	82%	83%	10%	8%	8%	10%							
Total Average		0.00	0.00	5.15	8.85	8.25	8.10	0.95	1.05	2.80	2.85	32.5	5.9	35.1	5.8	-0.19	-0.12	
Total%		0%	0%	43%	74%	69%	68%	8%	9%	23%	24%							

(NPD-w) and employers (NPD-e); A count of intermittent defectors for workers (IntD-w) and employers (IntD-e); A count of always-defectors for workers (AllD-w) and employers (AllD-e); A count of always-cooperators for workers (AllC-w) and employers (AllC-e); Mean utility level for workers (Util-w) with standard deviation (Util-w SD); Mean utility level for employers (Util-e) with standard deviation (Util-e SD); Mean market power level attained by workers (MPow-w); Mean market power level attained by employers (MPow-e).

The twenty runs in Table 5 are grouped together, first in accordance with their network distance (NetD), and second in accordance with the type of work-site behaviors expressed by the workers and employers. This grouping reveals that the runs are essentially clustered into two distinct *attractor states* comprising 18 runs in total, each run exhibiting a perfectly latched persistent network pattern (NetD=12). The remaining two runs {5,7} comprise a mix of recurrent and latched relationships and appear to be transition states between the two attractor states. The workers attain very low mean market power levels in the transition-state runs. This is due to the substantial offer costs they accumulate from refused work offers in the course of maintaining their recurrent relationships.

In the first attractor state comprising four runs {30,50,90,65}, 77% of the workers and 71% of the employers are AllCs (persistent cooperators). Despite the prevalence of AllC agent types, the employers attain an average mean market power level (MPow-e = -0.00) that is markedly higher than the corresponding level obtained by the workers (Mpow-w = -0.12). This is due to the offer costs incurred by workers in the process of forming and sustaining the persistent latched networks and to the modestly higher percentages of NPD (non-provoked defection), IntD (persistent intermittent defection), and AllD (persistent defection) exhibited by employers.

In the second attractor state comprising fourteen runs {60,35,...,70}, very high percentages of the workers and the employers are NPDs and IntDs. Interestingly, the workers and employers obtain similar average mean market power levels in this second attractor state (-0.20 for workers and -0.17 for employers). However, these levels are substantially lower than the average mean market power levels they attain in the first attractor state. Thus, in terms of this market power measure, the first attractor state Pareto dominates the second attractor state.

In parallel to Table 5, Table 6 reports persistent relationship type counts for treatment ZeroT sampled at generation 12. As in Table 5, data are reported for the two transient-state runs {5,7} plus the eighteen remaining runs grouped into the two attractor states.

The most striking aspect of Table 6 is the almost complete lack of mixed persistent relationships, i.e., relationships in which the participant worker and employer are expressing distinct types of behaviors. In particular, Table 6

Table 6: Presistent Relationship Type Counts---ZeroT Treatment, Generation 12

NetD	Run	MUTUALITY			MIXED CASES (w - e)						MARKETPOWER		NETWORK PATTERNS
		M-IntD	M-AllD	M-AllC	IntD-AllD	IntD-AllC	AllD-IntD	AllD-AllC	AllC-IntD	AllC-AllD	MPow-w	MPow-e	
5	40	10	1	6	0	0	0	0	1	1	-0.19	-0.06	Mix of latched pairs and recurrent relations
7	45	7	1	3	2	2	0	2	1	0	-0.36	0.02	
Average		**8.50**	**1.00**	**4.50**	**1.00**	**1.00**	**0.00**	**1.00**	**1.00**	**0.50**	**-0.27**	**-0.02**	
12	30	0	0	7	2	0	0	0	1	2	-0.29	0.13	Perfect latched pairs with high percentage of AllC Cooperators
12	50	5	0	6	0	0	0	0	1	0	-0.15	0.05	
12	90	2	0	9	0	0	0	0	1	0	-0.10	-0.07	
12	65	0	0	10	0	0	0	2	0	0	0.07	-0.10	
Average		**1.75**	**0.00**	**8.00**	**0.50**	**0.00**	**0.00**	**0.50**	**0.75**	**0.50**	**-0.12**	**0.00**	
12	60	10	0	0	1	0	0	0	1	[illegible]	-0.28	-0.01	Perfect latched pairs with high percentage of Int-Defectors
12	35	9	1	2	0	0	0	0	0	[illegible]	-0.23	-0.09	
12	95	9	2	0	1	0	0	0	0	[illegible]	-0.24	-0.11	
12	75	9	0	0	1	1	0	0	0	1	-0.30	-0.12	
12	15	9	1	0	0	1	0	0	0	1	-0.23	-0.12	
12	55	12	0	0	0	0	0	0	0	0	-0.21	-0.13	
12	85	11	0	0	0	0	0	0	1	0	-0.21	-0.13	
12	5	11	1	0	0	0	0	0	0	0	-0.26	-0.15	
12	10	7	0	3	0	0	1	1	0	0	-0.09	-0.18	
12	20	8	0	1	0	1	2	0	0	0	-0.10	-0.23	
12	80	10	0	1	0	0	0	1	0	0	-0.07	-0.24	
12	25	9	0	1	0	0	2	0	0	0	-0.10	-0.27	
12	0	8	3	0	0	0	0	1	0	0	-0.21	-0.28	
12	70	9	2	0	0	0	1	0	0	0	-0.20	-0.37	
Average		**9.36**	**0.71**	**0.57**	**0.21**	**0.21**	**0.43**	**0.21**	**0.14**	**0.14**	**-0.20**	**-0.17**	
Total Average		**7.75**	**0.60**	**2.45**	**0.35**	**0.25**	**0.30**	**0.35**	**0.35**	**0.25**	**-0.19**	**-0.12**	

reveals that the first attractor state comprising four runs {30,50,90,65} is dominated by mutual cooperation (M-AllC) whereas the second attractor state comprising 14 runs {60,35,...,70} is dominated by mutual intermittent defection (M-IntD). Mutual defection (M-AllD) is almost entirely absent.

The mean market power levels reported in Table 6 reveal, however, that the shirking rates expressed by the workers and employers in their M-IntD relationships in the second attractor state are not generally balanced in any given run. Rather, in about half the runs the workers shirk more than the employers, and in the remaining half the employers shirk more than the workers. Thus, although the average mean market power levels attained by workers and employers in this second attractor state are very close, this hides an underlying volatility in relative shirking rates across runs.

The characteristics reported in Table 5 and Table 6 for treatment ZeroT sampled at generation 12 are largely maintained in generation 50 and in generation 1000. One interesting observation, however, is that individual runs can traverse from one attractor state to another as time proceeds. For example, run 30 is in the first attractor state in generation 12, appears as a transition state in generation 50, and ends up in the second attractor state by generation 1000. Conversely, run 60 is in the second attractor state in generation 12 but ends up in the first attractor state by generation 1000.

A second interesting observation is that the number of runs lying in each attractor state evens out over time. In generation 12, the cooperative first attractor state comprises only four runs while the second attractor state dominated by intermittent defection comprises fourteen runs. By generation 50, the first attractor state comprises eight runs while the second attractor state comprises 11 runs. By generation 1000, each attractor state comprises exactly nine runs. Thus, on average, agents over time are improving their ability to coordinate on mutual cooperation.

As in treatment ZeroT, the twenty runs comprising treatment LowT, sampled at generation 12, can be clustered into two attractor states together with a collection of transition states. The first attractor state comprises six runs characterized by perfect latching and a high percentage of AllC agent types in M-AllC relationships. The second attractor state comprises eight runs characterized by almost perfect latching and a high percentage of IntD agent types in M-IntD relationships. The six transition-state runs each comprise a mix of latched and recurrent relationships and have a high percentage of IntD agent types in M-IntD relationships.

In contrast to treatment ZeroT, however, the number of transition-state runs is larger (six runs instead of two) for treatment LowT sampled at generation 12. This is consistent with the network distribution data reported in Figure 1. The latter data reveal that, for each sampled generation, the peak at network distance 12 (latching) for treatment LowT is less pronounced than the peak at distance 12 for treatment zeroT. This indicates that the workers and employers in treatment LowT take longer on average to coordinate into perfect latched networks than the workers and employers in treatment ZeroT.

Also in contrast to treatment ZeroT, the average mean market power levels attained by workers and employers in treatment LowT, sampled at generation 12, are not balanced in the second attractor. The employers attain a level of -0.08, whereas the workers attain a markedly lower level of -0.16. The second attractor is dominated by latched relationships, indicating that each worker is persistently incurring only one offer cost per trade cycle. Since each offer cost is small relative to trade payoffs, only 1.0, it follows that accumulation of offer costs does not explain this large discrepancy in market power. Rather, since the second attractor state is dominated by M-IntD relationships, this discrepancy indicates that the employers are managing to shirk at a substantially higher rate than the workers in these M-IntD relationships.

The outcomes for treatment LowT sampled at generation 1000 closely resemble the outcomes reported in Table 5 and Table 6 for treatment ZeroT sampled at generation 12. The first attractor state comprises nine runs strongly dominated by M-AllC relationships, and the second attractor state comprises seven runs strongly dominated by M-IntD relationships. (Hence, an increase in the size of the first attractor state is observed for treatment LowT in moving from generation 12 to generation 1000.) Mixed types of relationships are almost entirely absent in the two attractor states. In the first attractor state the workers and employers attain average mean market power levels of -0.04 and -0.03, respectively. In the second attractor state the workers and employers attain uniformly lower but balanced average mean market power levels of -0.15. As for treatment ZeroT, this balance hides an underlying volatility in shirking rates across runs.

Table 7 reports market non-participation rates, work-site behaviors, utility levels, and market power outcomes for the twenty runs constituting treatment HighT, sampled at generation 12. Table 8 reports persistent relationship type counts for these same runs, again sampled at generation 12. As for the previous two treatments, the twenty runs can be clustered into two attractor states together with a scattering of transition states. Moreover, once again the runs in the first attractor state exhibit perfectly (or almost perfectly) latched persistent networks with a high percentage of AllC agent types. Nevertheless, the nature of the second attractor state is dramatically different. Whereas in the previous two treatments the second attractor state was dominated by M-IntD relationships, now the second attractor state corresponds to complete or almost complete coordination failure. More precisely, the network distance for the runs in the second attractor state varies from 22 (only two persistent relationships) to 24 (no persistent relationships). With a high non-employment payment, agents are opting for non-employment rather than choosing to remain in M-IntD relationships.

Table 7: Non-Participation Rates, Work-Site Behaviors, and Welfare Outcomes---HighT Treatment, Generation 12

NetD	Run	NON-PARTICIPATION RATES AND WORK-SITE BEHAVIORS										WELFARE OUTCOMES						NETWORK
		UnE-w	Vac-e	NPD-w	NPD-e	IntD-w	IntD-e	AllD-w	AllD-e	AllC-w	AllC-e	Util-w	Util-w SD	Util-e	Util-e SD	MPov-w	MPov-e	PATTERNS
0	45	0	0	0	1	1	1	0	0	11	11	38.6	0.6	40.7	1.0	-0.04	0.02	Mostly recurrent
1	0	0	1	0	1	0	0	0	0	12	11	35.4	0.4	40.5	1.7	-0.12	0.01	relations. High
1	65	0	1	0	1	0	0	0	0	12	11	35.4	0.4	40.5	1.5	-0.12	0.01	percentage of
2	35	0	2	0	2	0	0	0	0	12	10	33.2	0.7	39.9	2.5	-0.17	0.00	AllC Cooperators
5	75	0	3	0	5	1	2	0	0	11	7	32.6	0.7	40.5	1.7	-0.19	0.01	
6	40	4	2	2	12	8	10	0	0	0	0	34.0	1.8	37.2	1.9	-0.15	-0.07	
Average		**0.67**	**1.50**	**0.33**	**3.67**	**1.67**	**2.17**	**0.00**	**0.00**	**9.67**	**8.33**	**34.90**	**0.80**	**39.90**	**1.70**	**-0.13**	**0.00**	
%		**6%**	**13%**	**3%**	**31%**	**14%**	**18%**	**0%**	**0%**	**81%**	**69%**							
12	5	0	0	0	0	0	0	0	0	12	12	39.8	0.0	41.0	0.0	-0.01	0.03	Mostly latched
13	10	1	1	1	0	0	0	0	0	11	11	39.1	2.3	40.2	1.6	-0.02	0.01	relations. High
13	50	1	1	1	0	0	0	0	0	11	11	39.0	2.7	40.2	1.6	-0.03	0.01	percentage of
13	80	1	1	1	0	0	0	0	0	11	11	39.0	2.7	40.2	2.1	-0.03	0.01	AllC Cooperators
14	85	3	4	5	4	3	5	0	0	6	3	33.3	2.5	39.6	2.7	-0.17	-0.01	
Average		**1.20**	**1.40**	**1.60**	**0.80**	**0.60**	**1.00**	**0.00**	**0.00**	**10.20**	**9.60**	**38.10**	**2.00**	**40.20**	**1.60**	**-0.04**	**0.01**	
%		**10%**	**12%**	**13%**	**7%**	**5%**	**8%**	**0%**	**0%**	**85%**	**80%**							
22	20	10	10	12	10	2	2	0	0	0	0	30.9	1.9	31.3	0.2	-0.23	-0.22	Almost complete
23	15	11	11	12	11	1	1	0	0	0	0	30.5	1.6	30.8	0.1	-0.24	-0.23	coordination
24	25	12	12	12	12	0	0	0	0	0	0	30.0	0.0	30.1	0.0	-0.25	-0.25	failure
24	30	12	12	12	12	0	0	0	0	0	0	30.0	0.0	30.1	0.0	-0.25	-0.25	
24	55	12	12	12	12	0	0	0	0	0	0	30.0	0.0	30.1	0.0	-0.25	-0.25	
24	60	12	12	12	12	0	0	0	0	0	0	30.0	0.0	30.1	0.0	-0.25	-0.25	
24	70	12	12	12	12	0	0	0	0	0	0	30.0	0.0	30.1	0.0	-0.25	-0.25	
24	90	12	12	12	12	0	0	0	0	0	0	30.0	0.0	30.1	0.0	-0.25	-0.25	
24	95	12	12	12	12	0	0	0	0	0	0	30.0	0.0	30.1	0.0	-0.25	-0.25	
Average		**11.67**	**11.67**	**12.00**	**11.67**	**0.33**	**0.33**	**0.00**	**0.00**	**0.00**	**0.00**	**30.20**	**0.40**	**30.30**	**0.00**	**-0.25**	**-0.24**	
%		**97%**	**97%**	**100%**	**97%**	**3%**	**3%**	**0%**	**0%**	**0%**	**0%**							
Total Average		**5.75**	**6.05**	**5.90**	**6.55**	**0.80**	**1.05**	**0.00**	**0.00**	**5.45**	**4.90**	**33.50**	**0.90**	**35.70**	**0.90**	**-0.16**	**-0.11**	
Total %		**48%**	**50%**	**49%**	**55%**	**7%**	**9%**	**0%**	**0%**	**45%**	**41%**							

Table 8: Persistent Relationship Type Counts---HighT Treatment, Generation 12

NetID	Run	MUTUALITY			MIXED CASES (w-e)						MARKET POWER		PATTERNS
		M-IntD	M-AllD	M-AllC	IntD-AllD	IntD-AllC	AllD-IntD	AllD-AllC	AllC-IntD	AllC-AllD	MPow-w	MPow-e	
0	45	1	0	37	0	0	0	0	0	0	-0.04	0.02	Mostly recurrent relations. High percentage of AllC cooperators
1	0	0	0	79	0	0	0	0	0	0	-0.12	0.01	
1	65	0	0	80	0	0	0	0	0	0	-0.12	0.01	
2	35	0	0	99	0	0	0	0	0	0	-0.17	0.00	
5	75	1	0	60	0	0	0	0	1	0	-0.19	0.01	
6	40	21	0	0	0	0	0	0	0	0	-0.15	-0.07	
Average		3.83	0.00	59.17	0.00	0.00	0.00	0.00	0.17	0.00	-0.13	0.00	
12	5	0	0	12	0	0	0	0	0	0	-0.01	0.03	Mostly latched relations. High percentage of AllC cooperators
13	10	0	0	11	0	0	0	0	0	0	-0.02	0.01	
13	50	0	0	11	0	0	0	0	0	0	-0.03	0.01	
13	80	0	0	11	0	0	0	0	0	0	-0.03	0.01	
14	85	3	0	4	0	0	0	0	2	0	-0.17	-0.01	
Average		0.60	0.00	9.80	0.00	0.00	0.00	0.00	0.40	0.00	-0.04	0.01	
22	20	2	0	0	0	0	0	0	0	0	-0.23	-0.22	Almost complete coordination failure
23	15	1	0	0	0	0	0	0	0	0	-0.24	-0.23	
24	25	0	0	0	0	0	0	0	0	0	-0.25	-0.25	
24	30	0	0	0	0	0	0	0	0	0	-0.25	-0.25	
24	55	0	0	0	0	0	0	0	0	0	-0.25	-0.25	
24	60	0	0	0	0	0	0	0	0	0	-0.25	-0.25	
24	70	0	0	0	0	0	0	0	0	0	-0.25	-0.25	
24	90	0	0	0	0	0	0	0	0	0	-0.25	-0.25	
24	95	0	0	0	0	0	0	0	0	0	-0.25	-0.25	
Average		0.33	0.00	0.00	0.00	0.00	0.00	0.00	0.00	0.00	-0.25	-0.24	
Total Average		1.45	0.00	20.20	0.00	0.00	0.00	0.00	0.15	0.00	-0.16	-0.11	

As also seen for treatments ZeroT and LowT, increased coordination on the first attractor state occurs over time for treatment HighT. In generation 12, the first attractor state comprises five runs, the second attractor state comprises 9 runs, and the six remaining runs are scattered across transition states. Also, in the first attractor state, an average of 9.8 out of the 12 persistent relationships in each run are M-AllC. By generation 1000, however, the first attractor state comprises 11 runs, the second attractor state comprises seven runs, and only two runs are in a transition state. Moreover, in the first attractor state, an average of 10.73 out of the 12 persistent relationships in each run are M-AllC.

Summarizing the relative market power outcomes of workers and employers in each treatment, the following regularities are observed. For every treatment, in each sampled generation, the employers consistently attain a higher average market power level than workers in the cooperative first attractor state. This difference is attributable to the relatively higher (although small) incidence of NPD, IntD, and AllD behaviors among employers and to the fact that offer costs are borne solely by the worker. Also, for treatments ZeroT and HighT, the workers and employers attain essentially the same average market power levels in the second attractor state in each sampled generation; and the same is true for treatment LowT when sampled in generation 1000. A balanced market power level in the second attractor state indicates either that workers and employers have essentially the same shirking rates on average (treatments ZeroT and LowT) or that all agents are persistently non-employed (treatment HighT).

With regard to market power in the cooperative first attractor state compared across treatments, the workers attain a modestly negative average market power level in each treatment in each sampled generation; the levels range from -0.12 to -0.02. Interestingly, treatments LowT and HighT have a lower average incidence of NPD behavior and a higher average percentage of M-AllC relationships per run than treatment ZeroT in this first attractor state. Nevertheless, these advantages are offset (in market power terms) by the higher average offer costs incurred by workers due to the longer time taken within each generation to establish a persistent network. (For example, as seen in Table 7 for treatment HighT sampled at generation 12, only one run in the first attractor state attains a network distance of 12, i.e., a perfectly latched persistent network.) In contrast to the workers, employers do not incur offer costs, hence they attain close to a zero average market power level in each treatment at each sampled generation in the cooperative first attractor state; the levels range from -0.02 to +0.03.

With regard to market power in the second attractor state compared across treatments, in each sampled generation both the workers and the employers attain their lowest average levels in treatment HighT. The second attractor state in treatment HighT is characterized by complete or nearly complete coordination failure.

4.5. *Never-Provoked Defection*

The importance of stance toward strangers and first impressions for determining subsequent outcomes in sequential interactions has been stressed by Orbell and Dawes [11] and by Rabin and Schrag [15]. In the present computational experiment, two sharply differentiated attractor states exist for each treatment, the first dominated by persistent mutual cooperation and the second dominated either by persistent intermittent defection or by persistent non-employment. Thus, outcomes are strongly path dependent, and stance towards strangers and first impressions could play a critical role in determining these outcomes. These aspects of agent behavior are captured by counts of never-provoked defection (NPD).

In treatments ZeroT and LowT, NPD is commonly observed in all sampled generations, particularly in the second attractor state dominated by persistent intermittent defection (IntD). For example, as seen in Table 5, for treatment ZeroT sampled at generation 12, 33% of workers and 38% of employers engage in NPD in the first attractor state, and these percentages rise to 52% and 83%, respectively, for the second attractor state. It would appear that these high percentages for NPD in the second attractor state might actually be inducing the resulting predominance of IntD as agents engage in retaliatory defections. Because the non-employment payment is lower than the mutual defection payoff in these two treatments, agents tend to defect back against defecting partners rather than simply refusing to interact with them.

Another interesting observation regarding treatments ZeroT and LowT is that the incidence of NPD for each agent type in each attractor state tends to be higher in treatment ZeroT than in treatment LowT. In treatment ZeroT, the non-employment payment 0 lies below all work-site payoffs, including the sucker payoff L=10 earned by an agent who cooperates against a defecting partner. Consequently, there is no risk of refusal on the basis of bad behavior alone, but only from unfavorable comparisons with other agents. In contrast, in treatment LowT the non-employment payment 15 lies between the sucker payoff and the mutual defection payoff D=20. In this case, then, an opportunistic agent faces a higher risk of refusal since non-employment is preferred to a sucker payoff.

In treatment HighT the non-employment payment 30 lies above the mutual defection payoff for the first time, and the impact of this change in payoff configuration is substantial. For example, as reported in Table 5, only 13% of workers and 7% of employers in generation 12 engage in NPD in the first attractor state characterized by mutual cooperation. In contrast, 100% of workers and 97% of employers engage in NPD in the second attractor state characterized by complete or almost complete coordination failure. The same pattern holds at generation 50 and generation 1000. Agents are now much pickier with regard to their partners; an early defection from a partner drops that partner's expected utility assessment below the non-employment payoff and hence below minimum tolerability.

5. Concluding Remarks

As detailed by Roth [17], recent advances in experimental methods and game theory using both human subjects and computational agents are now permitting economists to study a wide variety of complex phenomena associated with decentralized market economies. Examples include inductive price discovery, imperfect competition, buyer-seller matching, and the open-ended co-evolution of individual behaviors and economic institutions.

One interesting branch of this literature is the attempt to exploit synergies between experiments with human subjects and experiments with computational agents by means of parallel experimental designs. The few parallel experimental studies to date have largely focused on financial market issues.[9] However, we conjecture that parallel experiments will ultimately prove to be even more valuable when applied to economic processes such as labor markets in which face-to-face personal relationships play a potentially strong role in determining market outcomes.

The preliminary ACE labor market study at hand highlights the need to carefully align parallel experimental designs to ensure valid comparability. For example, transaction costs must be properly scaled across experiments to ensure comparable agent incentives, and horizons need to be aligned to ensure that short-run and long-run effects are properly distinguished.

In future ACE labor market studies, we intend to calibrate our parallel experimental designs to empirical data. Salient aspects of actual unemployment benefit programs will be incorporated, and findings from previous empirical studies of unemployment benefit programs will be used wherever possible. In addition, the recent construction of linked employer-employee (LEE) data sets is an exciting development facilitating the empirical study of outcomes generated by worker-employer interactions; see Hammermesh [5]. LEE data sets complement beautifully the focus of ACE labor market studies on worker-employer interaction patterns. Consequently, LEE data should permit careful

---

[9] See http://www.econ.iastate.edu/tesfatsi/aexper.htm for pointers to research using parallel experiments.

empirical testing of computational findings related specifically to interaction effects, such as strong path dependence and the existence of multiple attractors.

Acknowledgments

The authors are grateful for helpful comments received from an anonymous referee, from Peter Orazem, from Marshall Van Alstyne and other participants in the UCLA Computational Social Sciences Conference held in May 2002 at Lake Arrowhead, California, and from Richard Freeman and other participants in the Harvard University Colloquium on Complexity and Social Networks held on April 7, 2003.

References

1. D. Acemoglu and R. Shimer, Productivity Gains from Unemployment Insurance, *European Economic Review* **44,** 1195 (2000).
2. F. D. Blau and L. M. Kahn, Institutional Differences in Male Wage Inequality: Institutions versus Market Forces, O. Ashenfelter and D. Card, editors, Handbook of Labor Economics **3A**, Elsevier Science B.V., 1399 (1999).
3. R. Freeman, War of the Models: Which Labour Market Institutions for the 21st Century?, *Labour Economics* **5,** 1 (1998).
4. D. Gale and L. Lloyd Shapley, College Admissions and the Stability of Marriage, *American Mathematical Monthly* **69**, 9 (1962).
5. D. Hammermesh, LEEping into the Future of Labor Economics: The Research Potential of Linking Employer and Employee Data, *Labour Economics* **6**, 25 (1999).
6. L. Ljungqvist and T. J. Sargent, The Unemployment Dilemma, *Journal of Political Economy* **106**, 514 (1998).
7. W. B. MacLeod and J. Malcomson, Motivation and Markets, *American Economic Review* **88**, 388 (1998).
8. D. McFadzean, D. Stewart, and L. Tesfatsion, A Computational Laboratory for Evolutionary Trade Networks, *IEEE Transactions on Evolutionary Computation* **5**, 546 (2001).
9. D. McFadzean and L. Tesfatsion, A C++ Platform for Evolutionary Trade Networks, *Computational Economics* **14**, 108 (1999).
10. S. Nickell and R. Layard, Labor Market Institutions and Economic Performance, O. C. Ashenfelter and D. Card, editors, Handbook of Labor Economics **3C**, Elsevier Science B.V., 3029, (1999).

11. J. Orbell and R. M. Dawes, Social Welfare, Cooperator's Advantage, and the Option of Not Playing the Game, *American Sociological Review* **58,** 787 (1993).
12. M. Pingle and L. Tesfatsion, Non-Employment Benefits and the Evolution of Worker-Employer Cooperation: Experiments with Real and Computational Agents, Iowa State University Economic Report No. 55, (2001).
13. M. Pingle and L. Tesfatsion, Non-Employment Benefits and the Evolution of Worker-Employer Cooperation: A Human-Subject Experiment, Working Paper, (2002).
14. M. Pingle and L. Tesfatsion, Evolution of Worker-Employer Networks and Behaviors under Alternative Non-Employment Benefits: An Agent-Based Computational Study, Anna Nagurney, editor, *Innovations in Financial and Economic Networks,* Edward Elgar, Cheltenham, U.K., 256 (2003).
15. M. Rabin and J. Shrag, First Impressions Matter: A Model of Confirmatory Bias, *Quarterly Journal of Economics* **114**, 37 (1999).
16. A. Roth and M. A. Sotomayor, Two-Sided Matching: A Study in Game-Theoretic Modeling and Analysis, Cambridge University Press, Cambridge, UK, (1992).
17. A. Roth, The Economist as Engineer: Game Theory, Experimentation, and Computation as Tools for Design Economics, *Econometrica* **70**, 1341 (2002).
18. L. Tesfatsion, A Trade Network Game with Endogenous Partner Selection. H. Amman, B. Rustem, and A. B. Whinston, editors, Computational Approaches to Economic Problems, Kluwer Academic Publishers, Dordrecht, The Netherlands, 249 (1997).
19. L. Tesfatsion, Preferential Partner Selection in Evolutionary Labor Markets: A Study in Agent-Based Computational Economics, V. Porto, N. Saravanan, D. Waagan, and A. E. Eiben, editors, Evolutionary Programming VII, Springer-Verlag, Berlin, 15 (1998).
20. L. Tesfatsion, Structure, Behavior and Market Power in an Evolutionary Labor Market with Adaptive Search, *Journal of Economic Dynamics and Control* **25**, 419 (2001).
21. L. Tesfatsion, Hysteresis in an Evolutionary Labor Market with Adaptive Search, S.H. Chen, editor, Evolutionary Computation in Economics and Finance, Physica-Verlag Heidelberg, 189 (2002).
22. L. Tesfatsion, Economic Agents and Markets as Emergent Phenomena, *Proceedings of the National Academy of Sciences U.S.A.* **99**, Supplement 3, 7191 (2002).
23. L. Tesfatsion, Agent-Based Computational Economics, Francesco Luna, Alessandro Perrone, and Pietro Terna, editors, Agent-Based Theories, Languages, and Practices, Routledge Publishers, to appear, (2004).

EARLY RETIREMENT FROM THE LABOUR MARKET: POLICY EXPERIMENTS IN THE ITALIAN CASE

PIETRO A. VAGLIASINDI

Department of International Economics, Finance and Law, University of Parma
e-mail: pvagli@unipr.it

MARZIA ROMANELLI

Sant'Anna School of Advanced Studies - LEM
Pisa, e-mail: romanelli@sssup.it

CARLO BIANCHI

Department of Economics, University of Pisa,
e-mail: cbianchi@ec.unipi.it

The substantial changes in the Italian pension system over the last decade subsequent to the Amato, Dini, Prodi and Berlusconi reforms have given raise to a renewed debate on re-designing pension system and in particular seniority pensions. Workers respond quickly to different incentives present in the pension systems and to expected government policies, especially through their retirement choices. These reactions, in turn, can or should inform government policy design to contrast the consequences of the ageing process. Based on the not fully satisfactory way of addressing such issues, this paper aims to shed some new light on the transition from one pension regime to another. After a brief review of the economic literature, this paper presents a bit more evidence on early retirement and its future evolution using dynamic ageing methodology, considering an economy, with heterogeneous workers, whose retirement age depends on expected utility. We examine behavioural changes estimating the age of retirement along the current pension reform path, assuming different behavioural regimes and policies, using a model calibrated to reproduce the main Italian demographic and economic features and retirement dynamics. We find a tendency to postpone the exit from labour market, especially when workers maximise their benefits flow coming from all incomes, instead of sole pension benefits. In this case, pension expenditures grow faster, because savings, due to retirement postponement, are compensated by higher benefits. Finally, we consider how future trends of inequality and poverty among pensioners can be negatively affected by the government seniority pension reform and propose possible remedies.

1. Introductory remarks on the Italian case

It is well known that before the '90^{ies} the Italian pension system experienced changes that extended eligibility rules (even for seniority pensions), increased the generosity of pension benefits and proposed the use of pre-pensioning scheme (e.g. temporary lay-off, like the "cassa integrazione guadagni") as a safety net.[a] The generosity of benefits and early retirement options often had perverse intra and intergenerational redistributive features and moved the pension system towards persistent structural deficits (also due to population ageing and increasing dependency ratio).[b]

The legislative innovations of the '90[ies] — the Amato (L.503/92), Dini (L.335/95) and Prodi (L.449/97) reforms — responded to these difficulties with gradual cuts, and a long term transition towards a new sustainable regime, cf. Brugiavini and Fornero [14]. Pensions are now indexed to inflation (rather than to wages), the most generous pensions' eligibility and computation rules are going to be slowly but steadily abolished during a long transition phase (the so called "mixed regime") towards a new contribution based regime ("contributivo").[c] In this way a great part of the burden has been placed on the shoulders of younger and future generations. Moreover, the elimination of minimum pensions and wage indexation for social pensions opened larger role for welfare benefits. In this context, the present government (L.448/01) has recently raised social allowances for disadvantaged elders.

In this work we are mainly interested in assessing the consequences of the transition path on workers' retirement choices and incomes. As the Italian experience showed, workers' retirement choices respond quickly to pension systems reforms and to expected government policies.[d] These reactions, in turn, can or should inform government policy designed to reduce the burdens and distortions imposed on labour market. A rigorous assessment of the consequences of the policy shift towards the contribution based formula on retirements requires a careful consideration of the transition path and a realistic evaluation of the three main different schemes that compose the Italian pension

---

[a] They may have been also a political response to labour market shocks, affecting several elderly workers, not yet eligible for an old-age pension.

[b] Italy is the European country where the dependency ratio is expected to grow the most. Moreover, due to the generosity of existing public pension the old age dependency ratio may be greater than the retirees/workers ratio.

[c] The reforms safeguarded the rights already acquired not only by pensioners but also by mature workers. Currently, seniority pensions requirements are 57 years old and 35 years of contributions or 37 years of contributions (40 by 2008), regardless of the age.

[d] Retirement patterns are different if we consider the period before the reforms of the '90[ies], the period during the initial implementation of the reforms or the following years. Contini and Fornero [22] analysis highlights that mass exits at relatively young ages (up to 54) from the labour market are typical of the initial reform period, also characterised by highly variable exit rates and by mass withdrawals induced by the fear of new pension cuts. In fact, the 35-year contribution requirement, imposed for seniority pensions, has *de facto* recognised a retirement legal age of 55 as a sort of social "norm".

system.[e] It also requires looking at the evolution of three geographical areas (North, Centre and South).[f] In fact, another relevant feature of our country is the existence of strong socio-economic differences in the labour market and in the distribution of resources between the rich northern geographical area and the poor southern one.

Economists argued about the need to postpone retirement choices by increasing age requirements or reducing benefits for early retirements. The economic incentives of such schemes have been one the most studied aspect of the retirement behaviour. As a consequence, if pension rules are well defined in law, modelling workers' retirement should be easy. However, a number of different economic incentives must be considered and it is unclear whether labour market decisions are based on long-term considerations, or merely by short-term replacement rates.[g] Moreover, due to its peculiarities, the Italian case appears quite complex.

Also according to the detailed report by Contini and Fornero [22][h] the subject deserves a deeper analysis. Hence we aim to shed some light using a quantitative analysis that combines econometric and simulation methods, trying to reach the highest explanatory power.[i] Once validated and calibrated, the MIND (Micro Italy National Dynamics) dynamic microsimulation model, which has already allowed us to asses the implications of Italian demography and the redistributive consequences of fiscal reforms, is an ideal instrument to evaluate individual responses to systemic changes in the pension system.

The main aim of this paper is to discuss how the old age labour market transitions could be better modelled in Italy in a dynamic micro simulation model. This work can be conceived as a methodological companion for Vagliasindi, Romanelli, Bianchi [59] where we consider the effect of different

---

[e] We distinguish between the rules applied to public and private employees (FPLD) and to self-employed ones.

[f] Our recent research work already focused on topics related to agents' responses to pension reforms, evaluating alternative indexation systems (Bianchi, Romanelli, Vagliasindi, [7]), demographic changes and the ageing process (Vagliasindi, Romanelli, Bianchi, [58]), and considering how governments respond to pensioners' behaviour, cf. Vagliasindi [60].

[g] A simple explanation may consider a one period comparison between work-related or retirement related financial compensations. More complex ones take into account the whole individual life cycle. Previous researches highlighted also spouse's effects on the timing of retirement.

[h] They estimated a reduced form model using explanatory variables such as pension wealth and its marginal variations, concluding with non univocal results: significant effects of pension wealth (presenting the expected signs), but disappointing outcomes for marginal variation in wealth.

[i] Structural and reduced-form retirement models have been successfully used in the literature. Structural models tend to perform better in terms of predictive ability, inferring future behavioural changes after comprehensive pension reforms, as in the Italian case. But, they are not easy to manage, due to the complex estimations and the difficulties to incorporate explanatory variables.

seniority pension reforms under two limiting "retirement behavioural rules". In the first case, under *individual rationality (1)*, the choice to retire depends only on the comparison between (i) the present value of the expected utility of the flow of the pension benefits obtained with an immediate retirement and (ii) the one obtained postponing retirement to the next period. Under *family bounded rationality (2)*, workers are eager to retire (valuing less the benefit from labour income), more myopic (using a higher discount rate for actualising future benefits streams) and influenced by the partner retirement decision.[j]

Hence, we start in section 2 with a brief review of the large literature on retirement,[k] keeping in mind the goal of modelling labour market for older workers in Italy, choosing among possible options to estimate retirement in a simple way. The rest of the paper is organised as follows. Section 3 discusses validation experiments on the behavioural reaction function for retirement choice. In section 4, we estimate, under alternative behaviours, retirement ages per area, employment and sex, "pensioners/workers' ratio" and the replacement rate, validating indirectly our model. Section 5, considers possible consequences on retirement ages, replacement rate and "pensioners/workers' ratio" of alternative seniority pension reforms as well as the impact, on inequality and poverty, of indexing income support allowances to prices. Section 6 summarizes the results and concludes with some final remarks.

2. Defining retirement and pensioners: motivations and modelling

In what follows we consider modelling issues relative to retirement choice in the Italian case. We start from the definition of retirement, its economic incentives and the modelling of dependence between spouses, also referring to the MIND microsimulation model.[l] Finally the strengths and weaknesses of structural and reduced-form models for retirement are considered. The choices we review are connected to: (***a***) the "work and incomes" module that estimates workers' incomes, and (***b***) the "social security" module that determines the retirement age and pension incomes using a reaction function.

Unfortunately, the definitions of pensioner and retirement are not clear-cut

[j] Precisely, we compared the current state of affairs with the reform proposed by the Italian Welfare Minister and with an anticipated start of the mixed regime, limited to seniority pensions. We do not describe these issues that has been instead included in the accompanying paper [59].

[k] For a longer reviews see Hakola [35] as well as Contini and Fornero [22].

[l] The MIND model allows considering the socio-demographic dynamics of the different Italian geographical areas, simulating the evolution of: (***a***) demographic and family structures, (***b***) phenomena related to work incomes and (***c***) retirement choice and pension incomes. See Vagliasindi [60].

and problem free. Decisions on working hours and benefits claims are separate, even if related. Referring to inactive individuals more than 60 years old would exclude workers taking advantage of early retirement options, i.e. the issue we intend to investigate. Since current pension regulations do not require full withdrawal from the labour force for claiming benefits, one cannot limit the working hours to zero. It might be more appropriate to define retirement as no longer working on a full-time basis.

On the other hand, the decision to stop working does not necessarily imply claiming retirement benefits. It can precede a benefit application.[m] People may withdraw from the labour market before being eligible for pension scheme or may use pre-pensioning scheme. Some income support activities have turned into such pre-pensioning schemes even without an explicit intention (e.g. extended unemployment benefits).[n] This would imply the modelling of the labour force withdrawal also through these channels.

According to Lazear ([41] and [42]) employment relationships are based on long-term, implicit contracts, where the value of compensation equals the marginal product over the work life, in terms of expected values. Since wage profiles are steeper than productivity profiles, at the end of the career wages are higher than productivity. Hence, there are opposite incentives: firms have an interest to terminate employment contracts and workers to stay. Mandatory retirement, non-actuarial pensions and others arrangements help to face this issue. Besides, retirement may be determined by a company crisis or restructuring strategies.[o] There are a number of firm specific variables that can affect retirement (e.g. changes in sales, experience-rating, cost of a specific type of labour).[p] Skill biased technological changes may differently affect the demand for various skill groups. Some of the skills can be age specific. Stories explaining the change in the demand structure of labour rely on technical progress (e.g. R&D intensity) and internationalisation (e.g. share of exports). In case of employers' lay-off, when individuals would not stop working, the traditional supply side model is wrong. Yet, in Italy there are fairly rigid

---

[m] Coile et al. [19] investigate delays in claiming social security benefits in the US, showing that they can be at times even optimal.

[n] Individuals that have derived income through an alternative source (e.g. health benefits) prior to qualifying for pensions are automatically transferred to the pension scheme when they reach the needed requirements.

[o] In fact, instruments such as early retirements or layoffs, markedly affect older workers. Often, final working years are marked by an irregular pattern of labour market activity, alternating several employment periods, or periods spent as employee and self-employee as well as on layoff lists, temporary lay-off or non-voluntary withdrawal from the labour market.

[p] Existing productivity controls tend to be occupation or task specific. Employer-employee data allow formation of firm specific controls. See Huttunen [40] and Hakola [34].

employment protection laws. Moreover, it is difficult to incorporate the demand side effects when modelling retirement on the basis of the utility maximisation; firm level data and information on the work conditions are rare or unavailable in the data sets. Hence, retirement models usually leave out the demand side, or just control for local unemployment.[q] These cases may count, but are difficult to tackle, if one is mainly interested in deriving behavioural parameters. Hence, the focus is on who takes up the pension directly from work.[r]

Let us now consider economic incentives; i.e. the most important explanatory variables in retirement models.[s] While higher wages encourage work, higher pension benefits encourage retirement. The most straightforward control for the economic incentives would then be the wage rate and/or the pension benefit (net of taxes).[t] Workers' pension benefits can be easily computed, differently from TFR benefits (to predict them, assumptions are needed on how long people stay with the same employer). But if these benefits are not taken into account, the incentive could be undervalued and we can overestimate the effect of the incentive variable on the probability of retirement. Also tax incentives should be considered. Pensioners (especially low-income ones) may be entitled to different tax allowances and benefits.[u]

There are alternative ways to model the economic incentives that can be considered. A first useful indicator may be the replacement rate — the ratio of the expected pension benefits and expected wages — if we believe that the ratio

---

[q] Since the demand side may have a direct effect on retirement, it is not enough to control for labour demand. Often, flexible work arrangements are more important for older workers. It is therefore critical to know employers' willingness to provide these opportunities. Flexibility may also be more common in specific industries and in small firms. Therefore controls for occupation, industry, and firm size can capture some demand side effects.

[r] Moreover, our analysis does not distinguish between full-retirement and partial retirement, counting both in the first category. Currently pensioners are encouraged to work. Nevertheless, most retirements still imply a final withdrawal from the labour market. Hence, this is our general assumption.

[s] Other variables, such as education, gender or industry, may be important, but their inclusion into the models is to a large extent straightforward.

[t] Accordingly, it is important to incorporate the demand side effects on relative wages especially considering a specific cohort. As a baby boom generation approaches retirement in most industrialized countries, the size of different cohorts and their substitutability (between each other and with capital) can affect the demand for old workers. A number of papers tried to estimate the effect of the cohort size on relative wages. Large cohorts can depress wages within the same skill cluster and increase demand and market opportunities. If a skill-age cohort is substitutable with others, the effect is dissolved across several cohorts. Hence, expected effects on wages are not easy to determine and the results differ greatly between different studies.

[u] In Italy we have national, regional and local taxes and we experienced year-to-year changes as well as major reforms. Tax calculations from income data are extremely difficult and future trends hard to predict, since allowances depends on costs and hence choices. Therefore, many chose not to consider the issue. Others (e.g. Palme and Svensson [48]) try to approximate taxes.

of the two income sources matters rather than their absolute levels. Replacement rates may suffer from the problem of the short time horizon that can be overcome simply stretching the horizon over which they are defined.

Social security wealth (*SSW*) considers the whole time path until the end of the life expectancy, summing up expected pension benefits and social security contributions (see Gruber and Wise, [26]). It may be represented as the difference between all discounted benefits (*SSB*) one expects to get from the pension system, and contributions (*SSC*) expected to be paid to it.[v] These are measures of public sector wealth accumulated by individuals and they control for wealth effect.[w] Predicted lifetime earnings can be an additional control for wealth effect in retirement models, while social security wealth controls for the public wealth. Presumably, higher lifetime earnings may imply higher private wealth, producing in general positive effects on retirement.

Hence we need incentive measures (that control for the substitution effect) such as *accrual rate*, *peak value* or the *option value*. The *accrual rate*, the change in the social security wealth (*SSW*) from one year to the next, measures the gains from working an additional year.[x] Instead, the *peak value* compares the present year's social security wealth with the maximum one.[y] In any case, previous measures consider expected returns not expected utilities.

The option value *OV* is similar to the peak value, but is defined by a difference between the utility values of the earnings streams (wages and benefits).[z] As shown in formulae (1) and (2), results depend on: (*i*) the functional form for the period specific utility function *U*, often with constant

---

[v] Survival probabilities, constructed from gender and age specific data are usually considered, as well as spousal benefits, i.e. spouse's survival probability, and the widow's benefits in the case the spouse is deceased.

[w] Wealth effect tends to increase the demand for leisure, while the substitution effect considers it's the relative price, comparing the possibility to retire now, with the opportunity to retire later with a higher pension benefit.

[x] It could be myopic and biased if there are discontinuities in *SSW* in the future. To capture these discontinuities we should consider larger time horizon to allow individual to wait for the highest benefits available in the future.

[y] Coile and Gruber [21] normalize the peak value by the expected stream of wages over the period between the maximal year and the current year. Hence, they measure the benefits of continuing work relative to the earnings in the same period. Consistent with earlier papers, they call this relative measure the tax/subsidy rate, cf. Diamond and Gruber [23]. The same normalization can be done as well for the accrual rate and the option value.

[z] Hence, changes in *OV* may depend upon the variation in wages rather than in the pension formula. Moreover, uncertainty is not incorporated in the concept. Rust and Phelan [51] allowed uncertainty with respect to mortality, health status, health expenditures, marital status, employment, and income, estimating complicated dynamic programming models. Berkovec and Stern [5] and Stock and Wise [56] do not allow for uncertainty, but capture the consumption-leisure trade-off in a lifecycle context.

relative risk aversion (given by coefficient γ), (*ii*) the difference between the utility derived from wages and from benefits (a constant k that reveals how much less individual values a euro from work income Y than a euro from pension benefits B) and (*iii*) the assumptions on the discount factor β, the maximum life length T and the conditional survival probability p. The variable k is a leisure control if the utility structure is correct.[aa]

$$OV_t(R) = E_t \sum_{s=t}^{R-1} \beta^{s-t} \left[Y_s^{\gamma} + \omega_s \right] + E_t \sum_{s=t}^{T} \beta^{s-t} \left[(kB_s(R))^{\gamma} + \xi_s \right] \tag{1}$$

The indirect utility functions for labour and pension incomes are respectively:

$$U_y(Y_s) = Y_s^{\gamma} + \omega_s \qquad\qquad U_b(B_s) = (kB_s(R))^{\gamma} + \xi_s \tag{2}$$

Lazear and Moore [43] defined the option value of retirement, but its use was widespread after Stock and Wise [56] structural model.[bb]

Retirement can be modelled using structural or reduced form models (discrete choice models or duration models),[cc] but only structural models can appropriately handle the presence of uncertainty and reforms in the pension system.

Butler et al. [16] note that duration models fit the data well initially, imposing only few assumptions, but their use is questionable in policy simulations, when rules change. Structural models are preferable if they were not complex in their application.[dd] Due to the complexity in estimation,

---

[aa] This is why Coile and Gruber [21] suggested that wages should be controlled for separately, rather than including them within the option value variable, and favoured their own measure, the peak value.

[bb] Since structural models are difficult to implement, *OV* were used in reduced form, cf. Börsch-Supan [12], [13], Samwick [52], Gruber and Wise [26].

[cc] Reduced form models (multinomial logit and competing risks duration model) effectively deal with many end states, but generally, assume independent channel choices. This independence assumption can be partially relaxed through additional explanatory variables. Hakola [34] use indicators for whether an alternative exit channel is available in order to control for the potential channel substitution.

[dd] The main purpose of the models is to predict retirement behaviour. Lumsdaine et al. [44] consider the in-sample and out-of-sample predictive power of a dynamic programming, an option value and a probit model. The predictive power of the dynamic programming and *OV* models were much better, using data on one big company. The *OV* model was more unsatisfactory, considering the whole population, see Harris [36]. But since explanatory variables were not included, it is not surprising that it worked better in a more homogeneous sample. Butler et al. [16] included a number of explanatory variables and assessed the predictive capability of similar models. The *OV* model provided best predictions both in- and out-of-sample. Spataro [55] seems to find a reduced-form duration model preferable to the structural *OV* model, considering log-likelihood values. However, as Butler et al. [16] noted there are better ways to compare non-nested hypothesis and Spataro's *OV* model had no explanatory variables.

structural models so far have limited the retirement decision to a "yes or no" option.

The MIND "social security" module determines the retirement age and pension incomes using a reaction function based on the *OV* model. [ee] Given the available information at time *t*, individuals calculate the differential benefit $OV_t(t+1)$ of postponing the retirement to the next year. If *OV* is positive the retirement will be postponed; otherwise the worker retires immediately. *OV* is estimated each year until the maximum age of retirement is reached.[ff]

In our model, in each period *t* workers calculate the differential benefit $OV_t(t+1)$ of postponing retirement to time $t+1$ and retire if $OV_t(t+1) \leq 0$. In particular, the value at time *t* to retire at time *R* depends on the actualised flows of incomes Y_s and pensions $D_s(R)$.[gg] Given our assumptions, each worker determines the age that maximises the value of retiring. In fact, the differential benefit monotonically decreases, reaching the maximum when it becomes null.[hh]

Many previous measures require predicting future wages. A simple method is to assume real earnings growth (e.g. 1% per annum, cf. Coile and Gruber, [21]), or to use the previous wage observations to impute a value, cf. Palme and Svensson [47]. These models can be too simplistic for capturing true wage dynamics of different types of people. To take this into account, we may use regression models. With cross-section data, the identifying variation would come from the differences between individuals. In panel data, time variation for the same individual can also be used.[ii] To produce a better fit for older individuals, with enough observations, one may limit the sample to aged

---

[ee] We reconstruct the history of wages and social contributions of each worker, necessary to calculate his pension, assuming the absence of individuals that temporarily suspend the payment of their contributions.

[ff] *OV* are calculated considering the different regimes (*retributivo*, *misto* for mature workers or *contributivo* for the new entrant workers) depending on individual characteristics, contributions and eligibility.

[gg] The indirect utility specification of labour and pension incomes are respectively $U_y(Y_s) = \alpha Y_s + \omega_s$ $(0 \leq \alpha \leq 1)$ and $U_b(B_s(R)) = B_s(R) + \xi_s$, with ω_s and ξ_s zero mean normal random variables whose variance can be estimated as in Stock and Wise [56]. For recent work on this topic see Gruber and Wise [26] and Peracchi [49]. See also Di Pino and Mucciardi [24] and Spataro [55].

[hh] For further details, see Vagliasindi, Romanelli, Bianchi [58].

[ii] Fixed effects panel data models insert an individual specific dummy for each individual in the sample that picks up the effect of all time-invariant explanatory variables. They are recommended in a specific sample. Random panel data effects models assume the problematic hypothesis of independence of errors from the explanatory variables, but produce results that are more easily generalized to larger samples, cf. Hsiao [37]. If we assume that there is a time-invariant error term, there is correlation between the actual error term and the lagged wage (i.e. one of the explanatory variables). Estimations bias can be removed by differencing all variables, and using lagged wages as instruments for wage differences, cf. Arellano and Bond [3]. Regression can be run on the differenced variables. A Hausman-Taylor transformation can be used to estimate coefficients on time- invariant variables, as in Hakola [33].

individuals. The aim is to predict wage expectations, however, we may assess the model comparing wage predictions to actual observations when both are available (e.g. considering their means, variances and mean squared errors).

Wages, among other things, affect retirement. However, it is very hard to find variables that affect wage expectations, but not retirement. Unfortunately, if a variable, say education, affects both at the same time, we cannot first predict wages and then estimate the effect of wages on retirement, since wage predictions using education will bring no new information.[jj] The "work and incomes" module estimates workers' incomes, based on cross sectional data, using the log-linear specification suggested by Mincer [46].[kk] It is also employed in the "social security" module to determine the reaction function based on the *OV* model.

Let us now focus on the assumptions behind the utility function and the calibration procedure used in our model to validate retirement from the labour market and to estimate the shape of the wage profiles and the parameter α, reflecting the utility of labour income (see Footnote 36).

In our simulation model we paid particular attention to the lifetime income estimation and the modelling of the retirement choice, since they are connected issues. In fact, the shape of the wage profiles, especially in the last part of the working career, is crucial to determine the incentive to retire. As discussed by the literature, the cross-section approach can hide cohorts (and also time) effects generating (upward) biases in the age polynomial estimates.[ll] Previous dynamic microsimulation models applied to Italy, such as Cannari and Nicoletti Altimari [17], have chosen a similar cross-section approach in estimating wage profiles. Since the panel has a very limited number of families with older workers to

---

[jj] In practice, even if it is difficult to find a satisfactory model, it is better to keep wage models relatively simple. Moreover, wage models that use many information may be unmanageable and unnecessarily complicated for a task that is only a small part of the retirement models.

[kk] We consider a structure diversified by *AGE*, AGE^2, *SEX*, *EDU* and *HOURS* for three occupational sectors (dependent, self-employed, public) and areas (North, Centre, South). Almost all the coefficients have the right sign and statistically significant at the 99% confidence level. For more details, see Andreassen, Fredriksen and Ljones [2] and Bianchi, Romanelli, Vagliasindi [6]. For the individual i, the forecast value ($\hat{y}_{it}$) at time t is obtained by replacing the individual characteristics ($\mathbf{x}_{it}$) in the equation $\hat{y}_{it} = e^{(xitb+\hat{u}i)}$ where, to avoid biases, the estimated residuals $\hat{u}_i$ are also included. Real income derived from: $\tilde{y}_{it} = \hat{y}_{it}\ (1+g)^{t-t_0}$, where g, the real growth rate, is 1% in the future (i.e. for $t > t_0$). The number of hours worked by entrants (*HOURS*) are estimated on the basis of the average number of hours worked (*HOURSA*) and the standard error (*Stderr*), depending on the sector and the area:

$$HOURS = HOURSA\ (AGE,\ SEX,\ AREAGEO) + (Stderr(AGE,\ SEX,\ AREAGEO) \times \mathbf{rd})$$

where $\mathbf{rd}$ is a random number with normal standard distribution which introduces a stochastic element.

[ll] Therefore a panel approach, together with the use of controls for white and blue collars is recommended to get unbiased estimates, e.g. with respect to educational variables.

produce reliable estimates (differentiated by gender, geographical area, kind of workers), we preferred to use the cross-section approach as well.

However, the utility function of labour and pension incomes and retirement choice were design in such a way that eventual biases in the shape of the wage profiles in the last part of the working career can be partially corrected in the calibration procedure. In this way the right incentives to retire may be determined. This is one of the main reasons why the fitting of the utility function to the data is performed maximising with respect to α, while the degree of risk aversion is set to one, assuming neutrality towards risk.[mm]

These choices may be questioned on several grounds, but they can also be justified. Let us start from the basic assumptions relative to the utility function of labour and pension incomes that determine retirement from the labour market. In the model, workers' expected utility functions depend only on incomes. Even if it is quite simple, this assumption is more realistic than that one adopted by a large part of the literature based on expected return. Linear utility may be an inadequate hypothesis, especially when analysing a decision, such as retirement, that crucially involves the leisure-income trade-off. However, following the option value approach (Stock and Wise, [56]) we specify two different (indirect) utilities for employment and retirement status, so that, after all, leisure is not ignored in the retirement choice. The presence of the parameter α, reflecting the disutility of labour (loss of leisure), alleviates the problem. In fact, it explicitly takes into account the average disutility of work experienced by older workers, given our linear utility specification.

Again, available estimates of the marginal utility of income in labour supply studies typically do not support a linear specification. In reality we do not presume utility to be linear but we use this device to try to estimate indirectly (through the validation and calibration procedures) the mean value of the relative benefit of income from labour, with respect to income from pension. The implied hypothesis that the average disutility of work experienced by older workers is approximately the same for everybody is indeed a strong one but can be jointly tested with the others present in the "work and incomes" module (where workers' future incomes are estimated), and the "social security" module (where on the basis of the utility function the retirement age is determined).

Retirement estimates and the effects of policy changes may be biased if the spouse effects are omitted or badly modelled.[nn] Namely, in a world where both

---

[mm] In our opinion a different choice would have required an explicit and detailed description of the risks faced by workers and pensioners that would have considerably complicated our analysis.

[nn] Since the husband is usually older than the wife, we would expect him to retire earlier. Instead there is a concentration of couples reporting the last date of full-time work in the same year. However, in the retirement literature, structural models have been estimated from individuals data,

husbands and wives are likely to work it is increasingly necessary to assess whether measures, which affect the retirement decision of one family member, can indirectly influence the retirement of the spouse.[oo]

One of the first econometric approaches, developed by Gustman and Steinmeier [30], was designed to recognize a number of interdependences in retirement decisions.[pp] They generated behaviours that bring the retirement dates of husbands and wives closer together, for about 11% of couples. Both the spouse retirement and the preference correlation explanation seemed significant.

In general, the way the influence of the spouse is taken into account through the explanatory variables may vary.[qq] Coile [20] includes all of the spouse's explanatory variables, but excludes indicators of the spouse's retirement status, arguing that, when one enjoys spending time with the spouse, this could be viewed as a control for the complementarity of leisure. The interaction of this variable with the incentive variable produces plausible results in her models.

An et al. [1] construct a bivariate proportional hazard model with three hazard functions that depend on individual characteristics. In particular, they estimate the baseline hazards for the husband and the wife, and additionally one for the incidence of joint retirement. Conditional on observables, all three hazard functions are mutually independent, an assumption not easily defendable.

Palme and Svensson [48] do not include spousal employment explicitly, but

---

ignoring the retirement decisions and status of their spouses, cf. Burtless and Moffitt [15], Fields and Mitchell [25], Gustman and Steinmeier [28] and [29], Stock and Wise [56] and [57], Berkovec and Stem [5] and Lumsdaine, Stock and Wise [44], [45]. Estimates of reduced form retirement equations, as in Clark and Johnson [18] and Hurd [39], suggested the importance of the spouse's retirement status. Pozzebon and Mitchell [50] were the first to analyse joint retirement in the context of a reduced form model.

[oo] In particular, there can be: ***i***) complementarity of leisure between spouses, ***ii***) cross-spouse effects of covariates, and covariate effects differing by the spouse's employment status (e.g. health), ***iii***) assortative mating on unobservables or correlation across spouses in unobserved tastes, and/or ***iv***) cross-spousal financial effects, cf. Hurd [38] and Blau [8]. A number of theoretical labour supply models accounts for the household labour supply decision, cf. Blundell and MaCurdy [11]. Empirical models used to estimate the spousal retirement behaviour range from simple probits or logits (e.g. Coile, [20]) to differences- in-differences estimates (Baker, [4]), or to structural models (Blau, [9], Blau and Riphahn, [10], Gustman and Steinmeier, [31] and [32]). Blau [9] and Blau and Riphahn [10] estimate dynamic multinomial probit equations, considering four discrete employment status of spouses. This model is, however, not only difficult to implement, but the results are also hard to interpret.

[pp] In the opportunity set, jobs may be selected with peaks in pension accrual profiles that encourage joint retirement. On the preference side, each spouse's utility may depend on the retirement status of the other spouse: the preferences of each spouse may be correlated. Each spouse may not decide independently, but may collude to insure jointly optimal retirement decision .

[qq] Economic incentives are often calculated separately for both spouses, in sub-samples, e.g. Blau [9], Blau and Riphahn [10]. A good predictor for spouse's retirement is the indicator of whether the spouse qualifies for early retirement and the age difference between spouses, cf. Hurd [39], An et al. [1].

account for the spouse in calculating the economic incentives.[rr] The spouse's lifetime earnings and social security wealth increase the retirement propensity of the partner. However, the complementarity of leisure, or the correlation between the unobservables are not account for.

Gustman and Steinmeier ([31], [32]) include an indicator of the spouse's labour market status explicitly and estimate a simultaneous probit model with truncated endogenous variables, focussing on a correlation in tastes for leisure and an additional value of retirement once the other spouse has also retired. Both effects were significant, but the joint value of leisure has a bigger impact.

We do not estimate a structural model of joint retirement decision, but we start considering this as a crucial issue, assuming that the wife's retirement decision takes as given the husband choice. This may be justified since benefit losses due to anticipated wives' retirement are generally minor

Moreover, retirement decisions are made in an uncertain environment. Uncertainty is also an inherent feature of the early retirement options. Finally, there is an increased chance to suffer from health shocks or loss of the spouse.

3. Validation of the retirement from the labour market

Similarly to the majority of agent-based models, the MIND model is calibrated, not estimated. The validation procedure of retirement from the labour market we adopt may also rise some doubts, e.g. due to the period (1996−1999) we consider. It can be argued that, because of distortions caused by announcements effects, "temporary stops" (imposed to seniority pensions only for temporary cash needs) and uncertainty due to the post-reform climate may have stimulated early retirement. For instance, 1996 is characterised by a big wave of exits, coming from people whose retirements were blocked by the Government in 1995, and 1997 by the Amato's reform, which again called for anticipated exits. Accordingly, statistics show cumulated hazards up to young age (before normal retirement age) in the reform period much higher than in the 80[ies]. On the other hand, focusing on the period 1996−1999 was in part a forced choice when we built the model. However, also in this respect we design our validation experiment in such a way that our calibration procedure - that leads us to an estimate for the parameter α - tries to avoid the biases brought by these relevant issues. In fact, the temporary phenomena that stimulated early retirement are relevant if considered on an annual basis, but less relevant if we

---

[rr] They account for the survival probability of both spouses and the survivor's benefits and control also for the spouse's lifetime earnings, its square and net social security wealth (all statistically significant in their models).

consider the entire period 1996–1999 of four years on the whole. In fact, the most relevant biases in this case are due to the peculiar phenomena that stimulated early retirement in 1999, which are in our opinion minors, since the situation was quite less uncertain and no announcements effects or "temporary stop" was operative. In this way, considering the evolution of pensioners by age, starting from 1995 data, more correct retirement behaviours are considered, confronting the entire population of pensioners with the one in the model. In fact, simulated retirements provide each year a limited number of observations differentiated by gender, geographical area, kind of workers. That is also another reason why we calibrate our model maximising with respect to the parameter α of the utility function and why we consider a very simple utility function. Moreover, the calibration of the utility function to the data is performed also with respect to the discount rate r and has been improved by considering as well family ties.

Let us now verify that our database evolves with the same path as the observed data, i.e. it mimics the trend of the percent change in the quota of workers retired between 1996 and 1999. When retirement is postponed, the problem whether (and to which extent) workers take into account the wage income earned in the following period arises, i.e. which is the proper value chosen for α.[ss] In practice, the utility of income from labour may be lower than the utility gained from pension benefits. This justifies a value of α less than one.

The validation of the social security module is carried out trying alternative values for the parameter α until we reach the lowest difference between simulated output and official data.[tt] In performing our analysis we also try to disaggregate the results, as far as possible, by considering sex and occupational sector (dependent, D, and public, P, employees and, self-employed, SE,) of the agents. In Table 1 we report the R^2 coefficient calculated comparing the results achieved using different values of the parameter with respect to the ISTAT and INPS data, coming from *Casellario INPS.* Our results show a high correlation between the simulated output and the official data.

They also illustrate that almost all the times the R^2 reaches its maximum when the parameter is equal to 0.25. In general low values of α (from 0 to 0.25)

[ss] The indirect utility specification of labour and pension incomes are respectively $U_y(Y_s) = \alpha Y_s$ $(0 \leq \alpha \leq 1)$ and $U_b(B_s(t)) = B_s(t)$.

[tt] In particular we consider the time period between 1996 and 1999 and compare the simulated and official percent change in the quota per age class of the individuals retired and still alive in 1999. Obviously we do not consider the right to cumulate pension benefits with labour income, which was not feasible in that period. In this respect, our estimate of α can be considered as an upper bound for the real future value. In fact, there are now stronger incentives to anticipate retirement given the possibility to enjoy both the wage and the pension benefit.

provide the best fitting.[uu]

Table 1. R^2 for different values of α.

α	MALES			FEMALES		
	D	SE	P	D	SE	P
0.00	0.894	0.874	0.918	0.985	0.954	0.848
0.125	0.894	0.877	0.916	0.977	0.983	0.843
0.25	0.894	0.892	0.915	0.973	0.987	0.842
0.50	0.887	0.950	0.892	0.976	0.961	0.816
1.00	0.836	0.524	0.677	0.986	0.879	0.673

The good fit of the simulation output with the official data clearly emerges in Fig. 1, where we report the simulation results using different values of the parameter α. This is particularly true for small values of α, except for the case of the public sectors (especially for females).

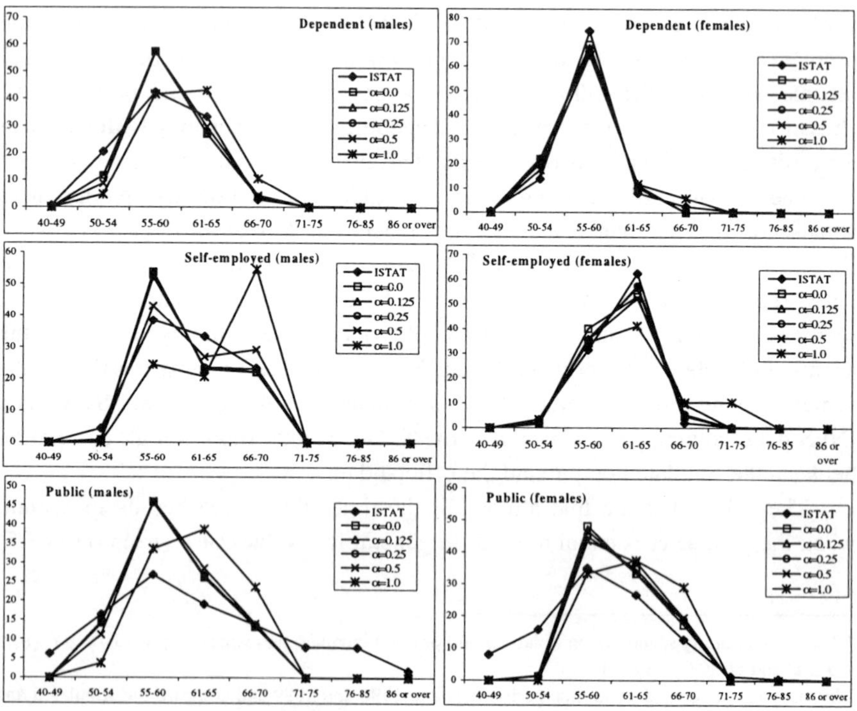

Figure 1. Change in quota (%) for different sectors.

[uu] However, for formerly self-employed males, the best fitting is for $\alpha = 0.5$, even if lower values of the parameter do not produce strong distortions with respect to the official data.

It must be also observed that our model seems to concentrate the values around the modal classes.[vv]

Similar conclusions can be drawn if we consider the results disaggregated at the regional level (in appendix A, Fig. A1 reports the results setting the parameter equal to 0.25). The regional profiles produced by the model are quite similar to the national ones except for some categories in the South[ww] where they exhibit different patterns.

So far, the calibration of the utility function has been performed maximising only with respect to α. However, it is interesting to asses if our calibration procedure is robust with respect to a different value of the discount factor, representing a more myopic behaviour. Table 2 reports the corresponding value of the R^2 coefficient under this new hypothesis (discount rate set equal to 8%).

As it clearly emerges from the results in Table 2, the differences in the fitting determined by a different value of the discount factor are really minor. Also in this case, the value of the parameter α that better assures a good replication of the official profiles seems in general to be enclosed in the interval between 0 and 0.25.

Table 2. R^2 for different values of α if the discount rate is set equal to 8%.

α	MALES			FEMALES		
	D	**SE**	**P**	**D**	**SE**	**P**
0.00	0.897	0.876	0.918	0.992	0.954	0.850
0.125	0.896	0.874	0.918	0.987	0.954	0.850
0.25	0.894	0.877	0.916	0.980	0.977	0.846
0.50	0.892	0.946	0.913	0.968	0.969	0.816
1.00	0.822	0.442	0.631	0.982	0.905	0.673

Another factor that we intend to analyse is the possible presence and effect of *family bounded rationality* in terms of retirement decision. In particular we assume that the wife will anticipate retirement with a probability $\pi = 20\%$ if the husband is already retired.[xx] In Table 3, we report the results for the R^2 under this new hypothesis as well as for $\pi = 10\%$, for female workers.

[vv] In particular, the model does not replicate completely the phenomenon of "young pensioners" (workers who decide to retire before the age of 50) especially in the public sector, for female workers. This may be due in part to the tendency, in a period perceived as uncertain, to retire early in order to avoid future restrictions as well as to take advantage of economies of scope of the family and of possibilities offered by the informal sector.

[ww] In particular in four cases (dependent males, self-employed and public females) the results show different modal classes with respect to the INPS and ISTAT statistics.

[xx] Specifically, a public dependent wife will anticipate retirement with a probability of 30% if the husband is already retired.

Table 3. R^2 for different values of α under *family bounded rationality* (females only).

α	π = 20%			π = 10%		
	D	SE	P	D	SE	P
0.00	0.832	0.550	0.906	0.905	0.739	0.947
0.125	0.827	0.540	0.897	0.921	0.674	0.942
0.25	0.825	0.568	0.904	0.895	0.745	0.951
0.50	0.788	0.608	0.921	0.878	0.775	0.935
1.00	0.791	0.574	0.948	0.785	0.622	0.975

Even in this case, the value in Table 3 shows a high correlation between the official data and the simulation results. However, it emerges a clear reduction in the goodness of fitting, except in the case of public employees, for which there is an increase, ranging from 5% to 10%, in the explained variability. The higher correlation with official data produced by the *family bounded rationality* in the case of female public workers is also illustrated in Fig. 3

Even if our calibration procedure does not seem to support the *family bounded rationally* for non public female workers, this behaviour cannot be rejected *a priori*, as it will be shown in the next section.

Although acceptable for a methodological exercise, obviously calibration per se is not well founded in inferential statistics (even if it is connected to simulation-based estimation techniques, if properly extended).

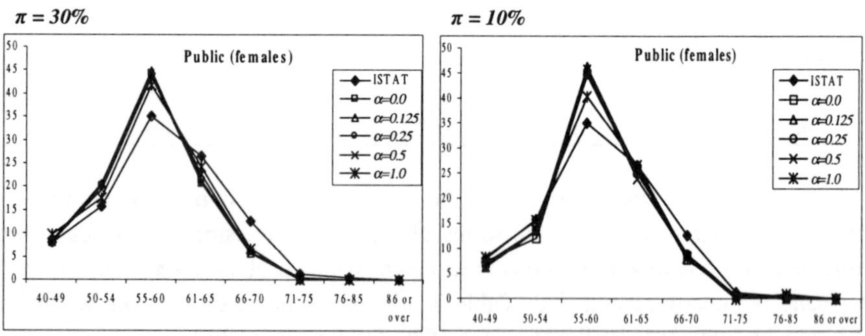

Figure 3. Change in quota (%) for female public employees (*family bounded rationality*).

The main problem appears to be "identification". In fact, if we calibrate the standard utility function proposed in Stock and Wise (1990), there could be several parameters' configurations that closely mimic actual behaviours.[yy] Even

[yy] Moreover, different variables can be used to calibrate the model; e.g. the absolute variation in the quota of retirees over workers, average retirement age, replacement rate, etc.

if they are more or less equivalent in term of replicating some observations, still they might have different implications in terms of policy simulation.

What we are really interested in is the future retirement behaviours in the transition phase and the workers' reactions to policy changes. Given the very relevant topics we address and the policy oriented character of our research work, it is important to ensure that retirement behaviours and reactions to policy changes are not biased. Unfortunately, these important issues cannot be fully answered. However, there are some possible facts (about retirement ages, replacement rate and "retirees/workers" ratio) that may fit into the picture, hinting that our choices of functions and parameter cannot be easily dismissed as biased or unrealistic.[zz]

4. Economic consequences of different retirement choices

The MIND model can be used for many purposes, including the evaluation of: (*i*) retirement ages per area, employment and sex, (*ii*) replacement rate and "pensioners/workers' ratio", (*iii*) pension expenditures and the average individual pension benefits, (*iiii*) poverty and concentration of gross incomes (net of capital incomes) among families with at least one pensioner. In particular, the introduction of a reaction function for modelling the retirement decisions allows us to consider alternative hypotheses on retirement behaviour, depending on whether workers: (*1*) determine their retirement age following *individual rationality*, maximising their individual benefits flow coming from labour (with $\alpha = 0.25$) and pension incomes; (*2*) decide their retirement age (with $\alpha = 0.125$) when *family bounded rationality* applies. Although acceptable for a methodological exercise, obviously calibration per se is not well founded in inferential statistics (even if it is connected to simulation-based estimation techniques, if properly extended).

These two alternatives may be useful as boundary cases in the context of retirement choice, since they are able to encompass a number of intermediate behaviours. In order to reduce the variance induced by the dynamic ageing approach, the reported results are mean values of 10 Monte Carlo replications. Considering mean values, we substantially reduce the uncertainty introduced by the dynamic ageing approach by 90%. This reduction can be performed using other "ad hoc" techniques, such as *selective sampling* and *side walk* methods. However, the use of such techniques may have some drawbacks, e.g. altering the

---

[zz] Accordingly, it is essential to reproduce as well as possible the actual trends of retirement not only focusing on the estimation of the true value for some parameters.

probabilities of the events.[aaa] Although acceptable for a methodological exercise, obviously calibration per se is not well founded in inferential statistics (even if it is connected to simulation-based estimation techniques, if properly extended). For the two above mentioned behavioural scenarios, the mean retirement ages (Table 4), simulated for the period 2004–2024, disaggregated by gender, geographical area, kind of workers, reflect some regularities that we may expect, at least in the short run. In fact, in the period 2005–2007, one is expecting males in the private sector (both employees and self-employed) to retire later than females, while in the public sector retirement ages are very close, being the males' slightly higher than females'.[bbb]

Table 4. Retirement age (mean values) per area, employment and sex.

	individual rationality						*family bounded rationality*					
	MALES			FEMALES			MALES			FEMALES		
	D	SE	P	D	SE	P	D	SE	P	D	SE	P
NORTH												
2005-2007	58	59	59	59	60	60	58	59	59	56	58	57
2008-2010	57	60	58	59	62	60	57	60	58	57	59	57
2011-2013	58	60	59	58	62	61	58	60	59	57	58	58
2014-2016	57	59	59	59	60	61	57	59	58	58	59	58
2017-2019	58	59	59	61	63	62	57	58	58	58	59	58
2020-2022	59	62	62	61	64	63	58	59	60	58	60	59
2023-2024	59	61	62	61	65	63	58	59	59	58	60	60
CENTRE												
2005-2007	59	59	60	60	59	61	59	59	60	58	57	57
2008-2010	59	59	59	59	60	60	59	60	59	57	57	58
2011-2013	58	60	60	59	60	60	58	60	60	57	58	58
2014-2016	60	61	60	61	60	61	59	60	59	59	59	59
2017-2019	59	63	61	61	61	65	58	60	61	59	60	61
2020-2022	62	63	62	62	62	65	59	60	59	59	59	61
2023-2024	63	64	61	63	61	66	59	59	60	59	60	61
SOUTH												
2005-2007	61	62	60	62	60	63	61	62	60	57	58	59
2008-2010	60	62	60	61	60	63	60	62	60	59	58	58
2011-2013	60	61	61	61	62	62	60	61	60	59	59	59
2014-2016	62	62	61	61	62	63	61	62	60	60	60	60
2017-2019	62	62	61	63	63	64	60	61	60	59	61	61
2020-2022	62	62	62	62	65	65	60	61	61	60	61	62
2023-2024	63	62	63	63	65	66	60	61	62	59	61	61

Moreover, in a longer run there are reasons to think in favour of a convergence between the mean retirement age of males and female and between different types of workers: working careers are expected to be more similar between genders and differences in minimum requirements and in pension

[aaa] On this topic, see Gupta and Kapur [27] chapters 17 and 18.

[bbb] To avoid corner solutions, we have set a social constraint to retire at 66 for employees at 67 for public and 68 for self employed.

computation are expected to disappear in the future.

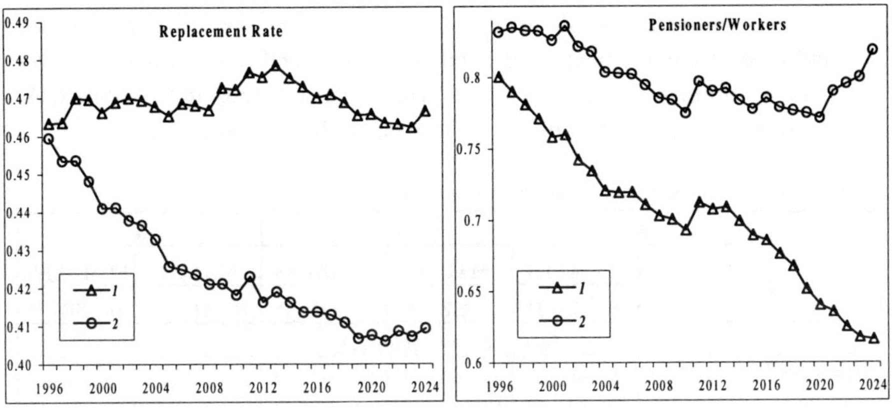

Figure 4. Average replacement rate and “retirees/workers” ratio.

To further investigate the issue of validation and calibration of the MIND model, it is useful to consider (as in Fig. 4) the trend of the ratio “average pension over average wage” and the ratio “retirees/workers” in both the *family bounded rationality* (*2*) scenario and the *individual rationality* (***1***) hypothesis.

The average ratio “pension/wage” strongly decreases under hypothesis *2* (a total reduction of almost 5%), whereas it remains constant under hypothesis ***1***, over the whole period. On the other hand, whereas the “pensioners/workers” ratio is steadily decreasing under ***1***, the scenario **2** presents a more realistic profile: an initial slight decreasing trend that is reversed after 2020. Moreover, the oscillation band is quite narrow in comparison with the alternative scenario.

5. Seniority pension reforms and their economic consequences

Once calibrated and validated, the model can be used to compare alternative social security policy scenarios from 2004 to 2024.

5.1. *Retirement trends and the economic impact of alternative policies*

Let us consider retirement under the policy scenarios (***B***, ***M*** and ***A***) of the companion paper [59]. In the basic scenario (***B***) the current state of affairs remains the same, while in the modified scenario (***M***) the government reform is applies to all sectors. Finally in the ***alternative scenario*** (***A***) consists in an immediate switch to the mixed regime for all the workers entitled to seniority pensions who decide to retire earlier, from 2005. All scenarios will be evaluated under the two behavioural rules analysed in the previous sections: *individual rationality* and *family bounded rationality*.

Table 6 reports the trends of the average retirement age, disaggregated for sex and type of employment. In general both males and females tend to delay more their retirement under scenario ***M***. This is not the case under scenario ***A***, which presents profiles very similar to those under the basic scenario ***B***.

Table 6. Retirement age (mean values) per employment and sex

	B						M						A					
	MALES			FEMALES			MALES			FEMALES			MALES			FEMALES		
	D	SE	P	D	SE	P	D	SE	P	D	SE	P	D	SE	P	D	SE	P
Individual rationality (1)																		
2005-2007	59	60	59	59	60	61	59	60	59	59	60	61	59	60	59	59	60	62
2008-2010	58	60	59	59	61	61	59	62	61	60	61	64	58	60	59	59	61	62
2011-2013	59	60	60	59	62	61	60	61	62	60	62	63	59	60	60	59	62	62
2014-2016	59	61	60	60	60	62	60	62	62	60	61	63	59	61	60	60	61	62
2017-2019	59	61	60	61	62	63	60	62	62	62	62	64	59	61	60	61	62	63
2020-2022	60	62	62	62	64	64	61	63	63	62	64	65	60	62	62	62	64	64
2023-2024	61	62	62	62	64	64	62	63	63	63	64	65	61	62	62	62	64	64
Family bounded rationality (2)																		
2005-2007	59	60	59	57	57	58	59	60	59	57	58	58	59	60	59	57	58	58
2008-2010	58	60	59	57	58	58	58	61	59	58	58	58	58	60	59	57	58	58
2011-2013	59	60	60	58	58	59	59	61	60	58	59	59	59	60	60	58	59	59
2014-2016	59	60	59	58	59	59	59	61	60	59	60	60	59	60	59	58	59	59
2017-2019	58	60	60	58	60	60	58	61	60	59	60	60	58	60	60	58	60	60
2020-2022	59	60	60	59	60	60	59	61	60	59	60	61	59	60	60	59	60	60
2023-2024	59	60	60	59	60	60	59	62	60	59	61	61	59	60	60	59	60	60

When workers follow *individual rationality*, in the long run there is a strong tendency for both sexes to postpone the exit from labour market. In particular, the male and female average retirement ages increase significantly after 2008. Delaying retirement, indeed, allows workers to enjoy higher wage incomes for a longer period, compensating in this way the relatively lower pension benefits granted by the new pension rules. If *family bounded rationality* is considered, there is instead a weak tendency for both sexes and all geographic areas to postpone retirement. The average retirement age remains quite stable after 2008, since workers have limited benefits from higher wage incomes, and wives tend to anticipate retirement. This also explains a reduced increase of females retirement age, especially for those working in the public sector.

In Fig. 5 and Fig. 6 we report the trend of the replacement rate and the ratio "retirees/workers" for the two behavioural rules under the three policy scenarios.

The trend of the replacement rate is quite different depending on which behaviour is adopted. In general, the "pension/wage" ratio partially reflects the evolution of the total pension expenditure. According to our simulation, if *individual rationality* (case ***1***) is assumed, the ratio "pension/wage" rises under the basic hypothesis ***B***, while it slightly decreases under scenario ***A***. Instead, under scenario ***M*** it first follows the same profile of the basic scenario, then, after a sharp decrease in 2008-2010, it has a sudden rise.

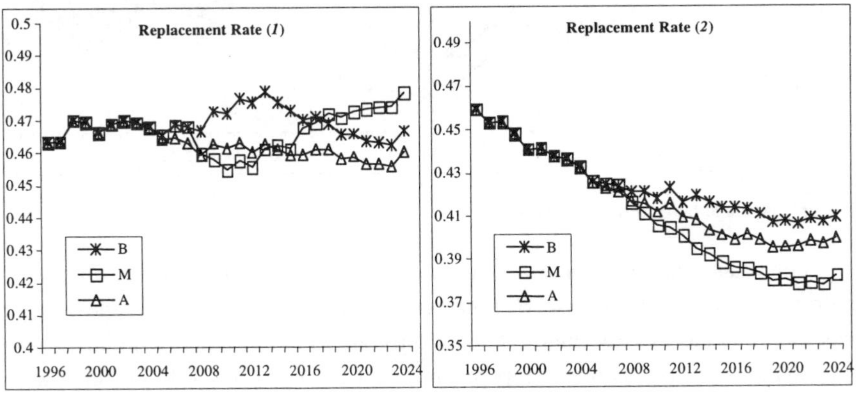

Figure 5. Replacement rate.

In particular, scenario ***M*** shows the minimum value in 2012, (that also reflects the peak in the reduction of the ratio "retirees/workers") allowing the maximum pension expenditure savings. Due to the rapid increase in the ratio after 2012, savings vanish by the end of the simulation period.

On the contrary, under *family bounded rationality* (case ***2***), the replacement rate shows a decreasing trend whatever is the scenario considered. In particular, differently from the case ***1*** (*individual rationality*), ***M*** is the most effective policy in reducing this ratio, due to the stronger negative effects on early retirement. The replacement rate is lower under ***A*** than under ***B***. However, under all scenarios the replacement rate remains stable from 2019 onwards.

As shown in Fig. 6, a visible reduction emerges in the "retirees/workers" ratio if *individual rationality* is assumed. This is particularly clear if the reform ***M*** is implemented, indicating that it represents a strong disincentive mechanism for early retirement.

This evidence is also present in the case of *family bounded rationality*, although less effective. In particular, under all scenarios, the family oriented retirement rule determines in the "retirees/workers" ratio only a slightly decreasing trend, that is even reversed after 2020. Its value is on average around

0.80 with a standard error of 0.02 (0.03 if *M* is considered).

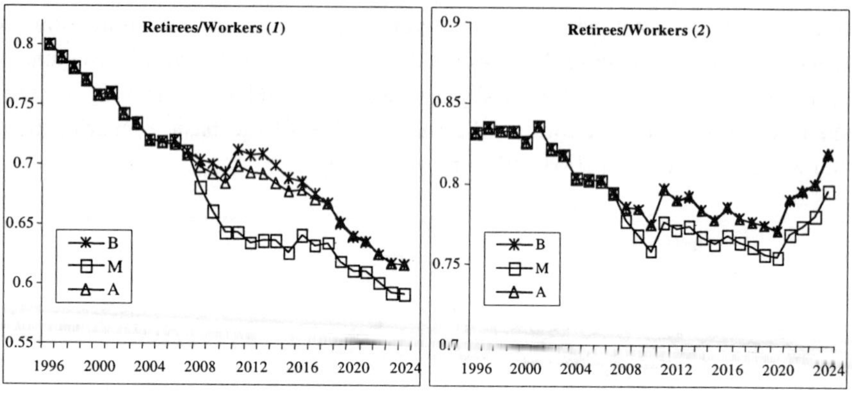

Figure 6. Average ratio "retirees/workers".

For what concerns scenario ***A***, the minor reduction of the "retirees/workers" ratio with respect to scenario ***B***, together with the trend of the average pension income, indicate that the main channel through which alternative policy ***A*** acts on savings, is by decreasing pension benefits rather than by incentivating workers to postpone retirement, independently from retirement behaviours.

Considering the impact of the three policy on poverty and gross labour incomes concentration among families with at least one pensioner, in the companion paper [59] we reached the following conclusions. (***i***) Government reform increases inequality among the families of pensioners in a permanent and more relevant way under *family bounded rationality*. (***ii***) Under the *individual rationality*, the reform mitigates poverty problems after 2008. The reverse is true under *family bounded rationality*. (***iii***) Under *individual rationality*, the alternative reform ***A*** slightly worsens poverty problems by increasing its diffusion and intensity. Assuming *family bounded rationality*, ***A*** has a lower negative impact on poverty than ***M*** the governmental proposal.

The negative impact on income concentration and poverty of the government reform under *family bounded rationality* represents a relevant drawback, that could be overcome indexing to prices the income support allowances established by the present government reform (L.448/01). This means to keep constant in real term the 516 € per month granted in 2001 to social pensioners at least 70 years old, whose income is under that threshold.

The effects of this new scenario (***P***) will be compared with the outcome of the proposed government reform (***M***) in term of impact on poverty and income concentration.

However, to have an overall view of the effects of ***P*** it is important to assess first the burden induced on pension expenditures. In Fig. 7 we report the total pension expenditure (on the left) and the average pension benefit under scenarios ***B***, ***M*** and ***P***.

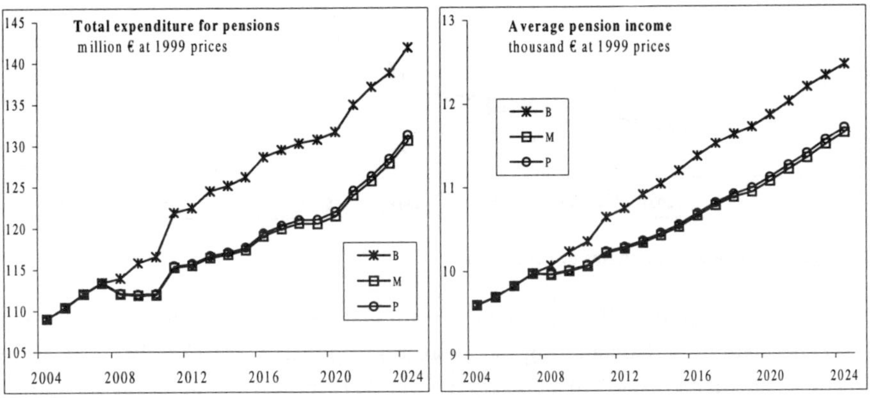

Figure 7. Aggregate expenditure for pensions and average benefit under scenario ***M*** and ***P***.

As it clearly emerges, ***P*** produces a minor rise on average expenditure (on average +0.25% only). Hence, the implementation of this "accompanying measure" (indexing to prices the income support allowances) together with the reform ***M*** still guarantees high savings.

5.2. *The distributive impact of seniority pensions reforms*

As pointed out, the ***P*** manoeuvre intends to alleviate the negative distributive effects produced by the government proposal. In what follows we analyse its impact on income concentration and poverty.

As shown by the Gini index[ccc] in Fig. 8, inequality increases over the whole period by 2.6% (from a level of 0.343 to 0.352) under ***B***, and even more (up to 0.357), about 4.3%, under ***M***. Even scenario ***P*** produces a sensible increase of income concentration (+3.7%), but always smaller than that realized under ***M***. In both scenarios with the proposed government reform, with (***P***) or without (***M***) indexing the income support allowances to prices, the rise is mainly realized after 2008, as the age requirements increase for seniority pensions.

[ccc] The ***Gini index***: $G(\mathbf{y}) = \sum_{i=1}^{n-1}(p_i - q_i) / \sum_{i=1}^{n-1} p_i = \frac{1}{2n(n-1)m} \cdot \sum_{i=1}^{n}\sum_{j=1}^{n} |y_i - y_j|$ (with $1 \le i \le n$) can be expressed as a function of the cumulated fractions of population p_i and of the equivalent family incomes q_i and represents the average difference of all equivalent family incomes y_i.

Figure 8. Gini index for families of pensioners.

However, policy ***P*** was meant to alleviate poverty rather than reducing income inequality. Considering the diffusion of poverty (see Fig. 9),[ddd] we see a slowly increasing trend till 2008 (and from 2012 onwards) under all scenarios. On the other hand, the trend has a sharp rise in 2012, as the diffusion of poverty increases from 0.11 till 0.15. The increase in poverty diffusion is slightly higher under ***M*** and ***P***, because of lower seniority benefits. Nevertheless, the impact of the indexation to prices of the social allowances on poverty diffusion is weak (with respect to ***M***) but persistent.

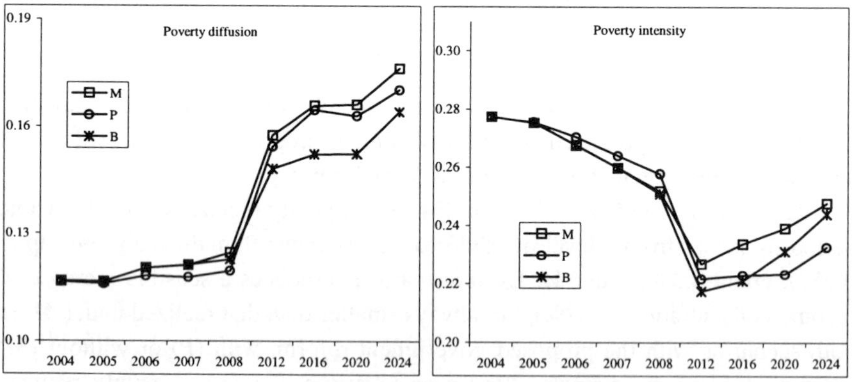

Figure 9. Poverty diffusion and poverty intensity among pensioners' families.

For what concerns poverty intensity ***M*** produces the highest values.

[ddd] Our ***poverty diffusion*** index is the usual ***head count ratio***, $H = q/n$ indicating the quota (q) of population under the poverty threshold, i.e. with an equivalent family income y_i below z_n.

Although it shows a decreasing profile,[eee] after 2012 its trend is reversed under scenarios ***B*** and ***M***, while scenario ***P*** strongly slows down this new increase.

The Sen index [53] modified by Shorrocks [54] summarises the poverty trend,[fff] showing how it slowly decreases till 2008 and then it apparently increases.

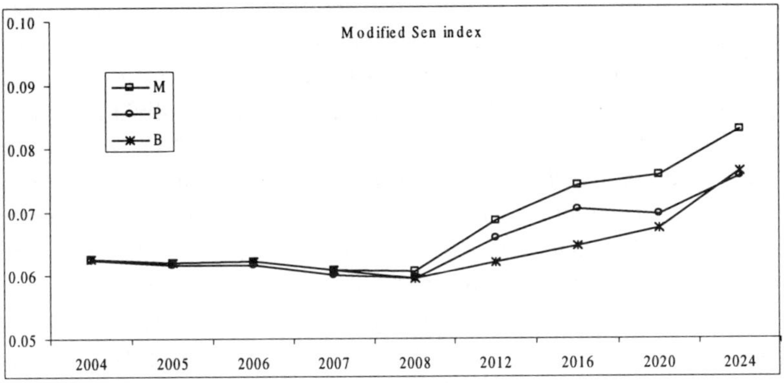

Figure 10. The modified Sen index for families of pensioners.

However, the increase of poverty is much higher under ***M*** because of the reduction in seniority benefits, whereas scenario ***P*** converges to the basic scenario in the end. From the previous simulation experiments, we can conclude that indexing the income support allowances to prices overcomes the strong negative impacts of government reform on poverty, partially contrasting the negative effects on concentration without an excessive additional burden.

If *individual rationality* is considered, the additional income support action ***P*** strengthens the positive consequence of the government proposal on poverty and alleviates partially the negative consequences on income concentration, without increasing significantly pension expenditures.[ggg]

The analysis uses Monte Carlo methodology: (***i***) to ensure more reliable results, since they are derived by the mean values of 10 replications, and (***ii***) to estimate the variances of the results. In particular, the estimated standard errors

---

[eee] To measure ***poverty intensity*** we use the ***income gap ratio***: $I = \left(\sum^{q} g_i / q \right) / z = \sum_{i=1}^{q} g_i / qz$ equal to the ratio between the average *poverty gap* $g_i = z - y_i$ and the poverty threshold.

[fff] The Sen index is based on the head count ratio H, the income gap ratio I and the Gini index for the poor G_p: $S = (2-H)HI+H^2(1-I)G_p$.

[ggg] Under *individual rationality*, looking at the modified Sen index, the government proposal (***M***) produces on average a decrease of 1.2% with respect to the current scenario (***B***). The additional income support action (***P***) determines a further reduction of 4.1%. Income concentration increases under policy ***M*** (+0.4% on average with respect to ***B***) whereas indexing income support allowances slows down this rise (-0.2%, compared to scenario ***M***).

are low and on average range between 0.7% and 2.8% of the mean value of the calculated indices, thus confirming the robustness of our results.[hhh]

6. Concluding remarks

Public activity and social security policies alter private choices, creating distortions in the individual budget constraint and affecting retirement behaviour, depending also on the generosity of early retirement provisions. In this paper we examined the economic consequences of individual retirement choices, providing new evidence on actual trends and on the results of alternative policies aimed at reducing early retirement from the labour market. Using dynamic ageing procedures, we consider the evolution of an agent-based economy, with heterogeneous agents, and endogenous retirement choice, modelled using the Stock and Wise [56] option value model.

Having already validated the demographic and socio-economic dynamics for geographical area (see Vagliasindi, Romanelli, Bianchi [58]), in this paper we calibrated the model as to replicate the retirement dynamics shown in the official data. The calibration has been performed also with respect to the discount factor and family ties. In this way we considered the possibility of more myopic behaviours and the existence of a family conditioning.

We estimated under different behaviours and policies the age of retirement, the replacement rate and the pensioners/workers' as well as total pension expenditures, pension benefits and the trend of poverty and gross incomes concentration among families with at least one pensioner, considering also the option to index income support allowances to prices.

In general, we see how (from 2005 to 2024) there is a tendency for both sexes, all geographic areas and all type of workers to postpone the exit from labour market, but the result may differ depending on whether workers follow *individual rationality*, i.e. they decide to retire maximising their expected benefits coming from labour and pension incomes (assuming the net benefit of 1€ from wages to be equivalent to 0.25€ from pensions), or *family bounded rationality*, and are eager to retire, valuing less the benefit form labour income (0.125€), more myopic (using a higher discount rate for actualising future benefits streams) and influenced by the partner retirement decision.

From 2004 to 2024, we consider both retirement rules (*individual rationality* vs. *family bounded rationality*) and compare the current state of affairs (***B***) with the reform proposed by the Italian Welfare Minister (***M***) and

[hhh] For a description and illustration of a criterion that allow distinguishing among alternative policies, see Vagliasindi, Romanelli, Bianchi [59].

with an anticipated start of the mixed regime limited to seniority pensions (***A***). The general tendency to postpone the exit from labour market is greater under scenario ***M***. The trend of the replacement rate is quite different depending on which behavioural rule is adopted. In general, it shows minor changes under *individual rationality* (case ***1***). On the contrary, under *family bounded rationality* (case **2**), it shows clear decreasing trends in all scenarios.

In the companion paper [59] we considered the redistributive effects of seniority pension reforms, showing negligible redistributive effects under *individual rationality*. On the other hand, under *family bounded rationality*, ***M*** increases income concentration in a permanent and more relevant way, as well as the diffusion and intensity of poverty. Nevertheless, the strong negative distributive effects of the government proposal ***M*** can be partially overcome incurring very low costs (+0.25% on average), by indexing the increase of welfare pensions to prices (policy ***P***).

Obviously, there are still wide margins for improvements. In particular, the shaping of workers' retirement behaviours deserve further effort that should be focused on the determinants of the wage profiles, the more appropriate form of the utility functions inside the *OV* model as well as the use of more sophisticated estimation and calibration procedures in modelling retirement decisions.

Finally, our results encourage us to face future challenges to incorporate and to verify individual "reaction functions", e.g. in the process of family creation, in the intertemporal choice of consumption and in the labour market.

Acknowledgments

MIUR financial support is gratefully acknowledged. We thank Maria Vagliasindi and the participants at the "Workshop on Industry and Labour Dynamics. The Agent-based Computational Economics Approach – Wild@Ace", held in Moncalieri (Turin) at LABORatorio Riccardo Revelli, on October 3-4, 2003, and in particular to Robert Axtel, Michele Belloni and Matteo Richiardi. We are also grateful to two anonymous referees for helpful comments and suggestions. All remaining errors and omissions are our own. Notwithstanding the strong interaction between the authors, section 4 and 6 could be attributed to C. Bianchi, sections 1, 3 and the appendix to M. Romanelli and sections 2 and 5 to P. A. Vagliasindi.

Appendix A: Calibration at the regional level

a) NORTH

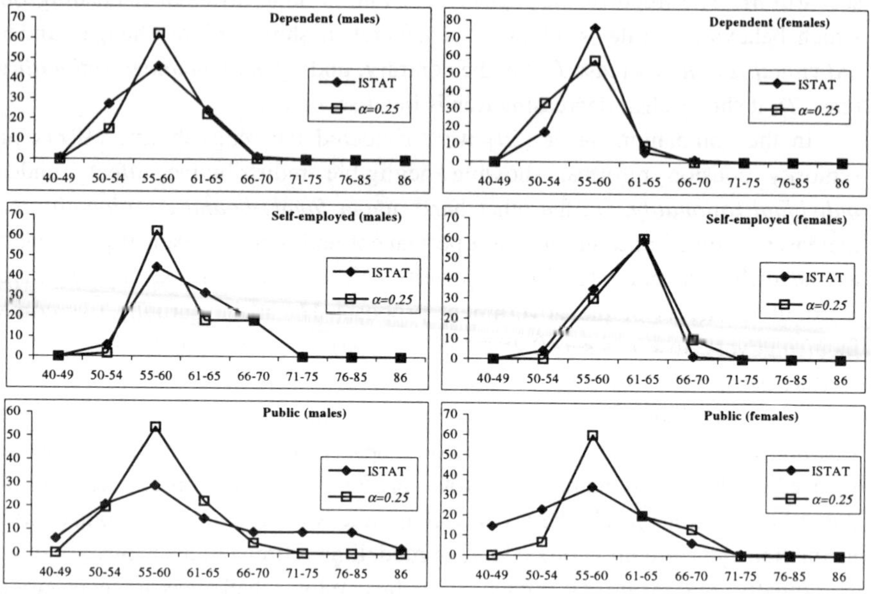

b) CENTRE

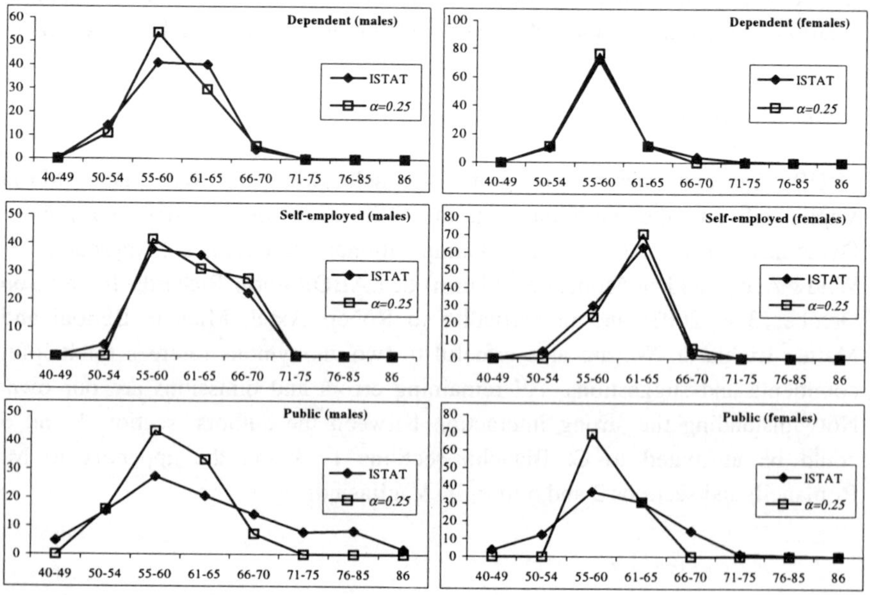

c) SOUTH

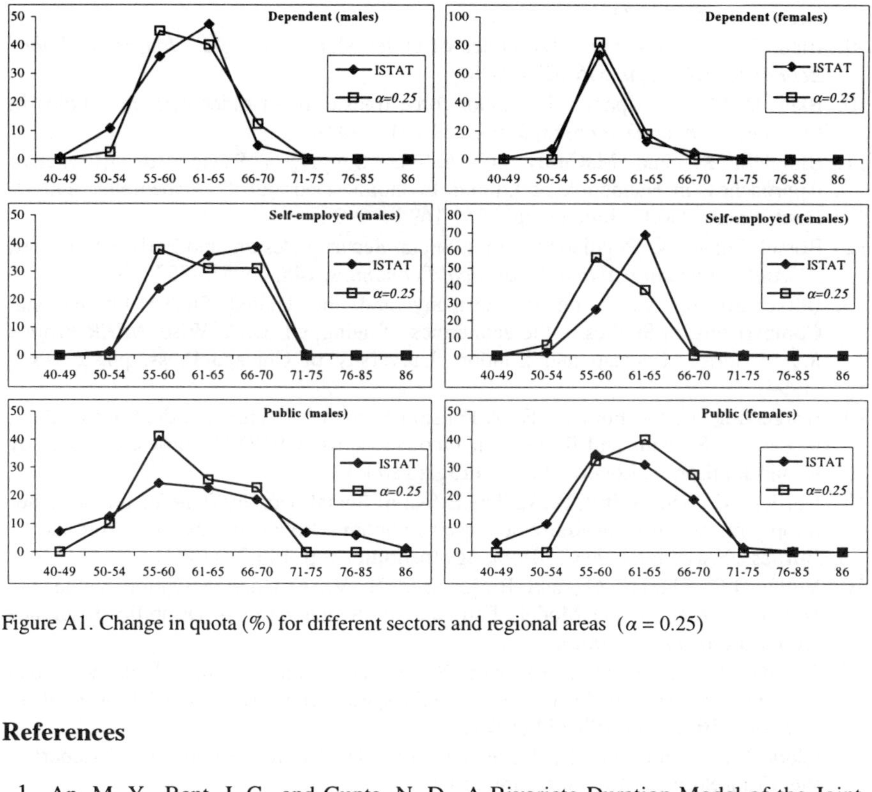

Figure A1. Change in quota (%) for different sectors and regional areas ($\alpha = 0.25$)

References

1. An, M. Y., Bent, J. C., and Gupta, N. D., A Bivariate Duration Model of the Joint Retirement Decisions of Married Couples, *Centre for Labour Market and Social Research*, WP 99-10 (1999).
2. Andreassen, L., Fredriksen, D. and Ljones, O., The future burden of public pension benefits: a microsimulation study, in Microsimulation and Public Policy, ed. A. Harding, North-Holland, pp.~329-357 (1996).
3. Arellano, M. and Bond, S., Some tests of specification for panel data: Monte Carlo evidence and an application to employment equations, *Review of Economic Studies*, **58**, pp. 277-297 (1991).
4. Baker, M., The retirement behavior of married couples: evidence from the spouse's allowance, *NBER WP 7138* (1999).
5. Berkovec, J. and Stern, S., Job Exit Behavior of Older Men, *Econometrica*, **59**, 1, pp. 189-210 (1991).
6. Bianchi, C., Romanelli, M., Vagliasindi, P. A., Inequality and poverty among pensioners: microsimulating the role of indexing lowest pensions to wages, *ECOFIN Discussion Papers*, Università di Parma (2001). www.unipr.it/arpa/defi/papers/brve.pdf
7. Bianchi, C., Romanelli, M., Vagliasindi, P. A., Microsimulating the Evolution of Italian Pension Benefits: the Role of Retirement Choices and Lowest Pensions Indexing, *Labour*, **17**, Special Issue, pp. 139-173 (2003).

8. Blau, D. M., Social security and the labor supply of older married couples, *Labour Economics*, **4**, pp. 373-418 (1997).
9. Blau, D. M., Labor Force Dynamics of Older Married Couples, *Journal of Labor Economics*, **16**, 3, pp. 595-629 (1998).
10. Blau, D. M. and Riphahn, R., Labor force transitions of older married couples in Germany, *Labour Economics*, **6**, pp. 229-251 (1999).
11. Blundell, R., and MaCurdy, T., Labour Supply: a Review of Alternative Approaches, in Handbook of Labour Economics, eds. O. C. Ashenfelter and D. Card, Vol 3a, North Holland, pp. 1559-1695 (1999).
12. Börsch-Supan, A., Population Aging, Social Security Design, and Early Retirement, *Journal of Institutional and Theoretical Economics*, **148**, pp. 533-557 (1992).
13. Börsch-Supan, A., Aging in Germany and the United States: International Comparisons, in Studies in the economics of aging, ed. D. A. Wise, *NBER Project Report series*, Chicago and London, University of Chicago Press, pp. 291-325 (1994).
14. Brugiavini, A., and Fornero, E., A Pension System in Transition: the Case of Italy, in Pension Systems and Retirement Incomes across OECD Countries, eds. Disney R. and Johnson P., London, Edward Elgar (2001).
15. Burtless, G., and Moffitt, R. A., The Effect of Social Security Benefits on the Labor Supply of the Aged, in Retirement And Economic Behavior, eds. H. Aaron and G. Burtless, Washington, D.C., Brookings Institution, pp. 135-74 (1984).
16. Butler, J.S., Gumus, G., and Burkhauser, R. V., Comparing Option Value and Dynamic Programming Models Estimates of Social Security Disability Insurance Application, *mimeo* (2002).
17. Cannari, L. and Nicoletti Altimari, S., A microsimulation model of the Italian household's sector, in Le previsioni della spesa per pensioni, ISTAT, *Annuali di statistica*, **10**, 16, pp. 103-134 (1998).
18. Clark, R., and Johnson, T., Retirement in the Dual Career Family, Final Report to the Social Security Administration (1980).
19. Coile, C., Diamond, P., Gruber, J. and Jousten, A., Delays in claiming social security benefits, *NBER WP 7318* (1999).
20. Coile, C., Delays in Claiming Social Security Benefits, Universite Catholique de Louvain, *CORE Discussion Paper* **29** (2000).
21. Coile, C. and Gruber, J., Social Security Incentives for Retirement, *NBER DP 7651* (2000).
22. Contini, B., and Fornero, E., Labour and retirement choices of the elderly in Italy, Center for Research on Pensions and Welfare Policies, *mimeo* (2003).
23. Diamond, P., and Gruber, J., Social Security and Retirement in the United States, in Social Security and Retirement around the World, eds. J. Gruber and D. A. Wise, Chicago, University of Chicago Press (1999).
24. Di Pino A. and Mucciardi M., The retirement decisions in Italy: a logistic model, paper presented at the Seminar "Socio-demographic factors and the future of the Welfare State in Italy", Villa Mondragone (Frascati) March 16-17 (2001).
25. Fields, G. S., and Mitchell, O. S., Retirement, Pensions and Social Security, Cambridge, MIT Press (1984).
26. Gruber and Wise, D. A., eds., Social Security and Retirement around the World, Chicago, University of Chicago Press (1999).

27. Gupta, A. and Kapur, S., eds., Microsimulation in Government Policy and Forecasting, North-Holland, Amsterdam (2000).
28. Gustman, A. L. and Steinmeier, T. L., A Disaggregated, Structural Analysis of Retirement by Race, Difficulty of Work and Health, *Review of Economics and Statistics*, **67**, 3, pp. 509-513 (1986).
29. Gustman, A. L. and Steinmeier, T. L., A Structural Retirement Model, *Econometrica*, **54**, 3, pp. 555-584 (1986).
30. Gustman, A. L. and Steinmeier, T. L., Retirement in a Family Context: a Structural Model for Husbands and Wives, *NLS Discussion Papers*, **94-17**, U.S. Department of Labor , Bureau of Labor Statistics (1994).
31. Gustman, A. L. and Steinmeier, T. L., Retirement in Dual-Career Families: a Structural Model, *Journal of Labor Economics*, **18**, 3, 503-545 (2000).
32. Gustman, A. L. and Steinmeier, T. L., Social Security, Pensions and Retirement Behavior within the Family, *NBER WP 8772* (2002).
33. Hakola, T., Race for Retirement, *VATT-Research Reports 60*, Helsinki, Finland (1999).
34. Hakola, T., Economic Incentives and Labour Market Transitions of the Aged Finnish Workforce, *VATT-Research Reports 89*, Helsinki, Finland (2002).
35. Hakola, T., Alternative approaches to model withdrawals from the labour market: a literature review, *Working Paper*, **4**, Uppsala University, Dep. of Econ (2003). www.nek.uu.se/Pdf/wp2003_4.pdf
36. Harris, A. R., Modeling Retirement Behavior: a Test of the Optional Value Model Using the Health and Retirement Study, Congressional Budget Office, *mimeo* (2001).
37. Hsiao, C., Analysis of Panel Data, *Econometric Society Monographs*, **11** (1986).
38. Hurd, M. D., Forecasting the Consumption and Wealth of the Elderly, in Social Security and Private Pensions: Providing for Retirement in the 21st Century, ed. S. Wachter, D.C. Health, and Co., pp. 47-69 (1988).
39. Hurd, M. D., The Joint Retirement Decision of Husbands and Wives, in Issues in the Economics of Aging, ed. D. Wise, University of Chicago Press, Chicago, pp. 231-254 (1990).
40. Huttunen, K., Trade, technology and the skill structure of labour demand in Finland, *Studies*, **85**, Labour Institute for Economic Research (2002).
41. Lazear, E., Why Is There Mandatory Retirement?, *Journal of Political Economy*, **87**, 6, pp. 1261-84 (1979).
42. Lazear, E., Pensions as Severance Pay, NBER Reprint No. 501, published in Financial Aspects of the US Pension System, eds. Zvi Bodie, John Soven and David A. Wise, University of Chicago Press, Chicago (1986).
43. Lazear, E., and Moore, R., L., Pensions and Turnover, in Financial Aspects of the US Pension System, eds. Zvi Bodie, John Soven and David A. Wise, Chicago, University of Chicago Press (1986).
44. Lumsdaine, R., Stock, J., and Wise, D., Three Models of Retirement: Computational Complexity versus Predictive validity, in Topics in the Economics of Aging, ed. D. Wise, Chicago, University of Chicago Press, pp. 19-57 (1992).
45. Lumsdaine, R., Stock, J., and Wise, D., Pension Plan Provisions and Retirement: Men & Women, Medicare, and Models, Cambridge, *mimeo* (1992).
46. Mincer J., Schooling, Experience and Earnings, New York, Columbia University Press (1974).

47. Palme, M., and Svensson, I., Social Security, Occupational Pensions, and Retirement in Sweden in Social Security and Retirement around the World, eds. J. Gruber and D. Wise, Chicago, University of Chicago Press, pp. 355-402 (1999).
48. Palme, M., and Svensson, I., Income Security Programs and Retirement in Sweden, *mimeo* (2002).
49. Peracchi, F., Specificazione e stima di modelli microeconomici di pensionamento, Riunione scientifica del gruppo MURST su "Fattori economico-demografici e futuro dello stato sociale in Italia", Messina, *mimeo* (1999).
50. Pozzebon, S., and Mitchell, O. S., Married Women's Retirement Behavior, *Journal of Population Economics*, **2**, 1,. pp. 301-53 (1989).
51. Rust, J., and Phelan, C., How Social Security and Medicare Affect Retirement Behavior in a World of Incomplete Markets, *Econometrica*, **65**, 4, pp. 781-831 (1997).
52. Samwick, A. A., New Evidence on Pensions, Social Security, and the Timing of Retirement, *NBER WP 6534*, National Bureau of Economic Research (1998).
53. Sen, A. K., Poverty: an ordinal approach to measurement, *Econometrica*, **44**, pp. 219-231 (1976).
54. Shorrocks, A. F., Revisiting the Sen Poverty Index, *Econometrica*, **63**, pp. 1225-1230 (1995).
55. Spataro, L., New Tools in Micromodeling Retirement Decisions: Overview and Applications to the Italian Case, *Computing in Economics and Finance*, **109**, Society for Computational Economics (2002).
56. Stock, J. H. and Wise, D. A., Pensions, the option value of work, and retirement, *Econometrica*, **58**, 5, pp. 1151-1180 (1990).
57. Stock, J. H. and Wise, D. A., The Pension Inducement to Retire: an Option Value Analysis, in Issues in the Economics of Aging, ed. D. A. Wise, Chicago: University of Chicago Press, pp. 205-224 (1990).
58. Vagliasindi P. A., M. Romanelli and C. Bianchi, Demographic Evolution and Inequalities among Families of Pensioners in Italy: Microsimulating Regional Dynamics, *Genus*, **1**, in print (2004).
59. Vagliasindi P. A., M. Romanelli and C. Bianchi, Reforming the Italian Pension System in the XXI Century: the Issue of Seniority Pensions Once Again, *Advances in Complex Systems*, forthcoming (2004).
60. Vagliasindi, P. A., Effetti Redistributivi dell'intervento Pubblico: Esperimenti di Microsimulazione per l'Italia, Giappichelli, Torino (2004).

Section 3
Understanding Firm Behavior

BUSINESS CYCLE FLUCTUATIONS AND FIRMS' SIZE DISTRIBUTION DYNAMICS

DOMENICO DELLI GATTI,[a] CORRADO DI GUILMI,[b] EDOARDO GAFFEO,[c] GIANFRANCO GIULIONI,[b] MAURO GALLEGATI,[b*] ANTONIO PALESTRINI,[d]

[a] *Institute of Quantitative Methods and Economic Theory, Catholic University of Milan, Largo Gemelli1, I-20123 Milan, Italy*

[b] *Department of Economics, Università Politecnica delle Marche, Piaz.le Martelli 8, I-60121 Ancona, Italy*

[c] *Department of Economics, University of Trento, Via Inama 5, I-33100 Trento, Italy*

[d] *Department of Law in Society and History, University of Teramo, Via Crucioli 120, I-64100 Teramo, Italy*

Abstract

Power law behavior is an emerging property of many economic models. In this paper we emphasize the fact that power law distributions are persistent but not time invariant. In fact, the scale and the shape of the firms' size distribution fluctuate over time. In particular on a log-log space both the intercept and the slope of the power law distribution of firms' size change over the cycle: during expansions (recessions) the straight line representing the distribution shifts up and becomes less steep (steeper). We show that the empirical distributions generated by simulations of the model presented by [11] mimic real empirical distributions remarkably well.

* Corresponding author. E-mail: gallegati@dea.unian.it (M. Gallegati).

1. Introduction

Starting with the pioneering work of Gibrat [24], economists have long been interested in the relationship between the size and the expected growth rate of firms, and its implications for the firms' size distribution (FSD). While conventional wisdom received from the seminal studies of e.g. Hart and Prais [25], Simon and Bonini [47] and Mansfield [35] holds that the FSD is significantly right-skewed and approximately log-normal, recent empirical research has suggested that a Pareto-Levy (or power law) distribution returns a better fit to the data [42; 45; 3; 22]. This result is particularly intriguing since it implies a hierarchical organization of industrial systems echoing notions, like complexity, self-organization and scale invariance, largely applied in the hard sciences - for instance in physics - but generally neglected in economics. In fact, cross-fertilizations between statistical physics and financial economics have been recently organized into a promising brand new field, *econophysics* [34]. In this paper we inquire whether, starting from the observation that firms are Pareto distributed, the above mentioned notions can be of any help in addressing major questions in macroeconomics such as e.g. the origin and nature of business cycles. Summarizing our conclusions, the answer is likely to be a qualified yes.

The occurrence of a power law may be read as a symptom of self-organizing processes at work. In the self-organized criticality (SOC) framework [4; 41], scaling emerges because the sub-units of a system are heterogeneous and interact, and this leads to a critical state. Dynamic departures from such a state can be of any magnitude, from mild oscillations to major fluctuations driven by avalanches and domino effects. Alternatively, power laws can be generated by scale free growth processes.

The basic idea goes back to Simon's model [46], where Gibrat's law is combined with an entry process to obtain a Levy distribution for firms' size. Furthermore, recent work by physicists (e.g. [36; 2]) has shown that power laws emerge naturally extending Simon's scheme to account for direct or indirect interaction among units.

Regardless of the model generating it, the discovery of power law behavior over a wide range of values of economic variables is far from surprising, as soon as one realizes that an economy is probably the most complex of all complex systems [29][a]. Econophysicists [34] claim that economics should

[a]In the realm of economics, besides returning a good fit on the empirical FSD, power laws have proven useful in modeling the distribution of city sizes [6; 19], of stock price

share with other complex disciplines, like physics, biology and ecology, also the universality of critical phenomena. Briefly, this means that systems so disparate as firms, cities and countries show a common scale invariant behavior (that is, a quantitative similar scaling exponent), since they obey common mechanisms of microscopic interactions. This assumption turns out to be strikingly true in many cases. However, our point is that there is no compelling reason why universality should strictly hold also on a time dimension. In other words, power laws are not necessarily time invariant. On the contrary, the scale and the shape of the FSD and other economic distributions do fluctuate over time, and these fluctuations - or, in other terms, microeconomic distribution dynamics - are the key to a proper understanding of the business cycle. The structure of the paper is as follows. Section 2 outlines some stylized facts about FSD dynamics, which question the hypothesis of universality over time. Section 3 then discusses why one should naturally expect such dynamics when analyzing economic data. Section 4 briefly discusses a recently proposed macroeconomic model based on mean-field interactions among heterogeneous firms, while Section 5 examines some of its simulation properties and its ability to mimic the data. Section 6 concludes.

2. FSD Dynamics for Business Cycle Analysis: ...

Roughly speaking, a discrete random variable Z is said to follow a Pareto-Levy (also known as Rank-Size or power law) distribution, if its complementary cumulative distribution function takes the form:

$$\Pr\left[Z > z_j\right] = \left(\frac{z_0}{z_j}\right)^{\alpha} \tag{1}$$

with $z_i \geq z_0$. The scaling exponent $\alpha > 0$ is also known as the shape parameter, while z_0 (the minimum size) is the scale parameter. On a log-log space, this distribution yields a downward sloping straight line with slope -α. The special case $\alpha = 1$ is known as Zipf Law.

Recent empirical research has shown that equation (1) returns a remarkably good fit to empirical data for the FSD for the U.S. [3], Japan [42], Denmark [28] and an international sample of corporate firms [45; 22],

---

and exchange rate fluctuations [31; 33; 38], of returns from innovation activities [27;48], and of profits and sales in markets for information goods [14; 23].

using different measures of firms' size (e.g., employment, sales, total assets). Brock [7] and Durlauf [16], however, point out that a good linear fit in the log–log space should be interpreted with great care, since these distributions are unconditional objects and many conditional data generating processes are consistent with them.

Taking this criticism into account [22] conditioned FSD analysis on business cycle episodes. As a result, they could address the question of whether the statistical models driving firms growth change during upturns and downturns or, in other terms, whether firms long-run growth processes are influenced by short-run fluctuations.

They found that there are significant shifts of the FSD during the different phases of the business cycle, the mean and the standard deviation of firm size being bigger during expansions. In particular, the scaling exponent is on average bigger during recessions than during expansions. In spite of this variability a power law scaling behavior emerges as an invariant feature of the FSD, regardless of the proxy used for size or the phase of the business cycle conditioning the distribution. Furthermore, the scaling exponents for the unconditional distributions appear to be a weighted average of the conditioned scaling exponents in expansions.

Further evidence on FSD fluctuations over time is offered in table 1, where we report the time series of the (log of the) scale and the shape parameters of the FSD for Italy over the time period 1992-2001, as given by the data-set Amadeus. Firms' size has been proxied by employment, real value added and total assets, respectively. Estimates have been obtained by OLS linear fitting on a log-log space. After getting rid of finite sample biases, each regression explains more than 98% of the total variance.

All series display a significant variability of the scale and shape parameters, which are strongly correlated in each case. Notice also that FSDs measured with different proxies do not tend to move together. If size is measured by employment, the power law shifts inward and presents a decreasing slope during the recession of the early 1990s,[b] while both the minimum size and the exponent of the power law increase during the long expansion of 1994-2000. Movements in the opposite direction are displayed by the FSDs proxied by value added and total assets.

These results should be read in the light of previous empirical and theoretical work. Amaral *et al.* [1], for instance, present evidence on the

[b] According to the business cycle chronology calculated by the Economic Cycle Research Institute, Italy experienced a peak in February 1992 and a trough in October 1993.

Table 1. Estimates of the scale parameter and of the shape parameter obtained by OLS regression in a log-log space for the size distribution of a sample of Italian firms, Italy 1992-2001. The data source is Amadeus. Size has been measured by employment, value added and total assets.

Variable	Year	Rsq	Scale parameter	Shape parameter
Employees	2001	0,995	5,6842	-1,0124
Employees	2000	0,994	5,8751	-1,0506
Employees	1999	0,993	5,8661	-1,0459
Employees	1998	0,994	5,7265	-1,0398
Employees	1997	0,999	5,6927	-1,0684
Employees	1996	0,999	5,4761	-1,0002
Employees	1995	0,993	4,8773	-0,8861
Employees	1994	0,996	4,8776	-0,9307
Employees	1993	0,982	4,7038	-0,9092
Employees	1992	0,986	5,4980	-1,1719
Value added	2001	0,999	7,6245	-1,0089
Value added	2000	0,999	7,6606	-1,0112
Value added	1999	0,999	7,8269	-1,0492
Value added	1998	0,999	7,8352	-1,0749
Value added	1997	0,999	7,9600	-1,1244
Value added	1996	0,999	7,7207	-1,0761
Value added	1995	0,994	7,5666	-1,0849
Value added	1994	0,995	8,2971	-1,2854
Value added	1993	0,992	7,5989	-1,1401
Value added	1992	0,982	7,4505	-1,0869
Capital	2001	0,997	7,8530	-0,9166
Capital	2000	0,997	7,8761	-0,9197
Capital	1999	0,996	7,7369	-0,8917
Capital	1998	0,997	7,7465	-0,9170
Capital	1997	0,996	7,9642	-0,9784
Capital	1996	0,997	7,9203	-0,9803
Capital	1995	0,998	8,3322	-1,1097
Capital	1994	0,998	8,3103	-1,1264
Capital	1993	0,999	8,1654	-1,1124
Capital	1992	0,998	7,9953	-1,0615

probability density of firms' size (measured by sales) for a sample of U.S. firms from 1974 to 1993, showing that the distribution is remarkably stable over the whole period. Amaral and his co-authors claim that "[...] there is no existing theoretical reason to expect that the size distribution of firms could remain stable as the economy grows, as the composition of output changes, and as factors that economists would expect to affect firm size (like computer technology) evolve" ([1], p.624). On the contrary, Axtell [3] maintains that stability is exactly the outcome one should expect. Using a random growth process with a lower reflecting barrier studied by Malcai *et al.* [32], he calculates theoretical power law exponents for the U.S. FSD measured by employees in each year from 1988 to 1996. It turns out that the hypothesis of a Zipf Law can not be rejected at any standard significance level. He obtained a similar finding for 1997 using more than 5 million data points from the Census Bureau. It must be noticed, however, that Axtell's calculations - and therefore his conclusions about the stability over time of Zipf Law - are biased towards detecting Zipf Law due to the way the smallest size is specified [c]. Our main points, however, go well beyond this technical drawback. In the following section we shall argue that:

(1) Provided that the Pareto distribution represents an attractor for the FSD dynamics regardless of the proxy one uses to measure firms' size, there are indeed theoretical reasons to expect its position and shape to fluctuate over time. Furthermore, even small fluctuations can have important effects;
(2) There are also compelling theoretical reasons to expect the FSD fluctuations to diverge as we measure firms' size by recurring to different proxies. Furthermore, such differences represent a key for understanding the nature of the business cycle.

Analytically, let the cumulative distribution of firms' size at time t be given by $F_t(x)$. Time is assumed to be discrete. Following [43] to each F_t we attach a probability measure λ_t, so that $\lambda_t\left((-\infty, x]\right) = F_t\left(x\right), \forall x \in \Re$. Given that we are working with counter-cumulative distributions, we introduce a complementary measure μ, so that μ_t = 1 - λ_t = 1 - F_t. The dynamics of the counter-cumulative FSD is then given by the stochastic difference

---

[c]The reason lies in the fact that in Axtell's calculation, the minimum size s_0 has been assumed fixed and equal to 1. From the argument reported in Blank and Solomon [5], who discuss a paper by X. Gabaix [20] which makes use of the same assumption, it emerges that the formula (4) in [3] implicitly returns the Pareto exponent α if and only if the minimum size is assumed to be a constant fraction c of the current average of firms' size $\langle s\rangle$, so that one should pose $s_0 = c\langle s\rangle(t)$, which clearly varies in time.

equation:

$$\mu_t = V\left(\mu_{t-1}, \varepsilon_t\right)$$

where ε is a disturbance, while the operator V maps the Cartesian product of probability measures with disturbances to probability measures. The empirical evidence discussed above suggests that the invariant FSD is Pareto so that, for sufficiently large intervals $(s_2 - s_1)$ and h, we impose that:

$$\frac{\sum_{s=s_1}^{s_2} \mu_s}{s_2 - s_1} = \frac{\sum_{s=s_1}^{s_2} \mu_{h+s}}{s_2 - s_1}$$

while at the same time asking whether there exist theoretical reasons to expect the operator V to fluctuate around its "mean form" as business cycle phases alternate.

3. ... Does It Make Any Sense?

Despite some research on the dynamics of Pareto distributions carried out during the last decade by physicists (see among the others [9; 26; 17], economists have largely neglected such an issue. Notable exceptions are Brakman *et al.* [6], who report a time series for the scaling exponent of the distribution of Dutch city sizes over more than four centuries; Di Guilmi *et al.* [15], who find a downward-sloping time series for the scaling exponent of the world income distribution over the 1960-1998 period; Mizuno *et al.* [36], who find that the cumulative distribution of the profits of Japanese companies shifts during the 1970-1999 period, while the scaling exponent of the right tail obeys Zipf Law;[d] Nirei and Souma [40], who show that income distribution for U.S. and Japan from 1960 to 1999 is Pareto distributed, and that the scaling exponent fluctuates over time. In what follows we further elaborate on this issue, focusing in particular on FSD fluctuations over the business cycle.

3.1. *Power laws' shifts*

When striving to apply the methods and concepts of physics to economics, one has always to keep in mind that: *i*) economic agents, differently from

[d]Mizuno *et al.* [37] prove this last result only by means of visual inspection: no calculations of the scaling exponents are explicitly reported.

particles, form expectations about the future, learn from their past experience and interactions, and adapt to them; *ii*) economics, and macroeconomics in particular, deals with non-stationary processes. Despite the former fact gives rise to several interesting implications (e.g., processes are path dependent, the system is far from equilibrium, and so on) which deserve to be explored at length, here we want to emphasize the second caveat: if economic growth is a non-stationary process then FSD shifts become the key for understanding business cycles and growth.

Shifts of the FSD on a log-log space are related to a change of the system's minimum size (z_0 in equation (1)), which in turn may reflect a change of the minimum efficient scale (MES) of operating firms. There are many theoretical reasons to expect the MES to change over the business cycle. Furthermore, changes of the MES over the cycle depends on the proxy we use to measure the operating scale (i.e. the size). The adoption of a new technology, for instance, may generate primarily a shift of the FSD measured by added value, while shifts of the FSDs by employment and capital should be less marked.

According to this approach, one should look at the various distributions not in isolation, but in terms of their relative movements. Relative movements of employment, capital and value added can be immediately translated into changes of productivity, although these movements should be appropriately disentangled to be fully appreciated. Figure 1 reports the relation between labor productivity (roughly measured as the ratio of added value to employment) and firms' size by total assets for Italy over the 1996 – 2001 period, while figure 2 reports the labor productivity probability density plot on a log-log space.

Three facts clearly emerge from the data. First, there is no clear correlation between labor productivity and firms' size. From the viewpoint of business cycle analysis, the choice of the proxy one uses to measure firms' size is far from neutral. Second, labor productivity is Pareto distributed. In other words, labor productivity shares the same distributive features of the FSD. Third, the distribution of labor productivity shifts over time. As shown in [13], a unifying explanation to these facts can be given along Schumpeterian lines. The typical cyclical dynamics has the following structure: firms follow a technical change path by accumulating capital that allows the production of the same output using less labor as input. The growth of firms' size implied by labor-saving innovations generates a wage increase, due to a positive wage-firm size relationship and, consequently, a shift towards south-west of the firms' size power law distribution in a log-log space.

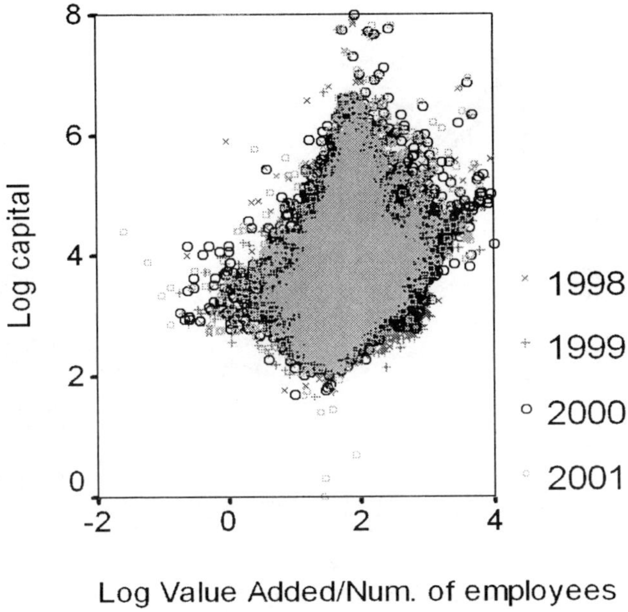

Figure 1. Labor productivity *versus* firms' sizes, Italy 1998-2001. Corporate firms: Source Amadeus.

After the wage level has reached its peak, the capital accumulation re-start to grow, while wages diminish and the power law shifts towards north-east. FSD may also shift because of firms' demography. In particular, a major cause of exit is due to bankruptcy, which is likely to affect firms at different scale of operation, as recent examples in U.S. and Italy have taught. Nevertheless, a large amount of empirical evidence has shown that smaller firms are in general more financially fragile [18].

3.2. *Power laws' changes in slope*

The evidence reported in table 1 highlights that movements of the FSD over time are due not only to changes of the intercept but also of the slope - that is, the scaling exponent – of the power law.

This fact has important implications for a proper understanding of industrial and macroeconomic dynamics. In fact, fluctuations of the scaling exponent translate into fluctuations of the Hirschman-Herfindahl In-

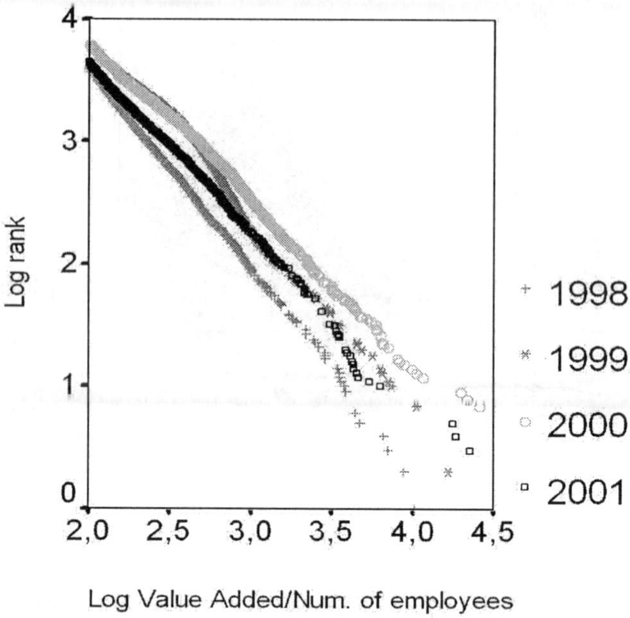

Figure 2. Distribution shifts of labor productivity in Italy 1996-2001. Corporate firms: Source Amadeus.

dex (HHI) of industry concentration [39]: the lower the estimated scaling exponent α, the higher the degree of concentration. Under the simplifying assumptions of an economy consisting of firms playing a homogeneous Cournot game and of a constant elasticity of demand, fluctuations of the HHI may in turn be associated to fluctuations of the weighted average of the firms' price-cost margins [10], that is fluctuations of markups and profits.

The possibility of slope changes conditioned to business cycle phases for a power law distributed FSD can be easily demonstrated. For instance, let the process generating industrial dynamics be given by a simple random multiplicative law:

$$k_i\,(t+1) = \lambda_i\,(t)\,k_i\,(t)$$

where $k_i(t)$ is the size of firm i (measured by its capital stock) at time t, and $\lambda_i(t)$ is a random variable with distribution $\Lambda(\lambda,\sigma^{\,2})$. The total number of firms N increases according to a proportionality rule (at each t, the number of new-born firms ΔN , each one with size k_{min}, is proportional to the increase of the economy-wide capital stock K), while firms which shrink below a minimum size (once again k_{min}) go out of business. Blank and Solomon [5] show that the dynamics of this model converges to a power law distribution, whose scaling exponent is implicitly defined by the following condition:

$$F = \frac{\Delta K}{k_{\min}\Delta N} = \frac{1}{(1 - \frac{1}{\alpha})}$$

where F is the inverse of entrants' contribution to total capital accumulation. F is likely to increase during recessions (when the number of entrants generally shrinks) and to decrease during expansions. If this assumption is correct, this simple model implies that the scaling exponent of the FSD fluctuates over the business cycle, to assume lower values during recessions and higher values during expansions, as in real data.

4. An Agent-Based Model

The Blank-Solomon model, that we have used for expositional convenience, is clearly too simple to capture the complexity of a real industry, not to talk of a macroeconomy. Interestingly enough, however, its basic results - and the ones on FSD's shifts discussed above as well - still hold as one adopts a more complete model, putting more structure on the behavioral foundations of firms' dynamics.

Delli Gatti *et al.* [11] (henceforth DG) model a multi-agent network of interacting heterogeneous (for size and financial conditions) firms. The model consists of only two markets: goods and credit. In order to simplify the analysis as much as possible, it is assumed that output is supply driven, i.e. firms can sell all the output they produce.

In each period, there is a "large" (but far from constant, due to endogenous entry and exit processes) number of firms which differ according to their financial conditions. The financial robustness of a firm is proxied by the equity ratio, i.e. the ratio of its equity base or net worth to the capital stock $a_{it} = A_{it}/K_{it}$. Since firms sell their output at an uncertain price they may go bankrupt. Bankruptcy occurs if net worth at time t becomes negative, i.e. if the individual price falls below a critical threshold. The probability of bankruptcy turns out to be an increasing function of the interest rate and the capital stock, and a decreasing function of the equity base inherited from the past.

In this setting, the problem of the firm is the maximization of expected profits net of bankruptcy costs. The optimal capital stock turns out to be a decreasing function of the interest rate and an increasing function of the equity ratio. Output follows the evolution over time of the capital stock, which in turn is determined by investment.

Firms can raise funds only on the credit market. For the sake of simplicity, DG assume that many heterogeneous firms interact with the banking sector (as an aggregate). As to demand, investment is financed by means of retained earnings and by new debt: Therefore the demand for credit of each firm is a function of the interest rate and financial robustness. In order to determine the supply of credit and its allocation to each firm, DG assume that there is a risk coefficient - i.e. a threshold ratio of bank's equity to credit extended - that the bank tries to target, either because of a strategy of risk management or as a consequence of prudential regulation on the part of the monetary authorities. Therefore the aggregate supply of credit turns out to be a multiple of bank's equity.

Credit has to be allotted to the heterogeneous firms. DG assume that each firm obtains a portion of total credit equal to its relative size, i.e. the ratio of the individual capital stock to the aggregate capital stock: highly capitalized (i.e. collateralized) borrowers have a high credit supply and vice versa. The rate of interest charged to each firm is determined in equilibrium when the demand for credit is equal to the credit extended by the bank to that firm. The equilibrium interest rate is generally decreasing – investment and output therefore are generally increasing – with the bank's and the firm's net worth.

The bank's equity base, which is the only determinant of total credit supply, increases with the bank's profits, which are affected, among other things, by firms' bankruptcy. When a firm goes bankrupt, i.e. its net worth becomes negative because of a huge loss, the bank has a "bad debt". This is the root of a potential *domino* effect: the bankruptcy of a firm today is the source of the potential bankruptcies of other firms tomorrow via its impact on the bank's equity.

5. Results

Applying the econophysics approach to macroeconomics, a micro-founded model should be able to replicate – among other things – significant income fluctuations from idiosyncratic shocks and a power law distribution for firms'size.

The DG framework builds upon firms' heterogeneity and their interactions to accomplish this task, with firms' and banks' balance sheets conditions driving output dynamics in an asymmetric information setting. Given its complex structure, the model has been explored by means of numerical simulation. In what follows, we compare the empirical evidence derived from balance-sheet data for a sample of Italian firms over the 1992-2001 period and simulation results. The capability of the model to replicate the stylized facts concerning FSD - both qualitatively and quantitatively - is striking.

A key source of heterogeneity both in real data and in the DG model is the degree of firms' financial fragility. While largely neglected in the macroeconomics literature, it turns out that financial heterogeneity is essential to a proper understanding of business cycle fluctuations. One finding that stands out from figure 3 is that the financial robustness or solvency of firms, here proxied by the average equity ratio a over dimensional classes, increases with size. Furthermore, the variance of solvency is heteroskedastic with respect to the size, with the equity ratio of bigger firms more volatile that that of smaller ones, although the variance increases with size at a lower rate than the average.

The information gathered from the distribution of the equity ratio over firms' size is essential to the study of industrial dynamics and its interactions with the business cycle, as we find that financial ratios are invariably a good predictor of firms failure, and therefore of exits due to bankruptcy. In particular, both the empirical evidence and the model show that the equity ratio deteriorates almost monotonically as the date of bankruptcy approaches (figure 4).

Combining the last two facts, one should expect smaller firms to have a higher probability to go bankrupt and, as new-comers generally enter at a small scale, young firms to have a higher probability to fail than older ones. While both predictions are considered well-known regularities in the industrial organization literature – see e.g. [50] and [8] - our empirical and simulated findings are somehow puzzling.[e] The distribution of exits by age turns out to be in all cases exponential, signaling that in our real and simulated data the probability to fail is independent of time (figure 5)[f].

The reason for this is likely to be different as we consider in turn real and simulated data. With regards to the empirical distribution, it should be stressed that the sample we employed consists of middle to large firms,

[e]But see also [19], who provides evidence based on Japanese data showing that the distribution of bankrupted firms conditioned to age is exponential.

[f]Recall that the exponential distribution is characterized by a constant hazard function, meaning that the probability to fail remains constant with time.

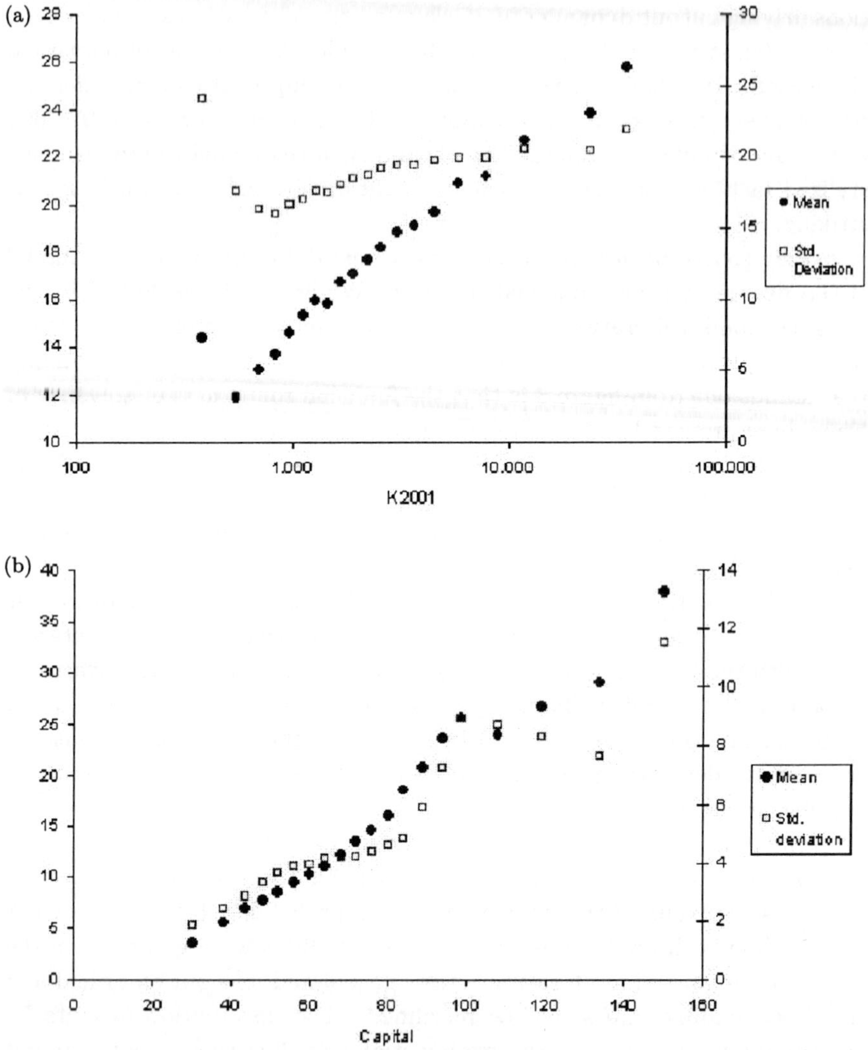

Figure 3. *a*) Equity ratio *vs* firms' size, Italy 1996-2001. Corporate firms: Source Amadeus. *b*) Comparable results from simulations.

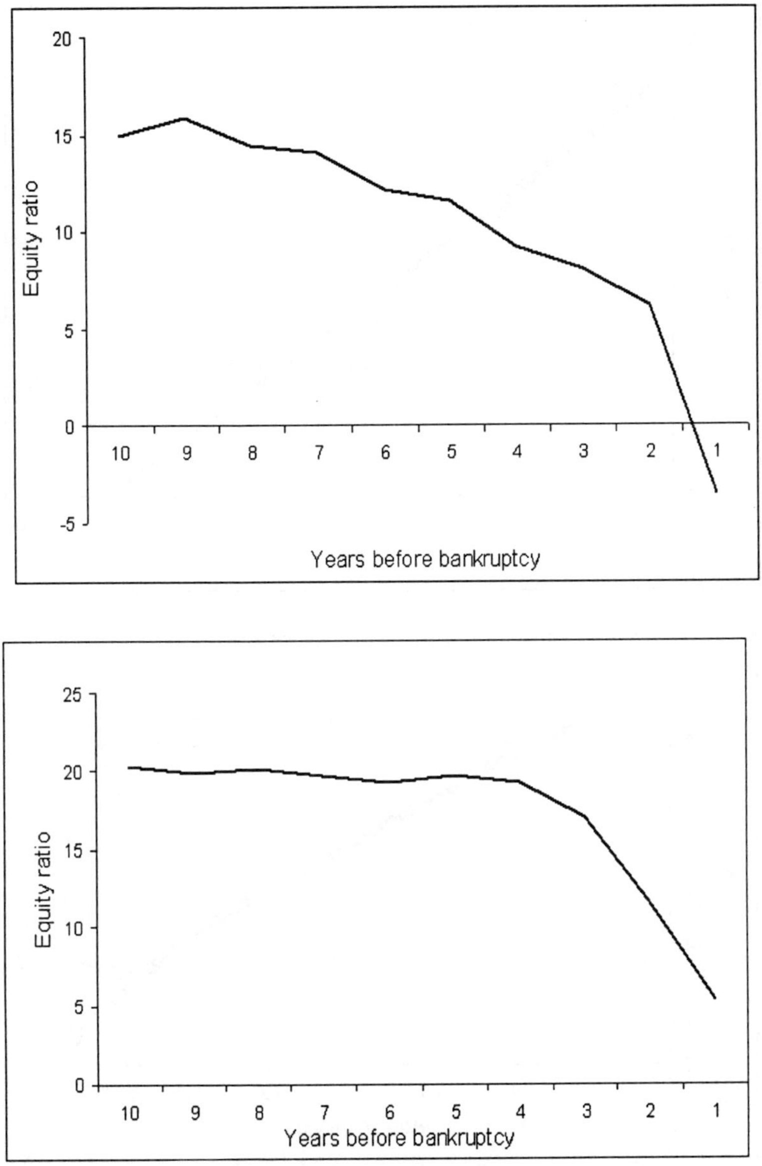

Figure 4. *a*) Equity ratio *n*years before bankruptcy. Italy 1996-2001. Corporate firms: Source Amadeus. *b*) Comparable results from simulations.

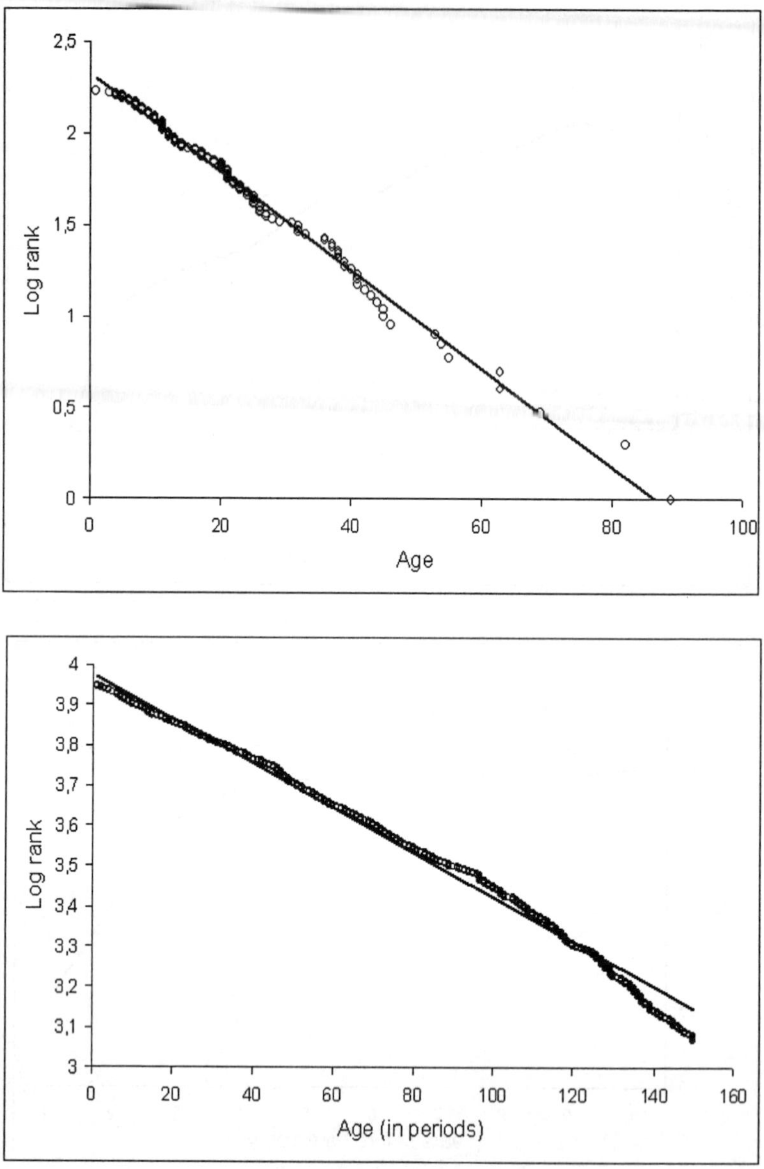

Figure 5. *a*) Exits by age. Italy 1992-2001. Corporate firms: Source Amadeus. *b*) Comparable results from simulations.

so that we are focusing on the right tail of the universe of bankrupt firms. Our empirical evidence for the right tail is therefore fully consistent with a left tail of the whole distribution (where younger firms are likely to be concentrated) characterized by an hazard function decreasing with age.

In the literature, five financial reasons have been put forward to explain bankruptcy [43]: asynchronicity of the cash-flow cycle, unbalanced current assets, excessive operating leverage, excessive financial leverage and unbalanced debt maturity. Only one is considered in the DG model, namely a negative equity ratio (i.e., excessive financial leverage), that is the one most likely to affect equally firms of all size and maturity. Thus, when compared to previous findings the probability to fail conditioned to age we report in figure 5 is likely to be biased towards older firms because of a small-sample bias (5*a*) and of the mechanism assumed to force firms to go out of business (5*b*), respectively. Besides signaling the DG model's ability in capturing what is going on in the right tail of the empirical distribution, one should stress that the lack of consistency between the evidence and simulation results for small firms remains a topic for further research.

The pivotal role of the equity ratio in linking industrial dynamics and business cycle fluctuations is further confirmed by its relationship with the profit rate. In fact, the DG model is capable of replicating quite well the available empirical evidence, according to which: (*i*) the rates of return on capital and equity ratio are positively correlated; (*ii*) a higher equity ratio is associated with a lower volatility of profits, and (*iii*) the distribution of the profit rate with respect to a is asymmetric. The empirical distribution of *bad debt*, that is the amount of unpaid loans due to bankruptcies extended by the banking sector, is characterized by a Pareto right tail [12], another feature mimicked by the model.

Moving on to *real* stylized facts, note that both the total output standard deviation and its autocorrelation are within the 5% confidence interval with respect to quarterly real data for the G7 group of countries. The distribution of firms' growth rates is approximated by an asymmetric tent-shaped curve (Laplace distribution). All the growth rates, sorted in bins depending on firm's dimension, collapse on the same curve. In agreement with the results reported in [30], the data obtained from simulations reveal a correspondence between the distribution of aggregate output and the one of firms' growth rates. Furthermore, expansions and recessions measured as trough-to-peak and peak-to-trough of the GDP growth rates, are distributed as a Weibull [15].

Simulations show that the model does a remarkably good job also in mimicking the empirical evidence on the real interest rate, albeit the model's standard deviation turns out to be some 10% higher than the actual one. In particular: (*i*) the rate of interest is *a*- or moderately *pro*-cyclical; (*ii*) there is no correlation between the rate of interest and debt; (*iii*) the ratio between firms' and banks' capital is approximately constant; and, (*iv*) the distribution of the amount of loans is power law.

It should be further noted that, once one rejects the *non-interacting-RA* methodological straightjacket, several non-traditional results emerge. Among them, probably the most interesting one is that the system becomes time-irreversible, so that economic policy is asymmetric. For instance, the main effect of a contractionary shift in monetary policy consists in deteriorating firms' financial conditions by rising their debt commitments: as some firms are forced to leave the market due to bankruptcy, it would be almost impossible that a decrease of the interest rate would restore exactly the previous situation (i.e., that new entrants equal in number and size the firms gone out of business). As far as the properties of the FSD's lower moments are concerned, we point out that: (*i*) the variance of the aggregate growth rate is lower than that of the individual firms [20], and (*ii*) there exists a *Taylor's rule* [51] according to which the mean and the variance of some firms' characteristics (here, capital, employment and added value) evolve linearly through time.

As figure 6 shows, the FSD measured by capital stock (but the same is true also for employment and added value) is characterized by persistent heterogeneity, and it is well approximated by a power law distribution. Given that the invariant distribution is fat tailed, small idiosyncratic shocks may generate aggregate large fluctuations or, in other terms, *distributions matter* [20; 12]. The FSD from the model shifts over the business cycle like the empirical one. During expansions, the FSD shifts towards north-east, while recessions are associated with movements in the opposite direction (i.e., shifts of the curve towards the origin). Moreover, during downturns the scaling exponent (as estimated by OLS in the log-log plane) decreases. As discussed in Section 3, this means that the concentration of firms tends to decrease during upturns, and to increase during contractions.

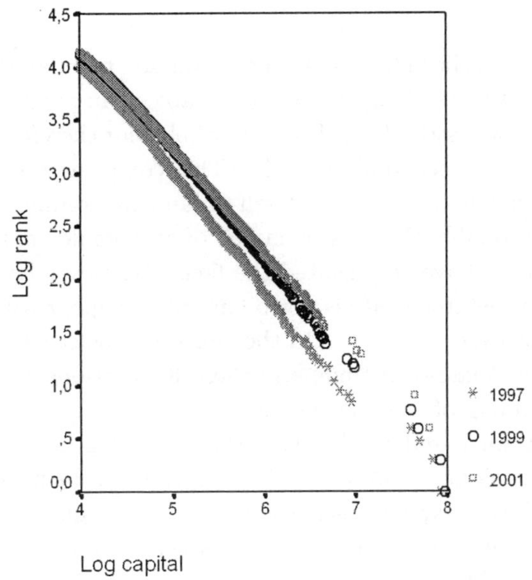

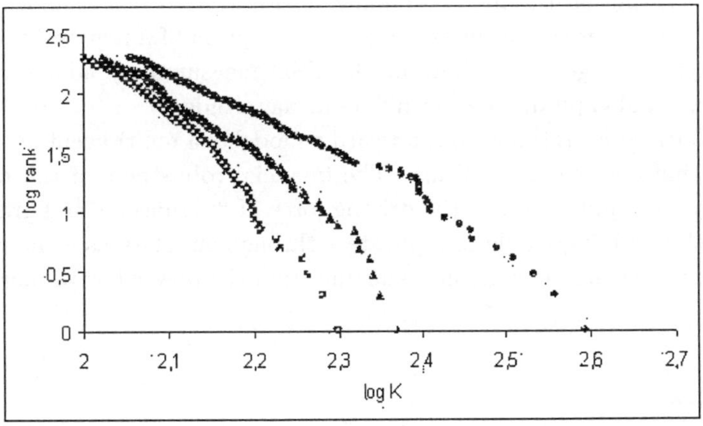

Figure 6. *a*) Firms' capital distribution shift in Italy 1997, 1999, 2001. Stock of capital of corporate firms. Source Amadeus. *b*) Comparable results from simulations. Data are presented for a representative cycle, with triangles and circles depicting the FSD during two consecutive expansions, and squares representing the FSD during the amid recession.

6. Conclusions

It is an established stylized fact that, in an economy populated by heterogeneous interacting agents, many economic variables – in particular firms'size – follow a power law distribution. Power law behavior therefore is an emerging property of many economic models. This comes as no surprise since power law behavior is a symptom of self-organizing complex systems and the economy is probably the most complex of all complex systems.

In this paper we have emphasized the fact that power law distribution is persistent – i.e. heterogeneity is not bound to disappear with the passing of time – but not time invariant. On the contrary, the scale and the shape of the FSD do fluctuate over time, and these fluctuations are the key to a proper understanding of the business cycle.

In particular we found in the data that on a log-log space both the intercept and the slope of the power law distribution of firms'size change over the cycle: during expansions (recessions) the straight line representing the distribution shifts up and becomes less steep (steeper).

Shifts of the FSD may reflect a change of the minimum efficient scale (MES) of existing firms. There are many theoretical reasons to expect the MES to change over the business cycle. The adoption of a new technology, for instance, may generate shifts of the FSD measured by added value, employment and capital, albeit of different magnitude.

Delli Gatti *et al.* [11] have put forward a model of a multi-agent network of interacting heterogeneous firms. The financial robustness of the firms, proxied by the equity ratio, is the driving force of fluctuations and growth. The model is strikingly able to replicate – through simulations – the properties of many economic variables, starting from the power law property of FSD.

References

(1) Amaral L., Buldyrev S., Havlin S., Leschhorn H., Maas P., Salinger M., Stanley E. and M. Stanley (1997), Scaling Behavior in Economics: I. Empirical Results for Company Growth, *Journal de Physique*, **7**:621-633.

(2) Amaral L., Buldyrev S., Havlin S., Salinger M. and E. Stanley (1998), Power Law Scaling for a System of Interacting Units with Complex Internal Structure, *Physical Review Letters*, **80**:1385-1388.

(3) Axtell R. (2001), Zipf Distribution of U.S. Firm Size, *Science*, **293**:1818-1820.

(4) Bak P. (1997), *How Nature Works.* Oxford: Oxford University Press.

(5) Blank A. and S. Solomon (2000), Power Laws in Cities Population, Financial Markets and Internet Size (Scaling in Systems with a Variable Number of Components), *Physica A*, **287**:279-288.

(6) Brakman S., Garretsen H., Van Marrewijk C. and M. van den Berg (1999), The Return of Zipf: Towards a Further Understanding of the Rank-Size Distribution, *Journal of Regional Science*, **39**:183-213.

(7) Brock (1999), Scaling in Economics: A Reader's Guide, *Industrial and Corporate Change*, **8**:409-446.

(8) Caves R. (1998), Industrial Organization and New Findings on the Turnover and Mobility of Firms, *Journal of Economic Literature*, **36**:1947-1982.

(9) Conti M., Meerson B. and P. Sasorov (1998), Breakdown of Scale Invariance in the Phase Ordering of Fractal Cluster, *Physical Review Letters*, **80**: 4693-4699.

(10) Cowling K. and M. Waterson (1976), Price-Cost Margins and Market Structure, *Economica*, **43**:267-274.

(11) Delli Gatti D., Di Guilmi C., Gaffeo E. and M. Gallegati (2003*a*), Bankruptcy as an Exit Mechanism in Models with a Variable Number of Components, arXiv: cond-mat/0401495v1.

(12) Delli Gatti D., Di Guilmi C., Gaffeo E., Gallegati M., Giulioni G. and A. Palestrini (2003*b*), A New Approach to Business Fluctuations: Heterogeneous Interacting Agents, Scaling Laws and Financial Fragility, *Journal of Economic Behavior and Organization*, forthcoming.

(13) Delli Gatti D. Gaffeo E., Gallegati M. and A. Russo (2004), Productivity Dynamics in an Agent-Based Macroeconomic Model, mimeo.

(14) De Vany A. (2001), *Hollywood Economics: How Extreme Uncertainty Shapes the Film Industry.* New York: Routledge.

(15) Di Guilmi C., Gaffeo E. and M. Gallegati (2003), Power Law Scaling in the World Income Distribution, *Economics Bulletin*, **15**:1-7.

(16) Durlauf S. (2003), Complexity and Empirical Economics, mimeo.

(17) Eng K., Feng X., Popovic D. and S. Washburn, (2002), Effects of a Parallel Magnetic Field on the Metal-Insulator Transition in a Diluite Two-Dimensional Electron System, arXiv:cond-mat/0112344v2.

(18) Fazzari S., Hubbard R. and B. Petersen (1988), Financing Constraints and Corporate Investment, *Brookings Papers on Economic*

Activity, **1**:141-196.

(19) Fujiwara Y. (2003), Zipf Law in Firms Bankruptcy, arXiv:cond-mat/0310062v1.

(20) Gabaix X. (1999), Zipf's Law for Cities, *Quarterly Journal of Economics*, **114**:739-766.

(21) Gabaix X. (2003), Power Laws and the Origins of Macroeconomic Fluctuations, mimeo.

(22) Gaffeo E., Gallegati M. and A. Palestrini (2003), On the Size Distribution of Firms: Additional Evidence from the G7 Countries, *Physica A*,**324**:117-123.

(23) Gaffeo E. and A. Scorcu (2004), Distribution Dynamics in the Book Publishing Industry, mimeo.

(24) Gibrat (1931), *Les Inegalites Economiques.* Paris: Librarie du Recueil Sirey.

(25) Hart P. and S. Prais (1956), The Analysis of Business Concentration: A Statistical Approach, *Journal of the Royal Statistical Society*, **119**:150-191.

(26) Joh Y., Orbach R., Wood G., Hammann J. and E.Vincent (1999), Extraction of Spin Glass Correlation Length, *Physical Review Letters.*

(27) Katz S. (1999), The Self-Similar Science System, *Research Policy*, **28**:501-517.

(28) Knudsen T. (2001), Zipf's Law for Cities and Beyond, *American Journal of Economics and Sociology*, **60**:123-146.

(29) Krugman P. (1996), *The Self-Organizing Economy.* Cambridge: Blackwell.

(30) Lee Y., Amaral L., Canning D., Meyer M. and E. Stanley (1998), Universal Features in the Growth Dynamics of Complex Organizations, *Physical Review Letters*, **81**:3275-3278.

(31) Lux T. (1996), The Stable Paretian Hypothesis and the Frequency of Large returns: An Examination of Major German Stocks, *Applied Financial Economics*, **6**:463-475.

(32) Malcai O., Biham O. and S. Solomon (1999), ,*Physics Review E*, **60**:1299-.

(33) Mandelbrot, B. (1997) Fractals and Scaling in Finance, Springer-Verlag, New York, 1997

(34) Mantegna R. and E. Stanley (2000), *An Introduction to Econophysics.* Cambridge: Cambridge University Press.

(35) Mansfield E. (1962), Entry, Gibrat's Law, Innovation; and the

Growth of firms, *American Economic Review*, **52**:1023-1051.

(36) Marsili M. and Y.-C. Zhang (1998), Interacting Individuals Leading to Zipf's Law, *Physical Review Letters*, **80**:2741-2744.

(37) Mizuno T., Katori M., Takayasu H. and M. Takayasu (2003), Statistical Laws in the Income of Japanese companies, arXiv:cond-mat/0308365.

(38) Muller U., Dacorogna M., Olsen R., Pictet O., Schwarz M. and C. Morgenegg (1995), Statistical Study of Foreign Echange Rates, Empirical Evidence of a Price Change Scaling Law and Intraday Analysis, *Journal of Banking and Finance*, **14**:1189-1208.

(39) Naldi M. (2003), Concentration Indices and Zipf's Law, *Economics Letters*, **78**:329-334.

(40) Nirei M. and W. Souma (2003), Income Distribution Dynamics: A Classical Perspective, mimeo.

(41) Nørrelikke S. and P. Bak (2002), Self-Organized Criticality in a Transient System, *Physics Review*, **68**:.

(42) Okuyama K., Takayasu M. and H. Takayasu (1999), Zipf's Law in Income Distribution of Companies, *Phyisica A*, **269**:125-131.

(43) Platt H. (1985), *Why Companies Fails.* Lexington, D.C. Heath and Company.

(44) Quah D. (1993), Empirical Cross-Section Dynamics in Economic Growth, *European Economic Review*, **37**:426-434.

(45) Ramsden J. And G. Kiss-Haypal (2000), Company Size Distribution in Different Countries, *Physica A*, **277**:220-227.

(46) Simon H. (1955), On a Class of Skew Distribution Function, *Biometrika*, **27**:425-440.

(47) Simon H. and C. Bonini (1958), The Size Distribution of Business Firms, *American Economic Review*, **48**:607-617.

(48) Scherer F., Harho D. and J. Kukies (2000), Uncertainty and the Size Distribution of Rewards from Innovation, *Journal of Evolutionary Economics*, **10**:175-200

(49) Stanley E., Amaral L., Gopikrishnan P. and V. Plerou (2000), Scale Invariance and Universality of Economic Fluctuations, *Physica A*, **283**:31-41.

(50) Sutton J. (1998), *Technology and Market Structure.* Cambridge: MIT Press.

(51) Taylor L. (1961), Aggregation, Variance and the Mean, *Nature*, **189**:732-735.

EFFECTS OF THE INTERACTION OF HETEROGENEOUS RATIONALITIES ON THE INNOVATION OUTPUT OF FIRMS — A MULTI-AGENT-SYSTEM APPROACH

ALEXANDER KAUFMANN
Systems Research Technology-Economy-Environment
ARC Seibersdorf research GmbH, A-2444 Seibersdorf, Austria
Phone: +43(0)50550/3889; Fax: +43(0)50550/3888
E-Mail: alexander.kaufmann@arcs.ac.at

Most innovations are the result of contributions from many agents. Not only the firm which eventually commercializes the innovation but also suppliers, service firms, customers, banks, venture capital providers, universities, contract research organizations or technology centres may have participated in this process. Often the collaborating organizations belong to different societal systems like business, science or politics. As a consequence, they face the problem how to deal with the different rationalities of these systems. They have to establish rules and routines how to integrate them in order to avoid conflicts and to benefit from the diversity of rationalities. As far as innovation is concerned there is a lot of evidence that the interaction between different rationalities, especially between the business and science systems, stimulates more advanced or so-called "radical" innovations. Far more ambiguous is the problem of organizing such multi-system based innovation projects. Two basic types of multi-system innovation processes can be distinguished: on the one hand, hybrid organizations which integrate two or more rationalities within the organization and, on the other hand, co-operations and market transactions between single-system based organizations. The aim of the paper is to present the concept of a simple multi-agent system model that simulates the effects of the interaction between the rationalities of the business and science systems on the innovation process of firms and that enables us to compare the two modes of organization — the internal mode of multi-system based hybrid organizations versus the external mode of co-operation or market transaction between single-system based organizations.

1. Introduction

In almost all cases firms are not innovating in an idiosyncratic and isolated way. There is hardly any innovation project without contributions from organizations external to the innovating firm like suppliers, service firms, customers, banks and venture capital providers, universities, contract research organizations or technology centres. Such innovation networks consist of two basic types of social entities: societal systems and organizational systems. Societal systems like business, science or politics are characterized by specific rationalities which comprise values, meaning, and communication modes that are shared throughout the community of individuals involved in these systems and that are typical only for this system. Societal systems are evolving by ways of self-organization. Organizational systems, on the other hand, like firms, universities, public administration or technology centres are characterized by specific rules and routines, stated objectives, resources and formal membership. From this theoretical point of view, an innovation network consists of a multitude of several societal systems and their interrelations. Organizational systems are usually either interacting with organizations belonging to other societal systems or are themselves involved in more than one societal system. As a consequence, they face the problem how to deal with the different rationalities of these systems. They have to establish rules and routines how to integrate them in order to avoid conflicts and to benefit from the diversity of rationalities. As far as innovation is concerned there is a lot of evidence that the interaction between different rationalities, especially between the business and science systems, stimulates more advanced or so-called "radical" innovations. Far more ambiguous is the problem of organizing such multi-system based innovation projects. Two basic types of multi-system innovation processes can be distinguished: on the one hand, hybrid organizations which integrate two or more rationalities within the organization and, on the other hand, co-operations and market transactions between single-system based organizations. The aim of the paper is to present the concept of a simple multi-agent system model that simulates the effects of the interaction between the rationalities of the business and science systems on the innovation process of firms and that enables us to compare the two modes of organization — the internal mode of multi-system based hybrid organizations versus the external mode of co-operation or market transaction between single-system based organizations.

2. On the Correlation between Innovativeness and Border-crossing between Societal Systems

In the course of a large European research project, investigating and comparing innovation systems at the regional level (see acknowledgement), we became interested in the more basic question concerning the nature of innovation systems. What type of system is this? What are the constituting elements? Are there subsystems? This has been discussed in more detail in Kaufmann, Tödtling[1]. In this paper I am going to highlight only the most important arguments and results.

In modern social systems theory, the concept of "self-referential" systems has become very influential. In short, it means that the behaviour of a social system is independent in interpreting external influences, organizing its internal structure, and behaving in the context of its environment. External stimuli cannot determine the system's responses. Insofar, the system is closed. Nevertheless, it interacts in numerous ways with its environment, using as well as providing resources and information. In this respect, the system is open. As a consequence, the environment restricts the set of alternatives of any system. Ultimately it may even destroy the system, but it can never control its behaviour.

In social systems theory there is an increasing interest in systems concepts based on self-reference and self-organization. Social systems are seen now as a way to reduce the complexity of the world human beings are confronted with. The reality an individual has to cope with is less complex within a system, because it can and must use the common set of interpretations concerning the part of reality which is relevant for the system. The interpretations are valid for all members of the system which, on the one hand, reduces ambiguity, but on the other hand, restricts alternative interpretations of the system-specific reality.[2]

It was primarily Luhmann[3] who tried to understand how social systems separate themseleves from the environment, how they maintain a boundary between their entity and the surrounding world. He argued that the identity of a certain social system is given by a common standard of communication both to interpret internal processes and external relations to the environment. This makes a social system distinct from its environment and other systems. Accordingly, any social system is distinguishable by different modes of interpretation, decision rules, objectives, and specific communicative standards (channels, methods, technical means, and so on). The common understanding of activities within the system, of influences on the system, and of behaviour against the environment separates the system from the environment. Communication is reproduced through the continuous process of sending or disseminating and processing relevant information. The central mechanism to separate system-relevant from irrelevant information is a system-specific medium (the most often quoted example is money for the business system). It contains only the system-specific information and it is coded in an unambiguous way so that it is understood by all individuals involved in the system. This enables a continuous chain of communication relations and, as a consequence, the continuous reproduction of the social system.

It is important not to confuse systems and organizations. Here the term system is applied to entities based on common standards of communication and information, a common set of interpretations, and a shared view of values and meaning (*Sinn*). An organization, on the contrary, refers to entities which are based on membership, specific tasks of the members (participants), certain methods to perform these tasks, explicit and impersonal rules, power to enforce the rules, and a formalized structure.[4] From this clarification follows that any individual is involved in several systemic contexts performing as many roles. As far as organizations are concerned, relations to more than one system are not necessary, but, actually, organizations linked to several systems are more the rule than the exception.

From the perspective of the self-referential model of social systems there is not one coherent innovation system but, on the contrary, several social systems are involved in the process of innovation. A single innovation system would have to have common sets of interpretations, the same decision rules, shared objectives, and identical ways of communication. Due to the fact, however, that there are very diverse actors taking part in the process of innovation — clearly reaching beyond industry — such a level of concurrence does not exist. There are important non-business and non-profit elements in many innovation projects, in particular science and politics. The business system is profit-oriented and communicates via the price mechanism[5]; the science system aims at the production of knowledge and communicates via publications. It is the exchange of formerly unrelated information belonging to a different systemic context that reinforces innovativeness. Crossing the border between different systems stimulates changes in the systems in general. In the particular case of industry–science interaction this might, among other things, result in product innovation.

It is very important to distinguish the relation between systems from the relation between or within organizations. The science and the business systems are based on different modes of interpretation, decision rules, objectives, and ways of communication. There is no overlapping of the systems, but there is interaction between the systems, either within one organization or between several organizations. This difference is rarely considered when arguing for the emergence of a new form of science, the so-called "entrepreneurial science" as a new type of science–industry interaction.[6] The concepts *system* and *organization* are confused, neglecting the fact that it is the clear distinction between the two ideal types of organizations *university* and *firm* which gets more and more blurred through profit-oriented contract research institutions, but not the distinction between the systems' operating principles.

From the perspective of self-referential systems theory the major impulse from the science system to initiate innovation in the business system is either due to the provision of new information, not accessible or available within industry, or the collaborative generation of new knowledge. Co-operation can also trigger the change of traditional perspectives, decision rules, and objectives of firms without actually adding knowledge. Inter-system communication can raise interest to discuss the objectives per se or their practical usefulness, i.e., an appropriate relation between objectives and results. Changes can be stimulated also in technical and organizational respects. Of course, all this is not restricted to one participating organization — the firm — only. It is obvious that interaction between science and industry also stimulates change in universities and research organizations. In any case, the stimulating effect is eventually a consequence of adding novelty and diversity to a specific organization's rules, modes of behaviour, and technologies.

The process of systems mutually influencing each other but maintaining their separate entity throughout this process can be called "border-crossing". Of course, interaction between different systems can also become routinized. In the context of innovation this might reduce the potential to stimulate change. This is a likely consequence of continuous relations between the same persons over a long period of time, because the novelty of exchanged information usually decreases once partners become locked into well-established routine interactions.[7] It follows that interaction between science and industry per se is not a guarantee for increased innovativeness. Routine relations like testing performed by research laboratories on behalf of firms do not add much to the firms' capacity to innovate.[8] Also in the case of inter-system innovation partnerships the organizational relations have to be kept flexible through weak ties to a broad range of innovation partners.[9]

That the interaction between the worlds of science and business matters with regard to innovative performance was also confirmed by empirical evidence deduced from data collected in the REGIS-research project (see acknowledgement). Using survey data for Wales (UK), Wallonia (Belgium), Baden-Württemberg (Germany), Styria (Austria), the Basque country (Spain), Aveiro (Portugal), and Tampere (Finland), the hypothesis was tested that firms which involve partners from science in their innovation processes are more likely to be able to realize more advanced innovations (i.e. develop products that are new to the market) instead of innovations which are only new for the firm. Accordingly, partners from the business system were expected to be more relevant for incremental innovation.

Table 1. The importance of partners and firm characteristics on innovativeness.

Binary Logit model	*Products new to the market versus products new for the firm only*		
	β	Probability	Significance
Innovation partners:			
Customer firms	-0.262	0.247	
Supplier firms	0.908	0.014	**
Consultants	1.225	0.016	**
Technology transfer organizations	-0.541	0.230	
Contract research organizations	-0.483	0.222	
Universities	0.994	0.047	**
Characteristics of the firms:			
Employment	0.000	0.155	
Region:			
Austria (Styria)	-1.215	0.036	**
Belgium (Wallonia)	-0.891	0.054	*
Finland (Tampere)	-2.040	0.000	***
Spain (Basque country)	-2.839	0.000	***
UK (Wales)	-0.908	0.052	*
Portugal (Aveiro)	-1.716	0.009	***
Industry:			
Food, beverages	-0.260	0.340	
Textiles, clothes, leather	-0.791	0.131	
Wood (products), paper	0.579	0.191	
Chemicals, rubber, plastic	-0.277	0.285	
Metal, metal products	0.122	0.399	
Machinery	-0.414	0.203	
Other industries	-0.265	0.344	
Transport equipment	-0.167	0.389	
Producer services	0.018	0.486	
Model significance:			
Number of cases		318	
r^2		0.164	
r^2 corr.		0.060	

Source: REGIS-survey (see acknowledgement).

As far as the aim of this paper is concerned, the following conclusions are important (see the grey lines in table 1): Universities stimulate or enable firms to introduce more advanced innovations whereas contract research organizations have no positive effects in this respect. "Pure" science seems to be more effective in stimulating advanced innovations than applied research focusing on commercialization. Institutions particularly designed to act as intermediaries between science and industry like technology transfer organizations do not seem to be effective in stimulating advanced innovations.

It can be seen that science-business interaction matters as far as more advanced innovations are concerned, but it is an open question how to organize this interaction effectively. Are market transactions sufficient or are co-operations between organizations involved in both the science and business systems better? Or should both systems' rationalities be integrated within one (so-called "hybrid") organization?

The open question of the adequate organization of science–business interaction was the motivation for developing the model outlined in this paper.

3. A General Multi-system Agent-based Microeconomic Model of Socio-economic Evolution

3.1. *Agent*

Any agent, individual person as well as organization, is defined by a set of objectives (O), routines (E, V, U), resources (R) and his address (L): {O, {E, V, U}, R, L}.

3.1.1. *Objective*

Objectives (O) consist of a stated goal (g) and either discrete or continuous target values (v). There are societal and organizational goals.

- Societal goals are shared within societal systems and differ between them. The target values, however, are not identical within societal systems.
- Organizational goals are stated by organizations. They are only valid within these organizations which means that they matter for those persons who are members of the respective organization.

3.1.2. *Routine*

Routines, in general, take the form of if-then rules consisting of the function (f) and parameters or weights (p). There are three basic types of routines which are necessary for any agent with learning capability (the only type of agent considered in this model). This set of routines comprises routines for expectation, evaluation and update. If all types of routines are present, the set is complete, in case of incomplete sets, routines for evaluation or update are missing.

- Expectation routines (E) consist of rules how the environment (or specific parts of it) will behave or change in a certain period of time and how own actions affect the environment.
- Evaluation routines (V) are rules how to compare realized effects with stated targets.
- Update routines (U) are rules where to search for new routines and how to update the old routines whose performance were deemed unsatisfactory.

3.1.3. *Resource*

Resources (R) comprise production factors other than manpower (human capital embodied in individual routines), i.e. financial and physical capital (buildings, machinery, materials), technology (disembodied knowledge) and other immaterial capital (e.g. copyrights).

3.1.4. *Address*

The address of an agent (L) contains his name and may contain, in case the spatial dimension of the network matters, his physical location.

3.2. *Action*

Any action (A) of an agent is the result of the application of a certain routine on specific resources available to the agent at this time. Corresponding to the three types of rules, there are three types of actions: A = E(R), A = V(O,R), A = U(E,V,U). Actions can be external (global as well as directed) and reflexive. External actions aim at the environment (including other individuals and/or organizations). The action can either be global: $A(x_1 \rightarrow Env)$. Or it can be directed towards certain other agents: $(Ax_1 \rightarrow x_2)$. Reflexive actions like updating rules refer to the agent himself: $A(x_1 \rightarrow x_1)$.

3.3. *Organization*

An organization is the structured set of inter-individual relations governed by organization-specific routines. Individuals and suborganizations are restricted regarding their set of possible actions (applicable routines) as far as they are members of the organization. On the one hand, only a fraction of their resources can be employed in the organization's context; on the other hand, resources beyond a member but within the stock of the organization may be made accessible by certain organizational routines. Organizations need internal as well as external routines:

- Internal routines govern specification (functions, restricted set of actions) and duration (one-time, limited, unlimited period) of relations between members of the organization.
- External routines govern relations with the organization's environment.

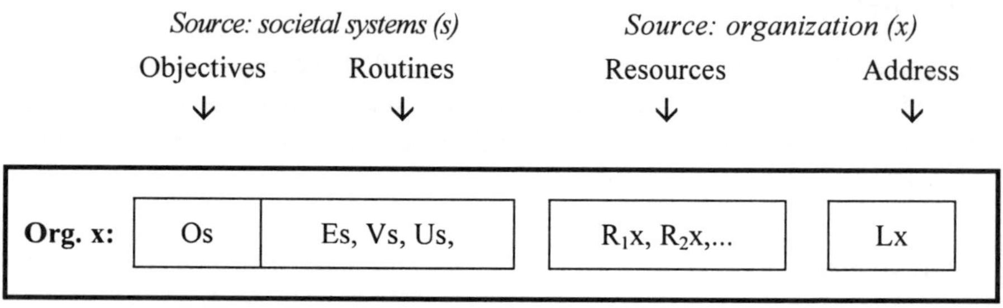

Figure 1. Formal description of an organization.

Thus an agent x is defined by the following set of variables:

$$\{Os, \{Es, Vs, Us\}, \{ R_1x, R_2x, \ldots\}, Lx\}$$

The new organization-specific routines can either belong to one of the societal systems of its members or belong to another system or even found a new system. The latter case is not considered in the present model.

3.4. *Societal Systems: The Global Pool of Routines*

Each routine of an individual or an organization is "stored" in respective societal systems. Any routine belongs to a specific societal objective and is stored in the corresponding system. If they belong to the same objective, both routines used by individuals and organizations, are added to the specific system's pool of routines.

Each routine is represented regarding the function as well as the parameters. Routines are represented according to their frequency, i.e. the number of agents (organizations) applying these routines. As a consequence, the more agents represent a certain routine, the higher is the probability that this kind of routine will be chosen by organizations looking for a better alternative.

If an agent looks for new routines because the old ones have been found inadequate, he does not necessarily choose only according to frequency (the more often a certain routine is represented, the more likely it will be adopted), but possibly also to proximity (the smaller the difference between old and new routine, the more likely it will be adopted) or other self-formulated rules.

3.5. *Evolution*

Evolution in a socio-economic context means the emergence of new and the change of existing organizations which is equivalent to the change of an organization's set of routines. As a consequence, the basic elements of evolution are routines, the entities of evolution are organizations. Two major evolutionary processes can be discerned:

- Change of routines in an organization which maintains its entity.
- Emergence of new and death of old organizations.

3.5.1. *Change of routines*

There are two possible causes why routines are changed:

- If the evaluation of a certain routine (more precisely, the executed action resulting from the application of this routine) is deemed unsatisfactory, the update rule is invoked and leads to a change in routine parameters or the search of new routines.

- In the process of setting up a new organization, new routines might becomme necessary (see 3.5.2.).

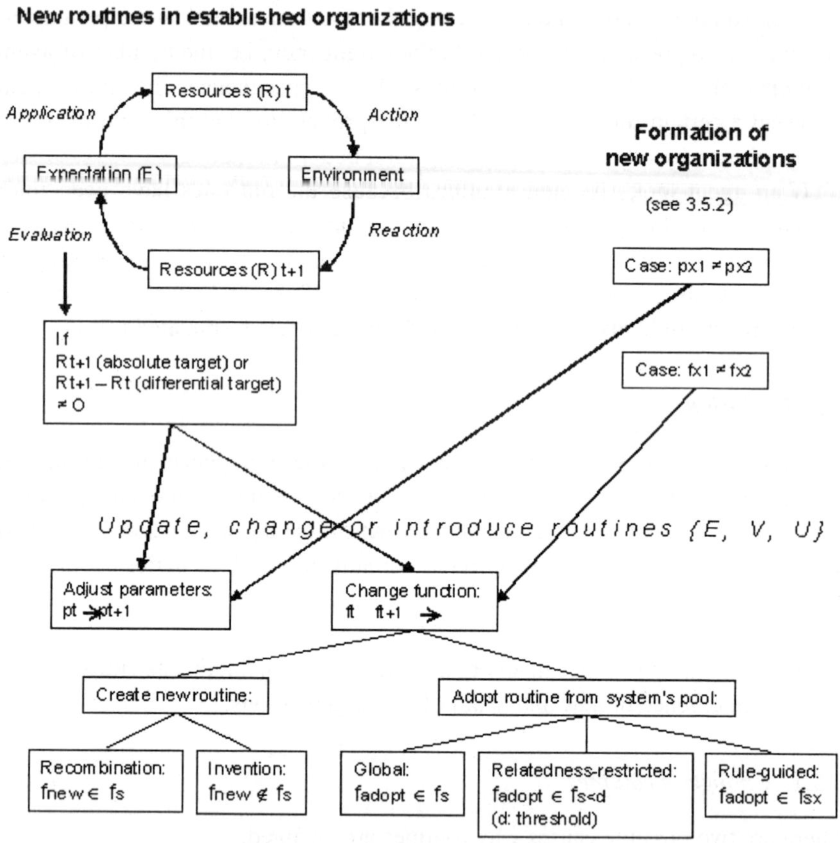

Figure 2. Adjustment, change and introduction of routines.

In both cases routines may be adopted or created:

- In the case of adoption, the pool of routines sharing the same objectives (i.e. belonging to the same societal system) is scanned and from this pool a new one is adopted, either globally by chance, restricted by proximity or according to a special condition of the update rule.
- New routines may be created either by recombining parts of existing routines or from scratch (i.e. unrelated to any existing routine). The latter case cannot be modelled (beyond random processes) and have to be given exogenously.

Concerning the societal acceptability of newly created routines, the minimum condition is that objectives remain the same (the evolution of societal objectives is beyond the described model). Further restrictions are possible, e.g. thresholds regarding to what degree of novelty (or degree of unrelatedness) the proposed new routine will be accepted within the societal system.

3.5.2. *Development of organizations*

Organizations are founded if individual persons or organizations expect to achieve a goal better (or only) in case they join with other agents forming a new (higher-level) organization. If this expectation is shared by other agents, the new organization will be established. For that routines have to be integrated (excluding ineligible individual routines, aligning useful individual routines) and, finally, the organization-specific set of routines has to be established. As a consequence of this final step, the original organizations dissolve. This concerns the organizational entity, but not the systemic routines. The latter ones evolve in an independent way, influenced by but not tied to the development of certain organizations.

Situation at t_0: Two organizations, each involved in one societal system only:

x_1:{Os_1,{Es_1,Vs_1,Us_1},{R_1x_1, R_2x_1},Lx_1}	x_2:{Os_2,{Es_2,Vs_2,Us_2},{R_1x_2, R_2x_2},Lx_2}

⇒ *Both organizations expect better goal achievment in case they join than in case they stay independent:*

Ex_1: $O(x_1 + x_2) > O(x_1)$	Ex_2: $O(x_2 + x_1) > O(x_2)$

⇒ *The additional benefit from joining can be due to:*

1 Pooling resources: ($Rx_1 + Rx_2$)	1.1 Market transaction:	Unilateral relation (i.e. the partners exchange different types of contributions (e.g. money against goods), one-time relation).
	1.2 Co-operation:	Bilateral relation (i.e. the partners exchange the same type of contribution (e.g. knowledge), limited period of time).
2 Integrating routines: ({E,V,U}x_1 + {E,V,U}x_2)	Hybrid organization:	New organization, unlimited period of time.

⇒ *In case of integrating routines (alternative 2), each partner's routines have to be matched in order to establish a new organization:*

"Merger matrix"		x1 E	x1 V	x1 U
x2	E			
	V			
	U			

If for a routine	*then*
$(f,p)x_1 = (f,p)x_2$	reduce routines
$fx_1 = fx_2$, $px_1 \neq px_2$	align parameters
$fx_1 \neq fx_2$	find new routine

⇒ *Establishment of a new organization:*

x_3:{Os^*,{Es^*,Vs^*,Us^*},{R_1x_1, R_1x_2, R_2x_1, R_2x_2},Lx_3}

The new organization can, but need not, be characterized by a new objective:

1 Single-rationality fusion:	$Os_1 + Os_1 \rightarrow Os_1$	(impossible in this example)
2 Multi-rationality take-over:	$Os_1 + Os_2 \rightarrow Os_1$	(possible)
3 Emergence of a new rationality:	$Os_1 + Os_2 \rightarrow Os_3$	(possible)

⇒ *Development or emergence of new routines and feeding back new routines to societal systems: see chart 2.*

Chart 3. The process of establishing a new organization.

4. The Innovation Model

4.1. *Innovation*

Product and technological (or process) innovations are both results of and driving factors in socio-economic evolution, but they are neither the elements nor the entities. They are the results from actions based on the application of routines and they are, in turn, resources at the disposal of the innovating or another benefiting agent. Two levels of innovations are considered in the model:

- Incremental innovations: These are products which are new in the respective firm's product range but have to compete with similar products (fulfilling the same functions or providing the same services) offered by other firms.
- Radical innovations: These are products which are new to the market. There are no competing firms or products available at the time of the introduction. The innovative firm has a temporary monopoly.

4.2. *The Societal Systems*

Two societal systems are considered in the model: business and science. Other systems with potentially high influence on innovation like politics are not included in the model at this stage.

Objectives and routines are still extremely simplified in this first model. The set of objectives and, in particular, routines can and will become much more diversified as the model is going to be improved.

4.2.1. *Objectives*

In both societal systems considered in this model — business and science — there exists only a single objective (see table 2). This system-specific homogeneity concerns only the goal but not the target values (see 3.1.1.).

Table 2. Objectives of the societal systems business and science.

	Business system	*Science system*
Objective (O, g):	Achieve profit target v: Sales – (production costs + innovation costs) → v (sales = price * market share)	Production of new knowledge: Number of articles in science journals → v

In the current model there is no third category of objectives. This is not only due to the fact that at present only two societal systems are considered, but also that for the time being the emergence of a new societal system out of the sector of hybrid organizations is ruled out.

4.2.2. *Routines*

Table 3. Routines of the societal systems business and science.

	Business system	*Science system*
Expectation (E, f):	a) Market development: Models estimating future demand (e.g. linear, exponential, logistic, conditional) b) Likelihood of innovation's success: b1) Models assessing the expected return on isolated innovation activities (without science participation) b2) Models assessing the expected return on joint innovation activities with science: - by market transaction - by co-operation - by setting up a hybrid org.	Likelihood of research results being published in a science journal: 1) Models assessing the expected return on isolated research activities (without business participation) 2) Models assessing the expected return on joint innovation activities with business: - by market transaction - by co-operation - by setting up a hybrid org.
Evaluation (V, f):	Targeted profit (v) – realized profit, with or without minimum difference for applying U	Targeted number of articles (v) – realized number of articles, with or without minimum difference for applying U
Update (U, f):	E.g. if targeted > realized profit by less than x%, then reduce profit target to realized level; if targeted > realized profit by x% or more, then look for new E; if else, no change	E.g. if targeted > realized number of articles by less than x%, then reduce target value to realized level; if targeted > realized number by x% or more, then look for new E; if else, no change

4.3. *The Actors*

The model consists of two basic and one emergent types of organizational actors:

- Firm (x_B): This is a single-rationality organization, exclusively involved in the business societal system. A firm has only business objectives and routines.

- University department (x_S): This is the other single-rationality organization, exclusively involved in the science societal system. A university department has only science objectives and routines.
- Hybrid organization (x_H): This is an organization which integrates the business and science rationalities in its objectives and routines in order to benefit from the combination of both rationalities. Routines may be combined in order to be applicable both for business and science objectives or it can be specified under which conditions a certain routine of a certain system will be applied.

The population comprises the following categories of agents:

- innovative firms without involvement of science (radical, incremental),
- innovative firms with involvement of science (radical, incremental),
- university departments involved in business innovation,
- university departments without links to firms,
- innovative hybrid organizations (radical, incremental),
- non-innovative firms

The resources that are available to the three types of agents are:

- For firms: production capital, innovation knowledge
- For science organizations: research personnel, research knowledge
- For hybrid organizations: production capital, research personnel, innovation / research knowledge

4.4. *The Interrelation between Inter-system Collaboration and Innovativeness*

The model consists of three feedback loops:

- The business cycle: Radical innovations lead to a temporary monopoly (i.e. a market share of 100%), incremental innovations increase the market share. Both types of innovations require funds and cause costs. Firms which do not innovate lose market share compared with innovators but can produce cheaper because they do not have innovation costs.
- The science cycle: The higher the funds available for research and the broader the knowledge (positively correlated with the number of

science-business projects), the more articles in scientific journals can be produced.

- The interrelation between the business and science cycles: Business-science innovation projects are more likely radical than incremental. The probability of an radical innovation and innovation costs depend on the type of organization. Pure business innovation projects are more likely incremental than radical. On the other hand, science-business innovation projects lead to more funds which means more research personnel as well as new knowledge too which, in turn, increases the number of publications.

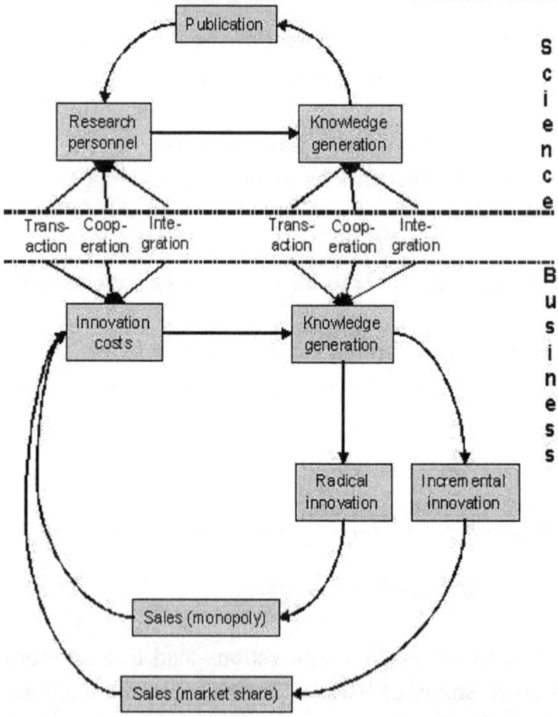

Figure 4. The feedback loops in the business-science innovation model.

4.5. *Types of Organizing Business–Science Interaction*

In the present model three basic types of organizing the collaboration between the worlds of business and science will be considered:

- Market transaction between single-rationality organizations: This type refers to a remunerated contribution (e.g., developing components, testing) of a certain organization (e.g., a manufacturing firm, a firm offering engineering services, a university department) to the innovation project of another organization based on an exact specification without further co-operation.
- Co-operation between single-rationality organizations: In this case two or more organizations establish a joint innovation project, sharing the same objective, pooling their resources, exchanging knowledge and producing new knowledge. The co-operation is limited for the time necessary to finish the project (or a specified range of projects).
- Hybrid organization integrating business and science rationalities: Here the business and science rationalities are integrated within a single institutional framework without temporal limitation.

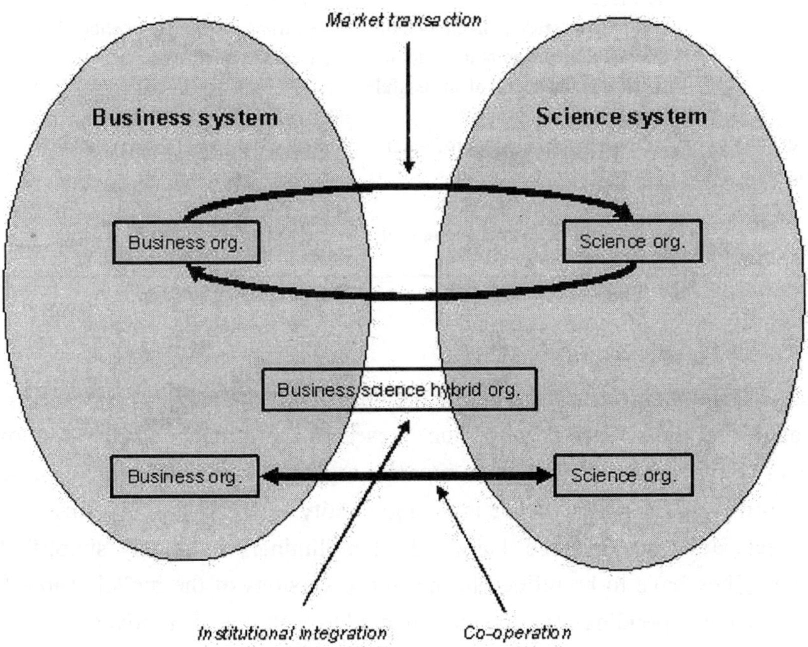

Figure 5. Three basic types of organizing business–science innovation collaboration.

These basic types of organizing the innovation-related interaction between the societal systems of business and science have two consequences:

- Firstly, they lead to different effects on the innovation process and the final outcome.
- Secondly, they cause costs of different magnitudes.

Table 4. Effects of different types of organizing joint innovation projects on business and science.

	Business	*Science*
Market transaction:	x_B: Receipt of a specific component or service for the innovation project without exchange or joint production of knowledge → Increase in likelihood of successful incremental innovation	x_S: Receipt of payments without gaining new knowledge (beyond the specification concerning the contribution required) → Funds for additional research personnel
Co-operation:	x_B: Exchange and joint production of knowledge → Strong increase in likelihood of successful incremental innovation, increase in likelihood of successful radical innovation	x_S: Exchange and joint production of knowledge → Strong increase in likelihood of successful publication
Hybrid organization:	x_H: Exchange and joint production of knowledge → Increase in likelihood of successful incremental and radical innovation	x_H: Exchange and joint production of knowledge → Increase in likelihood of successful publication

x_B: firm, x_S: university department, x_H: hybrid organization

Table 4 presents some effects of the organizational alternatives on the firms' innovation and the science organizations' research performance. In the case of the first two types the effects concern separate organizational entities, in the case of the third type, the effects occur in a single entity — the hybrid organization. The effects described in table 4 are only a preliminary extremely simplified selection. They have to be refined in the future versions of the model. Table 5 shows, in a corresponding way, the costs related to the three alternatives.

Table 5. Costs of different types of organizing joint innovation projects for business and science.

	Business	*Science*
Market transaction:	x_B: Price of the component or service → Small increase in costs of innovation	x_S: None
Co-operation:	x_B: Costs of setting up and organizing the co-operation → Strong increase in costs of innovation	x_S: Costs of setting up and organizing the co-operation → Increase in costs of publication
Hybrid organization:	x_H: Costs of integrating both rationalities in one organization → Increase in costs of innovation	x_H: Costs of integrating both rationalities in one organization → Increase in costs of publication

x_B: firm, x_S: university department, x_H: hybrid organization

5. Outlook

The innovation model presented in this paper is still preliminary. A lot of work has to be done before a model will be available which is adequate to make for interesting simulation results. What are the next steps?

- Empirical work has to be conducted concerning the routines in business, science and hybrid organizations that are actually used as far as innovation and R&D is concerned.
- Important issues are not yet included in the model. This concerns in particular the most basic agent and evolutionary processes. In the present model all agents are organizations, there are no individual persons. This is not satisfactory in two respects: Firstly, with the present model it is not possible to simulate the emergence of primary organizations, set up by individual people. Secondly, the model lacks the crucial role of people who are actually linking societal and organizational systems. Regarding evolutionary processes, much richer models of recombination and creation of new routines are required than those available at the moment.
- The simulation program has to be developed. This will be done at ARC / Systems Research, probably in co-operation with the Dipartimento di Informatica, Sistemistica e Comunicazione, Universita di Milano-Bicocca. At this institute a software for simulating multi-agent systems — L*MASS[10] — has been developed which seems very appropriate for the requirements of the model presented above.

- Finally, objectives and routines actually used in the real world have to be formalized according to the model requirements.

Running the final simulation model should enable us to compare the advantages and disadvantages of the three alternative ways of organizing innovation activities involving both business and science societal systems. This should make it possible to arrive at conclusions about the rationale and the potential of hybrid organizations in joint business-science innovation processes.

Acknowledgement

"Regional Innovation Systems: Designing for the Future" (REGIS), a research project co-funded by the European Union DGXII Targeted Socio-Economic Research programme. Co-ordinator: Ph. Cooke (U.K.), partners from Austria, Belgium, Finland, Germany, Italy, the Netherlands, Portugal and Spain, 1996–1998.

References

1. A. Kaufmann and F. Tödtling, Science-industry interaction in the process of innovation: the importance of boundary-crossing between systems, *Research Policy* 30, 791–804 (2001).
2. H. Willke, Systemtheorie: eine Einführung in die Grundprobleme der Theorie sozialer Systeme. Fischer, Stuttgart (1993).
3. N. Luhmann, Soziale Systeme: Grundriß einer allgemeinen Theorie. Suhrkamp, Frankfurt am Main (1991).
4. G. Reinhold, S. Lamnek and H. Recker (Eds.), Soziologie-Lexikon. Oldenbourg, München (1992).
5. N. Luhmann, Die Wirtschaft der Gesellschaft. Suhrkamp, Frankfurt am Main (1996).
6. H. Etzkowitz, A. Webster, C. Gebhardt and B. R. Cantisano Terra, The future of the university and the university of the future: evolution of ivory tower to entrepreneurial paradigm, *Research policy* 29, 313–330 (2000).
7. G. Grabher (Ed.), The embedded firm: on the socioeconomics of industrial networks. Routledge, London (1993).

8. F. Meyer-Krahmer and U. Schmoch, Science-based technologies: university-industry interactions in four fields, *Research policy* 27, 835–851 (1998).
9. M. Granovetter, The strength of weak ties, *American Journal of Sociology* 78/6, 1360–1380 (1973).
10. S. Bandini, F. De Paoli, S. Manzoni and G. Pavesi, A Language for Situated Multi-Agents Systems, unpublished.

MODULAR PYRAMIDAL HIERARCHIES AND SOCIAL NORMS.
AN AGENT BASED MODEL

ARIANNA DAL FORNO
UGO MERLONE*
Department of Statistics and Applied Mathematics, University of Torino, piazza Arbarello 8, Torino, 10122, Italy

We provide a model of hierarchical organization where artificial agents with limited individual capacities allocate their efforts in two activities. Different incentives schemes are considered and individual diversity and social norms are approached.

1. Introduction

The Moral Hazard literature approaches multi-agent relationships in different ways. Among them, the *joint production models* provide interesting insights in terms of income distribution among the agents. Another relevant aspect has been the comparison between centralized and decentralized structures as far contracting goes. For example, the literature provides conditions under which the situation where all the contracts are proposed by the principal (centralized organization) is superior to a more decentralized one.

Following the joint production approach, we consider a modular model of hierarchical organization. Specifically, we consider pyramidal structures. This particular structure is spread wise and, consequently, both the economic (see Beckmann [2] for a formal analysis) and simulative literature (for instance see Glance and Huberman[4]) finds interest. For an analysis of the different approaches to pyramidal structures see Merlone [7].

In our model, the organization consists of heterogeneous agents interacting in supervised teams with a Cobb-Douglas production function. We provide a theoretical analysis of the agents interaction in the modular element of the organization. Furthermore, we study the impact of heterogeneity of agents, social norms and incentive schemes in the organization. While in each team there exist infinite solutions to the optimal effort allocation problem, the presence of a social norm allows the selection of one of them.

When considering this simple model of supervised team embedded in a multi-layer organization, the complex dynamics between the agents call for the

*Corresponding author: merlone@econ.unito.it

simulation approach. The Agent-Based simulation model we consider allows the extension of the results obtained in the theoretical analysis of the supervised team. First, using the simulation platform we develop, it is possible to consider complex dynamics where agents adapt their efforts to different incentive schemes and to the observable variables. Second, it is possible to study the overall performance of organization when considering different characteristics of the agents, namely managerial capacity, individual capacity, sensitivity to different social norms and rewards. Finally, different adaptive managerial behaviors are compared.

Our results shed light on some aspects of interaction between individuals in complex environment and economic performance, and give insights in terms of observation of the performance measures in the organization. Furthermore, we prove that, while, in general, rewards that are based only on observable efforts by supervisor may lead to the underperformance of the organization, under certain circumstances, this kind of rewards allows to an improvement in the performance when a social norm is considered.

2. The Model

We consider a hierarchical modular model of organization. Each module consists of a supervisor and two subordinates as shown in the Figure 1.

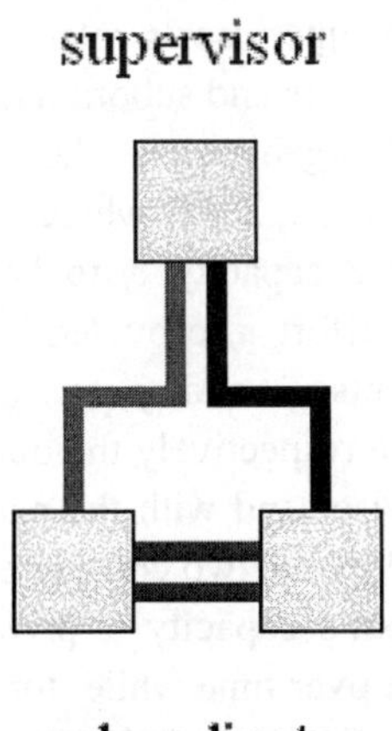

Figure 1 Organization module.

The organization we consider is modular i.e., each supervisor is paired with a same level one and both are in turn supervised by another manager. The organization may consist up to six layers of agents for a total of sixty-three agents. Obviously, the module is the most elementary organization, with only two layers. In Figure 2 we can see an example of a four layers organization where modules are well recognizable.

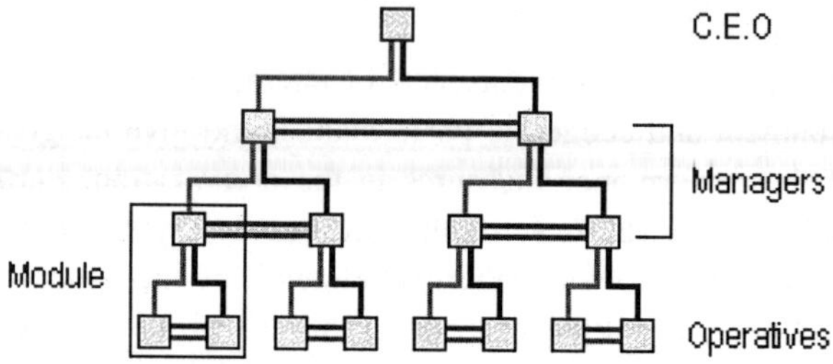

Figure 2. Four layers organization.

In the organization, bottom levels individuals are referred as operatives, middle level individuals are referred as managers and the top level individual is referred as the C.E.O.

As a consequence, in our hierarchy operatives play only the subordinate's role, the C.E.O. plays only the supervisor's role, while managers play both, i.e. they are at the same time supervisors and subordinates.

Let us consider a general organization where agents are identified by an index i belonging to the set $\{0, 1, \ldots, 2^N\text{-}2\}$ where $N \geq 1$ is the number of levels in the organization. Agent i has a capacity c_i to be allocated between effort l_i provided with its partner and effort u_i provided with its supervisor. The joint production function for agents i and j is $(u_i + u_j)^\alpha (l_i + l_j)^\beta$ where $0 < \alpha < 1$ and $0 < \beta < 1$ are respectively the output elasticity with respect to the joint effort with the supervisor and with the partner. Figure 3 illustrates the allocation of the efforts exerted by the two considered agents.

We assume that each agent's capacity is private information. For bottom level agents it remains constant over time while, for the others, it depends on the subordinates output. This is consistent to Quian [8] where the final output of the hierarchy is determined by a production function which is cumulative in the efforts of workers and managers at all levels. Furthermore, each agent can observe the level effort his/her partners provides but cannot observe the effort his/her partner provides with the boss. By converse, the supervisor can observe the joint output and the effort each agent provides with her. Finally, we assume that each agent knows the average efforts provided with partners and supervisors in his/her level.

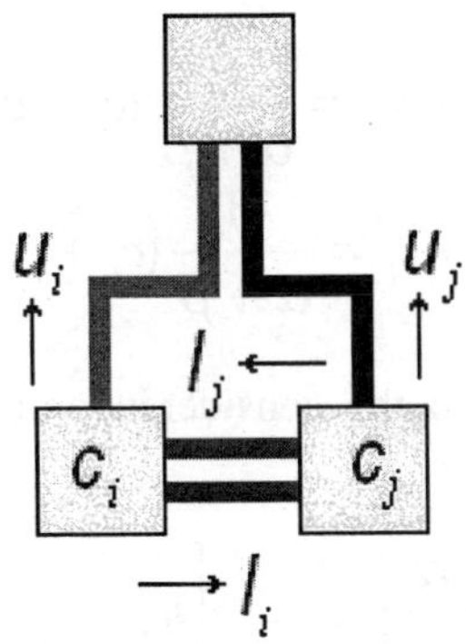

Figure 3. Effort allocations.

The agent's retribution is given by a fixed wage plus a linear incentive proportional to the joint output of the team and a linear incentive on the effort each agent exerts with the supervisor. The net output of the supervised team is the supervisor's capacity if she is up to work in some other supervised team, or the organization output if she is at the top of the organization.

Since, as we said above, a different place in the organization implies a different role, in the following we restrict our analysis to a single module, considering the agents' and the supervisor's problem.

3. The Agents' Problem

We start considering agents in the subordinate role case, i.e., agents that stay at the bottom of the hierarchy. The agents' problem is simple when retribution is proportional to the joint production and no social norm is considered. Assuming coordination and commitment between agents, for agent i the following problem must be solved:

$$\max_{u_i,u_j,l_i,l_j} \quad (u_i+u_j)^{\alpha}(l_i+l_j)^{\beta}$$
$$\text{sub} \quad u_i+l_i \le c_i \qquad (1)$$
$$u_j+l_j \le c_j.$$

By first order conditions it is easy to obtain

$$\begin{cases} u_i+u_j = \dfrac{\alpha}{\alpha+\beta}(c_i+c_j) \\ l_i+l_j = \dfrac{\beta}{\alpha+\beta}(c_i+c_j) \end{cases} \qquad (2)$$

There are infinite solutions to the considered problem, nevertheless, a rather natural effort allocation is

$$\begin{cases} u_i^f = \dfrac{\alpha}{\alpha+\beta}c_i \\ l_i^f = \dfrac{\beta}{\alpha+\beta}c_i \end{cases} \quad \begin{cases} u_j^f = \dfrac{\alpha}{\alpha+\beta}c_j \\ l_j^f = \dfrac{\beta}{\alpha+\beta}c_j. \end{cases} \qquad (3)$$

This allocation may be interpreted as a focal equilibrium in the sense of Schelling [11]. The solution sets are depicted as bold lines in Figure 4.

The process the agents use to reach this effort allocation is the following:

$$\begin{cases} (u_i^{t+1}, l_i^{t+1}) = BR(u_j^t, l_j^t) \\ (u_j^{t+1}, l_j^{t+1}) = BR(u_i^t, l_i^t) \end{cases} \qquad (4)$$

With any initial condition such that

$$(u_i^0, l_i^0) = \left(k_i \frac{\alpha}{\alpha+\beta}c_i, k_i \frac{\alpha}{\alpha+\beta}c_i\right) \quad (u_j^0, l_j^0) = \left(k_j \frac{\alpha}{\alpha+\beta}c_j, k_j \frac{\alpha}{\alpha+\beta}c_j\right) \quad k_i, k_j \in [0,1] \qquad (5)$$

the system converges to the natural effort allocation in one single step. From any other initial conditions the system oscillates in period-2 cycles. We are interested in conditions under which the system converges to the optimal allocation. To this purpose we consider different incentive schemes, social norms and individual diversity.

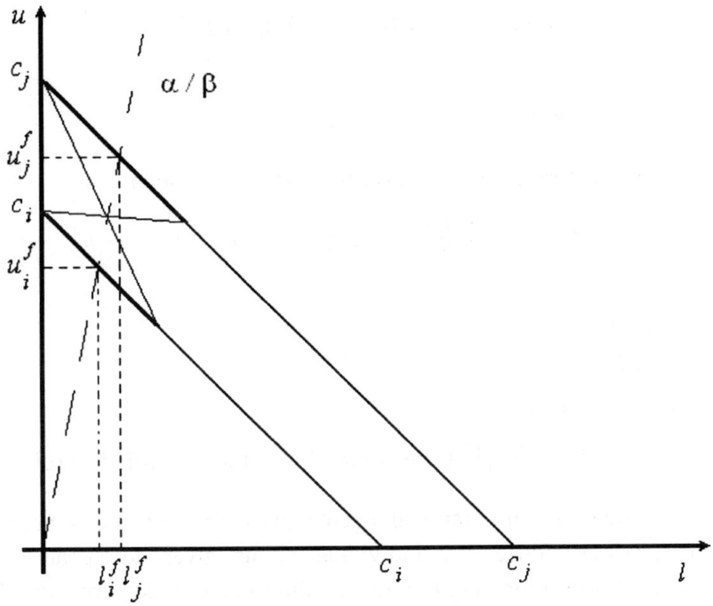

Figure 4. Solution set for the agents' problem.

4. The Supervisor's Problem

The supervisor's problem is to design a linear compensation scheme for the subordinates that induces them to use their capacity to maximize the team output. The supervisor can observe both the efforts u_i, u_j the subordinates exert with her and the team output i.e. $(u_i + u_j)^\alpha (l_i + l_j)^\beta$.

Subordinate i's compensation is $w_i = s + b_i u_i + b_t (u_i + u_j)^\alpha (l_i + l_j)^\beta$ (symmetrically for j) where s is a base salary sufficient to meet the participation constraint of the agent, while b_i, b_j are the incentives given to subordinates for their individual effort with supervisor and b_t is the incentive given them for team output. We assume that the supervisor declares the bonuses and that the subordinates decide their efforts in order to maximize their wage. Remark that when incentive effort is non-null the agent i's problem is modify as follows:

$$\begin{array}{ll} \max\limits_{u_i, l_i} & b_i u_i + (u_i + u_j)^{\alpha} (l_i + l_j)^{\beta} \\ \text{sub} & u_i + l_i \le c_i . \end{array} \tag{6}$$

Theoretically, the supervisor has to solve the following problem:

$$\max_{b_i, b_j, b_t} \quad (u_i^* + u_j^*)^{\alpha} (l_i^* + l_j^*)^{\beta} (1 - 2b_t) - b_i u_i^* - b_j u_j^*$$

$$\text{sub} \quad \begin{array}{l} 0 \le b_i \\ 0 \le b_j \\ 0 \le b_t \le 0.5 \\ (u_i^*, u_j^*) \text{ and } (l_i^*, l_j^*) \text{ are optimal for the modified problem} \end{array} \tag{7}$$

When considering fully rational agents insensitive to social norms, the solution is obvious. Since any individual bonus given to agents gives a suboptimal effort allocation, and null team output bonus makes for subordinates any allocation optimal, the optimal solution is

$$\begin{cases} b_i = b_j = 0 \\ b_t = \varepsilon > 0 \end{cases} \tag{8}$$

On the contrary, when considering social norms and/or bounded rationality agents the problem becomes complex.

5. Norms and Bounded Rationality

Literature devoted great attention to social norms and peer pressure. For example, Roy [10] documents quota restrictions in industrial workers, and documents peer-pressure in not exceeding some fixed levels of production.

In our approach, these important aspects are summarized by considering norms. In this case, individuals may have a disutility in effort allocation different from some common standards.

We assume that subordinates may be sensitive either to partner behavior or to the same level agents behavior. In particular, we consider two classes of behavior:

1. *partner's norm sensitive*: these agents have a disutility in being different from their partner level of behavior and their utility function (in the case of agent i) is

$$w_i = s + b_i u_i + b_t (u_i + u_j)^\alpha (l_i + l_j)^\beta - \delta_u (u_i - u_j)^2 - \delta_l (l_i - l_j)^2 \quad (9)$$

2. *same rank norm sensitive*: these agents have a disutility in being different from the agents at their level. In other words, we assume that each agent at level k knows both the average effort $\bar{l}$ exerted by his level agent with the partner and the average effort $\bar{u}$ exerted with their supervisor. The utility function for agent i is

$$w_i = s + b_i u_i + b_t (u_i + u_j)^\alpha (l_i + l_j)^\beta - \delta_{\bar{u}} (u_i - \bar{u})^2 - \delta_{\bar{l}} (l_i - \bar{l})^2 . \quad (10)$$

Nevertheless, norms may be interpreted in a different way. Laland [6] shows that for many animals adaptive behavior results in part from copying the behavior of others. "Do-what-others-do" is an effective heuristic in many situations. Animals probably do not copy other animals indiscriminately, although this has yet to be established empirically. Nonetheless, there is evidence that animals employ strategies such "Do-what-others-do" when they are uncertain, or, when there is no easier solution, they use "Do-what-the-majority-do", or "Do-what-the-successful-individuals-do".

In this sense we consider norms as a heuristics.

6. The Platform

We developed a software platform in order to study some interesting aspects of the model we presented and to perform simulations of pyramidal organizations with different incentive schemes and individual behaviors. Organizations with a number of levels from 2 to 6 may be studied and parameters may be interactively modified. For instance, it is possible to observe the organization performance under different values of α and β and under different linear incentives.

The organization performance is defined as the net capacity of the top manager. The theoretical performance of the organization and its inefficiencies may be monitored in real time considering the following variables:

1. *first best*: it is the total output when each agent optimally allocates his capacity and no bonus is paid;
2. *second best*: it is the output when each agent optimally allocates his capacity and all the bonuses are paid;
3. *third best*: it is the net total output with actual effort allocation and all the bonuses are paid.

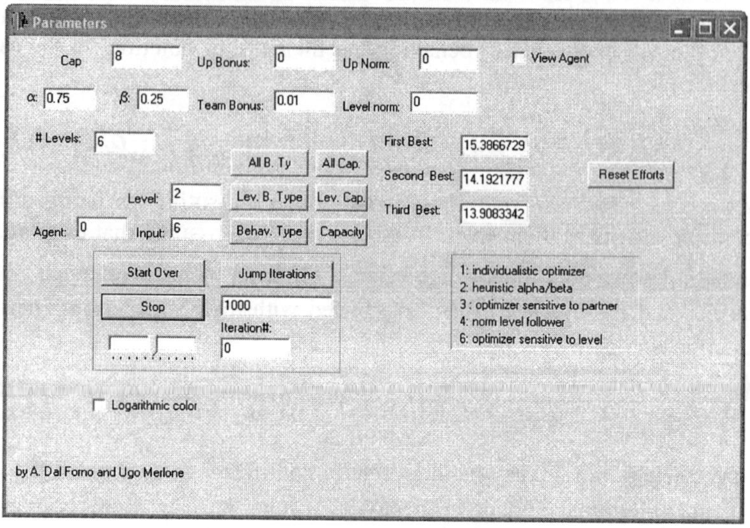

Figure 5. Platform control panel.

It is also possible to monitor single agent behavior using the output variables depicted in Figure 6. These variables may become especially interesting when considering a two levels organization. In this case the supervisor problem is to solve a two-level programming problem.

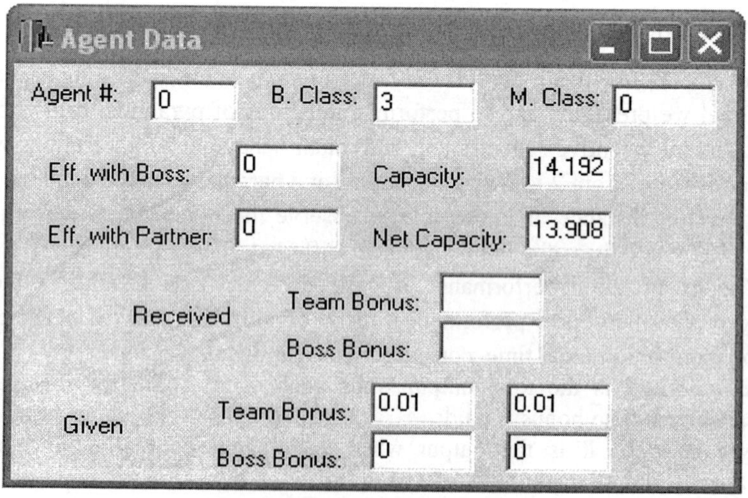

Figure 6. Agent monitoring panel.

The simulations allow the user to vary different levels of norms, both with same level colleagues and the supervisor. It is also possible to assign the agents to different classes of behavior.

7. Some Classes of Behavior

As it is evident, individual diversity plays a key role in real organization. As a consequence, besides the rational behavior, we are interested in considering also bounded rationality for the agents in our model of organization. Different behavioral classes of behavior have been implemented. At the moment, five kinds of behavior are available, but the platform is open to the introduction of further classes. In the following, we give a description of the available classes.

1. *Individualistic optimizer*: given last partner effort, this agent optimizes his effort without considering any social norm;
2. *Heuristic alpha/beta*: the relative proportion of effort between supervisor and partner is in the ratio alpha/beta;
3. *Optimizer sensitive to partner*: optimizes given last partner efforts;
4. *Norm level follower*: follows the norm of same level partner;
5. *Optimizer sensitive to level*: optimizes given last partner efforts but considers averages among society.

7.1. *Some Simulation Results*

The simulation we present here considers norms and individual incentives. In a two-levels organization (a module) assume the elasticities are:

$$\alpha = 0.75,\ \beta = 0.25.$$

While agent *1* has capacity 8, agent *2* has capacity 1. When the team bonus is 0.01, the ideal total output, since there are no incentives, is 5.128890, while the net performance is about 5.02631317. If operatives are sensitive to the social norm of effort provided with the supervisor ($\delta_u = 0.01$), the net total output decreases to 3.04729731, while, obviously, the ideal output of the organization is unaffected. Now, assume that the supervisor increases the team bonus up to 0.07. As expected, this incentive is needed to balance the social norm. In fact, this way, the total output increases to 3. 64866713. If the supervisor introduces in addition also an individual bonus of 0.06, then the performance has an extra improvement and it increases to 3.95921646. Therefore, individual bonus that is usually detrimental, in this case can help in improving the final net output of the organization.

8. Conclusion and Further Research

The model we provide allows the study of optimal incentive scheme and optimal allocation of individual capacity in a hierarchical structure.

The simulation platform allows the extension of the results provided by theoretical analysis to multilevel organizations. The agent-based model easily allows the extension of the analysis to heterogeneous agents. In particular, the platform can well be used to study the impact that different individuals have depending on their role in the organization. Simulations considering different kinds of incentive in order to improve non optimal situations can also be performed.

Another important aspect to consider is that, when the optimal incentive scheme is implemented, different capacity individuals may experience inequity (Adams [1]). We are currently studying the consequences of cognitive dissonance reduction strategies on the optimal effort allocation.

Further research is devoted in studying the impact of other factors in the organization, such as reneging and (mis)perception of behavior by colleagues.

References

1. J.S. Adams, "Injustice in social exchange". In: L. Berkowitz (Eds.), *Advances in experimental social psychology.* vol. 2. New York: Academic Press, (1965).
2. M.J. Beckmann, "Tinbergen lectures on organization theory", *Text and Monograph in Economics and Mathematical Systems.* Springer-Verlag (1988).
3. B.S. Frey and B.S. Oberholzer-Gee, "The cost of price incentives: an empirical analysis of motivation crowding-out". *The American Economic Review.* **87**(4), 764 (1997).
4. N.S. Glance and B.A. Huberman, "Social dilemmas and fluid organizations". In: *Computational Organization Theory.* Carley and Prietula Eds., Lawrence Erlbaum Associates, Publishers, 217 (1994).
5. D.M. Kreps, "Intrinsic motivation and extrinsic incentives". *The American Economic Review.* **87**(2), 359 (1997).
6. K.N. Laland, "Imitation, social learning, and preparedness as mechanisms of bounded rationality". In: Report of the 84th Dahlem Workshop on *Bounded Rationality: The Adaptive Toolbox*. Berlin, 233, (1999).
7. U. Merlone, "Organizations as Allocators of Human and Material Resources". Working paper. (2003).

8. Y. Qian, "Incentives and Loss of Control in an Optimal Hierarchy". *The Review of Economic Studies*. **61**(3), 527 (1994).
9. J.J. Rotemberg, "Human relations in the workplace". *The Journal of Political Economy*. **102**(4), 684 (1994).
10. D. Roy, , "Quota restriction and goldbricking in a machine shop",.*American Journal of Sociology*. **57**(5), 427 (1952).
11. T. Schelling, *The Strategy of Conflict*. Harvard University Press (1960).

Section 4

Industrial Clusters and Firm Interaction

GROWING SILICON VALLEY ON A LANDSCAPE: AN AGENT-BASED APPROACH TO HIGH-TECH INDUSTRIAL CLUSTERS*

JUNFU ZHANG

Public Policy Institute of California
500 Washington Street, Suite 800
San Francisco, CA 94111, USA
E-mail: zhang@ppic.org

We propose a Nelson-Winter model with an explicitly defined landscape to study the formation of high-tech industrial clusters such as those in Silicon Valley. The existing literature treats clusters as the result of location choices and focuses on how firms may benefit from locating in a cluster. We deviate from this tradition by emphasizing that high-tech industrial clusters are characterized by concentrated entrepreneurship. We argue that the emergence of clusters can be explained by the social effect through which the appearance of one or a few entrepreneurs inspire many followers locally. Agent-based simulation is employed to show the dynamics of the model. Data from the simulation and the properties of the model are discussed in light of empirical regularities. Variations of the model are simulated to study policies that are favorable to the high-tech economy.

Do not regard [Silicon Valley] as some sort of economic machine, where various raw materials are poured in at one end and firms such as Apple and Cisco roll out at the other, but rather as a form of ecosystem that breeds companies: without the right soil and the right climate, nothing will grow.

— The Economist, March 29, 1997

*This article appeared in the Journal of Evolutionary Economics, Vol. 13, pp. 529–548, 2003 and is reprinted with permission of Springer Verlag. I would like to thank Rob Axtell, Michael Dardia, Giovanni Dosi, Pat Norton, Olav Sorenson, and an anonymous referee for their comments, suggestions, and encouragement. I am grateful to Nikesh Patel for his superb assistance.

1. Introduction

Silicon Valley is the most salient example of high-tech industrial clusters. Public policy makers throughout the world would like to learn the secrets of Silicon Valley in order to build their own high-tech economies. The existing literature on industrial clusters, which traces back to Marshall (1920), focuses on the way in which firms benefit from locating in a cluster; it suggests that once a cluster comes into existence, it tends to reinforce itself by attracting more firms. However, a more important question is how to reach this critical mass in the first place. In contrast to the literature, evidence suggests that entrepreneurs rarely move when they establish high-tech start-ups (Cooper and Folta, 2000). This contradicts the notion that location choice analyses lead entrepreneurs to a high-tech cluster.

A high-tech industrial cluster such as Silicon Valley is characterized by concentrated entrepreneurship. Following Schumpeter, we emphasize the fact that "the appearance of one or a few entrepreneurs facilitates the appearance of others" (Schumpeter, 1934). We propose an agent-based computational model to show how high-tech industrial clusters could emerge in a landscape in which no firms existed originally. The model is essentially a spatial version of the Nelson-Winter model: Boundedly rational agents are scattered over an explicitly defined landscape. Each agent is endowed with some technology, which determines his firm's productivity (if he has one). During each period of time, an agent with no firm would make a decision as to whether he wants to start one. This decision is mostly affected by the behavior of his social contacts, who are all his neighbors. If an agent's neighbors are successful in their entrepreneurial activities, the agent is more likely to found a firm himself. An entrepreneur makes business decisions according to some rules of thumb. When an agent does start a firm and begin to make a profit, he spends part of his profit on R&D in order to improve his productivity, part on imitating other firms' technology, and the rest on capital accumulation. Entrepreneurs who lag behind in the Schumpeterian competition lose money and eventually fail; however, it is possible that they learn from their failures and try again.

We use an agent-based simulation to show that Silicon Valley-type industrial clusters will emerge spontaneously on the landscape. In addition, the model exhibits the following properties: 1) First mover's advantage: the first firm has a better chance to survive and grow; a region in which firms enter the market early tends to capture a large piece of the industry. 2) Path dependence: the more firms a region has, the more it tends to have; once a cluster is formed, it can hardly be toppled. 3) Clustering of entrepreneurship: firms are continuously forming and dying within clusters. 4) Clustering of innovations: the productivity in clusters is much higher than elsewhere because of the collective learning within clusters through innovation and imitation.

Data from the simulation and the properties of the model are discussed in light of empirical regularities. We also explore variations of the model in order to study the factors that determine the location of emerging clusters. We learn two lessons from the model. First, the conventional knowledge-spillover literature may only tell part of the story; the contagion of entrepreneurship through peer effects seems to be an important mechanism through which high-tech industrial clusters emerge and grow. Second, while many scholars have recognized the importance of "seed capital" for a budding high-tech regional economy, our model suggests that "seed entrepreneurs" may be even more important because they serve as local role models and inspire new entrepreneurs.

The main contribution of this paper is the application of a novel methodological approach to study the formation of industrial clusters and related policy issues. While agent-based computational economics has introduced new tools for economic analysis, we have yet to see applications of this approach in policy analysis. This paper intends to fill in the blank. As our model shows, the agent-based approach is particularly useful for dealing with dynamic economic systems. It is also flexible for testing the effects of alternative assumptions.

The remainder of the paper is organized as follows. Section 2 reviews related literature. Section 3 presents the model. The agent-based simulation of the model is described in Section 4. The last section concludes with some remarks.

2. Related Literature

Our model builds upon the intersection of several strands of the literature.

2.1. *The Nelson-Winter paradigm*

The term evolutionary economics has been used in different contexts and by various groups of economists, including institutional economists, evolutionary game theorists, and those who follow Nelson and Winter (1982).

The Nelson-Winter paradigm of evolutionary economics is a synthesis that integrates three sources of work: Simon's concept of "bounded rationality," Nelson's and others' work on invention and innovation (following Schumpeter), and Alchian's and Winter's work on "natural selection" in economic evolution.

A typical Nelson-Winter evolutionary model defines the state of the industry by a list of firm level state variables such as physical capital and productivity. Minimum environmental characteristics are specified, which may include input and output conditions, the space of innovations, and the way innovative search takes place. Based on these, the activities of the industry in the current period are calculated and in turn generate new values of state variables for the next period. New technology or new rules may be adopted if they increase expected profitability. Calculations are conducted for a series of periods and are used to study the evolution of technology, the application of rules, and other characteristics of the industry (Anderson et al., 1996). The Nelson-Winter paradigm provides a powerful and general theoretical framework for studying variety-creation and variety-selection within a given economic sector. Up until now, researchers within this tradition have worked with very simple examples; the potential of the general schema is far from fully exploited.[a]

2.2. *Agent-based computational economics*

Agent-based computational economics uses computer simulation to study the economy as an evolving system of autonomous interacting agents. Researchers in this field try to understand why certain macro-level regularities emerge and persist in decentralized market economies, despite the absence of any forms of centralized coordination. For example, the agent-based computational approach has been applied to the study of business cycles, trade networks, market protocols, the formation of firms and cities, and the diffusion of technological innovations. Computer programs are used to demonstrate constructively how those macro-level regularities might arise from the bottom up through repeated local interactions of autonomous agents. A methodological advantage of agent-based computational economics is that it enables social scientists to do "laboratory experiments" to test a theory, because computational models usually can be modified quite

[a]Nelson and Winter (1982) is a classic reference of their paradigm. Nelson (1995) gives a review of more recent developments in this area and related fields.

easily to study alternative socioeconomic structures and examine their effects on economic outcomes (Tesfatsion, 2001).

Using poker chips on a checkerboard, Schelling (1971) simulates the dynamics of racial housing segregation, which is generally recognized as the pioneering application of this approach in the social sciences. In a groundbreaking work, Epstein and Axtell (1996) investigate how social structures and group behaviors arise from the interaction of individuals. With agent-based simulations, they show how fundamental collective behaviors such as group formation, cultural transmission, combat, and trade can emerge from the interaction of individual agents following simple local rules. Axtell (1999) presents a model in which heterogeneous agents form firms. Agents join firms or start new firms when it is advantageous for them to do so. As firms grow, agents have less incentive to supply their efforts and tend to become free riders, which causes large firms to decline. At the micro level, firms grow and perish; at the aggregate level, the model produces data about firm sizes, growth rates, and related aggregate regularities that parallel empirical findings.

Epstein (1999) characterizes the agent-based computational approach with the following features: heterogeneous agents in terms of preferences, culture, social networks, etc.; decentralized autonomous behavior of agents; explicitly defined space; local interactions among agents; and bounded rationality. Because of these features, agent-based modeling is particularly useful when the population is heterogenous, when interactions among agents are complex and nonlinear, and when the space is crucial.

2.3. *Industrial clusters*

An industrial cluster is a geographic area in which many firms in an industry are located and interact with each other through competition and cooperation. Economists' interest in industrial clusters traces back to Marshall (1920), but we have seen a revival of this interest recently (see, e.g., Arthur, 1990; Krugman, 1991; and Porter, 1998). This line of research emphasizes the net benefits to firms located in a cluster, which are determined by the benefits and the costs of agglomeration. Sources of benefits include pooled labor forces, specialized suppliers, access to capital, proximity to customers, and knowledge spillovers, while diseconomies of agglomeration stem from increased competition, congestion costs, and knowledge expropriation. If positive net benefits are expected from an industrial cluster, new entrants tend to arise, further enhancing the geographic concentration.

Those works that focus on net benefits from agglomeration treat clusters as the result of firms' locational choices. Yet it is not clear whether firm owners or entrepreneurs engage in such searching and comparing exercises. Moreover, high-tech start-ups might have concerns different from those of manufacturing firms. Cooper and Folta (2000) point out that the primary determinant of a high-tech start-up is the prior location of its founder. In fact, entrepreneurs seldom move once they decide to start their new firms. This is understandable because, by staying where they are, entrepreneurs can utilize their existing network to seek investors, employees, customers, suppliers, and advisors; they can start on a part-time basis and defer full commitment until the start-up becomes more promising; and they may want their spouses to keep their current jobs. Given that entrepreneurs do not move, one doubts whether they intentionally take advantage of the benefits of geographic clusters.

Using data on U.S. manufacturing employment in the period of 1860-1987, Kim (1995) shows that industry localization patterns are negatively correlated with characteristics associated with external economies. In particular, high-tech sectors, which are believed to have more positive externalities than other sectors, are less agglomerated. This is inconsistent with the location choice literature.

Social scientists have long noticed that clusters, of individuals or firms, are the result of two types of behavior. One is a sorting process. For example, individuals' racial preferences could lead to housing segregation in which clusters of black or white residents are formed. The other is a behavior-adapting process. For example, smokers can convert their non-smoking friends into smokers, resulting in clusters of smoking behaviors. The existing literature on industrial clusters has studied the sorting process in which firms choose to locate close to other firms, but has neglected the other process. We argue that entrepreneurship may be contagious and that a person surrounded by entrepreneurs is more likely to start a firm himself. This provides an alternative theory of the formation of industrial clusters.

2.4. *The Schumpeterian entrepreneur*

The "Irish banker in Paris," Richard Cantillon, acknowledged by many historians as the first great economic theorist, first recognized the important role of entrepreneurs in economic life in the 18th century. The concept of the entrepreneur then appeared in the writings of many French economists, including Quesnay, Turgot, and Say. Yet within the British tradition, the dominant classical school made no distinction between capitalists—who provide the means for investment in production—and entrepreneurs—who explore possibilities of innovation, seek profitable opportunities, and assume risks. Thus the followers of Smith and Ricardo excluded the entrepreneur from economic analysis.

Today's economists learn the theory of entrepreneurs mainly from Schumpeter (1934). Schumpeter starts by describing the economic system as a circular flow within a Walrasian-like general equilibrium. To him, economic development is driven by the activities of a class of entrepreneurs who take it upon themselves to disrupt the circular flow by introducing new products, reorganizing labor forces and capital, and rearranging the processes of business life in the hope of making a profit from the disequilibria they create. To address the question of what drives entrepreneurs to exercise their talents, Schumpeter might have given the most romantic reasoning in economics: he states that entrepreneurs choose their way of life because of the dream and the will to found a private kingdom, the will to conquer, the impulse to fight, to prove oneself superior to others, to succeed for the sake not of the fruits of successes but of success itself, and finally the joy of creating, getting things done, or simply of exercising one's energy and ingenuity. Schumpeter uses his concept of the entrepreneur to explain business cycles. The introduction of new and untried products and processes causes "disturbances;" these disturbances that appear "in groups or swarms" constitute business cycles. Entrepreneurial activities appear in clusters because "*the appearance of one or a few entrepreneurs facilitates the appearance of others, and those the appearance of more, in ever-increasing numbers* [Schumpeter's italics]."

Schumpeter's theory of entrepreneurs has been renowned and influential. However, it is fair to say that its influence has remained outside of neoclassical economics. Schumpeter's entrepreneur is by definition an equilibrium-disturbing figure; his entrepreneurial activities constantly interrupt the tendency toward equilibrium in the economic system. Therefore, since neoclassical economics focuses on equilibrium analysis, there is no room for Schumpeter's entrepreneur. By contrast, the Schumpeterian entrepreneur plays a crucial role in our model.

3. The Model

Consider an $N \times N$ lattice graph, $\Lambda_N = (V, E)$, with periodic boundary conditions. V and E are the sets of vertexes and edges, respectively. Each vertex $i \in V$ represents an agent. An agent i is endowed with some human capital (technology) h_i.

At time 0, all agents are born and each agent's endowment of human capital is determined by a random draw: h_i^0.

In each period of time, an agent with no firm has to make a decision as to whether he wants to be an entrepreneur and start a firm. If he wants to do so at time t, he will raise some money to buy capital K_i^t. If agent i has a firm, his production function is

$$Y_i^t = h_i^t (K_i^t)^\alpha, \qquad \alpha < 1, \tag{1}$$

otherwise, he produces nothing: $Y_i^t = 0$. Capital is always obtainable at a fixed unit cost c. For simplicity, we deal with the single-factor production and do not bother with labor. This simplification may be understood in this way: each unit of capital is attached with a certain amount of labor according to a fixed capital-labor ratio and abundant labor is supplied at a constant price which is already included in c.

Aggregate supply in this industry is

$$S^t = \sum_i Y_i^t. \tag{2}$$

Aggregate demand D^t is given exogenously. Market price at time t is decided by

$$P^t = \frac{D^t}{S^t}. \tag{3}$$

If agent i produces, his profit is

$$\pi_i^t = P^t Y_i^t - cK_i^t. \tag{4}$$

Agents are boundedly rational; they act according to some rules of thumb. When an agent makes some profit, he will put part of it into R&D and spend the rest on capital accumulation. The R&D fund will be split again, with part of it being spent on technological innovation and the remainder on technological imitation. Each agent is born with two uniformly distributed random numbers $\gamma_i, \lambda_i \in (0, 1)$, which he takes as rules that govern his spending on technological innovation and imitation. If agent i makes profit $\pi_i^t > 0$, he puts aside $\gamma_i \pi_i^t$ for R&D. Among that amount, $\lambda_i \gamma_i \pi_i^t$ goes to technological innovation. Let IN_i and IM_i denote i's spendings on innovation and imitation, respectively. Then, if $\pi_i^t > 0$, then

$$IN_i^{t+1} = IN^t + \lambda_i \gamma_i \pi_i^t,$$
$$IM_i^{t+1} = IM^t + (1-\lambda_i)\gamma_i \pi_i^t,$$
$$K_i^{t+1} = K^t(1-d) + (1-\gamma_i)\pi_i^t;$$

if $\pi_i^t \leq 0$, then

$$K_i^{t+1} = K^t(1-d) + \pi_i^t. \tag{5}$$

Here $d > 0$ represents the rate of capital depreciation.

Technological innovation and imitation are costly. In addition, the larger a firm is, the more costly it is to improve its technology. Whenever agent i's spending on innovation exceeds $f(K_i)$, he gets a chance to draw a new h_i from the distribution of technological opportunities $F(h,t)$. This distribution function is independent of i's current technology, but its mean increases with time. If the new draw is greater than the old one, he will adopt the new one. Whenever agent i's spending on imitation exceeds $g(K_i)$, he gets a chance to copy the best technology from neighboring firms. It is more costly for large firms to upgrade technology, so $f'(\cdot) > 0$ and $g'(\cdot) > 0$. i's neighboring firms are those started by surrounding agents:

$$B_i = \{j | d(i,j) \leq 2 \text{ and } K_j > 0\}, \tag{6}$$

where $d(i,j)$ is the distance between i and j, which is defined as the number of edges that constitute the shortest path between i and j. Therefore, the mechanism of innovation and imitation can be summarized as follows:

$$\begin{aligned} &\text{If } IN_i^t \geq f(K_i^t), \text{ then } h_i^{t+1} = \max\{h_i^t, h_i'\}, \text{ where } h_i' \sim F(h,t),\\ &\qquad \text{and } IN^{t+1} = IN_i^t - f(K_i^t);\\ &\text{if } IM_i^t \geq g(K_i^t), \text{then } h_i^{t+1} = \max\{h_i^t, \max_{i' \in B_i} h_{i'}^t\},\\ &\qquad \text{and } IM^{t+1} = IM_i^t - g(K_i^t). \end{aligned} \tag{7}$$

If the firm simultaneously gets a random draw and a copy of the best technology in the neighborhood, the better one is adopted.

In addition, entrepreneurs learn from failures. Each time an entrepreneur fails, which means he keeps losing money and eventually does not have enough capital to operate, he earns a chance $\rho > 0$ to copy the best technology from neighboring firms. For the sake of parsimony, we use a single parameter, h, to represent technology, which should be understood as a combination of both management skills and production technology. A failed entrepreneur is likely to learn some management skills from the practices of nearby successful entrepreneurs. Similarly, he will likely recognize the better production technology used by neighboring entrepreneurs. This opportunity for a failed entrepreneur to copy a better technology from surviving firms may be interpreted as a chance for "zero-cost imitation." In this sense, we are assuming that imitation is easier for a re-starter than for an incumbent firm. Previous studies have shown that incumbent firms are less likely to adopt radical innovations because it is more costly for them to shift to a different technology standard (Foster, 1986; Christensen, 1997). But a failed entrepreneur who starts up a new firm faces no such costs.[b]

An agent's decision on firm-founding reflects his perception of risk and his evaluation of profitability. In turn, his attitude is affected by other agents in the society. We assume that social distance is proportional to physical distance and an agent's behavior is largely influenced by close neighbors. If many of his neighbors are entrepreneurs who make a lot of money, he will see the profitable opportunity and also get a psychological boost from their success. Hence, he is likely to choose to be an entrepreneur himself; otherwise, it is less likely that he will do so. A distant successful entrepreneur has smaller effects on an agent's decision. Specifically, the probability that an agent chooses to start a firm is defined as follows:

$$\Pr(K_i^{t+1} > 0 \mid K_i^t = 0) = \phi(K_{j_1}^t, K_{j_2}^t, \ldots),$$
$$\text{and } \frac{\partial \phi}{\partial K_j^t} \geq 0, \forall j \neq i; \quad \frac{\partial \phi}{\partial K_{j_x}^t} \geq \frac{\partial \phi}{\partial K_{j_y}^t} \text{ if } d(i, j_x) \leq d(i, j_y). \tag{8}$$

For simplicity, we have assumed that a failed entrepreneur has no negative effect on another agent's decision. Casual observation of the real world helps justify this asymmetry between the social effects of success and failure. For example, the limited liability corporation system creates an asymmetry between success and failure: a successful entrepreneur is usually worth millions but a failed one almost never loses much. Also, the media always gives more attention to successes than to failures, which further magnifies the relative psychological impact of successes. Research shows that even in the peak years of the Internet revolution, a large number of high-tech firms went out of business in Silicon Valley (Zhang, 2003). However, even the local media rarely covered such failures.

---

[b]For example, it is quite easy for a fresh starter to imitate Amazon.com, but not that easy for a conventional bookstore because its on-line service could hurt the position of its physical store. In this sense, it costs less for a failed bookstore owner to imitate Amazon's technology.

4. Agent-Based Simulation

Our dynamic model represents a complex Markov Process. To analyze it rigorously is a formidable task. We will proceed with an agent-based simulation to learn the properties of the model.

4.1. *Parameterization of the model*

One way to calibrate our model is to search for a set of parameter values, using methods such as the Genetic Algorithm, so that the outcomes of the model replicate some pre-selected empirical regularities. Since we will focus on the qualitative properties of the model, such a sophisticated method seems unwarranted. Instead, we take a simpler approach, that of picking a set of "reasonable" parameters through a few trials on the computer program. As you will see, the model works fine. This partly proves the robustness of our basic setup. The model is parameterized as follows:

- $N = 100$. That is, we have a population of 10,000 agents.
- Technology h_i^t is drawn in the way such that $\sqrt{h_i^t}$ follows $U(0, 1 + \frac{t}{2{,}500})$, a uniform distribution on $(0, 1 + \frac{t}{2{,}500})$. That is,

$$F(h,t) = \left(\frac{2{,}500h}{2{,}500 + t}\right)^2. \tag{9}$$

  This looks like a truncated normal distribution, which makes it difficult to attain a very efficient technology. Over time, the distribution expands to the right. This implies that a draw today is expected to yield a better technology than a draw yesterday. Therefore, the investment in technology, just as with the investment in capital, also depreciates.
- When agent i decides to start a firm, he simply takes money out of his savings and acquires capital $K_i = 5k$, where $k \in U(0, 1)$. We impose an arbitrary minimum capital requirement such that, if $K_i < 0.1$, the firm has to be shut down. The diminishing return to capital is captured by $\alpha = 0.995$.
- Aggregate demand is given exogenously to replicate the evolution of an industry that grows rapidly at an early stage and loses its momentum over time. We start with $D^0 = 10$. Its growth rate is

declining over the life cycle of the industry. Specifically, we define

$$g^t = \begin{cases} 0.03 & \text{if } D^t < 2{,}000; \\ 0.02 & \text{if } 2{,}000 \leq D^t < 10{,}000; \\ 0.01 & \text{if } 10{,}000 \leq D^t < 20{,}000; \\ 0.005 & \text{if } D^t \geq 20{,}000. \end{cases} \tag{10}$$

We also define a cyclical parameter as $b^t = \frac{1}{100}\sin\left(\frac{2\pi t}{40}\right)$, which simulates business cycles that span 40 periods (quarters).

In addition, we introduce random demand shocks in the form $\epsilon^t \in U(-0.01, 0.01)$.

The dynamics of aggregate demand follows

$$D^{t+1} = D^t(1 + g^t + b^t + \epsilon^t). \tag{11}$$

- If agent i is not producing at time t, the probability that he will choose to do so is

$$\begin{aligned} &\Pr(i \text{ starts a firm} |\ K_i^t = 0) \\ &= \frac{1}{25} \sum_{j|d(i,j)=1} \frac{K_j^t}{a_j^t} + \frac{1}{50} \sum_{j|d(i,j)=2} \frac{K_j^t}{a_j^t} + \frac{1}{50,000}, \end{aligned} \tag{12}$$

  where a_j^t is the age of firm j at time t. This says that i may choose to be an entrepreneur independently with a low probability; if his neighbors accumulated a great deal of capital in a short time, he is more likely to found a firm himself. Notice that closer neighbors have larger effects on an agent's choice and distant entrepreneurs have no effects.
- Profitable firms spend money on R&D and try to improve their technology through innovation and imitation. The parameters that affect the costs of R&D activities are $f(K_i) = 0.1(K_i)^3$ and $g(K_i) = 0.3(K_i)^3$. The chance of learning from failure is $\rho = 0.1$.

4.2. *Main results*

We start our simulation with a blank landscape with no firm. In this case, the emergence of the first entrepreneur is a pure chance event. He may not be an agent endowed with superior technology, but one thing is certain, he will make a large profit for his entrepreneurial move. Once the first entrepreneur emerges on the landscape, many of his neighbors will recognize the opportunity and follow suit; at the same time, others may start firms by chance. Those firms that make profits will upgrade their technologies.

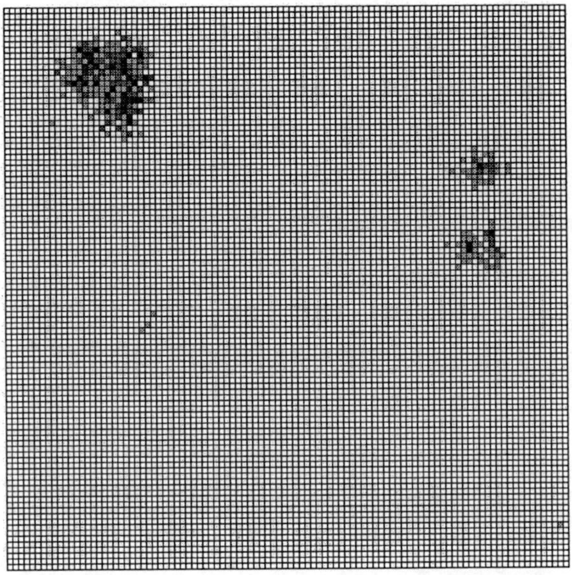

Figure 1. A Snapshot of Industrial Clusters

As more firms are founded and technology is improved, the market price for the product decreases sharply. Many new firms are born around profitable firms. Before long, one or more clusters form in certain regions. Some firms are forced to exit because they cannot keep up with others in technological progress, which may result from lower R&D expenditure or continuous unlucky draws from the distribution of technology. In the long run, we see a spatial pattern of industrial clusters as shown in Figure 1.[c] In Figure 1, a green cell represents a small firm ($K_i \leq 10$); a red cell represents a medium firm ($10 < K_i \leq 100$); and a blue cell is a large firm ($K_i > 100$). A cluster generally hosts firms of all types.

In this model, firms in a cluster do benefit from knowledge spillovers as they imitate better technologies possessed by nearby firms. However, we see that entrepreneurs do not move and they do not intentionally seek the benefits from knowledge spillovers. In fact, if it is cheap to improve the technology through independent research, industrial clusters still tend to emerge even if we shut down the channels for the inter-firm transmission of

[c]Interested readers may want to try the simulation by themselves. A Java Applet is available from the author upon request.

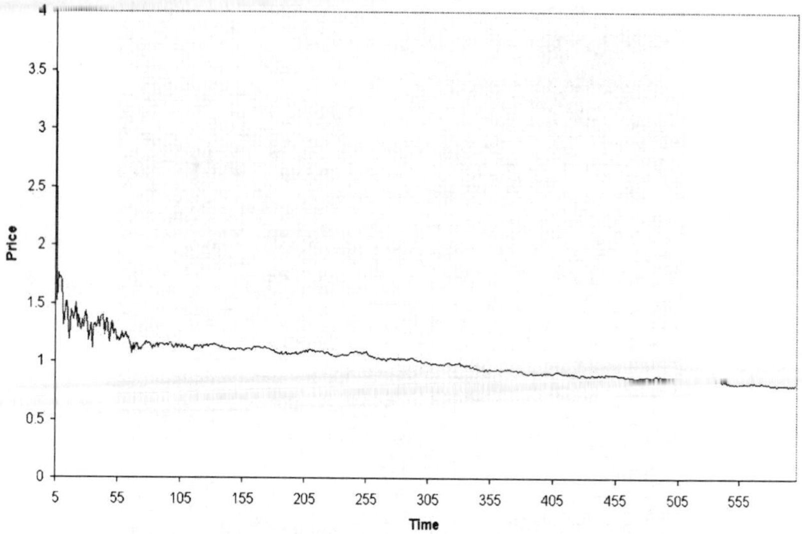

Figure 2. Price Series

technology.

Figure 2 shows the dynamics of market price. When the first firm enters the market, price is high. As capital is accumulated and production is expanded, market price is driven down quickly. Competition through entry of new firms continuously pushes the product price down to the cost of production. There is a cyclical pattern in the price series, which reflects the cyclical movement we have built in the demand.

Figure 3 shows the firm size distribution. Large firms are rare; small and medium firms dominate the industry. (Here we use output level to measure firm size. An alternative measure, capital stock, gives similar qualitative results.)

Since Gibrat's work in the early 1930s, it has been common practice to fit firm sizes with lognormal distributions (Sutton, 1997). A standard justification for the distribution is the so-called "law of proportional effect," which postulates that firms grow at random rates independent of firm size. This has now become well known as "Gibrat's law." A lognormal distribution is skewed to the right, meaning that firm sizes are concentrated on smaller values; in particular, the mean firm size is larger than the median firm size, and both are larger than the modal firm size. By definition, a

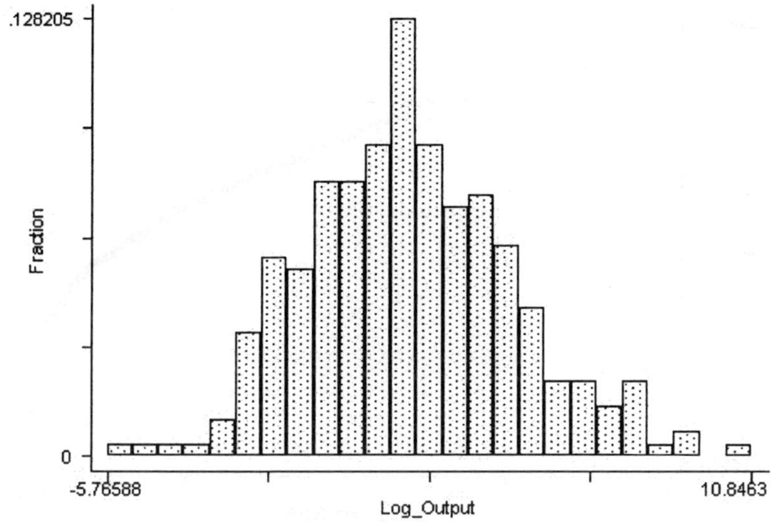

Figure 3. Firm Size Distribution

lognormal distribution of firm size implies a normal distribution of log firm size. Figure 3 roughly corresponds to a normal distribution.

The firm size distribution, especially its upper tail, has often been described by the Pareto law (Ijiri and Simon, 1977; Axtell, 2001):

$$sr^{\beta} = M, \tag{13}$$

where s is the size of a firm, r is its rank in an industry (or an economy) with the largest firm ranked 1, and β and M are constants. The power law implies a linear relationship between log firm size and log firm rank:

$$\log s = \log M - \beta \log r. \tag{14}$$

Figure 4 plots firm size over firm rank. Cutting off the lower quartile of the sample, we fit a straight line to the remaining data and obtain:

$$\log(firm\_size) = \underset{(0.125)}{12.33} - \underset{(0.028)}{2.11} \log(firm\_rank), \quad R^2 = 0.97. \tag{15}$$

It is almost a perfect fit. To compare this with reality, we do the same exercise for the 211 U.S. high-tech firms on the list of Fortune 1000 largest firms. The firm size-rank plot is presented in Figure 5. Since this data is

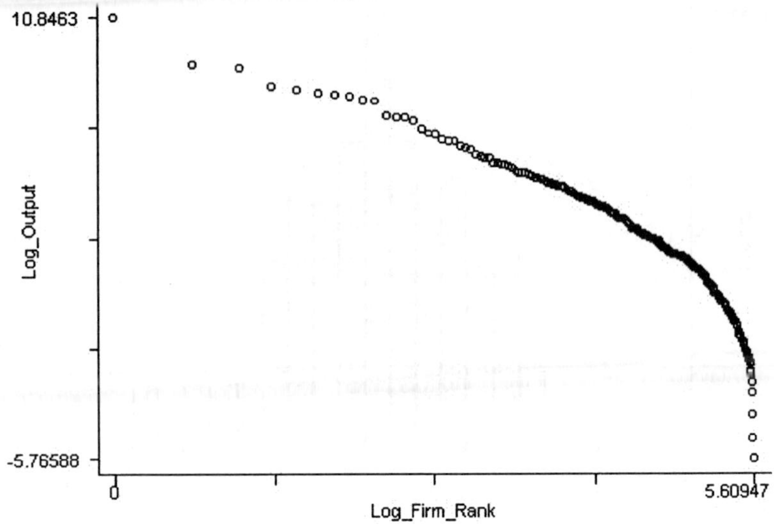

Figure 4. Firm Size-Rank Plot

already truncated from below, we fit a straight line to the whole sample. The results are:

$$\log(firm\_size) = \underset{(0.086)}{13.14} - \underset{(0.019)}{1.09}\log(firm\_rank), \quad R^2 = 0.94. \tag{16}$$

We see that the real data also fits a straight line very well, although its slope is smaller.

The curvature in Figure 4 corresponds to a feature that is repeatedly observed in real data. Ijiri and Simon (1977) propose two possible interpretations for the "departure" from the Pareto distribution: autocorrelation in firm growth rates and the effects of mergers and acquisitions. Our model does not allow for mergers and acquisitions, but we do have autocorrelated firm growth. Figure 5 only plots the upper tail of the real data, which gives no indication as to how the lower tail behaves. However, based on what we know, we are able to get a rough idea about the profile of the complete sample. Assume the smallest high-tech firm has an annual revenue of $0.01 million. By equation 16, we predict its rank is higher than 11.7 million. That rank is even larger than the total number of U.S. firms.[d] Therefore,

[d]According to the Census Bureau, the total number of U.S. establishments in 1999 was

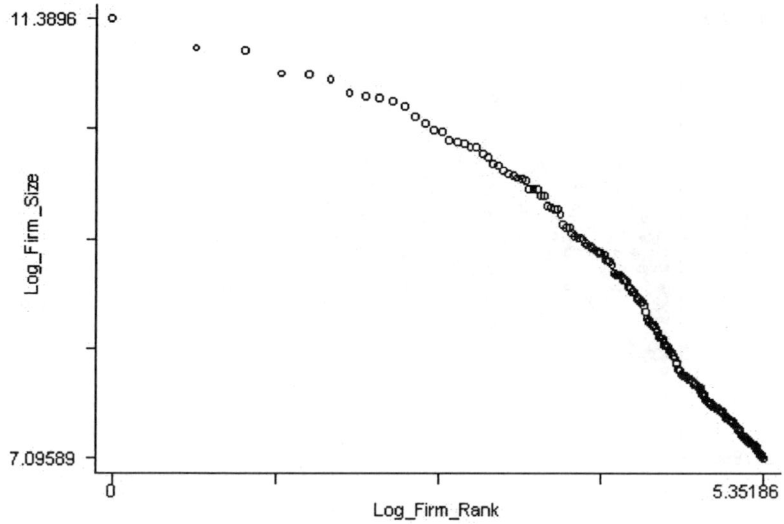

Figure 5. Size-Rank Plot for Fortune1000 High-Tech Firms

the lower end of the real data must bend down as do the simulated data.

By construction, a firm's growth rate is related to its size in our model. In particular, a small firm is assumed to be able to upgrade its technology more easily. This is a violation of Gibrat's law. However, our model is able to generate firm size data that is qualitatively similar to empirical findings. It reminds us that Gibrat's law is only one of the parsimonious interpretations of empirical data.

Figure 6 plots firm size over firm age. Interestingly, there is not a strong positive correlation between firm size and age. In fact, the largest firms are all relatively young. This is because once an old firm reaches a certain size, it slows down in upgrading technology due to the high cost. But, remember, the distribution of technology moves to the right. A newcomer draws technology from a better space, and so it is more efficient and will outgrow older firms under the same market condition. This reflects what happens in the high-tech sector in the real world. For example, in Silicon Valley, more than half of the top 40 technology firms in 2002 were not even founded two decades ago; only four out of 40 largest firms in 2002 were survivors from the top-40 list in 1982 (Zhang, 2003).

7,008,444.

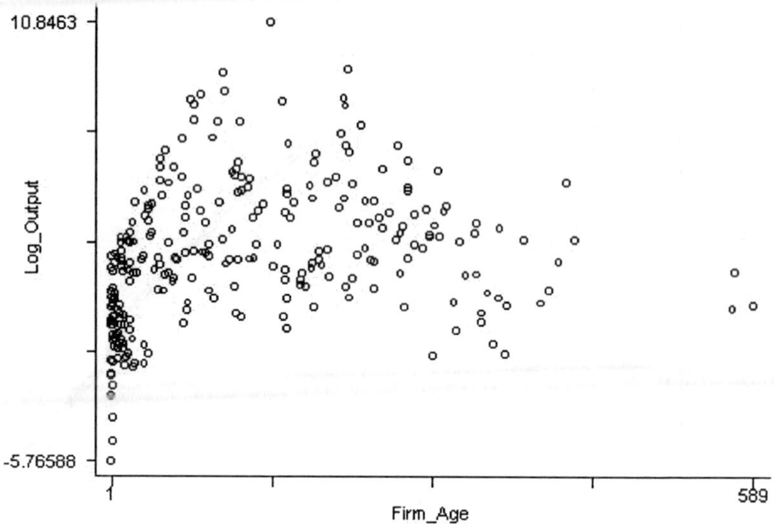

Figure 6. Firm Size-Age Plot

The model also exhibits the following properties:

The first mover's advantage

At the firm level, the first few entrepreneurs tend to make a lot of money and have good chances to grow into large firms. However, their survival is not guaranteed. Some late comers may be endowed with better technology that can drive the pioneers out of the market; the first mover may follow a rule that spends very little profit on R&D and eventually lags behind in the Schumpeterian competition; the first mover may be so unlucky that his research efforts fail to generate superior technology before his followers do. Therefore, the first mover does enjoy some advantage, but only in a probabilistic sense.

At the economic region level, an area that enters the market early (with a few firms already operating at the early stage) tends to capture a large piece of the whole industry. In a variation of the model, we differentiate regions by assigning to them different innovation spaces. In one region, firms search new technology in $(0, 1)$, but in another, firms are only allowed to innovate in $(0, 0.99)$. We find that if the disadvantaged region first occupies the market, its first mover's advantage can overcome the technological disadvantage and sustain the regional economy for a long time. The reason is that firms in the disadvantaged region can innovate and learn from each other and approach their potential quickly. They drive the product price to a low level and leave a slim profit margin for new firms. Not all agents in the advantaged region are endowed with superior technology. Even if an agent has a very advanced technology to start with, he may make little profit, and an economic downturn may drive him out of business. Although the bigger firms in the disadvantaged region also lose money in the downturn, they will not go bankrupt and will recover during the next upturn.

Path dependence

A region with many firms, on the one hand, will have more agents thinking of starting up new firms, and on the other hand, will become more advanced in technology because of R&D. This property of "increasing return" tends to lock the development of the industry into certain regions. Once clusters are established, other regions have little chance to catch up. In the real word, for example, it is very unlikely that other regions can surpass Silicon Valley in the semiconductor industry.

Clustering of entrepreneurship

Within the clusters, firms enter and exit the industry constantly. People in clusters try new ideas and found new firms. They may not succeed the first time, but they will try again and learn from their failures. This is the reason why a cluster differs from other regions, has so many firms, and becomes so technologically advanced. However, any snapshot of the industry tends to ignore the fact that cluster status is achieved through continuous learning by trial and error.

Clustering of innovation

As entrepreneurship is clustered, innovative activities are also unevenly distributed over the landscape. Firms in clusters spend a lot of money on R&D. They make technological progress through both innovative research and imitation. In the long run, almost all firms in clusters have mastered very advanced technology, which leaves any firm outside clusters little chance of survival.

4.3. *Location of clusters*

The way we start our simulation implies that industrial clusters can emerge in any area. However, it is particularly interesting to know what factors may determine the location of clusters. To study that, we try simulations with different initial conditions.

Technological advantage

Our simulation shows that a region that is quicker at finding, learning, and imitating better technologies (the distribution of technology is further to the right, and/or lower values of f' and g') is more likely to develop into an industrial cluster. In reality, different regions do have different capacities in terms of research and innovation. For example, California and Massachusetts together house 14.3 percent of the U.S. population, yet 43.3 percent of the National Academy of Science members and 34.6 percent of the National Academy of Engineering members are based in these two states. Not surprisingly, California and Massachusetts lead the U.S. high-tech economy. Universities, research institutes and labs have always been a major source of technological advancement. The recent development of the biotech industry further proved the importance of academic research for a regional high-tech economy. Almost all biotech firms either were founded by academic researchers or received advice from them. At the same time, universities continuously provide high-quality laborers to the high-tech sector. It is safe to say that high-quality research universities are a necessary condition for a vibrant high-tech center, if not a sufficient condition.

Knowledge spillovers

Innovation such as superior technology is always first acquired by a lucky few. Other firms have to keep up with the pace of innovation through imitation. We find that regions in which firms may easily "copy" advanced technologies (smaller g' and/or imitation allowed for more distant firms) tend to develop into an industrial cluster. In reality, a local culture that tolerates inter-firm knowledge and labor transfers allows firms to learn collectively, which is favorable for the development of a cluster (Saxenian, 1994). A legal infrastructure, such as the enforceability of "not to compete" covenants, also has big effects on technology transfers (Gilson, 1999). Thus the way we see knowledge spillovers is different from the way in which the existing literature sees them. In our model, spillovers do benefit firms within clusters, but do not attract firms into clusters, in contrast to what the new economic geography literature suggests.

Seed capital and seed entrepreneurs

In a variation of our model, we assume that in some regions entrepreneurs have difficulties raising capital. In such regions, when agent i decides to start a firm, he acquires capital $K_i = 2k$ instead of $5k$ as in other regions, where $k \in U(0, 1)$. Those capital-scarce regions are less likely to develop into industrial clusters. The availability of capital is important for fostering entrepreneurs, which is well recognized. Many scholars even suggest that local governments set up public funds to provide "seed capital" to potential entrepreneurs when the objective is to develop a high-tech regional economy.

In another variation of the model, we start by putting four "seed entrepreneurs" in four different regions and see whether that brings substantial advantage to those regions. Our simulation shows that, with a very high probability, one or more of the four regions will grow up into industrial clusters. In a different way, this proves first mover's advantage and path dependence. On the other hand, it also shows the importance of entrepreneurial leadership to a regional economy.

It is widely believed that the history of Silicon Valley traces back to the garage where Hewlett and Packard started their business in Palo Alto. Another frequently heard story is the departure of the "Traitorous Eight" from Shockley's Semiconductor Lab to found Fairchild. Those successes have inspired generations of entrepreneurs in the Valley. Almost every other high-tech center's history began with legendary entrepreneurs, who served as local heroes and role models who motivated others to pursue success in the same way. Famous examples include Ken Olson in Boston, Bill Gates in Seattle, and Robert Dell in Austin. It seems that the key to replicating the Silicon Valley model is to incubate such a heroic entrepreneur. Providing seed capital is certainly an important part of that game, but it is not sufficient. Although we know heroes in most cases spontaneously emerge, some local policies may facilitate their emergence. For example, local government may provide training program for those scientists and engineers who consider starting their own businesses. Favorable policies such as tax credits also help pioneers.

Trying, and learning by failing

A high-tech industrial cluster, by definition, is characterized by many successful firms. Our dynamic model allows us to see the other side of the story: clusters emerge on failures. Most successes are achieved through constant learning by trial and error. In fact, a region that does not tolerate failures (failed entrepreneurs not allowed to start over again or do not learn from failures ($\rho = 0$)) has a slim chance of success. Therefore, a cluster will most probably appear in a region where entrepreneurship is encouraged and failed experiences are valued (Saxenian, 1994).

5. Concluding Remarks

We have proposed a simplified Nelson-Winter model with an explicit space dimension to study the way in which high-tech clusters emerge on a landscape in which no firm exists originally. We use agent-based simulation to show the dynamics of the model.

Social scientists have long been interested in clustering behaviors, such as racial housing segregation, the concentration of poverty and unemployment in certain neighborhoods, the exceedingly high crime rates in certain areas, the extreme dropout rates in certain schools, etc. Mainly two types of explanations are raised for clustering behaviors. One contends that clusters result from a sorting process in which individuals alike choose to associate with one another; for example, the residential segregation phenomenon can be explained in this way. The other argues that peer effects cause individuals to conform to norms in a social group. Obviously, the two arguments are not mutually exclusive. In many cases, including all other examples mentioned above, the two arguments may work simultaneously. The existing literature on industrial clusters recognizes the sorting process in which firms choose to locate close to other firms in order to exploit the benefits from a cluster. However, it neglects the possibility that entrepreneurial spirit can spread among the people in a region through social effects. We believe this kind of social contagion story is close to the reality of high-tech industrial clusters that are characterized by concentrated entrepreneurship. Our model shows that one does not have to invoke the benefits of industrial clusters such as knowledge spillovers in order to explain the formation of clusters; the contagion of entrepreneurship through peer effects alone is able to account for the emergence of clusters.

Another point our model has highlighted is the importance of pioneering entrepreneurs for an emerging industrial cluster. Entrepreneurial life style is by definition creative and disruptive. It takes at least one charismatic, successful role model to demonstrate the profits of taking risks and the joy of "changing the world" through innovation. Such "seed entrepreneurs" that generate a swarm of followers locally can be identified in every major high-tech industrial cluster in the United States. We are aware that such pioneers are not picked beforehand; in fact, in most cases, it seems as though those leaders had appeared by chance. However, we can certainly increase the chance of seeing such leaders by creating a favorable environment for entrepreneurial activities. Providing "seed capital" is one measure that may work, especially when entrepreneurs face binding financial constraints. Yet that is not enough. Given that high-tech firms are often founded by scientists and engineers, who do not necessarily have the impulse or knowledge to start as entrepreneurs, policies that help convert those people into entrepreneurs are useful.

Despite the simplicity of our theoretical model, it is beyond our capability to analyze it mathematically. For this reason, we resort to an agent-based simulation to show the evolutionary dynamics of the model. We have built a prototype for studying the emergence of high-tech industrial clusters. The primary advantage of the simulation approach is that we are free to try many variations of the model. For example, some authors have recently shown that large incumbent firms are likely to spin off new businesses, which provide an alternative mechanism through which industrial clusters emerge and grow (e.g., Klepper, 2001; Klepper and Sleeper, 2002; Lazerson and Lorenzoni, 1999; Zhang, 2003). Although our model completely shuts off the spin-off channel, one can easily modify our simulation to incorporate such spin-off activities.[e] Our model can also be modified to allow firms to move into or out of clusters, to have more sophisticated agents, to introduce product innovation in addition to new technology, or to test the consequences of different social network structures. We leave these for future work.

References

1. Anderson, E. S., A. K. Jenson, L. Madsen, and M. Jorgensen, 1996. "The Nelson and Winter Models Revisited: Prototypes for Computer-Based Re-

[e]Indeed, early spin-offs in Silicon Valley, such as those from the Fairchild Semiconductor, inspired many employees at incumbent firms to follow suit and start their own businesses, which has been happening over many generations. This is an important thread of Silicon Valley's history (Saxenian, 1994).

construction of Schumpeterian Competition." DRUID Working Paper No. 96-2.

2. Arthur, B., 1990. "'Silicon Valley' Locational Clusters: When Do Increasing Returns Imply Monopoly?" *Mathematical Social Sciences* 19, 235-51.
3. Axtell, R., 1999. "The Emergence of Firms in a Population of Agents: Local Increasing Returns, Unstable Nash Equilibria, and Power Law Size Distributions." Working Paper, Brookings Institution.
4. Axtell, R., 2001. "Zipf Distribution of U.S. Firm Sizes." *Science* 293, 1818-20.
5. Christensen, C. M., 1997. *The Innovator's Dilemma.* Boston, MA: Harvard Business School Press.
6. Cooper, A and T. Folta, 2000. "Entrepreneurship and High-technology Clusters." In *The Blackwell Handbook of Entrepreneurship*, edited by D. L. Sexton and H. Landstrom. Malden, MA: Blackwell Business.
7. Epstein, J. M., 1999. "Agent-Based Computational Models and Generative Social Science." *Complexity* 4, 41-60.
8. Epstein, J. M. and R. Axtell, 1996. *Growing Artificial Societies: Social Science from the Bottom Up.* Washington, D.C.: Brookings Institution Press.
9. Foster, R. N., 1986. *Innovation: The Attacker's Advantage.* New York, NY: Summit Books.
10. Gilson, R. J., 1999. "The Legal Infrastructure of High Technology Industrial Districts: Silicon Valley, Route 128, and Covenants not to Compete." *New York University Law Review* 74, 575-629.
11. Grebel, T., A. Pyka, and H. Hanusch, 2003. "An Evolutionary Approach to the Theory of Entrepreneurship." *Industry and Innovation* 10, 493-514.
12. Ijiri, Y. and H. A. Simon, 1977. *Skew Distributions and the Size of Business Firms.* New York, NY: North-Holland.
13. Kim, S., 1995. "Expansion of Markets and the Geographic Distribution of Economic Activities: The Trends in U.S. Regional Manufacturing Structure, 1860-1987." *Quarterly Journal of Economics* 110, 881-908.
14. Klepper, S., 2001. "Employee Startups in High-Tech Industries." *Industrial and Corporate Change* 10, 639-74.
15. Klepper S. and S. Sleeper, 2002. "Entry by Spinoffs." Papers on Econonmics and Evolution 2002-07, Max Planck Institute for Research into Economic Systems.
16. Krugman, P., 1991. *Geography and Trade.* Cambridge, MA: MIT Press.
17. Lazerson, M. H. and G. Lorenzoni, 1999. "The Firms That Feed Industrial Districts: A Return to the Italian Source." *Industrial and Corporate Change* 8, 235–66.
18. Marshall, A., 1920. *Principles of Economics*, 8th edition. London: Macmillan.
19. Nelson, R. R. and S. Winter, 1982. *An Evolutionary Theory of Economic Change.* Cambridge, MA: Harvard University Press.
20. Nelson, R. R., 1995. "Recent Evolutionary Theorizing about Economic Change." *Journal of Economic Literature* 33, 48-90.
21. Porter, M. E., 1998. "Clusters and the New Economies of Competition." *Harvard Business Review* 76, 77-90.

22. Sexenian, A., 1994. *Regional Advantage: Culture and Competition in Silicon Valley and Route 128.* Cambridge, MA: Harvard University Press.
23. Schelling, T. C., 1971. "Dynamic Models of Segregation." *Journal of Mathematical Sociology* 1, 143-86.
24. Schumpeter, Joseph A., 1934. *The Theory of Economic Development.* Cambridge, MA: Harvard University Press.
25. Sutton, J., 1997. "Gibrat's Legacy." *Journal of Economic Literature* 35, 40-59.
26. Tesfatsion, L., 2001. "Introduction to the Special Issue on Agent-based Computational Economics." *Journal of Economic Dynamics and Control* 25, 281-93.
27. Zhang, J., 2003. "High-Tech Start-ups and Industrial Dynamics in Silicon Valley." Public Policy Institute of California, San Francisco, California.

SIMULATING KNOWLEDGE DYNAMICS IN INNOVATION NETWORKS[1] (SKIN)

PETRA AHRWEILER
Research Centre Media and Politics, Institute for Political Science, University of Hamburg, Germany

ANDREAS PYKA
University of Augsburg, Institute of Economics, Universitaetsstr. 16, D-86135 Augsburg, Germany

NIGEL GILBERT
School of Human Sciences, University of Surrey, Guildford, Surrey, GU2 7XH, United Kingdom

An agent-based simulation model representing a theory of the dynamic processes involved in innovation in modern knowledge-based industries is described. The agent-based approach allows the representation of heterogeneous agents that have individual and varying stocks of knowledge. The simulation is able to model uncertainty, historical change, effect of failure on the agent population, and agent learning from experience, from individual research and from partners and collaborators. The interactions between the agents occur on two levels: through a market with firms supplying and consuming goods for a price, and through the exchange of knowledge. A brief description of the implementation of the model and its user interface is given.

1. Introduction

Although the institutional approach in economics has introduced a sociological perspective to mainstream economic theory, sociologists such as Granovetter (1985), Willke (1995), Schneider and Kenis (1996), Weyer (2000) and others have criticised the approach, arguing that actual markets are shaped by social factors to a much larger degree than institutional economics allows. 'Social shaping' not only refers to the fact that real markets rely on the co-operative behaviour of their members, that is, on the institutional regulations that frame the interactions of the traders, but also refers to an equally important aspect, the social role of the networks of collaborations and contracts which are an integral part of most markets. Modern innovation economics, as framed in evolutionary economics, is considering the various dimensions that are shaping the organization of innovation processes in knowledge intensive industries.

[1] This work was partly supported by the German Academic Exchange Service and the British Council (ARC Programme, XVI-02/1) which provided funds to facilitate the authors' research collaboration on the modelling of innovation networks.

Networks are a mode of co-ordination that are particularly relevant in knowledge-based market sectors such as biotechnology and the ICT industries. The need for knowledge creation and transfer within markets is one of the main reasons for networking. Powell (1990: 304) suggests that it is impossible to put a price tag on qualitative features such as an innovation-friendly strategy, a special style of production, technological capacity, know-how or a zero-failure philosophy, none of which can be traded on the market. Combining knowledge resources in networks enables innovation and learning that are difficult to provide by other means (Summerton 1999). "In innovation networks, inter-organisational communications negotiate the features of new technologies and integrate user contexts. "Joint agendas and sometimes implementations generate various feedbacks of learning and innovation which reflect on the planning process" (Krohn 1995: 29). Thus, markets are more than places where goods are bought and sold within an institutional context: they are the arenas where innovation takes place, where knowledge is generated, communicated, re-combined and exchanged. The SKIN model to be described in this chapter aims to combine a sociological perspective with insights from evolutionary economics in order to characterise both the trading and the knowledge levels of high-tech innovation networks.

2. The Model

SKIN is a multi-agent model containing heterogeneous agents which act in a complex and changing environment. Its agents are innovative firms who try to sell their innovations to other agents and end users but that also have to buy raw materials or more sophisticated inputs from other agents (or material suppliers) in order to produce their outputs. This basic model of a market is extended with a representation of the knowledge dynamics in and between the firms. Each firm tries to improve its innovation performance and its sales by improving its knowledge base through adaptation to user needs, incremental or radical learning, and co-operation and networking with other agents. In the next paragraphs, the elements and processes of the model are described in further detail.

2.1. The Agents

A SKIN agent is a firm with an individual knowledge base. This knowledge base is called its *kene* (Gilbert 1997) and consists of a number of "units of knowledge". Each unit is represented as a triple consisting of a firm's *capability C* in a scientific, technological or business domain (e.g. biochemistry), represented by an integer randomly chosen from the range of 1..1000, its *ability A* to perform a certain application in this field (e.g. a synthesis procedure or filtering technique in the field of biochemistry), represented by an integer randomly chosen from the range 1..10 and the *expertise level E* the firm has achieved with respect to this ability (represented by an integer randomly chosen from the range 1..10). The firm's kene is its collection of C/A/E-triples.

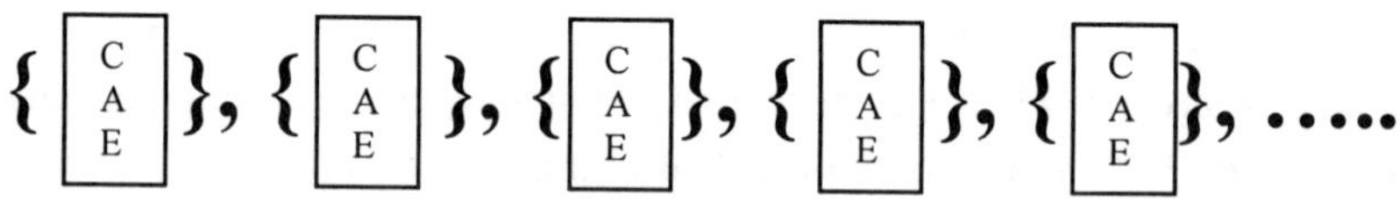

Figure 1: The kene of a firm

When it is set up, each firm has a stock of initial *capital*. It needs this capital to produce for the market and to improve its knowledge base, and it can increase its capital by selling products. The amount of capital owned by a firm is a measure of its size and also influences the amount of knowledge that it can support, represented by the number of triples in its kene.

Most firms are initially given a randomly assigned amount of starting capital, but in order to model differences in firm size, a few randomly chosen firms can be given extra capital (set using the "n-big-firms" slider on the interface - see Figure 5).

2.2. The Market

Firms apply their knowledge to create innovative products that have a chance to be successful in the market. The special focus of a firm, its potential innovation, is called its *innovation hypothesis*. In the model, the innovation hypothesis (IH) consists of a subset of the firm's kene triples.

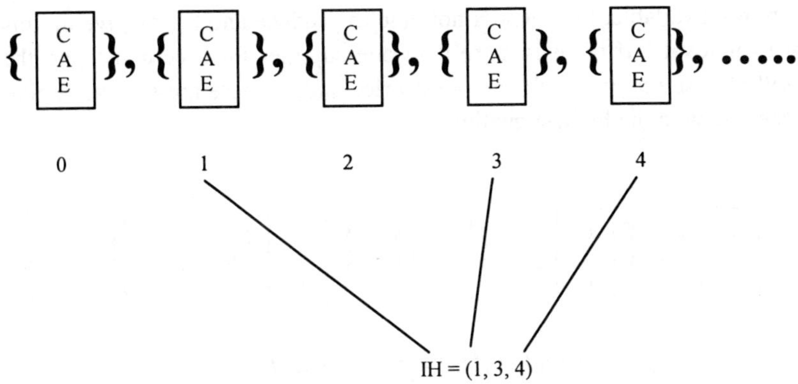

Figure 2: Forming an innovation hypothesis

The underlying idea for an innovation, modelled by the innovation hypothesis, is the source an agent uses for its attempts to make profits on the market. Developing the innovation hypothesis into a *product* is a mapping procedure where the capabilities and abilities of the innovation hypothesis are used to compute an index number that represents the product.

A firm's product, P, is generated from its innovation hypothesis as

$$P = (C_1 * A_1) + (C_3 * A_3) + (C_4 * A_4) + \ldots \text{ modulus } N \qquad (1)$$

(where N is the total number of products ever possible within the model)

The product has a certain *quality* which is also computed from the innovation hypothesis in a similar way, but using a product of the abilities and the expertise levels for each triple in the innovation hypothesis.

In order to realise the product, the agent needs some raw materials or more sophisticated inputs from other agents. What exactly it needs is determined by the underlying innovation hypothesis: the kind of material required for an input is obtained by selecting subsets from the innovation hypotheses and applying the standard mapping function (equation 1).

These inputs are chosen so that each is different and differs from the firm's own product. In order for an agent to be able to engage in production, all the inputs need to be available on the market, i.e. provided by other agents. If the inputs are not available, the agent is not able to produce and has to give up this attempt to innovate. If there is more than one supplier for a certain input, the agent will choose the one at the cheapest price and, if there are several similar offers, the one with the highest quality.

Input 1: $(C_1 * A_1 + C_2 * A_2)$ modulus N

Input 2: $(C_3 * A_3 + C_4 * A_4 + C_5 * A_5)$ modulus N

Figure 3: A firm's input requirements

If the agent can go into production, it has to find a price for its own product which takes account of the input prices it is paying and a possible profit margin. While the simulation starts with assuming that all agents have a product that they can sell and with the product prices set at random, as the simulation proceeds, a price adjustment mechanism ensures that the selling price will at least equal the total cost of production.

An agent will then buy the requested inputs from its suppliers using its capital to do so. It produces its output and puts it on the market in the next round. Agents follow a standard pricing strategy such that if a product sells, its price will be increased, while if it does not sell, the price is reduced each round, until the cost of production is reached. In this way, agents are able to adapt their prices to demand.

In making a product, an agent applies the knowledge in its innovation hypothesis and this increases its expertise in this area. This is the way that *learning by doing/using* is modelled. The expertise level of the triples in the innovation hypothesis is increased by 1 and the expertise levels of the other triples are decremented by 1. Unused triples in the kene eventually drop to an expertise level of 0 and are deleted from the kene; the corresponding abilities are "forgotten".

2.3. The Environment

Within the model, there are two world settings for the agents' environment. With the first, the model represents a closed market in which the agents trade only with each other as equals, sharing the same attributes and rules (see above). Each agent buys its inputs from other agents and itself produces an output which must then be bought by other agents (as part of their input requirements). The alternative world is a market where external sources and purchasers interact with the firm population. With this setting, the model includes some supplier firms and some customer firms. The supplier firms try to sell "raw materials", i.e. the basic elements necessary for the production of goods, to the other firms, but they do not buy anything. The customer firms are 'end users' who buy products without producing anything themselves. The implementation of the model allows for switching between these settings in order to experiment with the two market conditions (see the 'open-system' slider in Figure 5).

2.4. Learning and Co-operation: Improving Innovation Performance

In trying to be successful on the market, the firms are highly dependent on their innovation hypothesis, i.e. on their kene. If a product does not meet any demand, the firm has to adapt its knowledge in order to produce something else for which there are customers. In the model, a firm can choose between different ways of improving its performance, either alone or in co-operation, and either in an incremental or in a more radical fashion. All strategies have in common that they are costly: the firm has to pay a "tax" as the cost of applying an improvement strategy.

2.4.1. *Incremental research*

If a firm's previous innovation has been successful, i.e. the profit it gained was larger than a certain success threshold, the firm will continue selling the same product in the next round. However, if the previous profit was below the threshold, it considers that it is time for change. If the firm still has enough capital, it will carry out incremental research (R&D in the firm's labs). Performing incremental research means that a firm tries to improve its product by altering one of its abilities chosen from the triples in its innovation hypothesis while generally sticking to its focal capabilities. The ability in each triple is considered to be a point in the respective capability's action space. To move in the action space means to go up or down by 1 on the integer scale, thus allowing for two possible incremental "research directions". Initially, the research direction of a firm is set at random. Later it learns to adjust to success or failure: if a move in the action space has been successful the firm will continue with the same research direction within the same triple; if it has been a failure, the firm will randomly select a different triple from the innovation hypothesis and try again with a random research direction on the triple´s ability.

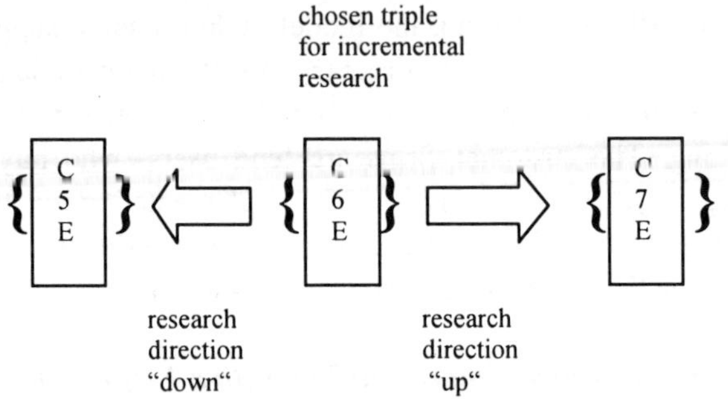

Figure 4: Incremental research

2.4.2. Radical research

A firm under serious pressure that is in danger of becoming bankrupt will turn to more radical means in order to prevent its exit from the market. In this situation, a firm can choose to perform radical research to explore a completely different area of market opportunities. In the model, an agent under financial pressure turns to a new innovation hypothesis after first "inventing" a new capability for its kene. This is done by randomly changing one capability in the kene for a new one and then forming an innovation hypothesis from its kene set.

2.4.3. Partnerships

An agent may consider partnerships (alliances, joint ventures etc.) and networks in order to learn from other agents, i.e. to exploit external knowledge sources. Within the model we can switch between a scenario where partnerships and networks are prohibited and a scenario where they are allowed (see Figure 5, slider "collaboration"). In the latter scenario, the decision whether and with whom to co-operate is based on mutual observations of the agents. The information a firm can gather about other agents is provided by a marketing feature: to advertise its product, a firm publishes the capabilities used in its innovation hypothesis. The firm's advertisement is then the basis for decisions by other firms to form or reject co-operative arrangements.

In experimenting with the model, we can choose between two different partner search strategies, both of which compare the firm's own capabilities in its innovation hypothesis and the possible partner's capabilities as seen in its advertisement. Applying the conservative strategy, a firm will be attracted by a possible partner that has similar capabilities; using a progressive strategy the attraction is based on the difference between the capability sets (see Figure 5, slider "partnership-strategy").

Previously good experience with former contacts generally augurs well for renewing a partnership. This is mirrored in the model: to find a partner, the firm will look at previous partners first, then at its suppliers, customers and finally at all others. If there is a firm sufficiently attractive according to the chosen search strategy (i.e. with attractiveness above the 'attractiveness threshold'), it will stop its search and offer a partnership. If the possible partner wishes to return the partnership offer, the partnership is set up.

The model assumes that partners learn only about the knowledge being actively used by the other agent. Thus, to learn from the partner, a firm will add the triples of the partner's innovation hypothesis to its own. It will take care that it will only take triples which are different from its own triples in the innovation hypothesis: the expertise levels of the triples taken from the partner are set down to 1 in order to mirror the difficulty of integrating external knowledge. If the partner has a similar triple in terms of capability and ability but a higher expertise level the firm will drop its own triple in favour of the partner's one; if the expertise level of a similar triple is lower, the firm will stick to its own version. Once the knowledge transfer has been completed, each firm continues to produce its own product, possibly with greater expertise as a result of acquiring skills from its partner.

2.4.4. Networks

If the firm's last innovation was successful, i.e. the amount of its profit in the previous round was above a threshold, and the firm has some partners at hand, it can initiate the formation of a network. This can considerably increase its profits because the network will try to create innovations as an autonomous agent in addition to those created by its members. It will distribute any rewards to its members who, in the meantime, can continue with their own attempts, thus providing a double chance for profits. However, the formation of networks is costly, which has two consequences: only firms with enough capital can form or join a network and no firm can be member of two networks at the same time.

Networks are "normal" agents, i.e. they get the same amount of initial capital as other firms and can engage in all the activities available to other firms. The kene of a network is the union of the triples from the innovation hypotheses of all its participants. If a network is successful it will distribute any earnings above the amount of the initial capital to its members; if it fails and becomes bankrupt, it will be dissolved.

2.4.5. Start-ups

If the sector is successful, new firms will be attracted into it. This is modelled by adding a new firm to the population when any existing firm makes a substantial profit. The new firm is a clone of the successful firm, but with its kene triples restricted to those in the successful firm's advertisement, and an expertise level of 1. This models a new firm copying the characteristics of those seen to be successful in the market. As with all firms, the kene may also be restricted because the initial capital of a start-up is limited and may not be sufficient to support the copying of the whole of the successful firm's knowledge base.

3. The Implementation

The model has been programmed using NetLogo (http://ccl.northwestern.edu/netlogo/) and is available from the authors.

With a complex model such as this one, extensive experiments have to be carried out to understand its behaviour and the sensitivity of the output to variations in the input parameters. This work has not yet been completed. Nevertheless, we can give an impression of how it performs using standard parameter settings.

The main graphic window (Figure 5) shows about 100 firms (represented by the small 'factory' shapes). Their position in the display window is not significant: a layout algorithm is used to move the factory icons to positions where they can best be seen. Factory icons in a lighter shade mark firms that were created after the start of the simulation (i.e. they are start ups) and those that are darker are network firms (firms producing on behalf of a network, with a kene based on the union of the kenes of the network members). The size of the icons indicates the amount of capital its firm possesses (the size is proportional to $\log_{10}$ of the amount of capital).

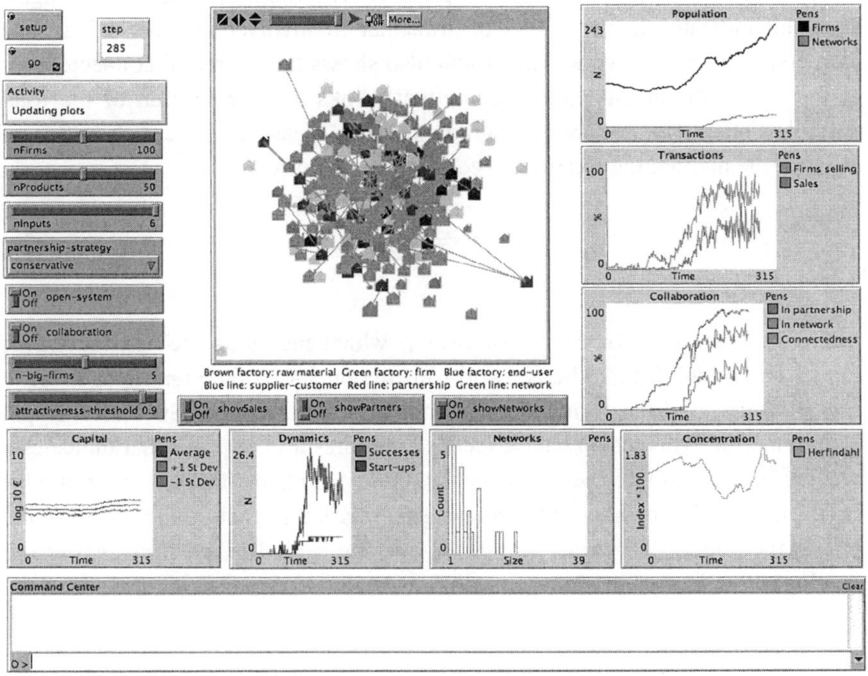

Figure 5: The interface of the model

The numerous lines indicate partnerships, supplier relationships and network linkages between firms. Those not involved in any relationship have been moved by the layout algorithm to the margins of the display. There is 1 network (having 14 members). The networks are shown with lines connecting all their members to the network firm. The medium grey factories are those producing 'raw materials' (these firms require no inputs from within the system in order to create their products); the dark grey ones are 'end-users' that produce no outputs.

The display is surrounded by graphs monitoring various aggregate aspects of the system. At the top right is shown the growth in the population of firms as start-ups are added, and the slow growth in the number of networks. The graph below shows the percentage of firms that have products on the market ('Firms selling') and the percentage that have made a sale ('Sales'); the latter is always less than the former because some firms are unable to find customers prepared to buy at the price proposed for the product. The third graph down the right-hand side indicates the percentage of firms that are involved in either at least one partnership or in a network. This graph also shows the degree of connectedness of the firms (the actual partner or network links as a proportion of the total possible links). The bottom right graph shows a measure of the distribution of funds in the market, the Herfindahl concentration index H_t,

$$H_t = \sum_n s_i^t \tag{2}$$

where s^t_i is the relative capital of firm i, which measures the distribution of capital among the firms. The Networks histogram shows the number of firms in each network, and the Dynamics plot indicates, on the upper Successes graph, the number of firms which have exceeded the threshold of profit that indicates a successful innovation (the 'success threshold') and, on the lower Start Ups graph, the number of new firms entering the market at each round. The Capital plot in the bottom left corner shows the average capital of the firms, expressed as a logarithm base 10.

4. Conclusions

The SKIN model is an attempt to improve our understanding of the complex processes going on in modern innovation. The model goes far beyond previous theoretical attempts in economics of analyzing the industrial organization of innovation processes (e.g. D'Aspremont and Jacquemin, 1988 and all model extensions, see Martin 2003 for an excellent survey). Instead of integrating strategic alliances and cooperative R&D in a standard equilibrium model of oligopolistic competition, insights coming from numerous case and industry studies are used to model the actors' decision procedures relating to innovation processes. Using an agent-based simulation framework allows the modelling of innovation processes through abstracting from reality without assuming away those essential characteristics of innovation processes (e.g. true uncertainty, historical time, heterogeneous agents learning experimentally, the consequences of failure, and learning from each other in partnerships and networks) that are heavily emphasized by modern innovation economists working in an evolutionary framework (e.g. Nelson, 2001).

SKIN allows the investigation of different industries in which there are differing strategies by altering the model's parameters. Parameters can be estimated econometrically from data sets describing an industry's cooperative behaviour. Such data sets are becoming increasingly available for e.g. the biotechnology-based industries and the information and telecommunication industries. Alternatively, the historical development of a particular industry can be reproduced by finding a set of parameters that gives a time trace that mirrors the development of the industry. Having reproduced the historical sequence in one industry, one can try to find the critical parameters which change the model's results so that they follow the historical sequence of another industry. With such exercises, which are on our agenda for future research, we will develop a much better understanding of the industries under consideration and will also be able to evaluate different policy measures and their efficacy for particular industries.

References

D'Aspremont, C., Jacquemin, A. (1988), Cooperative and Non-Cooperative R&D in Duopoly with Spillovers, *American Economic Review*, Vol. 78, 1133–1137.

Granovetter, M. (1985): Economic Action and Social Structure: The problem of Embeddedness. *American Journal of Sociology* 91: S. 481–510.

Martin, S. (2003), The Evaluation of Strategic Research Partnerships, *Technology Analysis & Strategic Management*, Vol. 15, No. 2, 159–176.

Gilbert, N. (1997): A Simulation of the Structure of Academic Science. In: *Sociological Research Online*, vol.2, no.2, <http://www.socresonline.org.uk/socresonline/2/2/3.html>.

Krohn, W. (1995): Die Innovationschancen partizipatorischer Technikgestaltung und diskursiver Konfliktregelung. IWT-Paper 9/95.

Nelson, R. (2001), Evolutionary Perspectives on Economic Growth, in: Dopfer, K. (ed.), *Evolutionary Economics, Program and Scope*, Kluwer Academic Publishers, Boston, Dordrecht, London.

Powell, W.W. (1990): Neither Market nor Hierarchy. Network Forms of Organization. *Research in Organizational Behavior* 12: S. 295–336.

Scheider, V. und P. Kenis (1996): Verteilte Kontrolle. Institutionelle Steuerung in modernen Gesellschaften. In: Kenis, P. und V. Schneider (Hg.) (1996): *Organisation und Netzwerk. Institutionelle Steuerung in Wirtschaft und Politik*. Frankfurt: Campus, S. 9–43.

Summerton, J. (1999): Linking Artifacts and Actors in Electricity. In: O. Coutard (Hg.) (1999): *The Governance of Large Technical Systems*. London: Routledge.

Weyer, J. (2000): Einleitung: Zum Stand der netzwerkforschung in den Sozialwissenschaften. In: Weyer, J. (Hg.) (2000): *Soziale Netzwerke. Konzepte und Methoden der sozialwissenschaftlichen Netzwerkforschung*. Wien/München: Oldenbourg, S. 1–34.

Willke, H. (1995): *Systemtheorie III. Steuerungstheorie: Grundzüge einer Theorie der Steuerung komplexer Sozialsysteme*. Stuttgart: UTB.

A GENERALISED COMPUTATIONAL MODEL OF FIRMS PRODUCTION AND INTERACTIONS: PRELIMINARY RESULTS ON INDUSTRIAL DYNAMICS*

TOMMASO CIARLI†

Università di Ferrara and University of Birmingham,
V. del Gregorio 13,
44100 Ferrara, Italy
ciarli@economia.unife.it

MARCO VALENTE

Università dell'Aquila,
P.le del Santuario 19,
67040 Roio Poggio (L'Aquila), Italy
mv@business.auc.dk

In the present work we describe a model of production processes, with a detailed representation of vertical interactions across sectors, in an input-output framework. Firms are heterogeneous agents, each with its competencies in production, using different inputs with different characteristics, acting in a specific sector. Firms within each sector produce similar goods, but with different quality features appealing to the sector's demand. We show, through different simulation settings, that the way in which the process is modelled is both extremely flexible and its results are robust under standard basic economics assumptions. As discussed in a methodological section we argue that those characteristics of the model are important in order to study the production structure to understand different industrial dynamics through a micro perspectives. In particular, we propose one particular framework, which synthesises the aspects of a broader research for which this model has been developed.

*We thank Prof. R. Sugden for useful comments on a first version. Any responsibility for the information proposed is ours.

†The author acknowledges the support of the PhD scholarship from the University of Ferrara.

1. Introduction

This paper is part of a broader research that aims at understanding the industrialisation (and innovation) processes in less developed countries, and how their different paths affect growth and capabilities to compete. Given the centrality of both individual actors and their interactions in shaping those emergent macro conditions, we partly (conceptually) draw on growth models based on micro evolutionary dynamics[1,2,3,4]. Nonetheless, we consider that firms do not operate in an aseptic environment; on the contrary, they are embedded in a particular institutional milieu that entails framework rules and other organisations not devoted to production. Thus, we aim at understanding how this system changes due to the interaction of local actors, how its proportion conversely affect their characteristics and interacting behaviour, and finally, how the relations with external systems (composed by other actors) are shaped, and conversely shape, the local features. We thus aim at building an agent based prototype that aims at replicating such a complex interacting system.

In the present contribution we draw from this general framework and focus on the modelling of the production process, with particular reference to elements that shape and are shaped by the relations among firms. In brief the model represents i heterogeneous firms, which produce in different sectors combining k inputs (with h_k quality features), with a vector of m competencies. That is, the production of a firm takes place combining the characteristics of the inputs with the firm's own competencies, and results in a vector of output characteristics. Firms are depicted as complex agents, but not as systems of interactions themselves (although there is an interaction between competencies and input, but not between agents). The output is represented in a Lancasterian fashion [5], following the conceptual framework redesigned by Ref. 6. In sum, the output consists in a vector of different features of a manufactured good. Final demand is a function of both prices and qualities of the firms in the final demand sector, weighted with exogenous elasticities.

This flexible representation of firms' activities allows a flexible representation of production processes by managing the technical coefficients that determine which input is used in each sector. Vertical interaction between buyers and sellers is modelled as the acquisition of an input vector with its own features, which it the outcome vector of the supplier. Thus, the features of the final goods depend on the features of the inputs used, eventually providing an incentive to both users and producers to co-operate (e.g.

knowledge exchange, input's features definition, etc.) [7], reducing their distance. The supplier is extracetd among the ones on the available market, proportional to its product features (quality and price).

We model the process by means of an agent based model in which variables co-evolve, causalities are defined, and the results portray the relevant emergent properties and interactions[a].

In the next section we present and discuss the methodological point of view adopted, anticipating some considerations on the results obtained and the model presented. In the third section we briefly describe the *general structure* of the economic system, for which the relevant model is built. In section four, we describe the formal construction of the *basic production model*, showing few examples of expected results provided by the model simulations. The fifth section extends the model to implement vertical input-output processes, and again presents some preliminary results. We conclude with some final considerations, suggesting potentially interesting future extensions.

2. Discussion on the Methodology of Simulations in Economics

The use of simulation models in theoretical economics is quite a controversial subject, and the more so for the type of models presented (and suggested) in this work. We claim our model to be a good representation of a quite complex reality, but we don't provide any support for the values used for the parameterization, nor compare our results with real world data. The reason is that we use our model as a "virtual world" that we can analyse in detail. We sustain that the phenomena emerging in our simulations and, most importantly, the motivations for such phenomena, provide useful insights on the much more complex real events. Since this method to present economic results is quite new, and likely to be controversial, in this section we discuss in some greater detail our methodological approach.

Traditionally, two types of simulation models are normally accepted as methodologically rigorous. A first type of models consist in building a quantitatively realistic representation of some real system, and is used to

[a]The language used to implement the model allows an easy management of the complicated model structure, in particular concerning the model initialization and the analysis of the results. For details on the language see Ref. 8, Laboratory for Simulation Development (LSD) (`http://www.business.auc.dk/Lsd`). Copies of the model can be requested to the authors.

forecast the state of the system after some time. These models can be evaluated with the traditional statistical tools testing for their adherence to the data of interest, and their results are judged according to the same criterion. For example, such models are used to study the behaviour of turbulent fluids. Concerning economic subjects, these "applied" models abound in the offices of central banks or consultants, willing to forecasts future directions of large or small systems.

A second type of simulation models concerns abstract systems that the standard set of analytical tools cannot describe. The simulation model provides a numerical estimation of the model properties, and the evaluation of the model is judged according to the robustness of the properties of the system against different parameterization and/or random events. Example of these models became popular in physics as the "Montecarlo" simulations. Like the mathematical theorems that such models surrogate, one does not necessarily need to understand the proof for appreciating the results.

In both methodological approaches described above the models themselves are considered as "black boxes". Once the code has been certified as correct (i.e. containing no programming error), all one is interested in is the input and output of the program, and the interest focuses on the relation between the two sets of data. Our approach is instead quite different. We use initialization that we consider "sensible", without being interested in using data as close as possible to a specific historical or geographical evidence. And we do not search for general properties of the model, to be found within a large part of the parameter space. Instead, we "open" the black box in order to study how the assembled elements of the model interact through time to produce the results. It is the explanations of the results which are of interest, rather than the results themselves. And it is the explanations that will be evaluated as more or less interesting, in both sense of being unexpected and relevant for deepening our understanding of real events.

Note that the methodology we used here is not alternative to the two mentioned earlier. One may actually apply all the three methodologies at the same time building a model that: i) closely represents a real system; ii) provides robust general properties, and iii) provides explanations for those general properties. Obviously, the right methodology to use depends on the goals one pursues: our goal is to set the stage to understand the mechanisms of creation (or failure to do so) of sustainable growth of knowledge in a productive system. This perspective does not require a strict adherence to a specific reality in a given time and place, since different contexts provide widely different measurements, or even definitions, of knowledge. Nor we claim to provide universal laws governing economic systems. Therefore, a qualitative and partial analysis provided by simulating a simplified system suffices for our goal.

Given the particular structure of the proposed methodology we may refer to it as *qualitative simulation modelling*. The goal of such methodology consists in analysing how particular configurations of the model emerge during a simulation run out of the interaction of the model elements. Referring once more to the terminology proposed by Ref. 9 we may say that qualitative simulation modelling is based on the study of the *emergent properties* of a system. In particular, we want to identify the explanations for such phenomena by replicating them in a simulated model and identifying their determinants. There may be two classes of explanations that can be conceptually considered, although most of the times they appear together: temporal and aggregative explanations. Temporal explanations consists in the temporal sequence of events that give rise to the emergent properties. Aggregative explanation consists in the list of the components making up the aggregate phenomenon. As already mentioned, these two classes of explanation are usually intertwined: an explanation is provided by listing a set of elements, their properties and their dynamics through time, providing an explanation for an aggregate property of the system.

Note that the explanations can only go up to a limit. In our case we provide explanations composed by the elementary routines and initial values used in the simulation that eventually produced the final result. The relevance of qualitative simulation results can hardly be measured by the usual instruments used to assess quantitative models, like the degree of fitting available data or robustness. Rather, it should be evaluated on the basis of how well the basic routines represent their purported reality.

This *un*-scientific approach does not depend on the method of research, but on the subject to which it is applied. The proposed methodology finds a natural application for research questions that pose the attention on *how* given phenomena occur, rather than on *what* actually occurs. Many of the phenomena of interest in Economics, in fact, can be formally explained with a plethora of generation mechanisms. That is, there are many different ways to explain each observed phenomena. The difficulty is in finding a generation mechanism that is both able to explain many of these phenomena at once and is compatible with the (generally scarce) evidence we have on what actually goes on in the real world. It is a difficult task because this entails to consider the interactions among many components makes difficult, if not impossible, to devise the aggregate outcome. In these cases, computers are a unique instrument to replicate, in a controlled environment, some of the complexity observed in the reality. We can build a program composed by many individual functions, possibly even quite simple, but whose interactions makes all but impossible to infer the behaviour of their aggregation through time. A simulation run provides such information, generating a virtual history of what happens to our artificial world.

However, the simple generation of data series resembling real ones is not enough. As said, the observed phenomena can be generated in many ways, and using a computer programs can be only yet another one. The advantage of computers is that we can re-run a simulation, add to the model variables to collect detailed statistics, observe step-by-step crucial moments of the simulated history, and use many other tools to interpret the results. Understanding the unfolding of the complexity in the artificial system can teach us something about the events taking place in the real world (and eventually be able to apply this knowledge). Cause-effect chains can be spotted in the model that are, at the same time, consequences of the model structure but, also, far from obvious before running the simulation. A successful simulation run is one that makes evident some implications of our model that are not obvious *and* appear of relevance in the real world. That is, we have gained knowledge by using the simulation model that we can apply in the real world.

Using simulation models consists in building artificial representation of portions of reality. This activity alone is worth attention because forces us to express rigorously concepts that frequently are defined in quite vague terms[b]. For the present version of the model we limited ourselves to study quite trivial types of results, and we checked that their generation reproduces the explanations normally used in elementary textbooks. Even in this stage, the mere attempt to provide a working representation of elementary economic events forced us to devise some less-than-elementary computa-

[b]See, for example, the concept of local system of production, which can be defined as a cluster, district, milieu, local innovation system, and so forth. Those concepts are used to promote industrial development in developing countries, but, having understood the theoretical background underneath, one would ask, on the basis of which elements they are implemented, apart from idiosyncratic learning-by-doing? Following the Italian district tradition of the seventies, the English district tradition of the 19th century, the clustering dynamics of biotech industries...? One should then carefully analyse which type of linkages endorses innovation[10], and how they can be promoted. Things get much more complicated if we expand the system toward relations that are external to it, but which have to be taken into account.

tional structures. These difficulties stem from the ways standard economics is generally taught in undergraduate courses. We are told the *properties* of economic systems, or agents' behaviour, such as the definition of equilibria or of optimal behaviour. But we are not even suggested how they actually can be implemented. Instead, a computer program consists of instructions to be executed, with the properties being the results of the computation. Our experience, shared by many simulation modellers, is that the very reasoning about the design of a model is a highly productive stage in terms of economic theoretical research. In fact, one cannot express in a computer language inconsistent statements, or overlook elements necessary for the working of the model, as one is allowed when describing verbally a model. Even mathematical representations highlight possible inconsistencies only during the elaboration of the model's equation. The very use of a computer language is a rigorous test of the viability of our theory, even before the first test run is executed. It is very frequent the case of adjustments, even radical, of a model caused by errors and mis-specifications emerged only when the model begins to be implemented.

Another advantage of simulation models consists in the possibility to build up gradually a complicated model starting from simple components (simple sub models). For example, our model already generates results that would be difficult to interpret, if we did not develop it gradually the different parts of the system. Testing each and every new equation and the changing to the overall results after the modification guarantees both that the new part is error-free, and that we can understand the results. However, this aspect relies heavily on the kind of language used for the implementation of the model. Technically, any computer language has the same power of expression. In principle one can choose whatever language and this should not affect the model represented or its results. However, experience shows that some languages are more adapt than others for simulation models. Object Oriented languages (originally designed on purpose for simulation models) have proved themselves to be the most adequate choice because they allow an easier modularization of a program, which, in turn, provides higher robustness against modifications due to error-fixes and extensions. Such questions may seem not relevant for economists, in that one may consider the implementation of model a mere technical task, to be delegated to an expert technician. After all, many economists (with little mathematical knowledge) rely on professional mathematicians (with little or no economic training) to produce theorems with important economic consequences. The economist is not interested in the proofs, as long as these are confirmed to be correct. However, for the kind of use of computer models proposed, this is not possible. In fact, we put forward that precisely in the technical inner workings of the simulation program lies the interest of the model. A technicians, however good as programmer, cannot have the sensitivity to appreciate the economic relevance of the model results.

While suggesting that economists should write their own simulation programs, we do not sustain that they need to become sophisticated programmers. In fact, a simulation program, like any program, is roughly made for 90% of lines implementing merely technical code, meant to deal with interfaces of various nature, and only a small portion of lines directly expressing the model dynamics. Writing a model with a generic computer language forces the programmer to write a whole program, which may require advanced technical skills. This is specially the case for the use of simulation models we propose. In fact, we need to have the possibility to observe the results in the greatest detail, accessing every component of the model and presenting its data in any desired format. As any programmer's know, writing human interfaces in a software is a highly difficult task, generally much more difficult than writing the code for the actual elaboration requested to the program. In general, if one limits himself to write only the code strictly related to the model's scientific content, the writing a model is quite simple, requiring only basic notions of programming concerning few algebraic-logical operations. The language we used to implement the model is in itself an attempt to promote our methodological approach. In Lsd a model writer needs to implement only the lines concerning the way variables are computed, basically the computational equivalent of a difference equation system. For our model it consisted of less than 400 lines of mostly trivial code, consisting in algebraic operations, cycles and IF-THEN-ELSE statements. Lsd envelops such model-specific code with many general-purpose layers providing sophisticated interfaces to initialize the model, checking for errors, inspect data during a run, analyse the results, etc. The resulting program is a professional software (basically a C++ implementation of the model) that any user with a minimal training can exploit to generate data and, most importantly for us, make sense of them.

Concluding this section, we have sustained that simulation models need not necessarily to produce a quantitatively convincing replication of reality, but that can be used to understand complex patterns in a controlled environment in order to shed light on similar events in the real world. Such knowledge takes the form of explanations, either temporal or aggregative, of configurations assumed by the model. The methodology proposed implies that economists get involved in the technicalities of building simulation programs. This implication, though crucial for extracting scientific knowledge from the models, does not require a high level of programming skills.

3. The general settings: the theoretical structure of the system

In line with the methodological argumentation discussed in section 2, the model presented in the remainder of the paper is a tool that can be implemented in order to understand the mechanisms underpinning complex phenomena. In the present section we describe the main features of the system to which we propose to apply it.

In practice, we model a process of production of manufacturing firms, which entails different features of competencies, input and output quality features, routines, productivity, and demand. Next, we model their *linear* input/output interaction.

Broadly speaking, we try to conceive an economic system that entails the analysis of "the economy as an evolving complex system" [11], which is characterised by: i) dispersed agents acting in parallel, the action of which, as well as their generated outcome, reflect on their behaviour in the following periods; ii) no global entity regulating the system, such as the Walrasian auctioneer; iii) different levels of interactions, which only to a certain extent are hierarchically coordinated, formed by different organisations and institutions (e.g. firms, public bodies, service providers, rules, norms, and the like); iv) agents learning from and adapting to the changing system in which they are embedded; v) conditions emerging from the continuous interactions, which are sometimes completely new with respect to the past (radical innovations); and vi) the existence of equilibrium only as a transitory condition, and not as a state.

Hence, we first concentrate on the construction of the main agents of the system: we model firms' production processes, and the way in which they evolve in an 'aseptic' environment. However, we consider enterprises as only one layer of an hypothetical economic system in which they are designed as the driving forces[c]. The following description of the system allows us to 'position' the agents theoretically, describe the possible implementation of the model in different settings, and propose one particular system

[c]We adopt the idea of the firm as the driving force from the neo-Shumpeterian literature (e.g. Ref. 3), which converesly also argues the importance of the system in which it is embedded (e.g. Ref. 12.

construction. With the latter we aim at showing the rationale underneath the model, and how the agent-based simulation can help the understanding of the 'emergent phenomena' we are interested in: process of industrial development in developing countries.

We conceive an 'economic system' as composed by four different levels, which we present in a hierarchical order, without clear-cutting among them: i) the firm; ii) the Local Production (Innovation) System (LPS); iii) the National Production (Innovation) System (NPS); and iv) the Global (international/open) environment.

The four levels can be thought as different "emergent hierarchical organisations" [9], thus as the emergent representation of the lower level agents interactions. Conversely, the upper levels represent some of the conditions to which the lower level agents react, according to their behavioural rules (routines, etc.), which are also shaped by the upper level. Moreover, the emergent systems are themselves interacting agents, which generate the following hierarchical level (e.g. firms interaction shape the LPS and the interaction between the different local systems generate the national conditions). Hence, there is a bi-univocal relation between the agents and their emergent properties (which has also been defined as the 'second order' emergent property (e.g. Ref. 13). Similarly, we recognise that firms should be considered as sets of interacting agents (e.g. Ref. 14, 15). Given that we need to stop the disaggregation at a certain level, we choose the firm as the lower one, and model it as a complex agent with internal routines.

Given the complexity and the infinite structure of the hierarchical systems, we concentrate on one intermediate level: the local system. We define two types of agents that interact in the system: local manufacturing firms and local non productive organisations (NPO). While the first are modelled as complex agents, the latter are exogenously given, do not have endogenous dynamics and provide local conditions. In short, they can be considered as the scaffolding organisations, described by Ref. 16 as those agents that support the overall local production system[d]. Moreover, we consider the relations between agents of the second hierarchical level (LPS), with agents in the global system, the fourth level: i.e. the interactions between local firms and foreign ones (external to the local and national system). Thus, the national system (third level) simply sets the macro conditions in which the two lower levels change and adapt, and is eventually set aside.

[d]Actually, the author refers to the structure of an Industrial District, which is considered in our structure one particular condition of the LPS

In all, in the particular system construction in which we want the embed the agents/firms, three kind of linkages will be considered:

- *Local manufacturing firms* ↔ *local manufacturing firms (vertical* and horizontal)
- Local manufacturing firms ↔ local non productive organisations
- *Local firms* ↔ *international firms (vertical)*

In particular, in the present paper we test a model for the first and partially the third interaction, for what concerns the input output relation.

The model is not purely agent based, as we include aggregate dynamics (i.e. the demand in the final market). Only local firms are actually modelled as: i) autonomous, each behaving according to personal rules; ii) with social ability, able to interact with other agents understand each other through a common language; iii) reactive to the environment in which they are embedded; and iv) proactive toward the environment, trying to change the environment and adapt it to their aims [17].

Thus, firms' action depend on their 'neighbours' status and action, but we differ from statistical (physical) interacting models in two main aspects: i) we consider proximity as a meta-dynamic feature, such that agents change their position with respect to one another (we refer in this case to communication and technological values more than to geographical ones), thus changing the type and extent of influence they exert, and ii) we are more interested in a firm model which allows the understanding of agents' action and reaction than their final outcome in itself.

To wrap-up with the rationale of the overall system structure (of which, we recall, this paper shows only the agent's modelling), the aim is to frame an 'artificial world' for the analysis of Local Production Systems (LPS) and the relations between its actors with external ones (traders, brokers, suppliers, foreign investors, etc.). We aim at understanding to which extent the local Network Structure (NS) and the LPS are evolving entities with an important role in explaining the industrialisation processes of a defined system (might be a locality or region). We argue that their initial conditions, the relations with the broader national system, and the way they are aligned with the international networks[e], shape their capability to compete. 'Competitiveness' refers not only to the single actors' efficiency or to macro

[e]We borrow the idea of alignment of networks at different levels (local, national and international) as a key variable to investigate and understand 'successful' industrialisation processes from Ref. 18.

indicators, but to the capability of the system to innovate and upgrade, approaching a leading role in 'production' (and innovation[f]). Defining the LPS, we refer to the concept of National Innovation Systems[g] transferred to the local or regional level, and its localised institutions and organisations. Finally, the concept of NS focuses on the linkages among the local players, in terms of strength, fluidity, extension, flexibility, etc.

Provided the overall structure to which we refer, in the remainder of the paper we first describe how we model the main agents of the system, the firms. Next, we extend the model to the first application, which entails the input-output relations between firms in different sectors. The model thus describes an industrial organisation composed of different interacting agents, the action of which directly or indirectly affects others behaviour and outcomes. The high flexibility of the model allows a wide number of implementations by imposing diverse initializations; we will present a set of results that are particularly relevant to the type of conceptual framework discussed above.

4. Production model and interpretation of the results

We describe in the present section the 'engine' of the overall model, a process of firms' production, aiming to describe and render operative a flexible production function. The scope of this first basic model is to replicate basic results of a production market, with no particular and unexpected behaviour, as it has no endogenous dynamics (i.e. no autonomous decision by the firms as direct reactions to changes in the market and of other firms). Firms react (adapt) to the demand in terms of formation of market shares, revenues and profit, but do not change their strategies when facing changes in the market results. Although some of the equations are defined for both the final sector and the intermediate goods' sectors, we introduce the lat-

[f]When referring to developing countries, it is usually difficult to talk about leading (radical) innovators; but we can still consider innovation at the local level, thus relative to the starting conditions. That is, innovation might be both radical and incremental when considering the single country, but is less likely when considering the international manufacturing system.

[g]The literature on national and regional innovation systems is becoming quite large, and analyses them under marginally different perspectives. On the first see for example Ref. 19, Ref. 7 and Ref. 12; on the latter for example Ref. 20 and Ref. 21. The central characteristic, which emerges through the various representations, is the view of the industrialisation process as a systematic evolution in which the interaction among the different actors characterises the pattern of each country/region (also through the interaction with external players).

ter only in the following section, as a model extension. In this section we consider firms producing competing products for final consumption.

The model wants to be a robust framework to represent a basic production process. Once we have convincingly implemented the model and its results conform to our expectations, we will be able to extend the basic version to include other aspects. As a matter of example, we list some of the possibly interesting extensions of the model that we have in mind, and that are, therefore, perfectly compatible with it.

We will neglect any direct interaction at the horizontal level, and reaction functions between firms, which produce only in function of the changes in the final demand. Nonetheless, we set the model such that the different relations with other agents, introduced step by step, can affect differently the dynamic of each firm. There is also no "demography" of firms (entry and exit), which would require further assumptions, for example on the financial conditions; firms can produce for a very small portion of the market, being still able to survive. Hence, firms produce a positive quantity as far as they have a share of the market (which never goes to zero), and hence make profits (provided that fix costs are low enough)[h]. We will also consider firms endowed with exogenous production capabilities; however, we will implement this generally slippery concept, in such a way that will be easy to implement an extension with endogenous capabilities.

4.1. *The basic production model*

The aim of this section is to describe the implementation of a production model with heterogeneous products. We will not propose revolutionary definitions, but rather we will limit our work to propose a working implementation of representations that, though widely known and appreciated in the past literature, have never been translated in a fully functioning model.

We consider a set of firms each of them producing the same type of product. That is, a product is represented in a Lancasterian fashion[5,22] as a vector of quality characteristics. All firms in a sector have therefore products defined over the same characteristics, although each product is differentiated in that it can have different quality levels on each characteristic. Thus, the product of firm i defined over m characteristics will be denoted as:

[h]Note that we are always referring to the final market.

$$\vec{y}_i = \{y_{1,i}, y_{2,i}, \ldots, y_{m,i}\}$$

Production takes place by combining inputs with firm-specific competencies. Each firm has a certain amount of initial resources and combines them to obtain the final product. Following the framework drawn by Ref. 22, and modified by Ref. 6, conceptually the output vector of characteristics $\vec{y}$ is produced through the combination of a set of vector of competencies $\vec{\vec{A}}$ and different vectors of technical characteristics $\vec{w}$ embedded into inputs (one vector for each input used), as in Figure 1. The production of one single product requires the use of different inputs (e.g. intermediate, primary goods and capital), each of which can be introduced in the production process given the existence of minimum competencies.

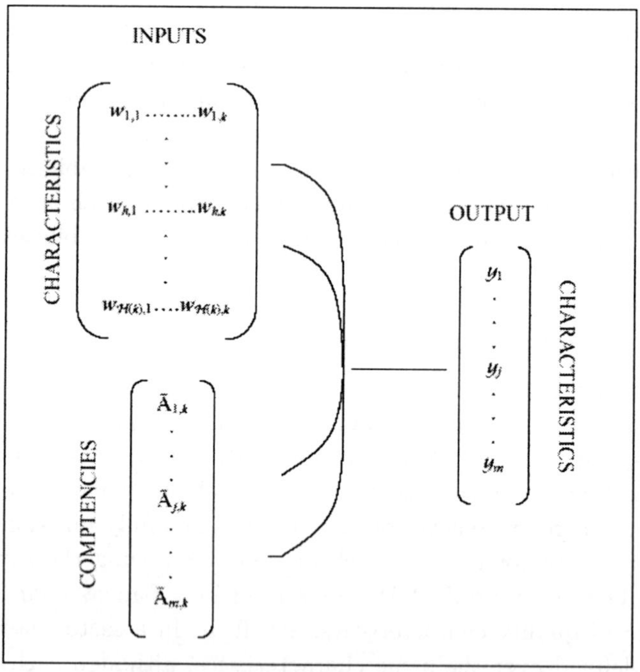

Source: Adapted from Ref. 6, p. 544

Figure 1. Qualitative representation of the production process: the combination of inputs (with their own features) and competencies result in a set of output characteristics

The schema in Fig.1 is implemented by representing each output's characteristic value as a linear combination of all characteristics of all inputs and the competencies of the firm. Let's consider a firm using K different inputs, defined respectively over H_1, H_2, ..., H_K characteristics. Thus, the generic input k is a vector of values $\vec{w}_k = \{w_{1,k}, w_{2,k}, \ldots, w_{H_k,k}\}$. The generic output characteristic y_j of the firm i is computed by averaging each input's characteristic using the competencies concerning this characteristic as weights:

$$y_j = 1 + \frac{\sum_{k=1}^{K} \sum_{h=1}^{H_k} a_{j,h,k} \cdot w_{h,k}}{\sum_{k=1}^{K} H_k} \tag{1}$$

where $a_{j,h,k}$ expresses the competence of the firm to manage characteristic h of input k in producing output characteristic j.

This modelisation is quite simple and flexible in the use of competences, which can vary for all inputs (e.g. general learning by doing at the firm level, or change in organisation, etc.) or for specific ones (e.g. increase in capital input quality, imports of specific materials, etc.). We normalise the values of the output in order to avoid having distorting large numbers from the multiplication of factors, which would arbitrarily change the weights of qualities and prices in the definition of market shares and of the final demand (see Eq. 2 and 4). For the same reason we scale the values to be greater than one.

The demand[i] for each firm is computed with a two-stages process. Firstly, total final demand is computed; secondly, this total is distributed among the firms of the sector. Both stages are based on the values of the individual products' qualities (and prices, whose inverse is treated as an additional product quality). Both steps are "smoothed" in respect of time, so that sudden changes in products' qualities take time to be reflected in actual market shares. Therefore, we have a "target" total demand, to which actual demand slowly adapts, and "target" market shares trailed with some lag by the actual market shares.

Target demand is computed following a Cobb-Douglas-like function of

[i]This basic implementation of the model does not consider stocks or rationing of demand, so that demand, sales and quantity produced are always identical.

the average product qualities:

$$D^* = H \cdot \left(1/\overline{p}_{t-1}\right)^{\alpha^p} \prod_{j=1}^{m} \overline{y}_j^{\alpha^j} \tag{2}$$

H is a constant, the over-lined symbols are the averages of prices and single product characteristics across all the firms (weighted by the quantities),

$$\overline{p}_t = \sum_{i=1}^{n} p_{i,t} \cdot ms_{i,t-1}$$

$$\overline{y}_{m,t} = \sum_{i=1}^{n} y_{i,m,t} \cdot ms_{i,t-1};$$

and the α^{y_m} and α^p stand for the sensitivity of the demand to each characteristic and to price, and are always positive.

The actual demand for firms in the final market is given by a smooth adjustment (s^D) to the target demand:

$$D_t = s^D D_{t-1} + \left(1 - s^D\right) D_t^* \tag{3}$$

The individual firm's demand in the the final market is computed as a share of total demand proportional to an index of 'competitiveness', which is determined by the relative price and qualities of firms in respect of its competitors. The procedure computes first the index of 'competitiveness' for each firm as:

$$I_i = \left(1/p_{i,t-1}\right)^{\alpha^p} \prod_{j=1}^{m} y_{i,j}^{\alpha^j} \tag{4}$$

where the elasticities α^{y_m} and α^p are the same used in the demand equation (2).

The indexes translate in target market shares. Considering a sector containing n firms, the target market share of the generic firm i is computed as:

$$ms_i^* = \frac{I_i}{\sum_{j=1}^{n} I_j}$$

The actual market share of firm at time t becomes, after the time smoothing,:

$$ms_t = s^{MS} ms_{t-1} + \left(1 - s^{MS}\right) ms_t^*$$

Finally, the actual level of sales of firms is computed by multiplying their market shares times the actual total demand:

$$q_t = ms_t * D_t \tag{5}$$

Given the level of sales, a firm determines the amount of inputs required by multiplying the sales times the technical coefficient for each input. As in Ref. 3 we use a Leontieff production function with fixed coefficients:

$$q_k^I = \beta_k \cdot q \tag{6}$$

where β_k represents the amount of input k required for the production of one unit of output. Consequently variable costs can be computed as the product of the amounts of all inputs used times their prices:

$$c^V = \sum_{k=1}^{K} q_k^I \cdot p_k^I \tag{7}$$

Assuming a monopolistic competition, provided the heterogeneity of the goods produced, on the base of the variable costs the price is computed adding a mark-up:

$$p = \frac{c^V}{q} (1 + mkp) \tag{8}$$

The profits of the firm as then computed as the revenues minus costs, assuming exogenous fixed costs c^F:

$$\pi = q * p - c^V - c^F \tag{9}$$

This implementation of production process potentially provides the opportunity to explore many issues concerning the evolution of the firm's knowledge resulting from R&D and innovation: i) increasing the $a_{k,h}$ competencies in order to improve one or more of the quality dimensions of the product (product innovation); ii) decreasing the quantity coefficients for the inputs to reduce the production costs (process innovation); iii) increase the quality of the inputs, searching for better ones, or giving incentives to providers to improve them. In respect to the first case (i), when there is no particular effort in the increase of internal competencies $\vec{A}$, the quality level of the inputs is directly reflected into a correspondent level of the output. On the contrary, when the level of internal efforts are sufficiently high, the output quality can be increased with respect to the input one. Nonetheless, it is more likely that the vectors are positively correlated, and firms with better competencies also look for better qualities inputs, and vice versa.

However, the model is already complex enough to require a testing exploration of its behaviour, that will be discussed in the next section.

4.2. *Some expected results and interpretation*

In this section we show some results obtained with different initializations. All the inputs used by the firms are bought on a general market and all firms sell to a common final market. The use of different initialisation on one side allows us to apply the model to different economic situations, and interpret their final outcome, under the methodological approach discussed above (section 2).

We start with the results obtained by initializing the model with an extremely simple set up. The main parameters on which the results of the simulations depend, and which are of interest for the direction of development of the model are: i) the quality features of the inputs (both price and qualities), ii) the competencies of the firms (both as overall competences and process capabilities), iii) the related consumers' sensitivity in the final market, which allows to distinguish the different markets faced by firms in different sectors and iv) the mark-up, or pricing strategy.

Before commenting on few selected cases, we provide some general model features, which apply to all the initialisations presented, and might be helpful in interpreting the results. Input features and prices are reflected in the respective values of the firms' output. Their role ultimately depends on the values of the consumers' preferences given by α^j and α^p. For simplicity, we assume that consumers react in the same way to the average values (on which they decide the quantity to demand) and to each firm changes (on which they determine firms' market share). We also assume that consumers response is equal for all the quality features (they do not have particular preference for improving one characteristic of the product). That is, $\alpha^j = \alpha$, $j = 1, 2, ..., m$. Both assumptions can be easily dropped from the point of view of the model construction and initialisation, even if it would increase the complexity of the results interpretation.

Given the way in which the price is defined (Eq. 8), the input prices play an indirect role also on the final profits, as they actually increase the value on which the mark-up percentage is applied. As we will observe, this is the case especially when consumers have low sensitivity to price ($\alpha^p < 1$): while firms with high final prices loose market shares, they still have a market niche large enough to obtain high profits. As an example of such market dynamics one might think of the same goods produced for two different market niches (high quality and low quality), or of basic products such as petrol for which the demand elasticity is low, and an increase in the input price alters only slightly the demand function.

We start by considering a sector whose product is made of $m = 5$ characteristics, containing $n = 10$ firms, using $K = 3$ inputs, each composed by $H_1 = H_2 = H_3 = 2$ quality characteristics. Further common initialization values are reported in Appendix A. In the next paragraph we comment upon the results produced by varying input qualities and firms' capabilities.

Sim1: representative agent (or, what the model is not aimed for)

As a first, didactic, example we look at what may be considered this model equivalent of a representative agent model: all firms and other conditions (i.e. inputs) are identical. Obviously, the result consists in all firms enjoying the same market shares. However, if we assign different initial market shares our model generates a gentle convergence toward the stable state, due to the smoothing of demand (see Fig 2).

This test simulation is not only a test of the correct technical implementation of the model. The smooth landing of the shares to their equilibrium value reminds us that the model is embedded in a real time flux, where the effects of any event (for the moment, just the starting in a disequilibrium) take time to unfold its effects. Such property of the model will generate realistic patterns when many events will be allowed to take place at the same time.

Sim2: different input prices and quality with high demand reactivity to prices and low reactivity to qualities

We consider now the case with differentiated inputs, both in terms of their qualities and prices, so that higher quality inputs are sold at higher prices (see parameter settings in Appendix A). This time the mechanism of the model will generate differentiated patterns, depending on which input is

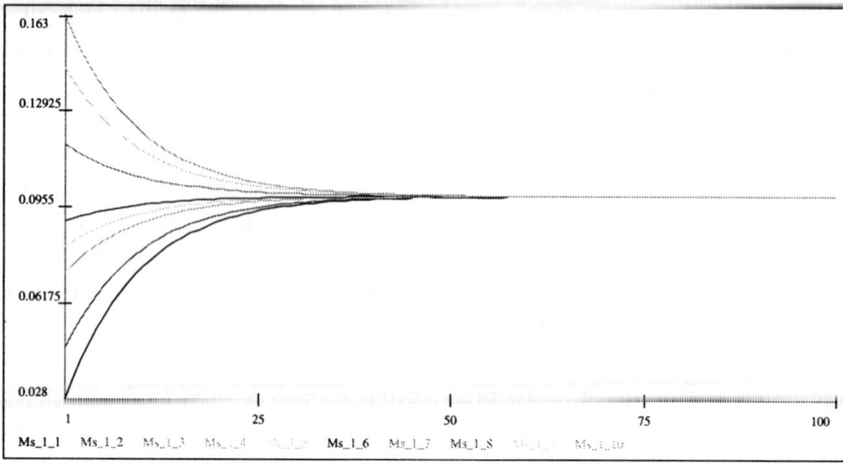

Sim1: market shares

Figure 2. Evolution of market shares through time (100 cycles), where 'Ms_1_1' indicates the market share of firm 1 (in the final market, which is the only one considered here) departing from different initial shares in the market.

used.

Ceteris paribus, with a high sensitivity to prices ($\alpha^p = 2$) and a very low one to qualities ($\alpha^j = 0.5$ for all characteristics), as expected the firms which gain the market are those who opt for low quality and low prices (e.g. Chinese shoe producers) (Fig. 3.a). Given the high sensitivity to prices the last firms (with high input prices) sell (produce) a very low quantity which cause lower overall profits, although the value added on their selling is higher.

The general conditions of the market also cause an increase of the overall demand (with the lag imposed by the smoothing mechanism), as the low price firms increase their share driving down the average price. Accordingly, both average quality and price in the market fall down, as a consequence of the interplay between the demand and supply features (Fig. 3,c d). High quality firms enjoy initially relatively high profits that start immediately falling. This is because their initial market shares are too generous. But as their shares shrink their profits decrease. Interestingly, the equilibrium values for their profits is slightly higher than a the lowest peak (Fig. 3,b)); that is, high quality firms first see their profits fall and then increase a bit. Why does this happen?

The reason is that the falling market shares for this firms is partly

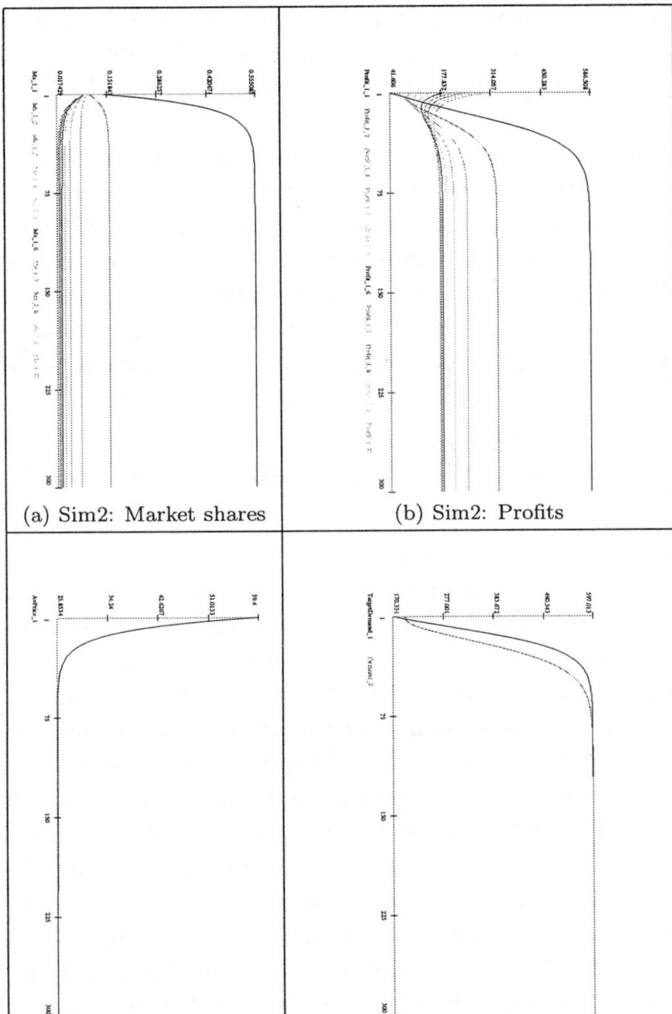

(a) Sim2: Market shares

(b) Sim2: Profits

(c) Sim2: Average price

(d) Sim2: Demand (target and real)

Figure 3. When consumers are highly sensitive to the price differences, the firms using low input quality and low input prices have an advantage which increases their market share (a) and their profits (b) relatively to high quality producers, which are penalised by the prices. Commodities are more suitable for this type of dynamics. Demand is driven by the firms that acquire the larger share of the market (d), and can impose their standard as average good: in a market with high elasticity to prices, firms with high price gain shares and reduce the average price (c).

compensated by an increase in the overall dimension of the market, driven by the increasing shares of low price firms. Given the adjustment lags used, the shares fall is faster than the market enlargement, and this is reflected in this firms' profits.

This simulation does not provide a terrific novel insight, but simply shows that the model does behave as an economist is entitled to expect. However, this is exactly the point of such model, at this stage of its evolution: at the very minimum, it must replicate obvious economic phenomena. Moreover, even in such simple settings, the model generate less than obvious dynamics as the result of the initialization. It is only by exploring such properties of the models in simple set ups that will permit to understand the results of the model with more elaborated initializations

Sim3: different input prices and quality with unit reactivity to prices and qualities

Let's compare the previous results with the case in which consumers' preferences are biased in favor to high quality (and high price) products, keeping constant all other values. This exercise suggests the various possibilities offered by the model in order to compare different scenarios by comparing firms' dynamics in different markets. In fact, the different values of α^j and α^p can be attributed to the market conditions (e.g. local market in a developing country or world market, with higher or lower competition, etc.) or sectoral patterns (e.g. standardised vs. innovative goods). The possibility to introduce different preferences for the average market and for each firm, would also allow to consider market segmentation and different niches of competition (provided we can specify the nature of the quality features).

We show below a comparison between the firms' average values and their relative positions (Fig. 4), as the simulation graphs would show figures similar to the above ones (*Sim2*), basically with inverted results[j].

From Figure 4 we note that with consumers neutral to price and qualities, market shares between firms are much more similar that in the previous configuration *Sim2*. As a result, the quantity sold is similar, but the differ-

[j]In the figure we compare results obtained with 10 competencies, and 15 input quality features. As argued before, this change somehow the relative weights of price and qualities, in the definition of the demand and market share. Yet, they do not change the general results presented here, as the patterns are very much similar when only 5 competences and 2 input features are included. The only observable difference is that in *Sim3* graph the market share curve would be decreasing monotonically, and not slightly convex (results available from the authors).

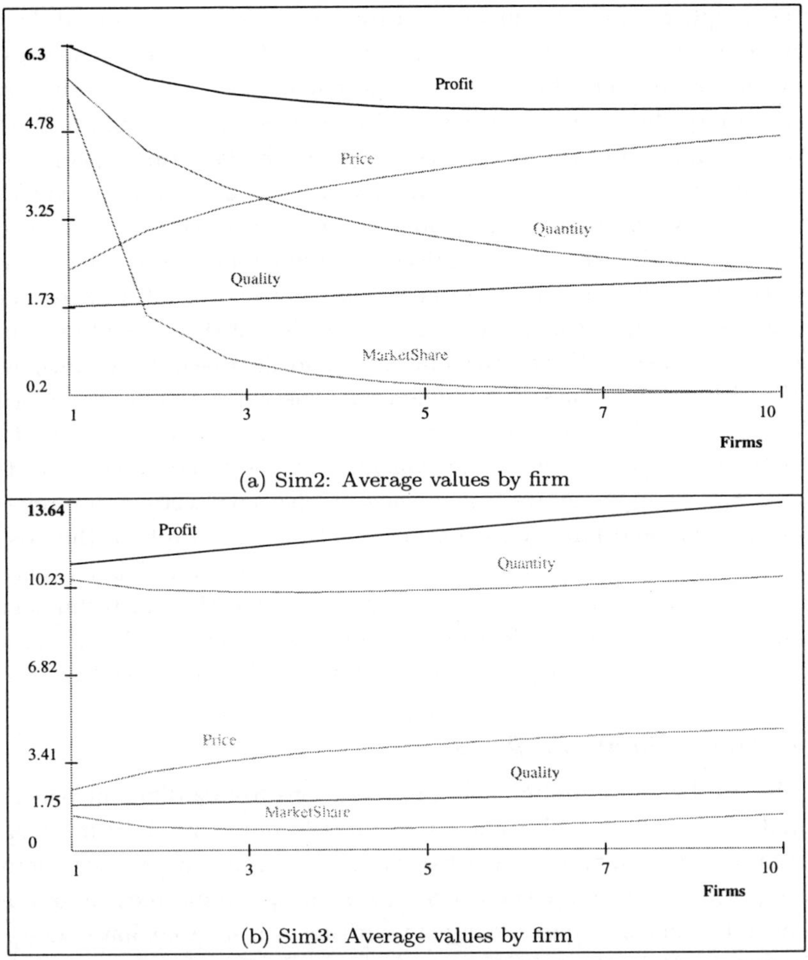

Figure 4. On the horizontal axis the graphs contain the 10 firms, and the vertical axis the reports the average values for the variables of each firm on the 300 periods simulated. Profits, price and quantities are expressed in natural log values, while the market share is scaled up by ten in order to have comparable unit of measure. While in *Sim2* market shares and profit are positively correlated, in *Sim3* they are negatively correlated.

ences in input/output prices now cause an inverse shape of the profits curve. Those results can yield to a preliminary interpretation on the differences between firms localised in a developing country producing for a local and an international market[k]. Local price elasticity, for non-basic goods is, on

[k]One application of the present model (extended) aims to analyse the relations between

average, higher, while the quality features are seldomly considered, by the great majority of the population (conditions in *Sim2*). This generates an argument for the importance of the export market, in which the incentive to increase qualities would be higher. Nonetheless, firms would have then to face a condition of price competition, given the low starting competencies in the production and low availability of high quality inputs, when not imported. It would then be quite straightforward to see the emergence of multiple equilibria, with the specialisation in different sectors (either based on price or qualities advantages) in which comparative advantages might play an important, distorting, role. Here are relevant the concept of technological complementarities between firms [23], and the role of local linkages [24], jointly with external ones [18], to understand the pattern they can enhance. In fact, some of the conditions that we assume in the above formalisation, are actually shaped by firms endowments and the interaction with other agents. For example, as we briefly show in the next section, the relation between inputs and final goods producers has a crucial role in the possibilities to compete of the latter. Conversely, also the given demand plays a crucial role, even greater when considering the 'position' of technological imitators held by firms in developing countries. In fact, as imitators it is difficult to change consumers' preferences, if not through price features.

Sim4-Sim5: Dominant firms

We discuss the above preliminary considerations from a different perspective,and parameter initialisation. In Figures 5 and 6 we show production dynamics in a locality in which two dominant firms with higher competencies ($a_{h,k}$), lower input coefficients (β_k), better (imported) inputs, and higher initial market shares, compete with local firms that have the same endowments set in the previous simulations (*Sim2* and *Sim3*). We show the resulting evolution through market share and profit indicators, in the international market (low price and high quality preferences) (a) and a local one (high price and low quality preferences) (b).

In figure 5 we provide an intuition that, when competing in the international market (assuming it is composed by two advanced companies and eight companies from the selected locality) where the condition of the demand require high products performance, the local firms are almost out of the market (a). The 0.05 remaining share of the market is likely to be the

firms at the local level and firms that buy or produce in the international market, both in terms of production, opportunity and knowledge/technology transfer.

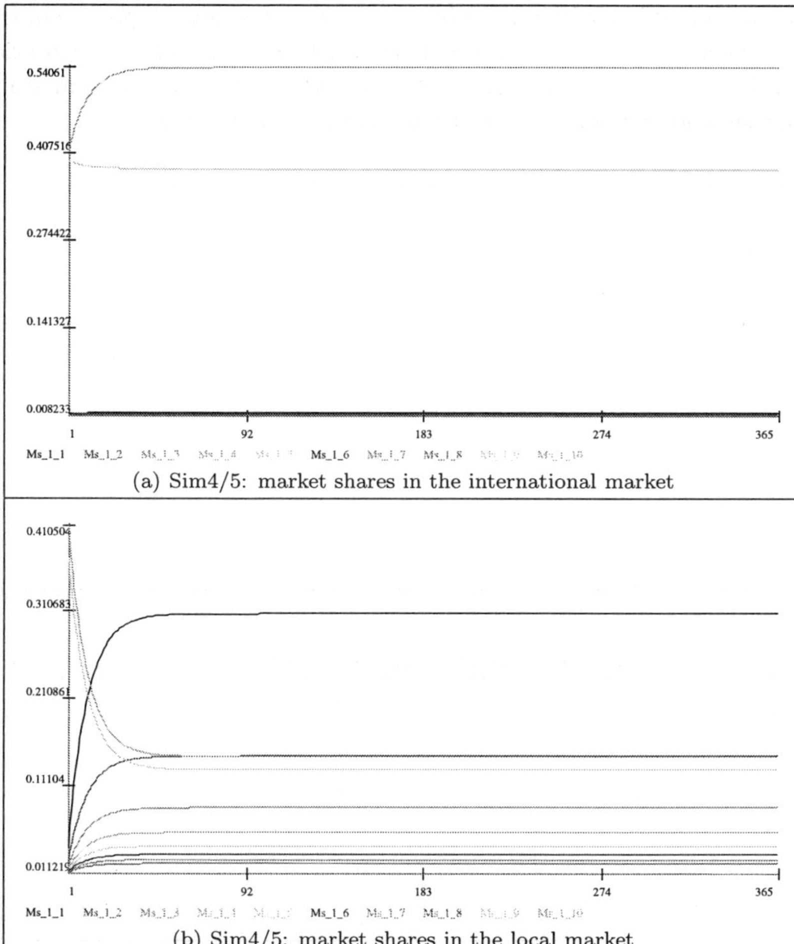

(a) Sim4/5: market shares in the international market

(b) Sim4/5: market shares in the local market

Figure 5. Evolution of market shares in two different markets. On the top market conditions in which $\alpha^i = 1.5, \forall i = 1, ..., m$ and $\alpha^p = 1$ (foreign market). On the bottom: $\alpha^i = .05 \forall i = 1, ..., m$ and $\alpha^p = 2$ (local market).

local one. On the contrary, when considering the local market, the high sensitivity to price hinders the possibility for advanced firms to maintain high market shares with higher price and quality goods (b). Nonetheless, as mentioned before, and shown in the next Figure 6, profits of the most advanced firms are higher in both markets, given their higher final mark-up. When considering conditions in the the first market, this result is again the outcome of an increasing demand (the demand increases given the increase in the quota of high quality goods and the low responsiveness to price changes). Once again, firms departing from such different conditions are likely to remain in their market niches, where they have a comparative advantage and can compete according to their endowments.

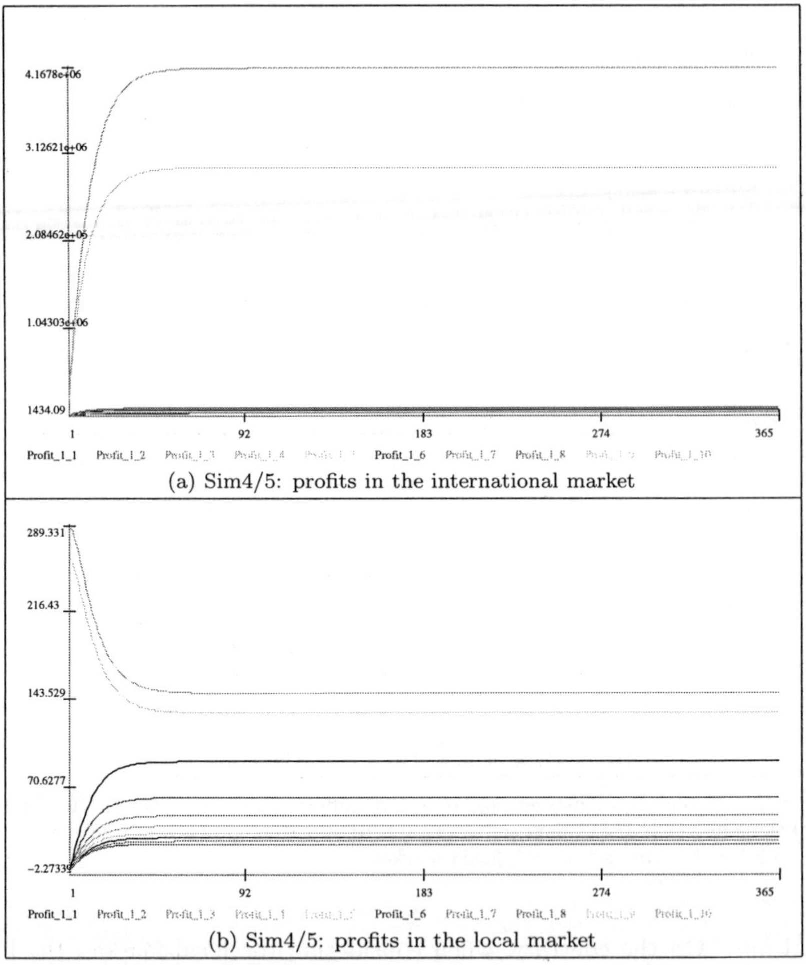

(a) Sim4/5: profits in the international market

(b) Sim4/5: profits in the local market

Figure 6. Evolution of profit distribution in two different markets. On the top market conditions in which $\alpha^i = 1.5, \forall i = 1, ..., m$ and $\alpha^p = 1$ (foreign market). On the bottom: $\alpha^i = .05, \forall i = 1, ..., m$ and $\alpha^p = 2$ (local market).

The exercises discussed in this section have shown that the model produces standard economic results as one should expect under the discussed conditions. These exercises can be used to compare different scenarios by twisting the representation of consumers' preferences. As such, the model provides the robust framework we demanded in order to extend our analysis to additional aspects.

In the next section we extend the basic model exploiting the fact that input goods are represented exactly in the same way as production goods. We will insert input sectors whose firms produce the input goods used by the producers in the final good sector. That is, we extend our model to implement vertically related production sectors.

5. A model with vertical interactions

One of the most important ways to introduce innovations in a system of production is to acquire intermediate products, or capital, with a higher technological content. In order to allow our model to represent this aspect we need to consider explicitly the vertical relations among firms in different markets. We begin by considering two markets for a final consumption good and for a generic 'input', an intermediate product used by firms producing the final consumption good. Each market contains several firms: $i_F = \{1, \ldots, n_F\}$, will be used to indicate firms in the final good market, and $i_P = \{1, \ldots, n_P\}$, referring to the intermediate good used as input by the final good producers. At any time t, each firm in the final good market uses as current supplier of the intermediate good one of the firms in the input market.

The major innovation of the model consists in the steps determining the quantities produced by firms in the input market. In fact, these firms assess the amount of production needed at each time step from the orders received by the their customers, the producers of the final good. In other terms, while the total demand for the final good is determined directly by the consumers' behaviour (as a function of the average price and qualities of the product), the total demand for the input market is obtained indirectly by summing the amounts of inputs required from the downstream sector, determined as in Eq. 6. Clearly, the production of the supplier firms depends indirectly on the level of the final demand. Nonetheless, the demand for each supplier is defined by the number of clients that choose it, their production level, and by the production coefficients of each firms.

The amount of production of firms in the input sector is computed according to an order book, in which all customers of the firms place the requested amounts of production.

$$q_{i_P} = OB_{i_P} = \sum_{j_F \in C_{i_P,k}} q^I_{k,j_F} \tag{10}$$

where $C_{i_P,k}$ is the set of all firms in the final good sector having firm i_P as supplier of input k.

Given the values of the production for each firm in the input sector, the model can then compute the total production for the sector and the market shares. Any other aspect of these firms (e.g. prices and quality levels) are computed as described in section 4.1.

The model assumes that the relations between producers (of the final good) and suppliers is based on contracts lasting over several periods, during which the supplier guarantees to provide the amount of input requested. When the contract expires, the producer searches for another supplier.

The initial suppliers at the start of the simulation have the same uniform probability of being chosen by producers of the final good. Instead, subsequent choices are based on a biased random draw in which each supplier has the following probability of being chosen:

$$P_{i_P,t} = \frac{I_{i_P,t}}{\sum_{j=1}^{n_P} I_{j_P,t}} \tag{11}$$

where the $I_{j_P,t}$ are the quality indexes defined in Eq. 4.

The timing of contracts (i.e. the frequency with which a final good producer searches for a new supplier) is randomly distributed over a range, such that not all producers change supplier at the same time.

Each time a supplier is selected by a customer, the latter adopts the input qualities of the new input chosen, as well as the price set by the supplier. This events therefore modify the appeal of the final product offered by the final good producers.

The dynamics of the sales of the input producing firms depend therefore on the dynamics of the final demand (which varies the amount requested by their customers) and on the modification of the customer portfolio.

5.1. *Preliminary results*

As an exercise to test this extension of the model, consider a simulation where 10 firms in the final good sector are initialized with slightly different values of capabilities (randomly drawn) and identical mark-up. When these firms use the same input supplier, they obtain slightly different market shares because of their differences in the qualities and costs of their competing products (as it is the case for the simulations discussed in the previous section, and in the first 60 steps of this exercise (see Fig. 8). We add an input sector composed by two firms, offering the same input product with slightly different qualities, again determined by small differences in their capabilities. The probabilities of choosing the supplier are proportional to their index of competitiveness, as defined in equation 4. The result of this test exercise are shown in Figures 7 and 8.

Figure 7 shows the time series of the market shares for the producers of the final good (b) and input good (a). The quite variegated dynamics in (b) are due simply to the modifications to the qualities of the competing products due to the use of the two different inputs. Such simple operation generates the complicated patterns because the same firm with the same input supplier will see its relative position (i.e. the market shares) at different levels depending on the input supplier chosen by the other firms.

In figure 8 we zoom on the first 120 periods, when all the firm have switched supplier at least once. First, we note that, although input change market position, firms' own endowments seem to influence more the results: e.g. firms 5, 8 and 10, which initially buy from the lower performing input provider (firm 1), achieve significantly different results before switching. The long period dynamics in Figure 7 confirm that the average results of the firms over the whole period largely depends on their own qualities. Secondly, we can appreciate the relative dimension of the results: when some of the firms start to change supplier, and consequently their own product features (sudden path change of market share), the market share of the remaining firms also have a smooth change. E.g. when the first firm switch to the worse input supplier, all other firms gain some of its lost share, although some of them loose it again in the following switch (Fig. 8, right after time period 60).

As a result, in this simple implementation all firms' actions are thoroughly interconnected. The choice of each of them, in whichever sector, and whichever stage of the production, influences the other's firms outcome. The model described so far can be considered a complete vertical production model, representing how production and trade is carried on in vertically (linearly) related markets for heterogeneous products, both final and intermediate. The results produced by this version of the model correspond to what one expects from such a model: competitiveness of a firm depends on the quality level of its product as compared to that of compet-

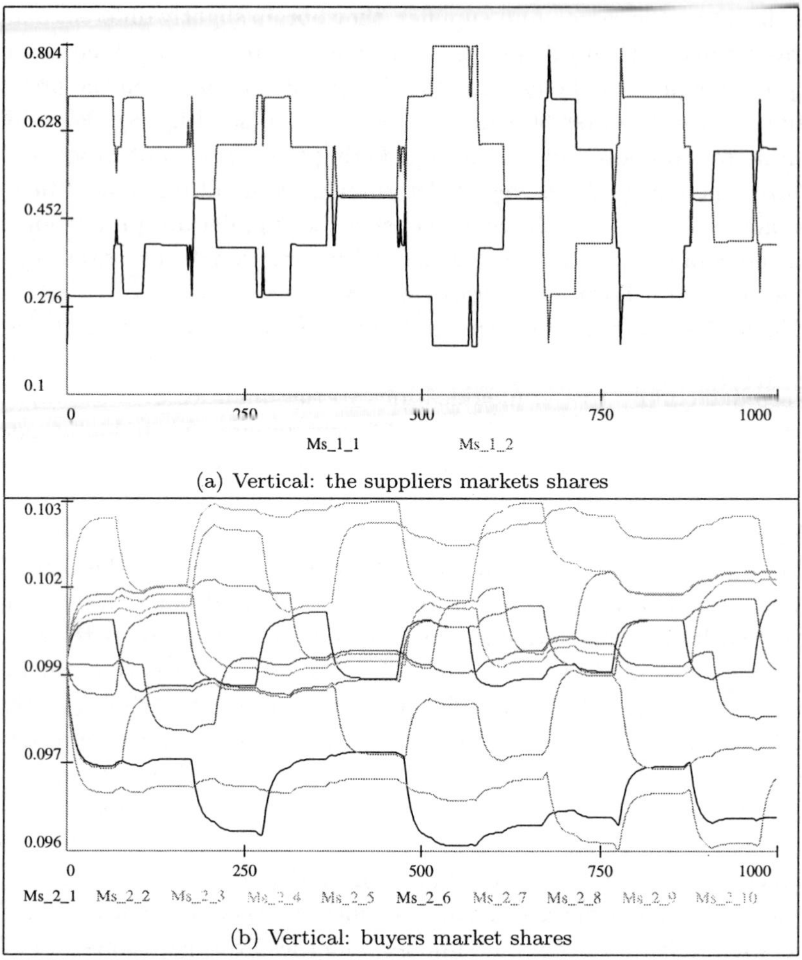

(a) Vertical: the suppliers markets shares

(b) Vertical: buyers market shares

Figure 7. Evolution of the market shares in two different markets, where ms_s_n respectively indicate sector and firm number. On the top we report the suppliers, and on the bottom the buyers (selling to the final market).

itors, with consumers' preferences assessing the relative importance of price and other qualities. Moreover, the model explicitly exposes the role of the internal capabilities of firms used to transform the inputs in the output, both in qualitative as well as quantitative terms. Such model will therefore permit comparative studies on the effects of different development patterns of the capabilities.

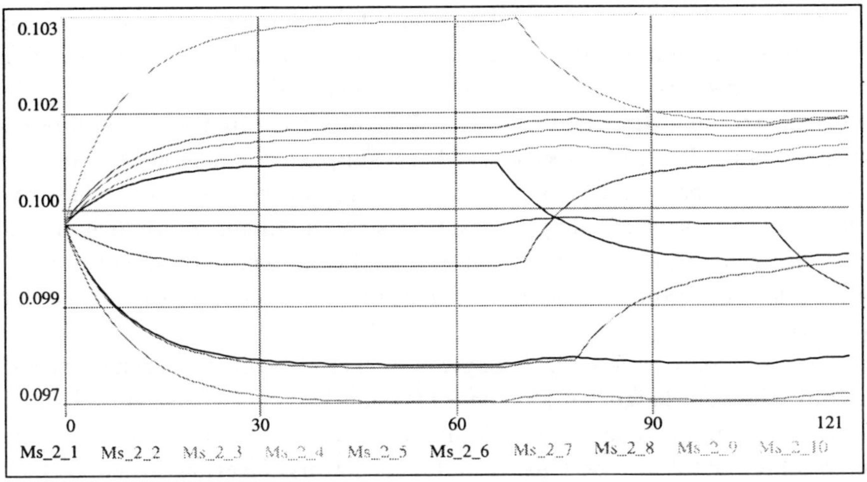

Figure 8. Evolution of the market shares in the final market in the first 120 periods, when all the firms have decided whether to switch the supplier. ms_s_n respectively indicate sector and firm number.

6. Extensions and final considerations

We have presented a computational model representing the production mechanisms of vertically related markets for heterogeneous products. The model explicitly represents the production process as the application of the firm capabilities to the inputs in order to determine quantity and qualities of the output. The exercises presented show that the model produces the results one expects once standard assumptions are applied. That is, keeping constant the capabilities, the performance of competing firms depends on the relative qualities of their respective products, with consumers' preferences determining the relative importance of different qualities. The way in which firms produce and the process of trade are represented in a very detailed way. For example, there is a specific parameter indicating the effect on each output characteristic of one input's characteristic. The model entails therefore a huge number of settings, with thousands of parameters available for initializations. The exercises presented in the paper show that nevertheless the model is very "docile", producing results that can easily be traced back to specific properties of the model equations and/or initialization. The power of the present version of the model resides in its manageability. Notwithstanding the dimension of the model, we can easily study the patterns produced by the model and trace them to their motivations.

The model suggests several directions of development. A first extension consists in extending the vertical interactions, in order to allow a higher number of sectors to interact in both a linear and 'circular' fashion. The vertical structure discussed in section 5 admits only unidirectional production relations. That is, a sector is either a supplier or a customer of another sector. However, this limitation is too strong in case one wants to use the model to represent strongly interacting sectors where, as usual happens, each firms is, at the same time, supplier and customer of other sectors. Allowing for this requires a complex simultaneous decision in the production patterns.

A second extension is the endogenisation of some of the parameters concerning the knowledge development of the market, such as learning channel. This can be implemented by building an interaction structure that encompasses horizontal interactions as well as other organisations (non productive), as briefly described in section 3. This would permit to undertake the analysis of the vertical interactions between local and external firms, both in terms of production and knowledge/information flows. Alternative production structures will be introduced, allowing for a comparative study of the results they produce in terms of levels and sustainability of knowledge growth and processes of industrial development. These future exercises will not only aim at producing more realistic patterns, but will be used to study the chain of events responsible for the emergence of specific phenomena, as suggested in the simulation methodology we called qualitative simulation modelling.

References

1. S. J. Metcalfe, Innovation, Growth and Competition: Evolving Complexity or Complex Evolution, in *Complexity and Complex Systems in Industry Conference*, University of Warwick, 19-20 September 2000.
2. S. J. Metcalfe, J. Foster, and R. Ramlogan, Adaptive Economic Growth, Working Paper mimeo, September 2002.
3. R. R. Nelson and S. G. Winter, *An Evolutionary Theory of Economic Change*, Harvard University Press, Cambridge, MA, 1982.
4. G. Silverberg and B. Verspagen, Evolutionary Theorizing on Economic Growth, Working Paper WP-95-78, IIASA, August 1995, Published in The Evolutionary Principles of Economics, edited by K. Dopfer, Norwell, MA: Kluwer Academic Publisher.
5. K. J. Lancaster, A New Approach to Consumer Theory, Journal of Political Economy **74**, 132–157 (1966).
6. F. Gallouj and O. Weinstein, Innovation in Services, Research Policy **26**, 537–556 (1997).

7. B.-A. Lundvall, Innovation as an Interactive Process: From User-Producer Interaction to the National System of Innovation, in *Technical Change and Economic Theory*, edited by G. Dosi, C. Freeman, R. R. Nelson, G. Silverberg, and L. Soete, Pinter Publisher, London, 1988.
8. M. Valente, Overview of Laboratory for Simulation Development - 4.1, Working Paper mimeo, Università dell'Aquila, January 27 2002.
9. D. Lane, Artificial World and Economics, Part I & II, Journal of Evolutionary Economics **3**, 89–108, 177–197 (1993).
10. U. Staber, The Structure of Networks in Industrial Districts, International Journal of Urban and Regional Research **25**(3), 537–552 (2001).
11. B. W. Arthur, S. N. Durlauf, and D. A. Lane, editors, *The Economy as an Evolving Complex System II*, Proceedings Vol. XXVII, SFI Studies in the Science of Complexity, Addison-Wesley, Reading MA, 1997.
12. R. R. Nelson, editor, *National Innovation Systems: A Comparative Analysis*, Oxford University Press, New York, 1993.
13. N. Gilbert and P. Terna, How to Build and Use Agent-Based Models in Social Sciences, Mind and Society **I**(1), 57–72 (2000).
14. M. Aoki, B. Gustafson, and O. E. Williamson, editors, *The Firm as a Nexus of Treaties*, Sage Publications, London, 1990.
15. R. Axtell, Non-Cooperative Dynamics of Multi-Agent Teams, in *International Conference on Autounomous Agents*, edited by AAMAS, pages 1082–1089, Bologna, July 15-19 2002, ACM Press.
16. D. A. Lane, Complexity and Local Interactions: Towards a Theory of Industrial Districts, in *Complexity and industrial Districts*, Montedison Foundation, Milan, 2001, Also in: "Complexity and industrial clusters: dynamics and models in theory and practice", Berlin, Springer, 2002.
17. M. Wooldridge and N. R. Jennings, Intelligent Agents: Theory and Practice, Knowledge Engineering Review **10**(2), 115–152 (1995).
18. S.-R. Kim and N. von Tunzelmann, Aligning internal and external networks: Taiwan's specialization in IT, Working Paper 17, SPRU Electronic Working Papers Series, January 1998.
19. C. Freeman, Japan: A New National System of Innovation?, in *Technical change and economic theory*, edited by G. Dosi, C. Freeman, R. R. Nelson, G. Silverberg, and L. Soete, Pinter Publishers, London, 1988.
20. P. Cooke, Regional Innovation Systems: An Evolutionary Approach, in *Regional Innovation Systems*, edited by H. Baraczyk, P. Cooke, and R. Heidenriech, London University Press, London, 1996.
21. P. Cooke and K. Morgan, *The Associational Economy: Firms Regions and Innovation*, Oxford University Press, Oxford, 1998.
22. P. P. Saviotti and S. J. Metcalfe, A Theoretical Approach to the Construction of Technological Output Indicators, Research Policy **13**, 141–151 (1984).
23. S. N. Durlauf, Nonergodic Economic Growth, Review of Economic Studies **60**, 349–366 (1993).
24. A. O. Hirschman, A Generalized Linkage Approach to Development, with Special Reference to Staples, Economic Development and Structural Change **25**(Supplement: Essays on Economic Development and Cultural Change in

Honour of Bert F. Hoselitz), 67–98 (1977).

Appendix A. Appendix: parameters and initial values

Table 1a. Initialisation values for one sector simulations.

Parameter	Description	all firms	Sim1[2]	Sim2[2]	Sim3[2]
H	Constant demand	20000	–	–	–
$D_{t=0}$[1]	lagged demand	–	59259.3	500	500
s^D	1 rate of adjustment to target demand	0.0			
s^{MS}	1 - rate of adjustment to target market share	0.9	–	–	–
α^p	Price 'elasticity'	–	1	2	1
α^i	Quality 'elasticity'	–	1	0.5	1
C^F	Fixed costs	–	100	10	10
$p_{t=0}$[1]	Lagged price	–	10.8	30	30
mkp	Constant mark-up	–	0.2	0.2	0.2
$ms_{t=0}$[1]	Lagged market share	–	0.02 0.04 0.07 0.07 0.08 0.09 0.12 0.15 0.15 0.17	0.1	0.1
$a_{i,h,k}$	Firms' competencies	–	1	1	1
β_k	Input quantity coefficient	3	–	–	–
p^I_k	Input price	–	1	1 1.5 2 2.5 3 3.5 4 4.5 5 5.5	sim2
$w_{k,h}$	Input quality features	–	1	0.75 0.8 0.85 0.9 0.95 1 1.05 1.1 1.15 1.2	sim2

1) Variables whose lagged value (at t=0) is used in the very first time step.
2) When more than one parameter is indicated, they represent the different values attached to different firms, ordered by firm number.

Table 1b. Initialisation values for one sector simulations.

Parameter	Description	all firms	Sim4[2]	Sim5[2]
H	Constant demand	20000	–	–
${D_{t=0}}^1$	lagged demand	–	500	500
s^D	1 - rate of adjustment to target demand	0.9	–	–
s^{MS}	1 - rate of adjustment to target market share	0.9	–	–
α^p	Price 'elasticity'	–	2	1
α^i	Quality 'elasticity'	–	0.5	1.5
C^F	Fixed costs	–	10	10
${p_{t=0}}^1$	Lagged price	–	30	30
mkp	Constant mark-up	–	0.2	0.2
${ms_{t=0}}^1$	Lagged market share	–	0.01 (x8) 0.4 0.44	sim4
$a_{i,h,k}$	Firms' competencies	–	0.7 (x8) 1.3 (x2)	sim4
β_k	Input quantity coefficient	3	3 (x8) 2 (x2)	sim4
p_k^I	Input price	–	1 1.5 2 2.5 3 3.5 4 4.5 5 5	sim4
$w_{k,h}$	Input quality features	–	0.75 0.8 0.85 0.9 0.95 1 1.05 1.1 1.4 1.5	sim4

1) Variables whose lagged value (at t=0) is used in the very first time step.
2) When more than one parameter is indicated, they represent the different values attached to different firms, ordered by firm number.

Table 2. Parameters initialisation for the two sectors simulation.

Parameter	Description	Input sector	Final good sector[2]
H	Constant demand	1	1
${D_{t=0}}^1$	lagged demand	100	100
s^D	1 - rate of adjustment to target demand	0.9	0.9
s^{MS}	1 - rate of adjustment to target m. share	0.9	0.9
α^p	Price 'elasticity'	1	1
α^i	Quality 'elasticity'	1	1
C^F	Fixed costs	1000	1000
${p_{t=0}}^1$	Lagged price	4000	4000
mkp	Constant mark-up	0.2	0.2
${ms_{t=0}}^1$	Lagged market share	–[3]	0.1
$a_{i,h,k}$	Firms' competencies	RND(.95, 1,05)	RND(.95, 1.05)
β_k	Input quantity coefficient	2	2
p_k^I	Input price[4]	1	1
$w_{k,h}$	Input quality features[k]	1	1
$i_{t=0,S_{F-1}}$	Input supplier at $t = 0$	–[5]	2 2 2 2 1 2 2 1 2 1

1) Variables whose lagged value (at t=0) is used in the very first time step.
2) When more than one parameter is indicated, they represent the different values attached to different firms, ordered by firm number.
3) Market share in the supplier market is determined after the goods have been produced and sold: there is non need for initial value.
4) Referred to the exogenous inputs.
5) Firms in the input market buy all their inputs from a common exogenous market.

LABOR MARKET, ENTREPRENEURSHIP AND HUMAN CAPITAL IN INDUSTRIAL DISTRICTS. AN AGENT-BASED PROTOTYPE

R. BOERO

Department of Sociology,
University of Surrey,
Guildford,
Surrey GU2 7XH, United Kingdom
E-mail: R.Boero@surrey.ac.uk

M. CASTELLANI, AND F. SQUAZZONI

Department of Social Sciences,
Via S. Faustino, 74/B,
Brescia 25122, Italy
E-mail: castella@eco.unibs.it, squazzon@eco.unibs.it

The paper describes an agent-based prototype that has been created to investigate relations among local labor markets, entrepreneurship and human capital in industrial districts. It basically describes the building blocks of the prototype, the agents acting in it and the forces that drive its most interesting dynamics. Some interesting hypotheses to investigate are sketched, too.

1. Introduction

The paper aims to describe an agent-based prototype that has been created to reproduce the functioning of an "idealized" industrial district (by now, ID), at the micro level of its constituencies. It allows to simulate some fundamental local dynamics, at the edge of labor market, entrepreneurship, technology and market adaptation, and to investigate some hypotheses concerning their relations[a].

[a]The Prototype has been created using SWARM libraries and Java programming language. SWARM is a toolkit for developing agent-based simulations (see: www.swarm.org) and it is used by a growing community of social scientists (see: Terna[36]). For descriptions and applications of SWARM to economic phenomena, see Luna, Stefansson[21] and Luna, Perrone[22]. For obtaining the simulation code, please

First of all, it is worth to say that we use the term of "prototype" to outline a substantial difference among modeling specific phenomena of an empirical reality (empirical-based models), modeling highly abstracted social mechanisms, such as, for example, cooperation-competition models in game theory (abstraction-based models), or modeling "ideal-typical" processes that work in a well defined family or class of phenomena, such as industrial districts in the case of this paper (ideal-types or prototypes). In the first case, it is a matter of modeling an empirical phenomenon, trying to reproduce as close as possible the space-time of reality; in the second case, it is an abstraction of some specific theoretical mechanisms that have no strong reference to the space-time dimension of reality and that, consequently, can say something with respect to a wide range of different phenomena or classes of phenomena; while in the third case, we are reproducing "stylized facts" that form each others the architecture of an ideal-type able to identify a general class or family of empirical phenomena.

In some foregoing papers, we used a prototype-like approach to understand some mechanisms of IDs, such as the role of inter-firm ties to explain different technological and market performance of ID firms, the impact of institutional agencies upon the adaptation capabilities of IDs (Squazzoni and Boero[34]), the role of cognitive processes and different behavioral attitudes at micro level of ID firms to explain different outcomes at macro-level of ID as a whole, and so on (Boero, Castellani and Squazzoni[8]).

In this paper, we take a quite different step: we go more deeply in the ID modeling, starting analytically not with ID firms, but with individuals that are embedded into a local labor market, which have a different life cycle, job, wage, knowledge, relational ties, which shape different ID firms, and so on. While the foregoing papers were based on the relation between the firms, as micro analytical units, and the ID and the external market as macro ones (with eventual institutional agencies as a meso level), this paper is based on individuals as the micro analytical units, firms as the meso ones and ID and external markets as the macro realities.

With this re-articulation of analytical levels, we try to understand the relation among labor market dynamics, emergence of entrepreneurship and technology and market adaptation of firms and of the ID as a whole. It is a matter of relationships that have been deeply discussed in the literature of IDs and industrial clusters, and that are conceived as driving forces of their evolution (for example, see: Saxenian[30]; Albertini[1]; De Propis[15]; Molina-

---

write to the authors.

Morales[25]; Russo[29]). According to such literature, diffuse entrepreneurship is viewed as the property of the flexibility of local labor markets and the result of specific cycles of human capital accumulation, life-death cycles of firms are viewed as adaptive dynamics with respect to unstable and volatile markets, and firms are viewed as a market segmentation within labor markets.

The paper is organized as follows: the second section shows how the prototype works, from the point of view of its building blocks, which are divided in agents and driving forces, while the third one suggests some hypotheses that we would investigate by creating different simulation settings, that is to say by giving rise to different but comparable motion pictures of the prototype. Because of the descriptive nature of the paper, the results will be reported in a further work.

2. How the Prototype Works

This section shows a description of agents populating the prototype and the leading forces that drive its dynamics. Agents are as follows: individuals, firms, external buyers, the service agency. They are units acting in the prototype at different levels of aggregation. The driving forces are fundamental processes that the prototype develops over time. They generate complex dynamics and relations that we want to investigate. They are: markets, technological evolution, production cycle and chains, human capital.

2.1. *Agents*

2.1.1. *Individuals*

Human individuals are the fundamental agent/unit of the prototype. They are heterogeneous, they have an autonomous life, they born and die, and they earn, spend and eventually cumulate economic resources. They inherit economic resources by their parents, they are embedded in a labor market, they can work in a firm, and they can give rise to new firms. If working they monthly receive a stipend, and they have capabilities to build wage expectations, connecting past situations, actual needs and future projections. Their position in the labor market basically depends on their human capital accumulation, while they retire from labor market after about 35 years of activity. They expect to be able to live following a "life style", which is the result of their human capital accumulation level that affects their needs and then their level of consumption. They can be employed or unemployed, they can become entrepreneurs, and as entrepreneurs they can move back to the employee status, too. The contract between firms and employees lasts for a fixed period (for instance two years). One month before the contract expiration, workers are engaged in a phase of wage bargaining with the firm, during which they can look around to seek for different contract conditions. During the bargaining period they try to fit the wage level offered with their wage expectations, and they can even become unemployed, according to a classical supply and demand dynamics. When they are unemployed, they can receive job offers, if there are firms searching for workers to assume. Workers are able to adapt their the wage level expectations (as said, they are mainly based on the workers' qualification and thus on their life style) depending on the easiness to get a job and, if they have a fresh experience in a firm, comparing their expectations with the wage levels encountered at work.

2.1.2. *Firms*

Firms are created by individuals and they are a collection of workers, raw materials and equipment. They belong to different classes, final firms and semi-manufactured firms, according to the given division of labor and of production segmentation which characterize the ID (see below).

They can born, grow assuming new workers, downsize themselves firing workers, collapse, and go through the hands of the family heir. The corporate governance structure is regulated by the traditional principles of the family ownership. The strategic, managerial and commercial control of a firm is in the only hands of the entrepreneur and of its successors, while the production is made by workers.

The simulations used to test the model start with an heterogeneous population of individuals: some of them immediately create new firms. During the simulation lifetime, firms emerge with the transformation of an employee in an entrepreneur. A worker can become an entrepreneur if some conditions are present: i) he has enough resources to sustain the costs for setting up a firm and for starting the production processes; ii) entrepreneurship seems to ensure a certain degree of profitability, which is calculated by observing some data of the old employing firm, such as the storehouse cycle (if the cycle is quick and the storehouse is minimized, then the market is supposed to thrive); iii) the worker wage expectations point out a period of future stagnation, which is perceived as a mismatch between offered wage level and subjective aspiration level in a phase of wage bargaining; iv) the employee perceives that, in other firms, other workers with similar status get higher wages than his own. Entrepreneurship thus depends on the intersection between a positive objective situation (market, resources, costs) and a supposed negative forthcoming personal situation. Furthermore, we assume that an employee, become an entrepreneur, starts a firm in the production specialization which he knows most.

The life of a firm is carried on by means of the articulation of different, interrelated and complementary functional areas. Areas are five and they are as follows: accounting, strategy, production, input-output, and human resources. The accounting area has the function of recording data, storing up daily information about costs generated by other functional areas, and generating semester data, with a report that contains information about revenues from sales, operative costs, investment costs, and profits.

The strategy area has the function of developing strategic decisions built upon the information available. This area can take five kinds of decisions (a, b, c,..), basing the choice on the presence of some conditions (i, ii, iii,..), as follows: Innovation through a technology break-up i) new technology available from external environment; ii) great variability in the profit dynamics of the firm in the last period of time (shortly, things are going too much well, or too much badly); iii) economic resources of the firm are much bigger than the requested to implement the new technology; iv) output storehouses are not full (shortly, an increase of productivity has sense because it seems that a demand for the produced good is present). Investment in human capital training i) economic resources are available, that is to say they are much bigger than costs of training, assuring the continuation of production in the near future; ii) there has been a light fall-off in profits in the last period of time considered. Employment of new workforce units i) output storehouses are empty; ii) economic resources are available; iii) profits show a light fall-off in the last period of time considered. Discharge a workforce unit i) more than one worker employed by the firm; ii) profits show a strong fall-off in the last period of time considered; iii) there are few economic resources, letting suppose that continuing production could be difficult in the near future. Liquidation i) there are not economic resources, and maybe indebtedness; ii) there is a loss; iii) the loss amount is growing in the last period of time considered.

The switch among strategic options conforms to the principle that the area can take just a decision per time, and that, for instance, if all conditions for taking the first decision are satisfied, then the other options are not even considered. The period of time considered in conditions can be the last six months between the completion of two reports, or the comparison of partial actual data with the last rectified.

The strategic option of technological innovation (option a, condition ii: "things are going too much well, or too much badly") lays upon some well-known cognitive mechanisms. The Simonian view of bounded rationality in terms of aspiration level adjustments argues in fact that agents decrease their aspiration levels, and/or increase search, when alternatives become difficult to find. Vice versa, if it turns out to be easy to find alternatives, agents increase their aspiration levels, and/or decrease search (Simon[33,32]). This well-known mechanism has been elaborated by many scholars within the decision making area, and revisited in the light of the relationship between the feedback of agents' decisions and their aspiration levels (what is often called ex-post rationality). This perspective shows that agents have a tendency to reason by correspondence or by a similarity-based viewpoint, comparing performances of related kind of decisions. In a sort of analogy with the Simonian theory, the main consequence of this relief is that aspiration levels of agents are influenced by previous performances, through their perception of what can be viewed as a failure (performance worse than aspiration level) or as a success (performance better than aspiration level). The mechanism shows that agents decrease aspiration levels in case of failure and increase them in case of success (March[23]; Elster[17]). This scheme has also been enlarged to the main interesting situations, the boundary ones, i.e. when agents are facing deep failures or big successes (high discrepancy between performances and aspiration levels on both sides).

In these situations things are observed to be not the same as just described. A frame which could be labeled as an "expanding model of satisficing search" (March[23]) shows that when agents face deep failure, they increase aspiration levels by means of a risk taking attitude, which pushes them to select (accept) high levels of risk in order to increase chances to reach the target (for a socio-cognitive experimental perspective with various task environment scenarios, see Castellani[11]). At the opposite circumstance, in front of big successes, agents tend to take greater risks because they can count on what March himself defines "large cushion", which in psychological terms recalls a sort of "euphoria effect" (agents think that everything will go as well as it's been going till now, despite high risk conditions) on one side, and, on the other, a mental condition that lead agents to underestimate the real "state of the world". Although the two boundary conditions present different characteristics (about the different aspiration adaptation, downward and upward, see Selten[31]), both of them show that agents act by playing upon high risk levels and choose a critical alternative, and so they increase aspiration levels. In conclusion, in our prototype, agents innovate through a technological break-up, which stands for a reactive respond to performances driven by the mechanism above described.

The production area allows firms to regulate their production operations. If the output storehouses are not full and if inputs, raw materials or semi-manufactured products, are available (stored in the input storehouse), the production daily goes on. The production process consumes inputs and work, and uses the equipment available (from the productivity point of view, equipments are different depending on the technology adopted). It allows to transform all production inputs into finished products (final goods or semi-manufactured products), according to the characteristics of the technology used, the availability of workers and their productivity level, which is the outcome of their human capital accumulation. Every worker has his own capability to transform inputs in outputs, according to the past experience on the process and to the amount of training received, i.e. to his human capital accumulation level. Daily activities produce units of finished products that go in storehouses, whilst un-finished products are overcharged to the activities of the day after.

The input-output is the fourth area. It has specific competence on the management of storehouses of inputs (raw materials or semi-manufactured products) and outputs (final goods or semi-manufactured products). It manages the purchasing and the selling activities, according to the rules which characterize the specific markets in which the firm operates. The maximum dimension of storehouses depends on the type and dimension of firm (final or subcontracted firm), as well as on the number of employees (the firm adapts the dimension of storehouses to its size). Final firms have threefold storehouses, according to the three kinds of semi-manufactured products that we assume are needed to be assembled to obtain a final good.

In the case of sub contracted firms, that area has the function of buying raw materials, whilst in the case of final firms it has the function of buying semi-manufactured products. While the price of raw materials is assumed to be exogenous and unique, because they come from a competitive market outside the ID, the price of semi-manufactured products is regulated according to a supply-demand dynamics emerging among firms, with a potentially unsteady price that goes up and down according to the degree of product availability.

The area sells products on markets, according to a threshold of price that fluctuates in accordance with the situation of storehouses (prices levels demanded are higher if storehouses are almost empty, lower if they are full) and the operative costs of production.

The input-output area has moreover the function of buying new machineries when the decision of adopting a new technology has been taken.

The last area is the human resources area. It has the function of managing internal human resources, paying wages, employing new workforce units, discharging them, as well as organizing training activities.

The recruiting activities follow market price dynamics. The salary policy of the firms is based on the interlacement among three mechanisms, as follows: the productivity level of the applicant (that is a proxy of his human capital accumulation level), the technology actually used by the firm, and a multiplier that is modified by the market information. It gradually increases the availability of the firm to converge towards the wage expected level of the applicant, if there have been difficulties to find new workforces, and decreases it, if the average level of wages offered by other firms is lower than its own (the other firms considered are the ones with which the company has recently had contact).

One month before the expiration of the agreement of work, the area notices it to the employee and offers a new agreement that should be higher than the older one, because of the supposed growth of human capital accumulated by the employee, over the period of work. Finally, the training costs are assumed to be exogenous, unrelated to the number of employees that are trained, and the value of human capital generated by the training is supposed to be equal for all the employees which are involved in.

The representation of firms as a collection of different specific functional areas does not imply the assumption of the presence of specialized organizational structures and roles, or a division of organizational labor, as in the bureaucratic business model.

It is rather as assuming that a firm, no matter what dimension it has, is a set of different but interrelated activities and practices that define its operational closure with respect to the environment and the plexus of its strategic decisions. For example, as several empirical investigations have pointed out (Albertini[1]), despite the familistic degree of their corporate governance structures, small and medium firms in IDs carry on human resource management policies, a strategy of human capital accumulation, even in absence of dedicated internal structures and specialized roles.

2.1.3. *External Buyers*

Outside the ID, there are many buyers in the global markets which are looking for ID final goods. They buy them from ID final firms, with specific expectations concerning the prices to offer. Buyers have an adaptive price level that they are able to offer to firms, and considering that these latters have also a dynamic demanded price level, the market of final goods results to be a competitive one, based on a supply and demand dynamics.

Everyday, a buyer can try to buy many products by ID final firms, trying to satisfy his need for goods. Buyers have a short memory of interactions, starting to explore the ID market by the final firms from which they have recently bought in the past.

2.1.4. *Service Agency*

Some exogenous services, needed by ID firms and bought in the global market outside the district, are offered in the prototype by a "meta-object" that is called "agency". Its functions are related to a set of services, such as machineries, raw materials, and so on.

Prices for setting-up firms and for buying raw materials are somehow related to the inflation trends (in terms of the average market price of final goods), while prices of machineries and training courses are related to inflation and to the technological paradigm.

2.2. *Driving Forces*

2.2.1. *Markets*

The functioning of IDs is based on the overlapping of markets that show a different typology, according to the degree of influence and interdependence that agents can exercise each others, along the interaction that constitutes the matter of the transaction. This is the reason why in the prototype there are three "many-to-many" and many "one-to-many" markets. The first type of markets includes:

- labor markets, which relate entrepreneurs and workers each others in job contracts (actors: firms in general and individuals);
- markets of semi-manufactured products, which relate firms each others along direct transactions of products (actors: firms producing final goods and firms producing semi-manufactured products);
- markets of final goods, which relate final firms and buyers each

others, along transactions of products (actors: external buyers and firms producing final goods).

Transactions in these markets are not based on an exogenously settled price, but on an endogenous one determined by means of direct interactions among agents, according to a dynamic interface and a mutual influence among parts that are involved in the transaction. Transactions in the second kind of markets (one-to-many) happen between ID firms and external service providers. They are based on a commonly known price, settled exogenously and thus ID firms can not strategically influence it. These markets are:

- materials markets, where raw materials are bought by firms producing semi-manufactured products; training markets, where training courses are offered to firms;
- machineries markets, where firms can find the equipment to adopt new technologies;
- set-up markets, where services in order to create a new firm are offered.

2.2.2. *Technological Evolution*

During the model lifetime, the technological paradigm is not static. But, looking at empirical studies on IDs, it is common to notice how the function of R&D of new technologies is outside the ID (Corò and Grandinetti[14]). IDs have no R&D functional structures or formalized activities, and thus ID firms buy technologies on global markets (Belussi and Gottardi[6]).

For these reasons, in our model the evolution of technology is exogenous and it is modeled as a random process that makes available new technologies after "long" periods of time (the length of the time period is the random part of the process).

Each new technology available lets the firm potentially increase its productivity over the level possible with older technologies. But the process of adoption of a new technological paradigm is a long one because it is not just the fact of buying new machineries, but also the one of training the workforce to exploit them. Shortly: the adoption of a new technology could mean for a firm a short term decrease in productivity and a bigger increase on the long term. Finally, new technologies give a potential increase of productivity that is not a fixed one: the amount of the increase is bigger for new technologies than for older ones.

2.2.3. *Production Cycle and Chains*

The ID production cycle lays upon a set of relations between outside markets and ID firms. The process of transformation of raw materials into finished products is what ID firms carry on, through a web of interactions that works according to a given division of labor among them (Carbonara, Giannoccaro, Pontrandolfo[10]). We assume the presence of four production activities. The first three concern semi-manufacturing operations, that is to say the transformation of raw materials into semi-manufactured products (thus there are three types of semi-manufactured products), while the last one concerns assembling functions, that is to say the final operation of assembling and making up the product to be sold in the market. This last one is the function of final firms.

The production cycle leading to a final good is made by two main steps. In the first one, a firm operating as a supplier of semi-manufactured goods, buys raw materials from external markets and using machineries and workforce transforms them in a semi-manufactured product of a particular kind. In the second step, a firm, operating as a final good assembler, buys at least one semi-manufactured product for each type (thus at least one for each of the three types in the model) and then, using machineries and workforce, produces the final good.

The production cycle is depicted in figure 1, where also the external relevant markets are shown. As a final remark, it is important to underline that firms, in the simulations used for testing the model, are specialized on a particular activity, thus they can be firms assembling the final good or producing one of the three semi-manufactured products. It is a constraint that obliges firms to be specialized on a particular activity, but it can be removed, letting firms developing more production lines or merging other companies.

The internal structure of the ID is dynamic and based on the exchange of semi-manufactured products. As said, these products are exchanged on a market generically driven by supply and demand. Firms assembling the final good have a short memory of past interactions, trying to find semi-manufactured products from their last supplier but, if they have failed to satisfy their demand with old suppliers, they search for new partners.

The market so sketched is a very competitive one and it is important here to underline how this is an option chosen for first tests of the model: for some IDs the internal market is more tied to the relational network that grows even outside the dimension of the "pure" economic rationality

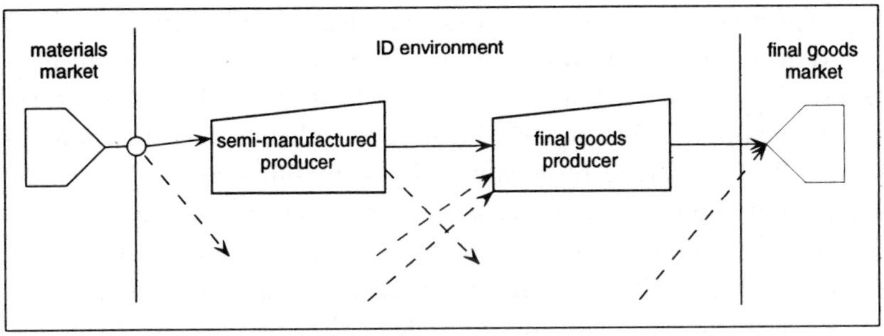

Figure 1. The production cycle.

(Albino, Garavelli, Schiuma[2]; Dei Ottati[16]; Mistri and Solari[24]; Piore[27]; Squazzoni and Boero[34]).

2.2.4. *Human Capital*

Human capital is one of the main intangible asset that affects the path of economic development of local industrial areas (Storper[35]; Hand and Baruch[19]). Since the seminal writings of Alfred Marshall, it is argued that a main essence of geographical clustering of firms can be found in the pooling mechanism of labor with specialized skills and knowledge accumulation (Becattini[4]). The literature has recently suggested some taxonomies of human capital mostly focused on the difference between generic and specific human capital, transferable and non-transferable knowledge (Becker[5]). To paraphrase the dichotomy suggested by Nonaka and Takeuchi[26], codified knowledge concerns the formation of human capital by formal educational institutions, training, learning seminars, and so on, and it is based on the transfer of highly manipulated symbolic knowledge. The latter concerns the formation of human capital by training on-the-job, direct mentorship among workers, learning by doing, and so on, and it is based on the transfer of specific tacit knowledge (Rullani[28]).

The case of labor market and inter-firm division of labor in IDs imposes strong limitations to the effectiveness of taxonomies above mentioned (for a critical view of these taxonomies, see Breschi and Lissoni[9]). Because of the complementarity-based production specialization, the inter-firm labor mobility, the diffuse entrepreneurship, and so on, which characterize IDs, the definition of transferable and non-transferable forms of human capital, as well as of codified and tacit knowledge, is a misleading one in a firm-level perspective of analysis (from firm to firm), while could be of a little help only if it is stated in a district-level perspective (from ID to external markets). For instance, fundamental knowledge of an ID could be rightly viewed as embodied into a tacit form of knowledge, but it is temporally and spatially transferred by means of labor mobility and relations among complementary specialized firms, as though it was codified by the language of the ID as a whole, as well as institutionally reproduced over time by means of specific institutional mechanisms working within the ID.

ID workers move within labor markets that are highly segmented by firms, because of the specialization-based division of labor, but, at the same time, highly inter-connected by the homogeneous kind of production at the ID level. This coupled mechanisms imply that workers can move along the segmentation levels of ID labor market, without loosing human capital and competencies they created by work experiences within specific firms, as though they were moving within the internal labor market of a large firm (Cingano[12]).

According to this perspective, our understanding of human capital starts with the analytical distinction between two different but interrelated forms of human capital, a generic and a specific one. By means of a linguistic analogy, generic human capital could be conceived as the acquisition of the general grammatical rules that allow to develop a language, while specific human capital as a specific vocabulary that allows to initiate and carry on a specific sub-set of linguistic communications (a metaphor of production activities), which, in our case, are spatially and temporally bounded within the ID, that is to say what define the ID itself. The former is the context, while the latter is the text. The former matters as a set of background principles, while the latter matters as a set of specific and appropriate instructions. The former can be enacted just because it requests the latter, whilst the latter needs the former to be formulated in appropriate and inter-subjective forms.

The first one refers to background and highly symbolic knowledge. It can be acquired in different ways, both with formal education, life experiences and cultural interests. It is a background that supports the creation, and fosters the accumulation, of specific forms of knowledge.

The second one refers to a specific set of competence-based specialized knowledge, instructions, domain-specific rules, that need to be acquired, for example, to use and manipulate in appropriate ways specific technology machineries. It can be achieved both with training on-the-job and off-the-job. It can have a tacit or explicit dimension, and it can be transmitted by means of direct contacts and interactions (for example, mediated by mentorship relations) or through formalized media (for example, using a handbook, or attending a workshop). It grows and spreads because it directly enacts forms of pre-requisite background knowledge.

These different forms of knowledge interact each other over the job, molding the level of human capital accumulation of individuals. It is usually assumed that, in the long term, a high level of accumulation of general human capital can foster the capacity of accumulation of forms of specific human capital, that specific human capital is closely related to technological learning and production activities and that it has a trajectory of growth, accumulation and dispersion that is closely coupled over time to cycles of innovation, exploitation and saturation of technological regimes which the firm moves within. Consequently, if generic human capital has a gradual and continuous positive accumulation over time and affects the level of specific human capital accumulation, as the experience of the worker cumulates over time, specific human capital accumulation conforms to the rule of decreasing returns and needs to be re-qualified according to specific technological trajectories defined by firm over time.

The cycle of human capital accumulation affects the professional trajectory of individuals and their level of productivity, connotes their position within the labor market, shapes their wage expectations in the phase of wage bargaining, and defines their lifestyle, affecting their cycle of economic resources accumulation.

Moreover, human capital is the principal intangible asset that affects the productivity of a firm as a whole, because it allows to tie technology absorptive capabilities developed by firm and productivity of organizational processes. It is one of the main object of policy of firms. Firm can choose to improve its human capital by organizing training courses, while, at the same time, the level of human capital becomes the crucial item upon which firm selects the applicant for a job and a proxy used to regulate and redefine the condition of the internal job agreements, that is to say the functioning of internal labor markets.

It is worth to notice that, for the time being, at this level of the prototypic stylization, we do not consider factors, such as the role of formal institutions (i.e., schools and educational institutes), both on the formation and accumulation of generic and specific human capital.

3. Some Hypotheses to Investigate

Simulations of the prototype should allow to investigate some hypotheses on the relations among waves of innovation, entrepreneurship and labor market dynamics in a local context, as follows:

- if firms work as a segmentation within labor markets, in the form of an operational closure between internal labor market and external labor markets, is there a relation between technology, innovation and labor market dynamics? and consequently, is there a close relation between emergence of entrepreneurship, innovations and labor market dynamics?
- finally, does entrepreneurship work as a driving force of adaptation of local markets with respect to global challenges?

These are some questions we should begin to investigate with the simulation of the prototype. Basically, they imply to focus our view on the relation among some macro emergent properties that the prototype allows to develop over time. But, there are a couple of more complex questions that we should be able to investigate, in a second time, too. They mostly concern the problem of the development of human capital in IDs, that is to say one of the most controversial issues in literature.

It is a matter of fact that, historically, forms of collective joint actions and local institutional engineering in IDs mainly apply to problems of "tangible assets", such as technological innovation and transfer, marketing, legal and financial issues (Bianchi and Giordani[7]; Cooke and Morgan[13]; Glasmeier[18]; Helmsing[20]; You and Wilkinson[37]), and so on, rather than to "intangible assets", such as knowledge and human capital management. Despite the fact that ID firms follow policies of human capital development, even if not formalized within specific and dedicated functional structures, they seem to be very far from recognizing the relevance of structuring joint actions in the field of human capital development and management (Albertini[1]). Why ID firms effectively institutionalize forms of strategic cooperation, along specific segments of their business chain, but not on human capital development and management?

If a sound answer should be formulated only after a set of comparative empirical studies that overcome our work, we would contribute in the next future by offering a computational analysis of the ID mechanisms about the process of human capital development and management, with the aim to figure out an evaluation of the possibilities given by institutionalizing such collective actions in IDs.

References

1. Albertini S. La gestione delle risorse umane nei distretti industriali. Lavoro e partecipazione nelle piccole e medie imprese, Etas Libri, Milano (2002).
2. Albino V., Garavelli A. C., Schiuma G. Knowledge Transfer and Inter-Firm Relationships in Industrial Districts: The Role of the Leader Firm, in Technovation, 19, pp. 53-63 (1999).
3. Amin A. The Emilian Model: Institutional Challenges, in *European Planning Studies*, vol. **7**, no. 4, pp. 389-405 (1999).
4. Becattini G. The Marshallian Industrial District as a Socio-Economic Notion, in Pyke F., Becattini G., Sengenberger W. (Eds.), Industrial Districts and Inter-Firm Cooperation in Italy, International Institute for Labor Studies, Geneva, pp. 134-141 (1990).
5. Becker G. S. Human Capital, The University of Chicago Press, Chicago (1993).
6. Belussi F. and Gottardi G. (Eds.) Evolutionary Patterns of Local Industrial Systems: Towards a Cognitive Approach to Industrial Districts, Ashgate, Aldershot Brookfield Singapore Sidney (2000).
7. Bianchi P. and Giordani M. G. Innovation Policy at the Local Level and at the National Level. The Case of Emilia-Romagna, in *European Planning Studies*, Vol. **1**, No. 1, pp. 25-41 (1993).
8. Boero R., Castellani M., Squazzoni F. Cognitive Identity and Social Reflexivity of the Industrial District Firms. Going Beyond the "Complexity Effect" with an Agent-Based Computational Prototype, in Lindemann G., Modt D., Paolucci M., Yu B. (Eds.), Proceedings of the International Workshop on Agent-Based Social Systems: Theories and Applications, Hamburg University, pp. 1-29, forthcoming for Springer Verlag, Berlin (2002).
9. Breschi S. and Lissoni F. Localised Knowledge Spillovers vs Innovative Milieux: Knowledge "Tacitness" Reconsidered, in *Papers on Regional Sciences*, **80**, pp. 255-273 (2001).
10. Carbonara N., Giannoccaro I., Pontrandolfo P. Supply Chains within Industrial Districts: A Theoretical Framework, in *International Journal of Production Economies*, **1**, pp. 1-18 (2001).
11. Castellani M. I livelli di aspirazione nel procedimento search and satisficing. Uno studio sperimentale di sociologia cognitiva, Department of Social Sciences, University of Brescia, Italy, Working Paper 5-03 (2003).
12. Cingano F. Returns to Specific Skills in Industrial Districts, in *Labor Economics*, **10**, pp. 149-164 (2003).
13. Cooke P. and Morgan K. The Associational Economy. Firms, Regions, and Innovation, Oxford University Press, New York (1998).
14. Corò G. and Grandinetti R. Industrial District Responses to the Network Economy: Vertical Integration versus Pluralist Global Exploration, in *Human Systems Management*, **20**, pp. 189-199 (2001).
15. De Propis L. Systemic Flexibility, Production Fragmentation and Cluster Governance, *European Planning Studies*, Vol. **9**, No. 6, pp. 739-754 (2001).

16. Dei Ottati G. Social Concertation and Local Development: The Case of Industrial Districts, in *European Planning Studies*, vol. **10**, no. 4, pp. 449-466 (2002).
17. Elster J. Sour Grapes. Studies in the Subversion of Rationality, Maison des Sciences de l'Homme and Cambridge University Press (1983).
18. Glasmeier A K. Territory-based Regional Development Policy and Planning in a Learning Economy: The Case of 'Real Service Centers' in Industrial Districts, in *European Urban and Regional Studies*, Vol. **6**, No.1, pp. 73-84 (1999).
19. Hand J. R. and Baruch L. (Eds.) Intagible Assets, Oxford University Press, Oxford (2003).
20. Helmsing A. H. J. Externalities, Learning and Governance: New Perspectives on Local Economic Development, in *Development and Change*, Vol. **32**, pp. 277-308 (2001).
21. Luna F., Stefansson B. (Eds.) Economic Simulation in Swarm: Agent-Based Modeling and Object-Oriented Programming, Kluwer Academic Publishers, Boston/Dordrecth/London (2000).
22. Luna F., Perrone A. (Eds.) Agent-Based Methods in Economic and Finance: Simulations in Swarm, Kluwer Academic Publishers, Boston/Dordrecth/London (2001).
23. March J.G. A Primer on Decision Making. How Decisions Happen, The Free Press, New York (1994).
24. Mistri M. and Solari S. Social Networks and Productive Connectance: Modeling the Organizational Form of the Industrial District, in *Human System Management*, **20**, pp. 223-235 (2001).
25. Molina-Morales F. X. Human Capital in the Industrial Districts, *Human Systems Management*, **20**, pp. 319-331 (2001).
26. Nonaka I. and Takeuchi H. The Knowledge-Creating Company. How Japanese Companies Create the Dynamics of Innovation, Oxford University Press, New York (1995).
27. Piore M. J. The Emergent Role of Social Intermediaries in the New Economy, in *Annals of Public and Cooperative Economics*, **72**, 3, pp. 339-350 (2001).
28. Rullani E. The Industrial District (ID) as a Cognitive System, in Curzio Quadrio A. and Fortis M. (Eds.), Complexity and Industrial Districts, Springer Verlag, Berlin (2002).
29. Russo M. The Effects of Technical Change in Skills Requirements: An Empirical Analysis, *Labor*, **5**, 1, pp. 45-74 (1991).
30. Saxenian A. Regional Advantage: Culture and Competition in Silicon Valley and Route 128, Harvard University Press, Cambridge, Massachussets (1994).
31. Selten R. Aspiration Adaptation Theory, in *Journal of Mathematical Psychology*, n. **42**, pp. 191-214 (1998).
32. Simon H. A. A Behavioral Model of Rational Choice, in *Quarterly Journal of Economics*, **69**, pp. 99-118 (1955).
33. Simon H. A. Bounded rationality, in J. Eatwell, M. Milgate and P. Newman (Eds.), The New Pelgrave: A Dictionary of Economics, Macmillan, London, vol.4 (1987).

34. Squazzoni F. and Boero R. Economic Performance, Inter-Firm Relations and Local Institutional Engineering in a Computational Prototype of Industrial Districts, *Journal of Artificial Societies and Social Simulation*, Vol. **5**, No. 1 (2002) ¡http://www.soc.surrey.ac.uk/JASSS/5/1/1.html¿.
35. Storper M. The Resurgence of Regional Economics, Ten Years Later: The Region as a Nexus of Untraded Interdependencies, in *European Urban and Regional Studies*, **2**, pp. 191-221 (1995).
36. Terna P. Simulation Tools for Social Scientists: Building Agent-Based Models with Swarm, *Journal of Artificial Societies and Social Simulation*, Vol. **1**, No. 2 (1998), ¡http://www.soc.surrey.ac.uk/JASSS/1/2/4.html¿.
37. You J.- I. and Wilkinson F. Competition and Cooperation. Towards Understanding Industrial Districts, in *Review of Political Economy*, **6**, 3, pp. 259-278 (1994).

THE ROLE OF SMALL BUSINESS BASED STRUCTURES IN PROMOTING INNOVATION, AND CREATING EMPLOYMENT, AS COMPARED TO OLIGOPOLISTIC BASED STRUCTURES

MEGAN KHOSHYARAN†

Department of Economics Catholic University of Leuven, Belgium.

The main idea of this paper is to prove that economic structures that are based on small businesses function better than oligopolies. Small business structures promote growth inducing innovation, while oligopolies seek incremental and continuous innovations. Thus the former system creates employment, and the latter modifies employment. To prove this claim, six propositions are introduced and analysed. The main argument used for the analysis is the nature of the tasks performed, and its relation to innovation. The six propositions use the variable of the tasks performed in various aspects of the comparison of the two systems.

1. Introduction

Innovation has become the new business obsession. Books like "The Innovation Dilemma" and ""Innovate or Die" often top the business bestseller lists. Though the crucial role played by innovation in driving economic growth, and creating employment is acknowledged, many economists do not share the new obsession. My intention is to shed some light on the topic of innovation. How can one define innovation? What are the main ingredients for innovation? What kind of economic environment encourages innovation? How innovation is related to employment? The premiss of this paper is that to encourage innovation businesses should stay small. The economy has to allow the entry of new small businesses, and even encourage it. Some economists believe that the industrial structure that best fosters productive innovation is oligopoly. I will prove to the contrary. Economic growth through innovation is only assured if in place of a few big companies competing with each other an environment could be created that allows many firms to compete in a free market.

In this paper my aim is to provide answers to the questions posed in the first paragraph by comparing an open market system that allows free entry and operation of small businesses, system (A), with a closed oligopolistic market system, system (B), in terms of each system's structural tendency towards innovation and its effects on employment. At the microeconomics level,

---

† E-mail: megan.khoshyaran@wanadoo.fr

innovation is related to the inherent nature of the tasks performed by the labour force in both systems. If I define a task as a force applied to a point, in system (A), each worker applies force in a multi-dimensional space. Thus, it is easy to form a complex functional. In other words, the labour force hired has to perform a spectrum of tasks in either the production process or the running of a business. This element offers a comprehensive knowledge of the nature of the product to the employees. The learning process eventually encourages one or more of the employees to come up with ideas for a new product or a complementary product. In system (B), each worker applies a linear force. In this case only linear projections are possible. Any function of this simple space has a simple form. In system (B), the labour force is highly specialised. Workers and specialists perform minuscule tasks when compared to the scope of the activities. The work force is short-sighted. This makes for innovations that are predictable, continuous and incremental. Proposition1: The scale of innovation is directly related to the degree of the complexity of the tasks performed.

The complex functional of the tasks performed in system (A) eventually results in two types of spin-offs: either 1) creation of complementary products or 2) creation of new products. Proposition 2: Given equal market conditions, innovations in system (A) always lead to either new products or complementary products; innovations in system (B) always translate to an incremental evolution of the same product. An important issue is pricing. Proposition 3: In system (A), price is a function of the tasks performed by labour and machine. In system (B), price is a function of the interaction among the market forces.

On the macroeconomics level, I prove Proposition 4: System (A) leads to a better distribution of the labour force, which leads to a balanced growth between innovation, productivity, and employment. To prove proposition 4, I take the two systems as two intelligent machines. Machine (A) starts from a nucleus of small sub-systems, and it propagates through diffusion and separation. Eventually, it develops into a large number of small intelligent sub-systems. There is always a slot for a new sub-system in machine (A). Each sub-system is made up of a number of self–organising particles or labour. When the equilibrium state in each sub-system is disturbed by exogenous factors, it experiences a phase transition. Some of its particles go through a diffusion process that eventually ends in a total separation and formation of a new sub-system. Machine (B) consists of a few large intelligent sub-systems. In system (B), any disturbance in the equilibrium state of each sub-system can only cause deformation. There is either expansion or contraction.

Extension of proposition 4 results in proposition 5: System (A) leads to multiple equilibrium points; while, system (B) leads to a single equilibrium point in the market. The advantage of a multiple equilibrium system is that it can function even if some of its sub-systems are not at equilibrium. In a single equilibrium case, once the equilibrium is disturbed, then it is unlikely that the system can continue. Finally, I will prove Proposition 6: Business cycles are directly related to the scale of a business, the larger the business the higher the occurrence of a business cycle. In system (A), business cycles are easily avoided. Any drop in demand can be considered as the factor causing the diffusion process. It can trigger innovation, and since any new diffusion can be supported by the system, it then allows companies to adjust their output. System (B) is more susceptible to business cycles. Since system (B) can only accept contraction, it becomes much harder for companies to make adjustments reflecting any decrease in demand.

2. The Microeconomic Aspect of Innovation in Small Business and Oligopolistic Structures

Everyone acknowledges that innovation plays a crucial role in driving economic growth. But the fact that innovation happens is mostly taken for granted; the how and why of innovation remain largely ignored. Innovation is directly dependent on the scale of production, which defines the division of labour. Innovation is thus perceived as a function of the division of labour. The more complicated the tasks performed, the more significant the scale of innovation. The larger the scale of production is, the more myopic the tasks become, and the less significant innovation becomes.

One of the most significant characteristics of the modern oligopolies has been the division of the labour force. In place of a worker, executing a composite and diverse number of tasks in a serial order, he performs a separated, isolated and a myopic task. Thus a product that could represent a composite work of several labourers becomes a social product representing the cooperative work of many workers, each of whom constantly executing the same myopic task [30-31]. The main feature of system (B) is its ability to reduce work to highly myopic tasks. In such an environment the worker is incapable of producing significant innovation; the best that can happen is a simple, continuous, and an incremental innovation. On the other hand system (A) attributes composite and often complicated tasks to their workers, and thus creates an environment where given the complexity of the task base, allows for innovations that add to economic growth. In the past the most primitive nucleus of a small business was a lone entrepreneur building some world-changing invention in his garage. Historically, such pioneers play an important role, particularly in devising radically new technologies. As the societies become more complex, and the products and the mode of production take a more intricate form, it is less and less possible to have from a garage to lab situation of the past pioneers. But, it is still possible to avoid the acute division of labour, and allow workers to perform composite tasks which in time provides them with the intellectual ability, and would encourage one or a number of workers in the business to innovate. It is to prove the above arguments and provide a more rigorous treatment of this topic that proposition one is introduced.

Proposition 1: The scale of innovation is directly related to the degree of the complexity of the tasks performed. Let's start by defining a task. A task is a force that is applied to a point to produce work. A task can be divided into two categories:

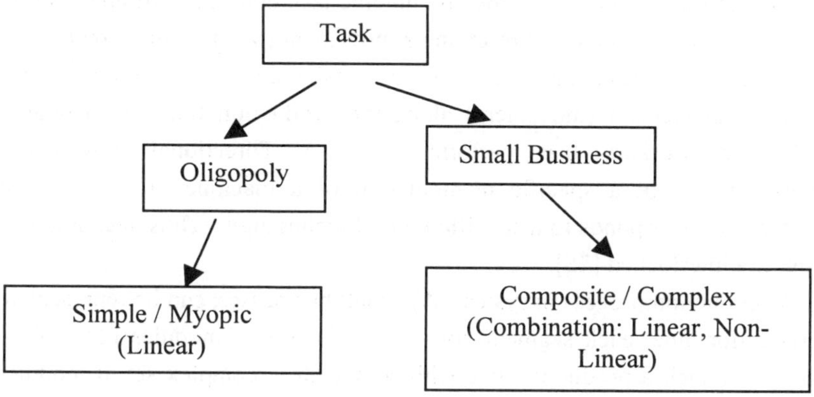

Figure 1. Task defined by an economic system

As is shown in Figure 1, each economic system imposes a certain type of task. In system (B), the workers are required to perform simple, myopic tasks. This implies that the physical movements relating to the production process are limited to simple directional displacements in the Euclidean space. While in system (A), workers perform composite and often complex tasks. There is a larger degree of freedom in the physical movements. Mathematically represented, myopic tasks are denoted by linear vectors in Euclidean space with rectangular coordinates; while composite tasks are denoted by vectors in non-Euclidean space with either affine or curvilinear coordinates.

A production line in system (B), oligopolies, can be represented by a linear sequence of modules depicted in Figure 2.

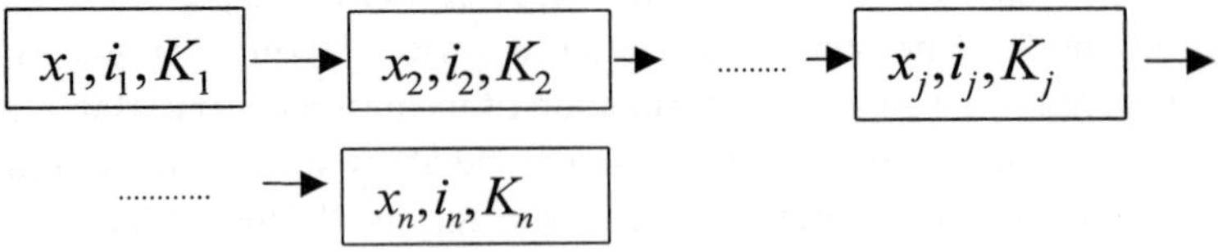

$$\sum_j K_j = N$$

$$x_j \cap x_k = 0$$

Figure 2. Production line in system (B)

Each module represents a specific myopic task done by a group of workers. (x_j, i_j) is a linear vector representing a movement (task) in direction (i_j). j is the index for the task number. N is the total number of workers making a specific displacement (movement) along the production line. K_j denotes the number of workers that perform task (j). Directional movement is representational of a specific manipulation of a machine or an instrument; therefore, it corresponds to a specific type of technology. Thus, technology and labour are interlocked [25].

A production process in system (A), small businesses, can be represented by a production line, each segment consisting of a set of modules [24, 26]. An example of such a production line with composite – complex set of modules is shown in Figure 3. Each set of modules that are connected by arrows represents a composite task and possess a specific geometrical shape.

Each $\overline{x}_l^k$ is a module or task which can be represented by a vector constructed from affine or curvilinear coordinates. A collection of modules ($\overline{x}_l^k$) constitutes a set. Each set is a graph that is connected by ($\overline{x}_l^k$) points and possesses a certain topology: This graph can be represented by a vector function $f\left(\overline{x}^k \mid \overline{x}^k = \overline{x}_l^k,\ l \in L_k\right)$. M is the total number of workers performing composite tasks. Innovation is the result of learning, experience, and intelligence. It is obvious that those who work in system (A), learn considerably more than those who work in system (B), simply by executing composite tasks that require the use of intelligence. They accumulate more experience simply because they do more.

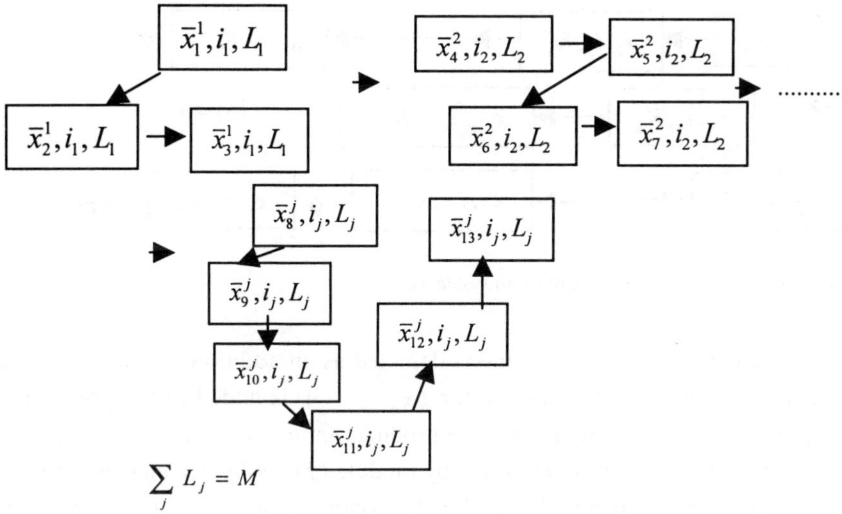

Figure 3. Production process in system (A)

Innovation is defined either as non-significant or significant depending on whether it occurs in system (B) or in system (A).

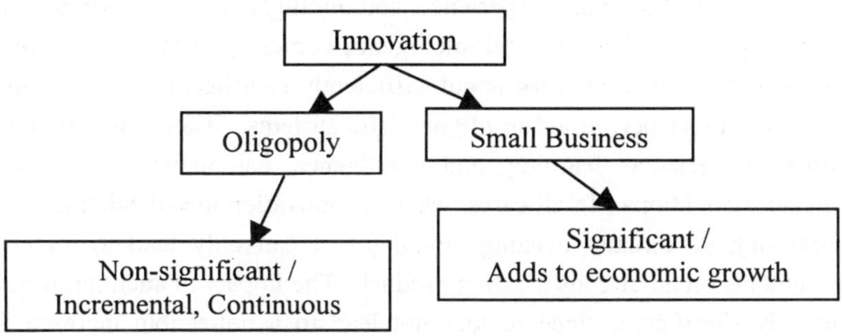

Figure 4. Innovation defined in oligopoly and small business systems

Non-significant innovation refers to a new technology or a technique that is capable of improving an already existing product. Non-significant innovations mainly occur in system (B), oligopolies. I identify two types of innovation in this case: 1) addition of a new module to the production line, 2) modification of an already existing module in the production line. Types one and two innovations can be demonstrated by Figure 5.

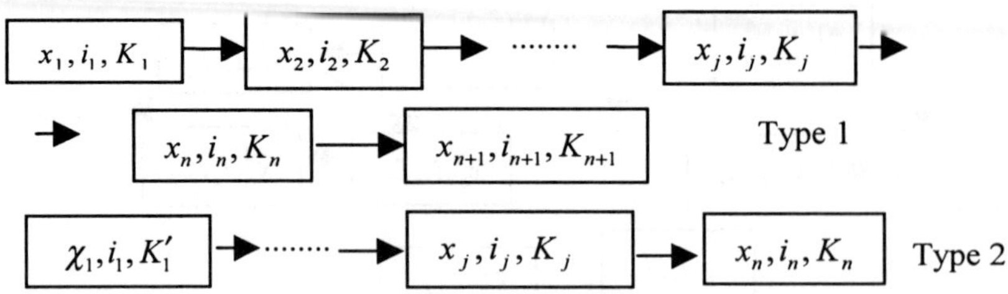

Figure 5. Types one and two innovations in system (B)

In figure 5 innovation type one is depicted as an addition of a new module in the production line. A linear vector (x_{n+1}, i_{n+1}) is added to the production line in order to modify and improve the product. Innovation type two is depicted by replacing modules (x_1), and (x_2) by module (χ). Whether innovation is an addition to or replacement of the already existing modules, it signifies linear projections. Both (x_{n+1}, i_{n+1}) and (χ) are linear functions of one or more of the modules in the production line or some new combination of linear movements (displacements) directed towards modifying a product; thus, they are a mapping from a linear space to a linear space. Innovations no matter whether they are an addition of a new module or a modification of an already existing module result from application of learning, experience, and intelligence. It is a worker who by using his experience, learning and intelligence comes up with a new innovation. But, experience gained at work is not sufficiently significant due to the myopic nature of the tasks performed in oligopolistic systems. Therefore, combination of narrow experience, learning, and intelligence, can naturally lead to non-significant innovations. In all cases, whether innovation means adding a module or improving on already existing module(s), it can only lead to incremental improvements on an already existing product. The impact of such innovations is not usually significant, since it does not lead to a noticeable increase in the employment level, and does not add to social wealth in any substantial way.

Significant innovations are the type of innovations that contribute to economic growth. These types of innovations are the technologies or techniques that allow for the production of new or complementary products. Significant innovations are more likely to occur in system (A), small business system. Innovation in the context of system (A) is: 1) Addition of a new set of modules, 2) Replace an existing set of modules with a new set of modules. This is done

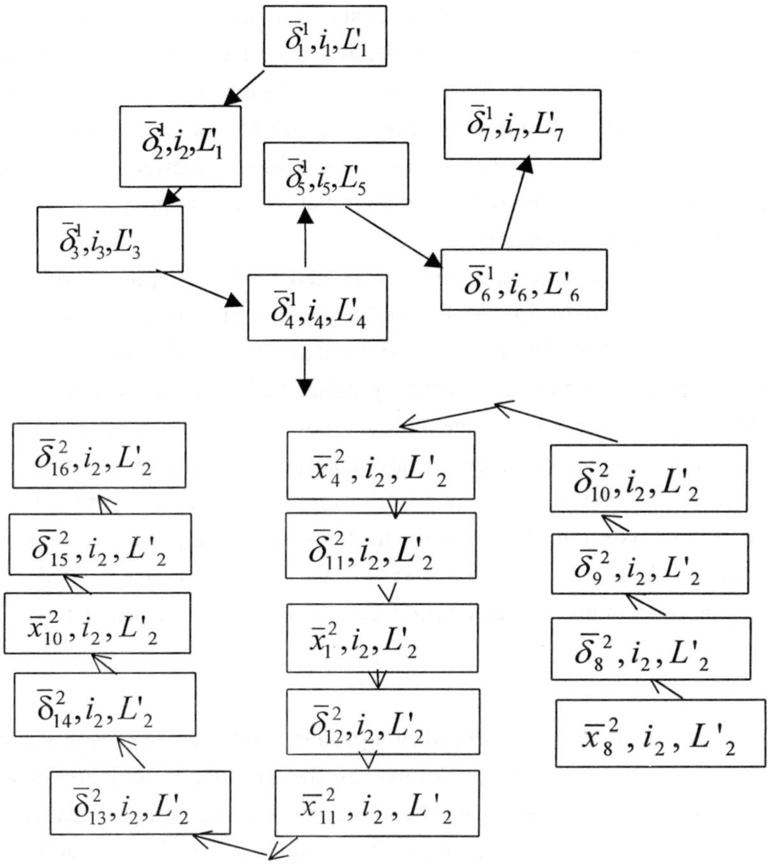

Figure 6. Types one, two, three innovations in system (A)

either by re-arranging one set of modules, or designing a new set of modules. 3) Design a brand new routine of a series of sets of modules, some of which are modification of old sets, some are new. Figure 6 depicts a new routine to replace the old routine of Figure 4. The new production line consists of two sets of modules. Set one consists of 7 new sub-modules, ($\bar{\delta}_1^1$, ..., $\bar{\delta}_7^1$). Set two consists of 16 sub-modules, of which 5 are the tasks from the old production line, ($\bar{x}_8^2, \bar{x}_4^2, \bar{x}_1^2, \bar{x}_{11}^2, \bar{x}_{10}^2$). Similarly to system (B), any addition or improvement is a function of already existing modules, or a combination of new set of modules. With one major exception that innovation in this context is a projection from a curvilinear or affine space to a curvilinear or affine space. A worker in system (A) draws a considerable experience from his environment working in a small business. This worker by using his intelligence, learning, and experience is capable of innovation that is significant; since the base experience he draws from is more complex than oligopolistic experience. It suffices to compare Figure 5, with Figure 6 to find out that innovation in system (A) is more complicated than in system (B).

The scale of innovation is directly related to the complexity of the tasks performed. This conclusion can be used to prove proposition 2. *Proposition 2:* Given equal market conditions, innovations in system (A) always lead to creating either new products or complementary products; whereas innovations in system (B) always translate to an incremental evolution of the same product. A product can be defined as manipulation of raw material by man and machine given a certain level of technology, into a specific form for a particular use. A product can be defined as a multiplication of the tasks along the production line by the raw material [5, 6]. Take system (B), and the production line as is defined in Figure 2 as an example, one can write a general formula for a product as follows.

$$Q = \Pi_{j=1}^{n} K_j x_j \times R \qquad (1)$$

Q represents quantity produced of a product, and R represents raw material. The equation above commonly known as the production function gives the maximum number of output given the input. In fact, this equation resembles the Cobb-Douglas production function, but with one major exception. The technology and labour are not two independent variables; rather these two elements are combined into tasks performed. For each level of technology a certain level and quality of labour is required. The interdependency of labour and capital or technology is denoted by the tasks performed along the production line. This is reflected on in Equation (1). Anytime a new innovation is introduced the shape of the production function changes. Thus, by comparing the graph of the production function before and after an innovation, one can conclude whether innovation has resulted in an improved product or a new product. Innovation is introduced by an addition of a new module, or replacement of an existing module, (Figure 5), then Equation (1), can be modified as follows:

$$\widetilde{Q} = \Pi_{j=1}^{\widetilde{n}} \widetilde{K}_j \lambda_j \times R$$

$$\lambda_j = \begin{bmatrix} x_j \quad \forall j = 1,2,\ldots,n \qquad if\ \widetilde{n} > n \\ or \\ \begin{bmatrix} \chi_j & \forall j \in J \\ x_j & \forall j \in \widetilde{J} \end{bmatrix} \quad if\ \widetilde{n} = n \end{bmatrix} \tag{2}$$

$\widetilde{Q}$ is the quantity produced of an improved product. The improved product is the result of a modification to the production process, namely, addition of (a) new module(s), or replacement of one or more modules with new ones. Obviously, the outcome of Equation (2) is different from Equation (1). Geometrically, Equation (2) and Equation (1) differ by a linear variation. In contrast, the production function in system (A) is given by equation (3):

$$\begin{aligned} \overline{Q} &= \Pi_{k \in \mathrm{K}} K_k f_k(\overline{x}^k) \times \overline{R} \\ \overline{x}^k &= \left(\overline{x}_l^k, l \in L_k\right) \end{aligned} \tag{3}$$

$\overline{Q}$ Represents quantity produced of a product in system (A), and $\overline{R}$ represents raw material. k is the index for the number of sets of modules. l is the index for the number of tasks in each set of modules. L_k, is the group of l's that are in set k. K_k is the number of workers executing a set of modules. $f_k(\overline{x}^k)$ is the vector function representing the graph of each set of modules in the production line. $K_k f_k(\overline{x}^k)$ is the labour-task input requirement. For a physical presentation you can refer to Figure 3. Introduction of an innovation transforms Equation (3) to Equation (4).

$$\begin{aligned} \widetilde{Q} &= \Pi_{k \in \widetilde{\mathrm{K}}} \widetilde{K}_k \widetilde{f}_k(\widetilde{x}^k) \times \overline{R} \\ \widetilde{x}^k &= \left(\widetilde{x}_l^k, l \in \widetilde{L}_k\right) \end{aligned} \tag{4}$$

$\widetilde{Q}$ represents the quantity produced of a product in system (A) after innovation. $\widetilde{f}_k\left(\widetilde{x}^k\right)$ is a new vector function representing the new graph of each set of modules after innovation . $\widetilde{x}^k$ represents either new modules or combination of old and new modules. $\widetilde{k}$ is the index for the number of new set of modules. Geometrically, Equation (3) and Equation (4) differ by a non-linear variation. The complexity of the change in the topological sense from the old graph points to a new product. In system (A), any innovation results in separation of the inventor from the firm. Firms stay small; there is no incentive to expand. The small business economy encourages new entries in the market. Therefore, Equations (3) and (4) are derived from two separate production lines, and producers; whereas Equations (1) and (2) are drawn from the same production line, at two different stages of its evolution with the same producer.

One of the major differences between an oligopolistic system, and a small business system is in the price setting mechanism of each respective regime. *Proposition 3*: In system (A) price is a function of the tasks performed by labour, and machine. In system (B), price is a function of the interaction among the market forces. Traditionally in system (A), small businesses, the objective of the producer, as long as no constraints are imposed, is to choose the optimal combination of (capital, and labour), which renders maximum profit. Formally, the producer's pursuit of monetary gains is formulated as the profit optimization problem with no constraints [8]:

$$\underset{C,T}{Max}\, \pi(C,T) = pQ(C,T) - wT - rC - f \tag{5}$$

In equation (5), π represents a profit function, (p) is price, (Q) is the production function, (T) stands for labour, (C) for capital or technology, (r) represents wages, (w) is return from capital, and (f) represents fixed costs. I should note that in this paper technology is synonymous to capital, since one needs capital to acquire technology; therefore, capital and technology are used interchangeably. In the conventional formulation, technology and labour are considered as two independent variables, as is shown in Equation (5). Price plays a detrimental role in finding what combination of capital and labour would maximise profit. The approach is somewhat different here. Pricing is based on how tasks along the production line are engineered. This main deviation from the traditional formulation of capital and labour reformulates Equation (5), where the production function $Q(C,T)$, is replaced by $Q($**Mod**$)$. The new production function is the function of tasks or set of tasks performed, or in other words, the modules (**Mod**).

$$\begin{cases} \underset{\mathbf{Mod},p}{Max}\ \pi(\mathbf{Mod}) = pQ(\mathbf{Mod}) - \boldsymbol{\alpha}(\mathbf{Mod}) - f \\ s.t. \\ Q(\mathbf{Mod}) = \Delta(p) \end{cases}$$

$$\boldsymbol{\alpha} = (\alpha_1, \alpha_2, \alpha_3, \ldots\ldots, \alpha_n) \tag{6}$$

$$\mathbf{Mod} = (\text{mod}_1, \text{mod}_2, \ldots., \text{mod}_n)$$

$\boldsymbol{\alpha}$ is a vector of monetary cost of a task. **Mod** is a vector of modules of a production line. Each (**Mod**) represents an engineered composite set of tasks. n refers to the number of modules along a production line. $\Delta(p)$ is the anticipated demand function. For a production routine several sets of tasks are engineered. The efficiency and the viability of each engineered set of tasks are tested by finding a price that corresponds to each designed set. The set is chosen that can maximise profit and its characteristic optimal price. Price plays an equally important role in the new formulation of the profit maximisation problem. Price determines the viability and the efficiency of the design of the tasks. The first order conditions calculate for what price the tasks designed are appropriate.

$$\begin{cases} \left(p + \dfrac{\Delta}{\Delta'}(p)\right)\dfrac{\partial Q(\mathbf{Mod})}{\partial \mathbf{Mod}} - \boldsymbol{\alpha} = 0 \\ Q(\mathbf{Mod}) = \Delta(p) \end{cases} \tag{7}$$

The system of equations thus obtained calculates the price of a product for a specific design of sets of modules. The impact of innovation in determining the price is evident from the formulation of the profit maximising problem. The vector (**Mod**) takes into account any type of innovation, since innovation is defined as either an addition of new modules, or modification of already existing modules, or designing new production routines. Evidently, innovation plays an important role in price setting procedure, and determining which tasks use capital, and labour most efficiently.

In system (B), oligopolies, competition is inherently a setting for strategic interaction. Therefore, the appropriate tool for its analysis is game theory. In the oligopolistic competitive model, firms choose their price simultaneously with constant returns to scale technologies. The commonly known model of this type is the Bertrand model, and its derivative the Cournot model. The critical part of this game-theoretic approach to pricing in oligopolistic markets is choosing the strategies and the payoffs of the firms. A particular attention is paid to demand, and the technological features of the market, and the underlying processes of competition. In oligopolistic environment, technology is a means of controlling output. For the sake of simplicity, let's consider an oligopolistic system with only two firms operating the market. Two firms simultaneously decide how much to produce, $Q_j(\mathbf{Mod}_j)$, and $Q_k(\mathbf{Mod}_k)$. Given the oligopolistic supply, price is adjusted to the level that clears the market, $p(Q_j(\mathbf{Mod}_j) + Q_k(\mathbf{Mod}_k))$, where $p(.) = \Delta^{-1}(.)$ is the inverse demand function. $p(.)$ is differentiable, $p'(.) > 0$, for all $Q \geq 0$. Firms produce output at a cost of $c>0$ per unit. The Nash equilibrium model of an oligopolistic (two firms) competition is a maximisation problem:

$$\underset{\mathbf{Mod}_j}{Max}\ p(Q_j(\mathbf{Mod}_j) + \tilde{Q}_k(\mathbf{Mod}_k))Q_j(\mathbf{Mod}_j) - c \cdot Q_j(\mathbf{Mod}_j) \quad (8)$$

replacing $c \cdot Q_j(\mathbf{Mod}_j)$ by $\alpha_j \cdot (\mathbf{Mod}_j)$, the following formulation is obtained:

$$\underset{Q_j}{Max}\ p(Q_j(\mathbf{Mod}) + \tilde{Q}_k(\mathbf{Mod}))Q_j(\mathbf{Mod}) - \alpha_j \cdot (\mathbf{Mod}_j) \cdot Q_j(\mathbf{Mod}) \quad (9)$$

$\tilde{Q}_k(\mathbf{Mod}_k)$ is the output level of firm k. In solving Equation (9), firm j acts like a monopolist with an inverse demand function. An optimal production plan for firm j given its rival's output $\tilde{Q}_k(\mathbf{Mod}_k)$ satisfies the first order condition which is the best –response function.

$$\left[p'(Q_j(\mathbf{Mod}_j) + \tilde{Q}_k(\mathbf{Mod}_k))Q_j(\mathbf{Mod}_j) + p(Q_j(\mathbf{Mod}_j))\right]\frac{\partial Q_j(\mathbf{Mod}_j)}{\partial \mathbf{Mod}_j} = \alpha_j \quad (10)$$

From Equation (10), one can deduct that $\mathbf{Mod}_j$ is a function of $\mathbf{Mod}_k$, and symmetrically, $\mathbf{Mod}_k$ is a function of $\mathbf{Mod}_j$. The best-response function of one firm depends on the choice and the architecture of linear tasks that comprise the production line of the other firm. The implication is that innovation in the context of oligopoly is geared towards modifications that rely on the strategic response of the other firm. An oligopolist does not take risks; innovation in an oligopolistic environment is always geared towards improving an already existing product. The market equilibrium is maintained by keeping a price level that is greater than the unit cost, and smaller than a monopoly price. This makes for innovations that are incremental, and continuous in nature.

3. The Macroeconomic Aspect of Innovation in Small Business and Oligopolistic Structures

Proposition 4: System (A) leads to a better distribution of the labour force, which leads to a balanced growth between innovation, productivity, and employment. To prove this proposition I start with the definition of the economic growth, and what are its main elements identified according to economists. Economic growth is defined as a continuous improvement of techniques of production and unlimited accumulation of means of production. The main elements identified as factors affecting the economic growth are: the rate of investment, the rate of savings, and the rate of consumption. This list is modified by Solow and Ramsey who add technology, labour, and capital to this list. The most significant aspect of technology in conventional economic growth theory is the assumption of increasing returns to scale which provides a favourable argument for the need for large scale firms and businesses. In proposition 4, it is argued that technology limited to increasing returns to scale is not sufficient to explain the ever decreasing level of productivity, and an ever increasing rate of unemployment experienced in many industrialised and third world countries.

In proposition 1, I argued that the scale of innovation is highly dependent on the complexity of tasks performed by workers. It is equally argued that the smaller the scale of a business, the more complex the tasks performed by employees. A task is complex if it is composite and non-linear. In *proposition 2*, I argue that the complexity of the tasks performed define innovations that eventually result in creation of either new products or complementary products, while increasing return to scale innovations due to their linear nature lead to improvements of the existing products. These arguments indicate that contrary to the common belief that the accumulation of wealth is the result of the increasing return to scale innovations, it is the economic environment that encourages productivity, and employment by providing a medium that allows the free entry of small businesses. To prove proposition 4, I employ theories and techniques from the physics of phase transitions.

I consider the two systems (A), and (B), the small business system, and the oligopolistic system, as two intelligent machines. Machine (A) starts from a nucleus of small sub-systems, and it propagates through diffusion and separation. Eventually, it develops into a large number of small intelligent sub-systems. A diffusion process is a displacement of either atoms or molecules of either gas, or liquid, or solid that determines the dynamics of a great number of transitional phases that make nucleation possible. Diffusion is a phenomenon that allows a system to reach equilibrium even if the system does not start from an equilibrium state. One can consider the economic environment as a solid medium (machine) consisting of a large number of sub- systems. Each time innovation occurs there is a separation from the nucleus or the sub-system. Each separation process possesses enough potential energy to allow the new sub-system to occupy a place among the other existing sub-systems, and reach an equilibrium position. There is always a slot for a new sub-system in machine (A). Each vacant slot is called a Lacuna [11], Figure 7.

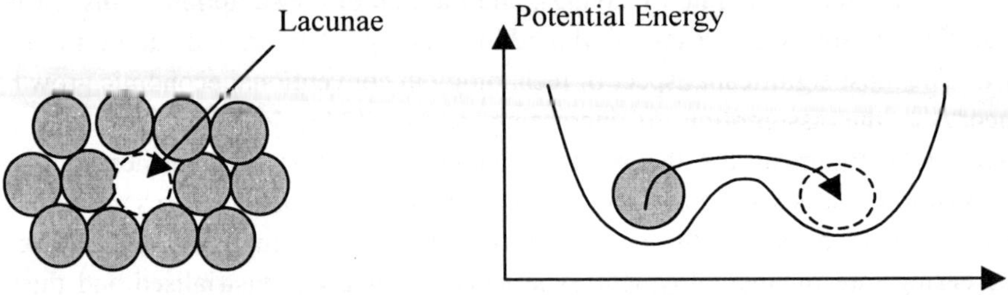

Figure 7. Depiction of a diffusion process

Each sub-system is made up of a number of self–organising particles or labour. When the equilibrium state in each sub-system is disturbed by exogenous factors, it experiences a phase transition. Some of its particles go through a diffusion process that eventually ends in a total separation and formation of a new sub-system. Exogenous factors causing a phase change are elements such as drop in the consumption level, dramatic changes in investment and savings, and unfavourable legislations. In this context innovation can be considered as the potential energy of the separation phase. Let's denote the change in free enthalpy of the energy of separation by ΔI_0. ΔI_0 represents the change in potential energy of innovation required to occupy a new Lacuna. The probability (P_0) that an innovation possess enough energy to effectuate a separation is a function of ΔI_0.

$$P_0 = C\exp(-\frac{\Delta I_0}{kD}) \tag{11}$$

where

$$C = \frac{V}{\eta}$$
$$V \to \infty \tag{12}$$
$$\eta \to \infty$$

V denotes the capacity or size of sub-systems (small businesses), η denotes the number of exogenous factors involved in the phase transition. $V \to \infty$, denotes the limit in the capacity of a sub-system. $\eta \to \infty$, denotes the limit in the number of exogenous factors. The free enthalpy of the energy of separation, ΔI_0 can be re-written as:

$$\Delta I_0 = \Delta H_0 - D\Delta S_0 \tag{13}$$

ΔH_0 is the change in the enthalpy of the sub-system. ΔH_0 is a function of the internal energy of the sub-system as it relates to the requirement for innovation such as the complexity of the composite tasks designed, and external pressure on the sub-system such as a drastic drop in actual demand. ΔS_0 is the change in the entropy of the sub-system. This is mainly the endogenous factors that hinder the occurrence of innovation such as inefficiently engineered tasks. D denotes anticipated demand for either a new product or a complementary product. k denotes a Boltzmann like constant. In the context of this argument, k represents the degrees of freedom of demand. The degree of freedom refers to the effect of independent parameters such as consumer utility, and price on demand. Substituting Equation (13) for the change in free enthalpy of the energy of separation, ΔI_0, Equation (14) is obtained:

$$P_0 = C \exp\left(-\frac{\Delta H_0}{kD} + \frac{\Delta S_0}{k} \right) \tag{14}$$

The probability of existence of a Lacuna is given as:

$$P_L = C \exp\left(-\frac{\Delta H_L}{kD} \right) \tag{15}$$

(P_L) is the probability that there exists a Lacuna. ΔH_L is the change in the enthalpy of a Lacuna. ΔH_L relates to the variables such as the anticipated potential energy of a new product to attract demand. The probability (P_D) associated with the diffusion mechanism is given by Equation (16). Both the enthalpy of innovation and the anticipated enthalpy of the new product are needed for the diffusion process to occur.

$$P_D = CP_0 P_L = C\exp\left(-\frac{\Delta H_0 - \Delta S_0 + \Delta H_L}{kD}\right) \tag{16}$$

Machine (B) consists of a few large intelligent sub-systems. The market environment is nearly closed since the existing firms almost saturate the market. New entries are highly unlikely due to severe competition, and high operation costs due to scale economies, and price level. Obviously, in this environment, there is very little possibility of occurrence of open slots, or Lacunas, thus, $(P_L) << \varepsilon$. Any disturbance in the equilibrium state of each sub-system is due to disequilibrium in the other sub-system, and can only cause deformation. This is easily deducted from proposition 1. In proposition 1, it is shown that the scale of innovation depends on the complexity of the tasks done. Since the tasks in oligoplolistic systems are shown to be linear, any innovation, which is the linear transformation of these tasks taken as basis, from a linear space to a linear space, is incremental, and continuous. Thus, the potential energy due to linear type innovation, characteristic of oligopolies is low. It can mainly cause deformation. There is either expansion or contraction. An expansion refers to the increasing return to scale innovation which usually results from a boom in the market, when households save less and spend more. Contraction refers to the decreasing return to scale innovation which is usually caused by a serious decline in market demand, or stringent government regulations.

Proposition 5: System (A), small businesses, leads to multiple equilibrium points; while, system (B) leads to a single equilibrium point in the market. Proposition 5 is an extension of proposition 4. Disequilibrium occurs due to exogenous factors such as change in the supply of the product, change in public spending, fall in consumer spending, etc. In system (A), disequilibrium leads to separation. A new sub-system is formed by occupying a Lacuna, which is independent of the parent sub-system. The new sub-system falls into a stable position till the next diffusion process. The probability of staying in an equilibrium position is derived in proposition 4, and is equal to (P_0). A generalisation of this idea is a situation where multiple diffusion processes occur simultaneously due to the availability of several Lacunas. In that case several Lacunas are filled at the same time with the condition that $\sum P_0^i = 1$, where (i), is the number of new sub-systems formed out of multiple^i diffusion processes. Each time a Lacuna is filled, the corresponding sub-system reaches equilibrium till the next diffusion process. This implies that diffusion and branching is time dependent, or specifically, there exists a stochastic branching random walk process [27]. Each new sub-system will have offspring (new innovations). Offspring either creates new products or complementary products. Therefore, one can assume that in time a branching phenomenon occurs that starts from the parent sub-system. By branching it is meant a stochastic random walk process where a new sub-system moves from position (x) to position (y). The branching phenomenon can be shown by imagining a lattice with few open slots or Lacunas as in Figure 8. When branching occurs

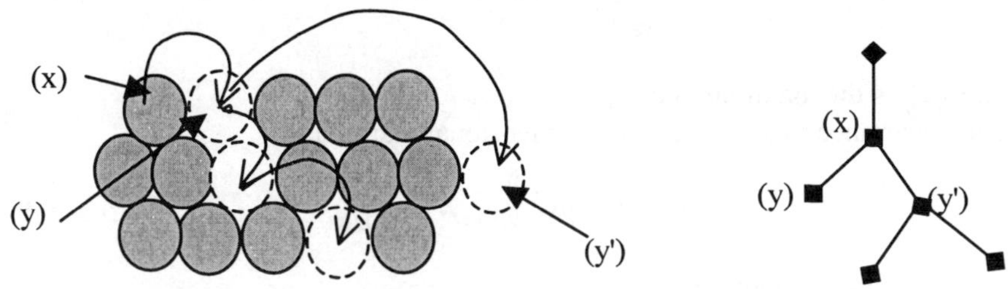

Figure 8. Depiction of a branching process

the new sub-system(s) branch out in either of two directions: 1) Towards producing a new product, position (y), or 2) Towards producing a complementary product, position (y'). Let $\mu = (\mu_n)_{n \geq N}$ be a random walk in discrete time on R_+^d, where d refers to those parameters that define a position. A transition kernel is defined as,

$$\alpha(x, y) := P\left(\mu_1 = y \middle| \mu_0 = x\right) = C \exp\left(-\frac{\Delta I_0(x, y)}{kD(y)}\right) = P_0(x, y) \quad (17)$$

The transition probability of the continuous time version μ is then given by:

$$\begin{aligned} \alpha_t(x, y) &:= \sum_{n \geq 0} \alpha_0^{(n)}(x, y) \frac{t^n e^{-t}}{n!} \\ \alpha_0^{(n)}(x, y) &= P_0^{(n)}(x, y) = \prod_{n=1}^{N} C_n \exp\left(-\frac{\Delta I_0^n(x, y)}{k_n D_n(y)}\right) \end{aligned} \quad (18)$$

where $\alpha_0^{(n)}(.,.)$ denotes the n-step transition probability. ΔI_0^n is the change in free enthalpy of the energy of separation for transition step (n), n=1,2,....,N.

$D_n(y)$ is demand at position (y); (y) is a generic notation for any new position. k_n represents the degrees of freedom of demand $D_n(y)$, at step (n). The following assumptions can be made on the discrete time kernel $\alpha(.,.)$

1. The matrix $\alpha(x,y)_{x,y\in R_+^d}$ is invariant under translation in space and is symmetric.
2. The kernel $\alpha(.,.)$ has finite second moments,

$$\sum_{x\in R_+^2} \alpha(.,x)\|x\|^2 < \infty \tag{19}$$

where $\|.\|$ is the maximum norm.

3.The covariance matrix of the one-dimensional marginals

$$X := \left(E\left[\mu_1^i \mu_1^j\right]\right)_{i,j\in(1,2,\ldots,d)} \tag{20}$$

with respect to distribution

$$P(\mu_1^1, \mu_1^2, \ldots, \mu_1^d) = \alpha(0,x) \quad x \in R_+^d \tag{21}$$

is assumed to be invertible, i.e., $\det X \neq 0$, implying that the matrix is $\alpha(.,.)$ irreducible.

The branching random walk in R_+^d is defined in terms of the random walk μ, life time parameter Ω, which represents the life time of the sub-system between two diffusion processes. The branching process starts with migration, and ends in branching.

Migration: Each sub-system starts from a slot $x\in R_+^d$ and moves according to the law of μ.

Branching: After a mean $1/\Omega$ exponential life time the sub-system either dies or is replaced by 2 new sub-systems resulting from a diffusion process.

Both situations occur independently for all sub-systems, independently from each other and independently of the initial configuration. Let Ψ be the random number of new sub-systems. The offspring behave as (Ψ) independent new sub-systems that start from the parent's sub-system's final position. In this way the initial system generates a population at time ($t>0$).

Let $(S_{s,t})_{t\geq s}$ be a transition kernel of (μ), which describes the expected position of a new sub-system at time (t), if it starts from a position say, (x), at time (s). A position represents either before diffusion or after diffusion (separation). The $(S_{s,t})_{t\geq s}$ can be written as:

$$S_{s,t}[f](x) := \mathrm{E}^{\delta_{x,s}}[f(\mu_t)]$$
$$f \in C_0(R^d) \tag{22}$$

Let (f) be defined as:

$$f = 1_Z$$

where (Z) represents a set of firms at time (s), with certain number of traits. $S_{s,t}[f](x)$ represents the probability of finding a descendent of a firm in set (Z), at the final position (x), and at time (t). An abbreviation $S_t := S_{0,t}$ defines a semigroup. Given Equation (18), the random walk generator (Δ_{RW}) of $(S_t)_{t\geq 0}$ on $C_0(R^d)$ is given by:

$$\Delta_{RW} f = \frac{d}{dt} S_t[f]\Big|_{t=0} = \sum_{y\in R_+^2} [\alpha(.,y) - \delta(.,y)] f(y) \tag{23}$$

where δ is a Dirac delta function.

Exogenous factors in system (B) induce linear type innovations that result in either expansion or contraction on the part of one large sub-system, inducing the other large sub-systems to react. A new equilibrium is achieved when a new unique Nash equilibrium price is determined through game theoretic type competition [5]. From proposition (3), as long as there is a unique Nash equilibrium price, the entire system remains in equilibrium.

Proposition 6: Business cycles are directly related to the scale of a business, the larger the business the higher the occurrence of a business cycle. Proposition 6 is a direct derivative of proposition 4. By definition business cycles are periodic fluctuations in the economic activity that are due to fluctuations in investment, and demand that bring about disequilibrium [10]. During business cycle elements such as labour, productivity, and stock level are adversely affected due to serious decline in demand.

The occurrence of business cycle triggers disequilibrium. What distinguishes system (A), small business system, from system (B), oligopoly, is the inventory level. In system (A), businesses have an upper ceiling on their size, thus their production level, never gets to the massive production level of oligopolies. Therefore, when business cycle occurs, it induces diffusion, i.e., innovation. This replaces halting of production to get rid of inventory, which is the trade mark of oligopolies. From proposition 4, once a new Lacuna is occupied, the new sub-system reaches equilibrium. The equilibrium in this case implies the optimal design of the production line through optimal design of the tasks performed which signifies optimal level of labour and productivity. This statement is possible since in propositions 1-3, labour and productivity are combined into one variable: the design of tasks performed, or in other words innovation. The following proposes a model of how a sub-system can expect to reach equilibrium by optimising the design of tasks performed in a business cycle situation.

$$\begin{aligned}
&\max_{\widetilde{x}} E_0 \sum_{t=0}^{T} \beta^t u\left((\widetilde{x}^k)_t\right) \\
&s.t. \\
&q_t \leq \left(\prod\nolimits_{k \in \widetilde{K}} \widetilde{K}_k \widetilde{f}(\widetilde{x}^k)\right)_t \cdot \widetilde{Q}_t \qquad (24) \\
&\widetilde{x}^k = \left(\widetilde{x}_l^k,\ l \in \widetilde{L}_k\right)
\end{aligned}$$

where E_0 is the conditional mean of experience acquired through performing composite-complex tasks on the production line. (β^t) refers to factors such as the level of education, and the level of intelligence. $u(\,.\,)$ is the utility function. $u(\,.\,)$ depends on the design of tasks performed ($\widetilde{x}^k$). (q_t) is the expected consumption level during the business cycle. Both variables $\left(\prod_{k\in\widetilde{K}} \widetilde{K}_k \widetilde{f}(\widetilde{x}^k)\right)_t$, the overall design of the tasks on the production line, and $\widetilde{Q}_t$, the production function are considered during the business cycle, thus the justification of the use of (*t*), the cycle period. *T* represents the totality of business cycle duration. The first order conditions will provide the optimal design of tasks performed. The variable, stock level, is not significant in system (A)'s optimization problem. New businesses do not start with an initial inventory level.

In system (B), periodic fluctuations in investment and demand have a significant effect. They always result in compression. Compression means significant dip in the production level, and massive layouts. The priority is to get rid of the already existing stocks; no modifications in the production line are envisaged unless the totality of the stocks is cleared out [29].

A good example of the resiliency of system (A) towards business cycles is the success of regional banks as compared to the big banks in America. Regional banks have avoided the worst effects of the recent slow down in the economy, while enjoying the best of its by-products. Unlike larger financial institutions, regional banks had little dealings with the stock market or the syndicated loans of large companies; consequently, the bankruptcies of oligopolies such as Enron, and WorldCom largely by-passed regional banks. Regional banks have found their free slots or Lacunas. They take clients such as small businesses that have no incentive to falsify their records or issue dodgy share options. Small or regional banks offer an alternative to the chaotic stock market, where customers can enjoy low fees, and are sure to have their money returned to them, when they ask for it. Regional banks have taken advantage of the decline in the interest rates, which are the reason for the boom in commercial property, which is a core lending business for regional banks [32].

4. Conclusion

The major contribution of this paper is to have shown that an economic system that functions based on small businesses performs better than an oligopolistic system. The main advantage of a small business system is in its ability to promote innovation. The reason is the nature of tasks performed by workers in the small business system. The limited scale of operation imposed on businesses, requires that workers perform complex – composite tasks. The combination of learning, experience, and intelligence results in innovation. Any disturbance in the market such as low demand will cause diffusion from the parent unit. Diffusion occurs when one or a group of employees come up with an invention. Inventors almost always separate from the mother company, and start up their own business. The economic environment allows for the emergence of new businesses. Many researchers have explored the design of production line from the view point of engineering design [24-26, 29]. The idea of relating the complexity of tasks to the size of a business is a new concept and has not been looked at by any researchers in the field. The paper is limited to theoretical analysis. From the practical aspect, the burden of proof is on performing experiments and investigation into the nature of the two systems through either laboratory simulation or data analysis.

References

1. Coriat, B., Weinstein, O., Les Nouvelles Théories de l'entreprise, Livre de Poche, 1995.
2. Henderson, J.M., Quant, R.E., Microéconomie, Dunod, 1972.
3. Picard, P., Elément de microéconomie, Montchrestien, 1994.

4. Leclercq, E., Les théories du marché du travail, Seuil, 1999.
5. Mas-Colell, A., Whinston, M., Green, J.R., Microeconomic Theory, Oxford University Press, Inc., 1995.
6. Varian, H., Microeconomic Analysis, W.W. Norton & Company, Inc., 1992.
7. Friedman, J.W., Game Theory with Applications to Economics, Oxford University Press, Inc., 1986.
8. Montoussé, M., Microéconomie, Bréal, 1999.
9. Arrous, J., Les théories de la croissance, Seuil, 1999.
10. Hairault, J.O., Analyse Macroéconomique, La Découverte, 2000.
11. Papon, P., Leblond, J., Meijer, P.H.E., Physique des Transitions de Phases, Dunod, 2002.
12. Montoussé, M., Macroéconomie, Bréal, 1999.
13. Michaud, Y., L'Economie, le Travail, l'entreprise, Odile Jacob, 2002.
14. Friedman, J.W., Game Theory with Applications to Economics, Oxford University Press, 1986.
15. Giraud, G., La théorie des jeux, Flammarion, Paris, 2000.
16. Smith, A., La Richesse des Nations, Flammarion, Paris, 1991.
17. Ricardo, D., Des principes de l'economie politique et de l'impôt, Flammarion, Paris, 1992.
18. Aubin, C., Norel, P., Economie internationale, Seuil, 2000.
19. Albertini, J.M., Silem, A., Comprendre les théories économiques, Seuil, 2001.
20. Mouchot, C., Méthologie économique, Seuil, 2003.
21. Généreux, J., Introduction à la politique économique, Seuil, 1993.
22. Malinvaud, E., Voies de la recherche macroéconomie, Odile Jacob, 1991.
23. Johnson, M., L. Meade, and J. Rogers, Assessing the Impact of Enterprise Engineering, Proceedings of the Society for Enterprise Engineering, Orlando, June, 1995.
24. Adams, S., J. Sarkis and D. Liles, The Development of Strategic Performance Metric , Engineering Management Journal, Vol. 7, No. 1, pp. 24–32, 1995.
25. Federico, C., Returns to specific skills in industrial districts, Labour Economics Volume 10, Issue 2 , April 2003, Pages 149–164.
26. Malcomson, J.M., Maw, J.W., McCormick, B., General training by firms, apprentice contracts, and public policy, European Economic Review Volume 47, Issue 2 , April 2003, Pages 197–227.

27. Winter, A., Multiple Scale Analysis of Spatial Branching Processes under the Palm Distribution, Electronic Journal of Probability, Vol. 7, (2002), Paper No. 13, pages 1–74.
28. Helbing, D., Modelling and Optimisation of Supply Networks: Lessons from Traffic Dynamics, Working paper.
29. Daganzo, C.F., A Theory of Supply Chains, Springer-Verlag Berlin Heidlberg, 2003.
30. Langlois, R., Schumpeter and the Obsolescence of the Entrepreneur, Working paper 91–1503.
31. Haag, G., Liedl, P., Modelling and Simulating Innovation Behaviour within Micro-based Correlated Decision Processes, Journal of Artificial Societies and Social Simulation, Vol. 4, No. 3.
32. "The Economist", April 5th–11th, 2003.

Section 5
Mathematical Tools

Section

A FINITARY APPROACH TO CLUSTERING *

U. GARIBALDI

IMEM-CNR, c/o Department of Physics, University of Genoa, Italy, via Dodecaneso 33, 16146, Genoa, Italy (e-mail: garibaldi@fisica.unige.it)

D. COSTANTINI AND P.VIARENGO

National Cancer Research Institute (IST), Genoa, Largo Benzi 10, 16132, Genoa, Italy and Department of Statistical Science, University of Bologna, Bologna, Italy (e-mail: paolo.viarengo@istge.it)

The clustering of agents in the market is a typical problem dealt with by the new approaches to macroeconomic modeling, that describe macroscopic variables in terms of the behavior of a large collection of microeconomic entities. Clustering has a lot of economical interpretations, that are often described by Ewens' Sampling Formula (ESF). Contrary to the usual complex derivations, we suggest a finitary characterization of the ESF pointing to real economic processes. Our approach is finitary in the sense that we probabilize a system of n individuals considered as a closed system, a population, where individuals can change attributes as time moves on. The intuitive meaning of the probability is the fraction of time the system spends in the considered partition. As ESF represents an equilibrium distribution satisfying detailed balance, some properties difficult to prove are derived in a simple way. Besides the mean distribution of the cluster sizes, we study the probabilistic time behavior of clusters, in particular the mean survival as a function of the actual size and the correlation between size and age.

1. Introduction

Thirty years ago, in the context of research devoted to population genetics, Ewens[1] introduced a distribution that later has been called the Ewens sampling formula (ESF)

$$P(\mathbf{z}) = \frac{n!}{\theta^{[n]}} \prod_{i=1}^{n} \left(\frac{\theta}{i}\right)^{z_i} \frac{1}{z_i!}, \tag{1}$$

*A shorter version of the paper, entitled "A finitary characterization of the Ewens sampling formula", was presented at the Wehia 2003 conference, Kiel, May 2003

$\theta > 0, \theta^{[n]} = \theta(\theta+1)...(\theta+n-1)$ is the Pochhammer symbol and $\mathbf{z} = (z_1, ..., z_n)$, $\sum_{i=1}^{n} iz_i = n$, is the partition vector to be defined later. ESF has been applied to a wide variety of models for reproduction. A description of (1), essentially due to Tavaré and Ewens itself, can be found in[2], together with structural properties, characterizations, estimation, relations with other distributions, approximations and applications. Among these we quote: Genetics, Bayesian statistics, permutations, Ecology, Physics, the spread of news and rumors, the law of succession, prime numbers, random sampling and combinatorial structures.

All the known characterizations of the ESF are either mathematically very sophisticated or appeal to the intuition *via* some urn scheme. They are essentially based upon populations being infinite both in the number of individuals and in that of categories.

In recent years (1) has been applied to Economics too (see for example [3 4]). Keeping in mind these new applications, we are suggesting a finitary characterization of the ESF pointing to real economic processes. One of the reasons to publish our characterization is that it has been used by Aoki[5]. This author in many occasions has quoted our finitary characterization known to him through a mimeographed working paper. This finitary approach allows comprehensible demonstrations, same of them collected in the Appendix.

1.1. *Some known characterizations of ESF*

In[2] only two kind of characterizations are taken into account. After quoting the pioneer work of Antoniak[6], who obtains ESF is in the field of sampling from a Dirichlet process, the main infinitary characterization is due to Kingman[7], who considers random partitions, an unconventional notion in fields other than Biology. The predictive approach starts with the prediction rule of Blackwell-McQueen[8], deepened by Donelly[9] with respect to Biology, interpreted by Hoppe's urn model[10], finally extended by Hansen and Pitman[11]. This approach can be traced to Johnson[12] and more recently to Zabell[13]

All these characterizations take for granted that the n individuals appearing in (1) are a sample from an infinite random population. This is essential from the Bayesian point of view, where the probability (1) is achieved as a mean of the likelihood over the initial (equilibrium) distribution on all possible infinite populations[7]. Also in the predictive approach it is essential that the population is at equilibrium, so that time plays no role.

Our approach is finitary in the sense that we want to probabilize our system of n individuals considered as a closed system, that is a finite population whose individuals change attributes as time moves on. Whatever the initial state may be, the probabilistic dynamics is able to drive the system into equilibrium. The intuitive meaning of the probability in (1) is the fraction of time the system spends in the state $\mathbf{z}$. To summarize this point we say that our characterization does not arrive at ESF as a distribution ensuing from a sampling procedure from some static superpopulation. We shall prove that ESF is the equilibrium distribution of a Markov chain ruled by a transition probability build up by exchangeable and invariant creation and destruction terms[14 15 16].

Our method is finitary in a second sense: the "infinite allele model" is obtained as a limit of a finite model. In this way, that can be traced back to Boltzmann, each assumption can be submitted to concrete inspection. This is of primary importance for applications. In fact a finitary characterization of a probability distribution can be concretely inspected. This allows to check whether the assumptions on which the statistical model is based hold good in the field where one wishes to apply it.

2. The Ehrenfest-Brillouin model

Consider a dynamical system composed of n entities and g categories (cells), whose state is described by the nonnegative integer occupation number vector $\mathbf{n} = (n_1, ..., n_i, ..., n_g)$, $n_i \geq 0$, $\sum_{i=1}^{g} n_i = n$. The system is closed (it is a population), but individuals may change their category at discrete times, so that occupation numbers change step-by-step. The dynamical discrete evolution of the occupation number random variable is a realization of a homogeneous Markov chain, whose stochastic matrix has elements $w(\mathbf{n}, \mathbf{n}') := P(\mathbf{N}_{t+1} = \mathbf{n}'|\mathbf{N}_t = \mathbf{n})$ not depending on time explicitly. A unary move makes an entity to change its state from the cell i to the cell k. $\mathbf{n} = (n_1, ..., n_i, ..., n_k, ..., n_g)$ denotes the initial state and $\mathbf{n}_i^k := (n_1, ..., n_i - 1, ..., n_k + 1, ..., n_g)$ the final one in terms of the coordinates of the starting vector. This transition (a destruction followed by a creation) can be split into two distinct operations[16 17]. The resulting (death-and-birth) transition probability is:

$$w(\mathbf{n}, \mathbf{n}_i^k) = P(\mathbf{n}_i|\mathbf{n})P(\mathbf{n}_i^k|\mathbf{n}_i) = \frac{n_i}{n}\frac{\alpha_k + n_k - \delta_{i,k}}{\alpha + n - 1} \tag{2}$$

with $\alpha = \sum_i \alpha_i$, and $\boldsymbol{\alpha} = (\alpha_1, ..., \alpha_g)$ is a vector of parameters that represent initial weights, and $\delta_{i,k}$ is the Kronecker symbol. The meaning of α_i is to allow the accommodation on void cells. We shall consider the case where all $\alpha_i > 0$. It is apparent that, starting from a given $\mathbf{n}$, by repeated applications of (2), each possible vector of $S_g^n = \{(n_1, ..., n_i, , ..., n_g) : n_i \geq 0, \sum n_i = n\}$ is reachable, $\#S_g^n = \binom{n+g-1}{n}$. Further all these states are persistent, as no absorbing state exists. It follows that the set of states is ergodic, the chain is irreducible and there exists an (unique) invariant measure $\pi(\mathbf{n})$ on the ergodic set[18]. In addiction (2) does not exclude $\mathbf{n}_i^k = \mathbf{n}$, that is the case $j = k$. Hence the chain is aperiodic, and the invariant measure $\pi(\mathbf{n})$ is also the equilibrium distribution on the ergodic set[19], that is

$$\lim_{t\to\infty} P(\mathbf{N}_t = \mathbf{n}|\mathbf{N}_0 = \mathbf{n}') = \pi(\mathbf{n}) \text{ whatever } \mathbf{n}'$$

The problem of finding the invariant distribution is solved by the detailed balance equations, which are satisfied by the generalized g-dimensional *Polya* distribution:

$$\pi(\mathbf{n}; \alpha) = \frac{n!}{\alpha^{[n]}} \prod_{i=1}^{g} \frac{\alpha_i^{[n_i]}}{n_i!}, \quad \mathbf{n} : \sum_{i=1}^{g} n_i = n \tag{3}$$

Thus $\pi(\mathbf{n}; \alpha)$ is dynamically invariant, and by uniqueness theorem is equal to the equilibrium distribution $\pi(\mathbf{n})$.

As $\{\alpha_i\} > 0$, accommodations are positively correlated with the occupation numbers $\mathbf{n}$. The correlation is large for small α , while it tends to zero for $\alpha \to \infty$, where the creation probability is $p_k = \frac{\alpha_k}{\alpha}$, independent on $\mathbf{n}$.

Very simple cases of (3) are: the Bose-Einstein distribution[14], which is uniform on all $\mathbf{n}$, obtained for $\alpha_i = 1; \alpha = g$; the Maxwell-Boltzmann distribution, obtained for $\alpha_i = c$, $\alpha = gc$, $|c| \to \infty$. The different behavior of the microscopic entities is ascribed to the vector parameter $\boldsymbol{\alpha}$, that determines the type of inter-entity correlation at the moment of choosing the new category, and to $|\alpha|^{-1}$, that fixes its strength. The deviation from independence, known in Economics as "herd behavior", depends on the ratio of the total initial weight α and the size of the population n.

Considering the mechanism of category change described by (2), the first part of the move is the drawing of an agent, and the first term $\frac{n_i}{n}$ gives the probability that the drawing occurs in the ith cell. This depends only on $\mathbf{n}$. The second part of the move is the accommodation of the moving agent into the final cell, and the term $\frac{\alpha_k+n_k}{\alpha+n-1}$ gives the probability that the final cell is the kth cell. This second term can be re-written as $\frac{\alpha p_k+(n-1)f_k}{\alpha+n-1}$, that is a mixture of the initial probability $\{p_k = \frac{\alpha_k}{\alpha}, \Sigma p_k = 1\}$ and of the current normalized occupation vector $\{f_k = \frac{n_k}{n-1}, \Sigma f_k = 1\}$ .The mixture can be interpreted as a randomization of two attitudes[20]. Suppose that the choice is performed in two stages: first the choice of an attitude (theoretical *vs* empirical, with weights α and $n-1$), followed by the choice of the cell given the distribution attached to chosen attitude.

In Economics this can be interpreted as following: if the agent chooses the theoretical distribution (he behaves as a "fundamentalist"), he is not influenced by his colleagues. In this case we have self-conversion[20] . If the agent chooses the empirical distribution (he behaves as a "chartist"), he chooses a colleague at random and he converts to its strategy[17].

2.1. *An auxiliary urn process*

Let us consider n random variables $Y_1, \ldots, Y_n$ whose range is $(1, \ldots, g)$. Suppose that $S_m = (m_1, \ldots, m_g)$ is the current occupation vector, that is $m_j = \#\{Y_i = j, i = 1, \ldots, m\}$. Let the conditional predictive distribution of Y_m be the following:

$$P(Y_{m+1} = j|m_j, m) = \frac{m_j + \alpha_j}{m + \alpha} \tag{4}$$

for $m = 0, 1, \ldots, n-1$. This is a simple urn (sampling) process (a Polya one, with initial weights $\{\alpha_j\}$) whose $n-$predictive distribution $P(S_n = \mathbf{n})$ is the same that the equilibrium distribution of our Markov chain $\pi(\mathbf{n}) = \lim_{t\to\infty} P(X_t = \mathbf{n})$.

2.2. *The approach to equilibrium of the mean occupation number*

The most elementary transition probability (2) refers to a unary move. A more complicated transition (a m-ary move)[16] is obtained when m units are drawn without replacement and then reallocated in the cells by recurring application of (4). Let the starting vector be $\mathbf{N}_t = \mathbf{n}$, and let $\mathbf{D}_{t+1} = \mathbf{d} = (d_1, .., d_g)$, $\sum_i d_i = m$ the frequency vector of the extracted units, classified by their categories. After the destruction, we reallocate the m units into the cells, and let $\mathbf{C}_{t+1} = \mathbf{c} = (c_1, .., c_g)$, $\sum_i c_i = m$ be the frequency vector of the "created" units. The resulting final occupation vector is:

$$\mathbf{N}_{t+1} = \mathbf{N}_t - \mathbf{D}_{t+1} + \mathbf{C}_{t+1} = \mathbf{N}_t + \mathbf{I}_{t+1} \tag{5}$$

where $\mathbf{I}_{t+1} = -\mathbf{D}_{t+1} + \mathbf{C}_{t+1}$ is the increment. Destruction is understood to precede creation. The probabilistic structure of the process is completely given, as $P(\mathbf{D}_{t+1}|\ \mathbf{N}_t)$ is a Hypergeometric distribution $H(m, \mathbf{n})$, while $P(\mathbf{C}_{t+1}|\mathbf{N}_t, \mathbf{D}_{t+1})$ is a Polya distribution $Po(m, \boldsymbol{\alpha} + \mathbf{n} - \mathbf{d})$.

Considering the marginal occupation number of the ith category, posing for simplicity $n_i = k$, and denoting by K_t,D_{t+1}, C_{t+1} and I_{t+1} the related random variables

$$K_{t+1} = K_t - D_{t+1} + C_{t+1} = K_t + I_{t+1}, \tag{6}$$

we calculate the regression of the increment, that drives the approach to equilibrium of the mean occupation number:

$$E\left(I_{t+1}|k_t\right) = -\frac{m\alpha}{n(\alpha + n - m)}\left(k_t - \frac{n\alpha_i}{\alpha}\right).$$

The mean increment vanishes if $\frac{n\alpha_i}{\alpha} = E(n_i) = \mu_i$, that we know to be the equilibrium value of the ith occupation number. It is apparent that

$$r = \frac{m\alpha}{n(\alpha + n - m)} \tag{7}$$

is the rate of approach to equilibrium, which depends on the size n, the total initial weight α and the number of changes m. Hence

$$E\left(I_{t+1}|k_t\right) = -r\left(k_t - \mu_i\right), \tag{8}$$

$$Cov\left(K_t, K_{t+1}\right) = (1 - r)\sigma_i^2,$$

where μ and σ_i^2 are the mean and the variance of the marginal Polya distribution. The autocorrelation of each occupation number is universal, that is

$$Corr\left(K_t, K_{t+s}\right) = Corr(s) = (1 - r)^s$$

Being a Markov chain, (5) behaves like an $AR(1)$.

The rate is rapidly increasing with m, and tends to 1 for $m = n$, where the destruction term is trivial and the creation term is just the auxiliary process of Section 2.2. In the domain $\alpha_i > 0$ the rate attains its maximum $(= \frac{m}{n})$ for $\alpha \to \infty$, while it tends to 0 for $\alpha \to 0$. Comparing this with the conclusions of the previous section, the process is fast in the independence limit, while it slows down for high "herd behavior". In this case the representative point needs a lot of transitions in order to move around all the possible states.

3. Infinite number of categories

In the Ehrenfest-Brillouin model[17 21] the distinctive feature of the system are the number of statistical entities n, the number of categories g, and the set of initial weights of the categories $\boldsymbol{\alpha} = (\alpha_1, .., \alpha_g)$. All these parameters are independent, so that they can vary independently, and represent very different scenarios. For instance it is well-known that in the continuum limit $n \to \infty$ (g and α fixed) the equilibrium distribution $Polya(n, \boldsymbol{\alpha})$ becomes $Dirichlet(\boldsymbol{\alpha})$. Now we want to investigate what happens when the number of cell tends to infinity being fixed the size n of the system and the total weight of the initial distribution α. Posing $\alpha_i = \frac{\alpha}{g}$, $\lim_{g\to\infty}\alpha_i = 0$, and $\lim_{g\to\infty} \sum_{i=1}^{g} \alpha_i = \alpha = \theta$ (for historical reasons:[1]). Note that in the limit $g \to \infty$ with fixed n any vector $\mathbf{n} = (n_1, ..., n_g)$ has infinite terms almost all vanishing, and some caution is necessary. We have shown in[17] that in the Ewens limit

$$P(\mathbf{n}_i^j|\mathbf{n}) = \begin{cases} \frac{n_i}{n}\frac{n_j-\delta_{i,j}}{\theta+n-1} & \text{for } j \leq k \\ \frac{n_i}{n}\frac{\theta}{\theta+n-1} & \text{for } j = k+1 \end{cases} \tag{9}$$

where the indexes $1, \dots, k \leq n$ relabel the categories initially occupied, and $k+1$ denote a "new" category $j \notin \{1, \dots, k\}$. Typical examples from Economics are n agents (firms)[5] and g sectors (or goods). The term $\frac{n_i}{n}\frac{n_j-\delta_{i,j}}{\theta+n-1}$ describes the probability that a unity leaves the ith cluster (strategy) and joins the jth, while $\frac{n_i}{n}\frac{\theta}{\theta+n-1}$ describes the probability of a change between an existing cluster and the foundation of new one. Summing over all possible starting clusters, we have that $\frac{\theta}{\theta+n-1}$ is the absolute probability of the emergence of a new cluster at each step. This is a constant, that does not depend on the occupation vector. Due to the absence of the initial weight α_j in the creation term, any state with $n_j = 0$ is an absorbing state; that is, once n_j becomes 0 it cannot undergo a rebirth. There is no equilibrium distribution on $\mathbf{n}$. In facts all the present k clusters sooner or later disappear, or better they go to the "equilibrium" value ($= 0$) with rate $\frac{\theta}{n(\theta+n-1)}$. All the mass will be transferred to new clusters. With probability 1 a new born cluster cannot be a reincarnation of old ones.

In order to represent these features by a homogeneous Markov chains there are two routes. The first is that of abandoning once for all the labels of the categories to introduce partitions $\mathbf{z} = (z_1, .., z_n)$, $z_i = \#\{n_j = i, j = 1, \dots, g\}$, with $k = \Sigma_{i=1}^{n} z_i$ and $\Sigma_{i=1}^{n} i z_i = n$. The Markov chain induced on partitions by (9) has indeed ESF as equilibrium distribution, but the demonstration is cumbersome (see Appendix). A second route is the following "label process", that is an improvement of a complex method suggested by Kelly[22].

3.1. *The label process*

If the population size is n, let introduce $g > n$ fixed labels. Suppose to start with $k \leq n$ distinct clusters. Label them with the first k labels, and $\mathbf{n} = (n_1, .., n_k, 0, \ldots 0)$. Define $A(\mathbf{n}) = \{i : n_i > 0\}$ the set of all active (occupied at the moment) labels, then $\#A(\mathbf{n}) = k$ is their number, and $g - k$ is the number of the inactive (unused at the moment) ones. We put $P(\mathbf{n}_i^j|\mathbf{n}) = \frac{n_i}{n}\frac{n_j - \delta_{i,j}}{\theta+n-1}$ for $j \epsilon A$ (that is $n_j > 0$), while we suppose that in case of innovation a new cluster will be randomly labeled by one of the $g-k$ available labels:

$$P(\mathbf{n}_i^j|\mathbf{n}) = \begin{cases} \frac{n_i}{n}\frac{n_j-\delta_{i,j}}{\theta+n-1} & \text{for } n_j > 0 \\ \frac{n_i}{n}\frac{1}{g-k}\frac{\theta}{\theta+n-1} & \text{for } n_j = 0 \end{cases} \tag{10}$$

The label process $\mathbf{L}_0, \mathbf{L}_1, ..., \mathbf{L}_t, ...$, where $\mathbf{L}_t = (n_1, .., n_k, \ldots, n_g)$, with the constraint $\sum_1^g n_i = n$, describes the random occupation vector with respect to the g categories. This curious procedure has the merit of producing an ergodic set of label states. In fact a label j that is inactive (and thus $n_j = 0$) can be reactivated, as it can be chosen in case of innovation. The transition probability (10) induces an irreducible aperiodic Markov chain, whose equilibrium distribution satisfies the detailed balance equations:

$$P(\mathbf{n}) = \frac{(g-k)!}{g!}\frac{n!}{\prod_{j\epsilon A} n_j}\frac{\theta^k}{\theta^{[n]}} = \tag{11}$$

$$= \frac{(g-k)!}{g!}\frac{n!}{\theta^{[n]}}\prod_{i=1}^{n}\left(\frac{\theta}{i}\right)^{z_i} \tag{12}$$

where in (12) we introduce the partition vector $\mathbf{z} = (z_1, .., z_n)$, $z_i = \#\{n_j = i, j = 1, \ldots, g\}$, with $k = \Sigma_{i=1}^n z_i$ and $\Sigma_{i=1}^n i z_i = n$. Now z_i is the number of active labels (representing clusters) with $n_j = i$, and k is the number of active labels (that is the number of clusters in $\mathbf{n}$). Note that $\prod_{j\epsilon A(\mathbf{n})} n_j = \prod_{i=1}^n i^{z_i}$. The label associated with a cluster is not intended to reproduce any physical characteristic of the cluster- it simply labels it. As time goes by, the same label will be used for different clusters, but after the extinction of a cluster an interval will elapse before its label is used again (due to $g > n$). Following the "history" of a label, each passage from 1 to 0 indicates the death of a cluster, and each passage from 0 to 1 indicates a newborn one.

An auxiliary urn process whose $n-$predictive distribution is (12) is very similar to the so-called Hoppe urn[10] (see Appendix). The label process has equilibrium distribution (11), and $E(n_j) = \frac{n}{g}$ for reasons of symmetry. As a consequence, all "true names" of the clusters are lost. This labeling process is analogous to that introduced by Hansen and Pitman in species sampling[11]: "it is just a device to encode species ... in a sequence of random variables". A very simple example is shown below (see Fig.1 to Fig.3.).

Now let us consider $\mathbf{z}$, the statistical description of clusters associated to a label state $\mathbf{L} = (n_1, .., n_k, \ldots, n_g)$. It is apparent that the number of distinct occupation numbers of n objects in g categories with the same $\mathbf{z}$ is $\frac{g!}{z_0!z_1!...z_n!}$, where z_0 is the number of empty categories. Hence the number of distinct label states with the same $\mathbf{z}$ is $\frac{g!}{(g-k)!z_1!...z_n!}$.

Further (12) depends only on $\mathbf{z}$, so that finally:

$$P(\mathbf{z}) = \frac{g!}{(g-k)!z_1!...z_n!} P(\mathbf{n}) = \frac{n!}{\theta^{[n]}} \prod_{i=1}^{n} \left(\frac{\theta}{i}\right)^{z_i} \frac{1}{z_i!} \tag{13}$$

(13) is the ESF[1], that appears as the equilibrium distribution on partitions generated by the label process $\mathbf{L}$. We can pose $g = n + 1$, that is the minimum number that allows to label unambiguously our death-and birth process.

Example 3.1. Consider a population of 5 agents, initially separated (they are all singletons). We need at least 6 labels, and we use A, B, C, D, E for labeling the 5 initial clusters.

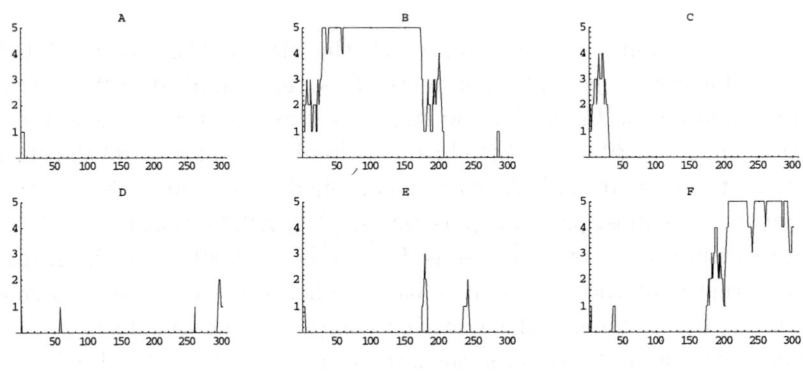

Figure 1. $\theta = 0.1$

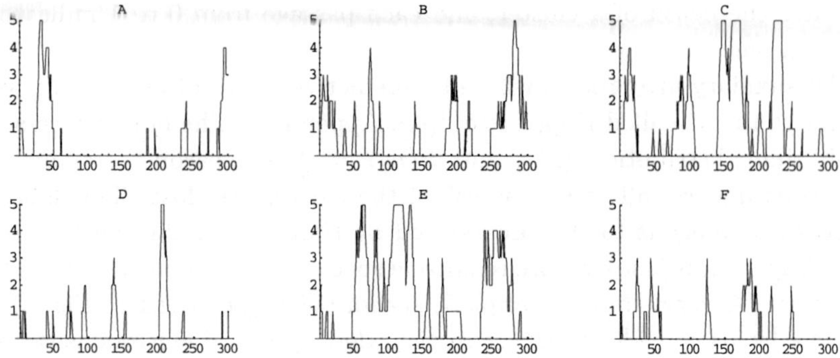

Figure 2. $\theta = 1$

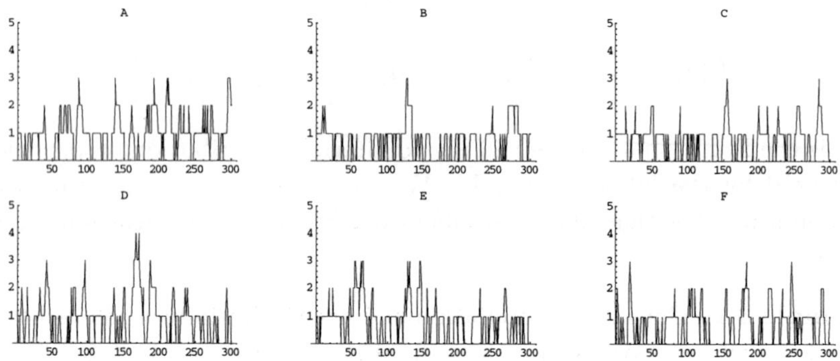

Figure 3. $\theta = 5$

The six graphics of Fig.1 represent the size of the clusters labeled $A, \ldots, F$ for 300 steps. The parameter θ is very small, $\theta = 0.1$, so that herding dominates. In the first 30 steps the clusters B and C are in competition, from $t = 30$ to 180 the cluster B dominates, at $t = 180$ the cluster F begins to compete with B, that is cancelled at $t = 200$, where after F dominates. The most probable partition is $(0, 0, 0, 0, 1)$, that is $z_5 = 1$. The theoretical mean life of a cluster is $E(k)\frac{(\theta+n-1)}{\theta} = 49$. The six graphics of Fig.2 represent the size of the clusters when the parameter θ is small, $\theta = 1$, so that herding and pioneering compete. The dynamics is faster, cluster mean life is shorter (the theoretical mean life is 11.4), all labels are really used. The time when $z_5 = 1$ is much shorter than before. This is an indication of the lowered strength of herding. The six graphics of Fig.3 represent the size of the clusters when the parameter θ is not small, $\theta = 5$, so that pioneering prevails. The dynamics is still faster, the theoretical mean life is 5.9. The system never experiences $z_5 = 1$. The time when $z_1 = 5$ is large. This is an indication of the strength of pioneer behavior.

3.2. *The probabilistic dynamics of a cluster*

It is noteworthy that the probabilistic dynamics of a cluster is independent of the rest of the system. In fact if a cluster has size i, then the probability of an increase or a decrease is:

$$\begin{cases} w(i,i+1) = \frac{n-i}{n}\frac{i}{\theta+n-1} & i = 1,\ldots,g-1 \\ w(i,i-1) = \frac{i}{n}\frac{n-i+\theta}{\theta+n-1} & i = 1,\ldots,g \end{cases} \tag{14}$$

$$w(0,1) = 0 \tag{15}$$

This behavior is a direct consequence of Johnson's sufficiency postulate[13]. Hence, given that $E(\Delta i|i) = w(i,i+1) - w(i,i-1)$,

$$E(\Delta i|i) = -\frac{i}{n}\frac{\theta}{\theta+n-1} = -ri \tag{16}$$

where r is the rate of approach of the mean to equilibrium(7) for unary changes. Note that (16) is a particular case of (8) when the equilibrium mean is null. Then each particular existing cluster is driven toward its extinction by (16).

The matrix $w(i,j)$ drives the evolution of the represented cluster. All states except 0 are transient, and the state 0 is absorbing. In order to study the time behavior of a cluster, we introduce $w^{(s)}(i,j)$, that is the transition probability from i to j after s steps. Then $w^{(s)}(i,0)$ is the probability that a cluster of size i is dead after s steps. Hence $w^{(s)}(i,0) - w^{(s-1)}(i,0)$ is the probability of dying at the sth step, and thus $\tau_i = \Sigma_{s=1}^{\infty} s(w^{(s)}(i,0) - w^{(s-1)}(i,0))$ is the expected duration time of a cluster of size i. Note that from (14) $w^{(s)}(i,0) - w^{(s-1)}(i,0) = w^{(s-1)}(i,1)/n$, as to die at the sth step is the same as to get the size 1 at the $(s-1)th$ step and then to die, with transition probability $w(1,0) = 1/n$ from 14. Hence

$$\tau_i = \Sigma_{s=1}^{\infty} s \frac{w^{(s-1)}(i,1)}{n} \tag{17}$$

where we pose $w^{(0)}(i,1) = \delta_{i,1}$. The expected duration time of a newborn cluster (of size 1, hence τ_1) is the mean life of a newborn cluster. It can calculated exactly by (17), but a shorter formula exists. In fact considering that $\frac{\theta}{\theta+n-1} = u$ is the innovation rate, that is the mean number of new clusters at each step, and posing $E(k)$ as the stationary mean number of clusters, it is apparent that the mean life of a cluster is just

$$\tau_1 = \frac{E(k)}{u} \tag{18}$$

where

$$E(k) = \sum_{i=0}^{n-1} \frac{\theta}{\theta + i} \tag{19}$$

is the mean number of clusters[2] as a function of θ and n. Theoretical values in Fig.1, 2 and 3 follow (18), while the empirical mean life is calculated as the arithmetic mean of the life durations of all the appeared clusters.

A recurrence relation exists for τ_i, so that it can be solved exactly avoiding the cumbersome (17). In fact if a cluster has size i (and its expected duration time is τ_i), at the following step we find three possibilities, and then three possible expected duration times, all increased by the duration of the step ($= 1$). Then

$$\tau_i = w(i, i+1)\{\tau_{i+1} + 1\} + w(i, i)\{\tau_i + 1\} + w(i, i+1)\{\tau_{i-1} + 1\},$$

that is

$$\tau_i = 1 + w(i, i+1)\tau_{i+1} + w(i, i)\tau_i + w(i, i-1)\tau_{i-1},$$

and substituting (14), reordering and introducing $\Delta_i = \tau_i - \tau_{i-1}, i \geq 2$

$$\Delta_i = \Delta_{i-1}\frac{n-i+1+\theta}{n-i+1} - \frac{n(n-1+\theta)}{(i-1)(n-i+1)}, \qquad \Delta_1 = \frac{E(k)}{u}$$

In Fig.4 we represent a simulation, and in 4.1 we show the age of the oldest cluster of the population as a function of time. The size of the oldest cluster in the temporal window $130 < t < 300$ is shown in 4.2. The parameters are $n = 7, \theta = 1$. It is apparent that the oldest cluster is the largest too only in a shorter temporal window ($190 < t < 250$): the correlation between these two order statistics deserves more investigation.

4. Conclusion

Economics is the field of application we had in mind. As showed by Aoki[4] the system could be that of shoppers waiting at one stall in an open air

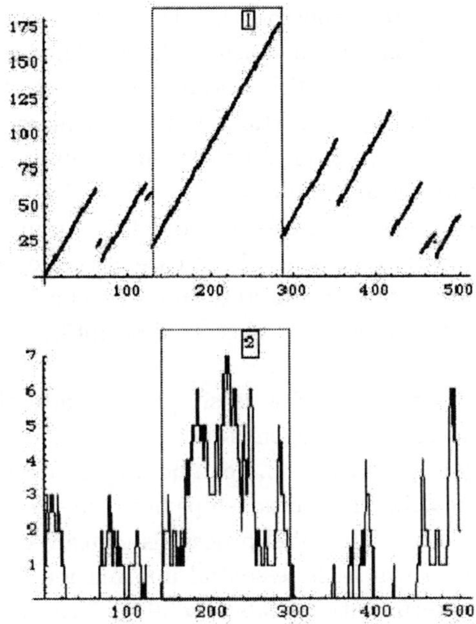

Figure 4.

market. The destruction probability is the probability that a stall loses a shopper, who decides to move to another one. On the contrary, the creation probability is the probability that a stall is chosen by a moving shopper. If we suppose that these probabilities are exchangeable and invariant the equilibrium is given by the generalized Polya distribution. In the case in which the number of stalls is much larger than that of the shoppers, that is when Ewens' hypothesis hold and the greatest part of the stalls have no shoppers, the induced equilibrium distribution on partitions is the ESF. Being strictly finitary our derivation is based on assumptions whose validity can be easily checked. In this ease rests the greatest advantage of the characterization we have suggested. Note that these derivations have nothing to do with sampling, and the resulting meaning of ESF is the fraction of time that the state of systems is described by some $\mathbf{z}$.

In Economics the interpretation is straightforward: you can think to a fixed number of agents (farms, costumers,...) that are wondering around a very large number of possibilities. The only important thing is the ratio between the "herd behavior" (proportional to n) and the pioneer behavior (proportional to θ), that controls the size and the number of existing clusters. In the Ewens limit, when an agent chooses "by himself", he is a pioneer, given the infinite possibilities of available choices. When he chooses the "herd", he joins clusters proportionally to their mass.

In Genetics the ESF comes out for the neutral infinite allele models. A treatise whose conclusions are similar to ours can be found in the Chapter 7 of the book of Kelly[22], where the ESF is derived as equilibrium distribution of a Markov process, that represent a limit case of the reproductive mechanism. Our treatise is confined to discrete times (it is a Markov chain), but about our chain we have a very satisfactory description of the approach to equilibrium.

Further from this point of view is simple to study the typical "life" of any particular cluster, that depends on its size, on n and θ. Computer simulations are easy to perform[17], and can be useful to study properties interesting to economics, like the relationships between size and age, duration time and size, and so on. The label process is conceived as the most natural environment from which the essential information about clusters can be extracted. This interpretation is also useful to derive some properties of the ESF in a very natural way.

Appendix

Partition Probabilistic Dynamics

We take the statistical description of clusters $\mathbf{z} = (z_1, .., z_n)$ (the "partition") as state variable of a homogeneous Markov chain. Let $\mathbf{u}$ be the initial partition, $\mathbf{v}$ the partition after the destruction and $\mathbf{z}$ the partition after the creation. If the destruction affects a unit belonging to a cluster of size i, then it transforms a cluster of size i in a cluster of size $i-1$, hence

$$v_i = u_i - 1, \quad v_{i-1} = u_{i-1} + 1;$$

Afterwards the created entity increases the number of clusters of size j if it joins to a cluster of size $j-1$, therefore $z_j = v_j + 1$ and $z_{j-1} = v_{j-1} - 1$.

Hence destructions in i are proportional to the number of entities belonging to an initial cluster of size i, that is iu_i, while creations in j are proportional to the number of entities belonging to a cluster of size $j-1$ after destruction, that is $(j-1)\,v_{j-1}$

$$P(\mathbf{z}|\mathbf{u}) = P\left(\mathbf{u}_i^j|\mathbf{u}\right) = \begin{cases} \frac{iu_i}{n}\frac{(j-1)v_{j-1}}{\theta+n-1} & \text{for } j>1 \\ \frac{iu_i}{n}\frac{\theta}{\theta+n-1} & \text{for } j=1 \end{cases} \tag{20}$$

as iu_i is the number of agents initially in some i-cluster, $(j-1)v_{j-1}$ is the number of agents in some $(j-1)$-cluster after destruction. If the agent joins to some of them, the number of j-clusters increases by one. Once again the transition probability (20) induces an homogeneous Markov chain irreducible and aperiodic, whose equilibrium distribution (the ESF) can be derived by the detailed balance equations, even if this case is more cumbersome than the label cases. The description $\mathbf{z}$ being statistical, it gives less information than the description $\mathbf{L}$. If two agents exchange their places, $\mathbf{z}$ is insensitive to this move, while $\mathbf{L}$ is not.

The auxiliary urn process of the label process

Let us consider n random variables $Y_1,\ldots,Y_n$, whose range is a set of labels $1,\ldots,n$. Suppose that the first r.v. is labelled 1, and that a new label is introduced sequentially whenever a new value appears. In this case the label j denotes the jth label that has been introduced. The model of this process is the so called Hoppe urn.

$S_m = (m_1,\ldots,m_k)$ is the current occupation vector, that is $m_j = \#\{Y_i = j, i = 1,\ldots,m\}$, and $k = \#\{m_j > 0, j = 1,\ldots,k\}$ is the number of present labels. If the conditional predictive distribution of Y_m is the following, for $m = 0,1,\ldots,n-1$:

$$P(Y_{m+1} = j|m_j, m) = \begin{cases} \frac{m_j}{m+\theta} & j \leq k \\ \frac{\theta}{m+\theta}, & j = k+1 \end{cases} \tag{21}$$

and hence $P(Y_1 = 1) = 1$ by definition.

This sampling process can be modelled by an urn process (the Hoppe urn, that can be traced back to A.De Moivre, following[13]) consists in an urn that contains initially a white ball whose weight is θ, with the following rule. a) Whenever the white ball is extracted it is painted with a colour not yet present in the urn; then a new white ball (of the same weight θ) is reintroduced into the urn, together with a ball (of weight 1) of the just painted colour. b) If a colored ball is extracted, it is reintroduced into the urn, together with a ball (of weight 1) of the same colour, just as in the Polya scheme. The probability of a sequence is derived by (21) and results:

$$P(Y_1,\ldots,Y_n) = \frac{\theta^k}{\theta^{[n]}} \prod (n_i - 1)! \tag{22}$$

where $n_j = \#\{Y_i = j, i = 1,\ldots,n\}$, and $k = \#\{n_j > 0\}$. The $n-$ predictive distribution is

$$P(S_n = \mathbf{n}) = \binom{n-1}{n_1-1}\binom{n-n_1-1}{n_2-1}\cdots\binom{n_{k-1}+n_k-1}{n_{k-1}-1}\frac{\theta^k}{\theta^{[n]}}\prod(n_i-1)!$$

$$= \frac{n!}{n_k(n_k+n_{k-1})\dots(n_k+n_{k-1}+\dots+n_1)}\frac{\theta^k}{\theta^{[n]}} \qquad (23)$$

called by Donnelly[9] "the size-biased permutation of the ESF".

For the label process, let us consider n random variables $Y_1^*, \dots, Y_n^*$ whose range is a set of $g > n$ labels $L = (l_1, \dots, l_g)$. Suppose that each type of label has almost n occurrences, so that in principle it is possible to label all the sample in the same way. To choose the type of the label to be attached, suppose that exists an urn U, that contains just g balls, each of them with printed a distinct name from $(l_1, \dots, l_g)$. When Y_1^* is extracted, we random chose a ball from U (without replacement) and we label Y_1^* with say l_{i_1}. Turning to Y_2^*, if $Y_2^* = Y_1^*$ it will be labeled by l_{i_1}, otherwise we make a second extraction from U, and a new label is given to Y_2^*, say l_{i_2} and so on. Proceeding this way all repeated values of Y_i^* are labelled in the same way, while different values have different labels.

Comparing the label urn process with the Hoppe urn scheme, we have that while $Y_1 = 1$ with certainty, $Y_1^* \in \{l_1, \dots, l_g\}$ equiprobably; and when the second label appears in the Hoppe scheme a new label will be extracted from U. The recursive predictive probability is

$$P(Y_{m+1}^* = j|\mathbf{m}) = \begin{cases} \frac{m_j}{\theta+m} \text{ for } m_j > 0 \\ \frac{1}{g-k(\mathbf{m})}\frac{\theta}{\theta+n} \text{ for } m_j = 0 \end{cases} \qquad (24)$$

where $k = \#\{m_j > 0, j = 1, \dots, m\}$. The probability of a sequence is derived by (24) and results

$$P(Y_1^*, \dots, Y_n^*) = \frac{P(Y_1, \dots, Y_n)}{g(g-1)\dots(g-k+1)}$$

Hence a sequence $Y_1, \dots, Y_n$ (that is not exchangeable[a]) is partitioned into $\frac{g!}{(g-k)!}$ exchangeable sequences $Y_1^*, \dots, Y_n^*$.

[a]Equation (22) depends only on $\mathbf{n}$, but this not implies $Y_1, \dots, Y_n$ to be exchangeable. In fact $Y_1 = 1, Y_2 = 2, Y_3 = 1$ and $Y_1 = 1, Y_2 = 1, Y_3 = 2$ are both admissible (equiprobable) with occupation vector $(m_1 = 2, m_2 = 1)$, while the permutated $Y_1 = 2, Y_2 = 1, Y_3 = 1$ is forbidden by construction. This is cleared by the multiplicity factor in $P(S_n = \mathbf{n})$ of equation (23). The fact that (22) is symmetric with regards to n_i, we have that $Y_1 = 1, Y_2 = 2, Y_3 = 1$ and $Y_1 = 1, Y_2 = 2, Y_3 = 2$ are equiprobable, but the number of sequences belonging to $(m_1 = 2, m_2 = 1)$ is greater than the number of sequences belonging to $(m_1 = 1, m_2 = 2)$

The $n-$predictive distribution on the occupation numbers on the g states is

$$P(S_n^* = \mathbf{n}) = \frac{n!}{n_1!\dots n_g!}P(Y_1^*,\dots,Y_n^*) = \frac{(g-k)!}{g!}\frac{n!}{\prod n_j}\frac{\theta^k}{\theta^{[n]}}$$

that is just same that the equilibrium distribution of the label Markov chain (11), that is $\lim_{t\to\infty} P(L_t = \mathbf{n})$

The mean number of clusters k is easily obtained by (21), and results $E(k) = \sum_{i=0}^{n-1} \frac{\theta}{\theta+i}$.

The marginal chain of the label

Each particular existing cluster is driven toward its extinction by (14) and (15). This is not true for its label, that conditioned to $\mathbf{n}$ can rebirth with probability $\frac{1}{g-k}\frac{\theta}{\theta+n-1}$, and hence depends on the rest of the system through $k = \Sigma_{i=1}^n z_i$. The equilibrium probability that the $j-$labelled cluster has size i, i.e. $P(n_j = i)$, is the marginal of (11), and can be calculated by the auxiliary urn process of the label process, provided that $i > 0$.

Now $P(Y_1^* = \dots = Y_i^* = j, Y_{i+1}^* \neq j, \dots, Y_n^* \neq j) = \frac{\theta}{g}\frac{(i-1)!\theta^{[n-i]}}{\theta^{[n]}}$, and due to exchangeability of $\{Y_k^*\}$

$$P(n_j = i) = \frac{n!}{i!(n-i)!}P\{Y_k^*\} = \frac{\theta}{gi}\frac{\theta^{[n-i]}/(n-i)!}{\theta^{[n]}/n!} \tag{25}$$

The probability that the label is found inactive or free, that is $P(n_j = 0)$ is obtained by difference, that is $P(n_j = 0) = 1 - \sum_{i=1}^n P(n_j = i)$

Observing that, due to (29), $\sum_{i=1}^n P(n_j = i) = \frac{E(k)}{g}$, we have

$$P(n_j = 0) = \frac{g - E(k)}{g} \tag{26}$$

that completes (25). The marginal rebirth probability of a label can be calculated by the detailed balance equation

$P(n_j = 0)w(0,1) = P(n_j = 1)w(1,0)$, and the result is

$$w(0,1) = \frac{1}{g - E(k)}\frac{\theta}{\theta + n - 1} \tag{27}$$

The transition probabilities (14) and (27) define a stochastic matrix $p_L = \{p(i,j), i,j = 0,\dots,n\}$ that drives the probabilistic motion of a label. The set of states $\{0,1,\dots,n\}$ is ergodic, and (25) together with (26) is the equilibrium distribution of the label.

Mean values of ESF from the Polya

1) As a simple application, from (20) we get that the probability of a newborn cluster, that is: $P(newborn) = \Sigma_{i=1}^{n} P(\mathbf{z}_i^1|\mathbf{z}) = \sum_i \frac{iz_i}{n}\frac{\theta}{\theta+n-1} = \frac{\theta}{\theta+n-1}$, is independent of the initial state $\mathbf{z}$. The probability of a cluster death is equal to the probability to destroy a cluster of size 1, that is $\sum_{\mathbf{z}} \frac{z_1}{n} P(\mathbf{z})$. For the balance equations, at equilibrium death and birth probabilities are equal, so that $\sum \frac{z_1}{n}\pi(\mathbf{z}) = \frac{\theta}{\theta+n-1}$ or $< z_1 >= \frac{n\theta}{\theta+n-1}$, where $\pi(\mathbf{z})$ is the ESF.

2) For all mean values $E(z_i), i > 1$, we use our finitary approach. Suppose n entities classified into g categories, that are symmetric $\alpha_1 = ... = \alpha_g = \beta$, $\alpha = g\beta$. Let us introduce the indicators

$$1_i(j) = \begin{cases} 1 & \text{if } n_j = i \\ 0 & \text{if } n_j \neq i. \end{cases} \quad j = 1, ..., g.$$

In words the i-indicator of a category is one if the category contains exactly i entities. The number of clusters of size i is then $z_i = \sum_{j=1}^{g} 1_i(j)$ and $E(z_i) = \sum_{j=1}^{g} P(n_j = i)$.

The equilibrium distribution is the symmetric $Polya(n;\alpha)$, all marginals are equal, and

$$P(n_j = i) = \binom{n}{i} \frac{\beta^{[i]}(g\beta - \beta)^{[n-i]}}{(g\beta)^{[n]}}.$$

Hence

$$E(z_i) = g\binom{n}{i} \frac{\beta^{[i]}(g\beta - \beta)^{[n-i]}}{(g\beta)^{[n]}}.$$

In the "Ewens limit" $\beta \to 0$, $g \to \infty$, $g\beta \to \theta$

$$\frac{\beta^{[i]}(\theta - \beta)^{[n-i]}}{\theta^{[n]}} \simeq \frac{\beta(i-1)!\theta^{[n-i]}}{\theta^{[n]}}$$

and

$$E(z_i) = \frac{\theta}{i}\frac{n!}{(n-i)!}\frac{\theta^{[n-i]}}{\theta^{[n]}}. \tag{28}$$

3) As regards to second moments:

$$z_i^2 = \sum_{j=1}^{g} 1_i(j) \sum_{k=1}^{g} 1_i(k) = \sum_{j=1}^{g} 1_i(j) + \sum_{j\neq k}^{1,g} 1_i(j)1_i(k),$$

$$E(z_i^2) = E(z_i) + \sum_{j\neq k}^{1,g} P(n_j = i, n_k = i) = E(z_i) + g(g-1)P(n_j = i, n_k = i)$$

for i integer $\leq \frac{n}{2}$. Otherwise the second term is null.

$P(n_j = i, n_k = i)$ is $Polya(n; \beta, \beta, (g-2)\beta)$, and in the Ewens limit

$$E\left(z_i^2\right) = \begin{cases} E\left(z_i\right) + \left(\frac{\theta}{i}\right)^2 \frac{n!}{(n-2i)!} \frac{\theta^{[n-2i]}}{\theta^{[n]}} & \text{if } i \text{ integer} \leq \frac{n}{2} \\ E\left(z_i\right) & \text{otherwise.} \end{cases}$$

In the same way

$$E\left(z_i z_j\right) = \frac{\theta^2}{ij} \frac{n!}{(n-i-j)!} \frac{\theta^{[n-i-j]}}{\theta^{[n]}} \qquad i+j \leq n$$

The usual derivation of these formulas is fairly complicated[23].

4) As for the frequency spectrum: for $n >> \theta$ we have $\frac{\theta^{[n]}}{n!} \approx \frac{n^{\theta-1}}{(\theta-1)!}$,then $E\left(z_i\right) \approx \frac{\theta}{i}\left(1-\frac{i}{n}\right)^{\theta-1}$, $E\left(z_i^2\right) \approx E\left(z_i\right) + \left(\frac{\theta}{i}\right)^2\left(1-\frac{2i}{n}\right)^{\theta-1}$, $E\left(z_i z_j\right) \approx \frac{\theta^2}{ij}\left(1-\frac{i+j}{n}\right)^{\theta-1}$ and so on.

In the continuum limit $n \to \infty$, introducing the fraction $x = \frac{i}{n}$, the density for $E\left(z_x\right)$ is $E\left(z_x\right) = \frac{\theta}{x}\left(1-x\right)^{\theta-1}$, the frequency spectrum. The meaning of $\frac{\theta}{x}\left(1-x\right)^{\theta-1} dx$ is the mean fraction of clusters whose fractional size is from x to $x+dx$, while $\theta\left(1-x\right)^{\theta-1} dx$ is the mean fraction of the mass that is allocated in clusters whose fractional size is from x to $x+dx$.

5) the simplest distribution is obtained for $\theta = 1$. In this case $E\left(z_i\right) = \frac{1}{i}$, $E\left(iz_i\right) = 1$: different sizes are visited proportionally to $\frac{1}{i}$, and the mass is uniformly distributed on all sizes (on average).

Mean values of ESF from the L- Process

Suppose n entities classified into $g > n$ categories. Let us introduce the indicators

$$1_i(j) = \begin{cases} 1 & \text{if } n_j = i \\ 0 & \text{if } n_j \neq i. \end{cases} \quad j = 1, ..., g.$$

In words the i-indicator of a category is one iff the category contains exactly i entities. The number of clusters of size i is then $z_i = \sum_{j=1}^{g} 1_i(j)$ and

$$E\left(z_i\right) = \sum_{j=1}^{g} P(n_j = i) = gP(n_j = i) \tag{29}$$

due to the equidistribution of the g categories.

$P(n_j = i)$ is the marginal of (11), and can be calculated by the auxiliary urn process of the label process.

Now $P(Y_1^* = \ldots = Y_i^* = j, Y_{i+1}^* \neq j, \ldots, Y_n^* \neq j) = \frac{\theta}{g} \frac{(i-1)!\theta^{[n-i]}}{\theta^{[n]}}$, and due to exchangeability of $\{Y_k^*\}$

$$P(n_j = i) = \frac{n!}{i!(n-i)!} P\{Y_k^*\} = \frac{\theta}{gi} \frac{\theta^{[n-i]}/(n-i)!}{\theta^{[n]}/n!} \tag{30}$$

where from (28) follows. As regards to second moments the demonstration is similar, considering that, denoting by R a sequence of $n - i - j$ values different from both a and b,

$$P(Y_1^* = \ldots = Y_i^* = a, Y_{i+1}^* = b, \ldots, Y_{i+j}^* = b, R) =$$

$$= \frac{\theta^2}{g(g-1)} \frac{(i-1)!(j-1)!\theta^{[n-i-j]}}{\theta^{[n]}}$$

Comparison with Kelly's method

Kelly's method, with the substitution of transition rates with transition probabilities, is the following

$$P_K(\mathbf{n}_i^j|\mathbf{n}) = \frac{n_i}{n} \frac{n_j(1-u) + (n - n_j - 1)\frac{1}{g-1}}{n-1}, \tag{31}$$

where i is the type where the death occurs, j is the type where the birth occurs, u is the mutation probability and g are the possible type of alleles. It is understood that any living entity has the same probability to die and to generate, and that mutations are equiprobable on all categories. (31) looks different from our fundamental (2). In facts introducing

$$\alpha_i = \frac{(n-1)u}{g(1-u) - 1}, \tag{32}$$

and $\alpha = \frac{g(n-1)u}{g(1-u)-1}$, we find that $P_K(\mathbf{n}_i^j|\mathbf{n}) = \frac{n_i}{n} \frac{\alpha_j + n_j}{\alpha + n - 1}$, that is the two formulations appear identical. In facts Kelly's equilibrium distribution is just $Polya(n, \boldsymbol{\alpha})$, though not explicitly recognized. Ewens limit $g \to \infty$ is performed on $P(\mathbf{z}) = \frac{g!}{z_0! z_1! \ldots z_n!} Polya(n, \boldsymbol{\alpha})$. The combinatorial factor is correct due to the equiprobability of all occupation numbers with the same abundances (they are exchangeable with respect both to times and categories). Hence all contents of the quoted chapter are deducible in our frame, when n, g and α,(or u) are fixed.

But there is a fundamental question hidden in (32): in our treatise n, α_i and g are independent parameters, while in this application the free parameters are n, g and u, hence α_i depends on n, g and u. In the Ewens limit $\alpha = \theta = \frac{(n-1)u}{1-u}$, or $u = \frac{\theta}{\theta+n-1}$, that is just the probability of a newborn mutant. At the end of the story, if one supposes that the mutation probability is an individual parameter independent of the population size, the previous model of "herding" or "pioneering" must be considered with much care. When all parameters are fixed, a mutant can be seen as a "pioneer", but when the population size is changed θ must change too, if we want that u is constant.

A similar question arises when comparing our treatise[17] to that of Kirman about the behavior of ants. In this case posing the "pioneer" weight equal to θ and the "herding" weight equal to $n-1$ appears more satisfactory than Kirman's original one[20], that is the same of Kelly for Genetics.

References

1. Ewens W. J. (1972) "The sampling theory of selectively neutral alleles" *Theoretical Population Biology* **3** 87-112.
2. Ewens W. J., Tavarè S. (1997) "The Ewens Multivariate Distribution", in *Multivariate Discrete Distributions,* Johnson N. L., S. Kotz, and N. Balakrishnam Eds., Wiley New York.
3. Aoki M. (1996) *New Approaches to Macroeconomic Modeling: Evolutionary Stochastic Dynamics, Multiple Equilibria, and Externalities as Field Effects,* Cambridge University Press, New York.
4. Aoki M. (2000) "Cluster Size Distributions of Economic Agents of Many Types in a Market", *Journal of Mathematical Analysis and Applications* **249**, 32-52.
5. Aoki M. (2002) *Modeling Aggregate Behavior and Fluctuations in Economics,* Cambridge University Press, Cambridge, UK.
6. Antoniak CE. (1974) "Mixtures of Dirichlet processes with applications to bayesian nonparametric problems", *The Annals of Statistics* Vol.2 **6**, 1552-1174.
7. Kingman J. F. C. (1978) 'The representation of partition structures', *Journal London Mathematical Society* **18** 374-380.
8. Blackwell D. and MacQueen, J.B. (1973) "Ferguson distribution via Polya urn scheme", *The Annals of Statistics,* Vol.1, 353-355.
9. Donelly P. (1986) "Partition structures, Polya urns, the Ewens Sampling Formula, and the ages of alleles", *Theor. Popul. Biol.* **30**, 271-288.
10. Hoppe F.M. (1987) "The sampling theory of neutral alleles and an urn model in population genetics", *J. Math. Biol.* **25**(2), 123-159.
11. Hansen B. and Pitman J. (2000) "Prediction rules for exchangeable sequences related to species sampling", *Statistics and Probability Letters* **46**, 251-256.
12. Johnson W. E. (1932) *Probability: The Relations of Proposal to Supposal; Probability: Axioms; Probability: The Deductive and the Inductive Problems* Mind 41, 1-16, 281-296, 409-423.
13. Zabell S. (1992) "Predicting the unpredicatable" *Synthese* **90**, 205-232.

14. Costantini D. and Garibaldi U. (1997) "A probabilistic foundation of elementary particle statistics. Part I", *Stud. Hist. Phil. Phys.* **28,** 483-506.
15. Costantini D. and Garibaldi U. (1998) "A probabilistic foundation of elementary particle statistics. Part II", *Stud. Hist. Phil. Phys.* **29,** 37-59.
16. Costantini D. and Garibaldi U. (2000) "A purely probabilistic representation for the dynamics of a gas of particles", *Found. of Phys.* **30**, 81-99.
17. Garibaldi U., Penco M.A. and Viarengo P. (2003) "An exact physical approach for market participation models", Cowan,R. and Jonard, N. Eds, "Heterogeneous agents, Interactions and Economic Performance", Lecture Notes in Economics and Mathematical Systems, Volume 521, Springer.
18. Penrose O. (1970) *Foundations of Statistical Mechanics*, Pergamon Press, Oxford, pages 72-75.
19. Sinai Y.G. (1992) *Probability Theory. An introductory Course.* Springer-Verlag Berlin Heidlberg.
20. Kirman A. (1993) "Ants, Rationality and Recruitment", *The Quarterly Journal of Economics*, **108**, 137-156.
21. Costantini D. and Garibaldi U. (2004) "The Ehrenfest fleas: from model to theory", to appear in *Synthese,* April 2004 issue (139,1).
22. Kelly F.P. (1979) *Reversibility and Stochastic Networks*, John Wiley&Sons.
23. Watterson G. A. (1976) "The stationary distribution of the infinitely-many neutral alleles diffusion model", *J. Appl. Prob.*, **13**, 639-651.

Conclusions

OPEN PROBLEMS IN USING AGENT-BASED MODELS IN INDUSTRIAL AND LABOUR DYNAMICS

NIGEL GILBERT

CRESS, Department of Sociology, School of Human Sciences, University of Surrey, Guildford, Surrey, GU2 7XH United Kingdom
n.gilbert@soc.surrey.ac.uk

The preceding papers have shown the impressive versatility and potential of agent-based modelling in developing an understanding of industrial and labour dynamics. The main attraction of agent-based models is that the actors - firms, workers, and networks - which are the objects of study in the 'real world', can be represented directly in the model. This one-to-one correspondence between model agents and economic actors provides greater clarity and more opportunities for analysis than many alternative modelling approaches. However, the advantages of agent-based modelling have to be tempered by disadvantages and as yet unsolved methodological problems. In this brief summary drawn from the discussion at the closing session of WILD@ACE, I review three of these open problems in the context of the papers presented at the conference: How can agent-based models be empirically validated? What criteria should be used to evaluate the explanatory success of agent-based models? And how can the conclusions of research on similar topics be integrated?

1. Can agent-based models be empirically validated?

Agent-based simulations are typically used to model complex social and economic phenomena. This implies that the behaviours of individual agents and, in particular, their interactions, give rise to emergent macro-level patterns. For example, Tesfatsion (this volume) shows that a model of workers' and employers' individual behaviours yielded relatively simple relationships between levels of unemployment and wage rates. It is such macro-level patterns (sometimes called 'stylised facts' by economists) which are usually of primary interest. However, the same macro level patterns can often be generated by a number of different micro-level behaviours. This means that to validate a model completely, it is necessary to confirm that both the macro-level relationships are as expected *and* that the micro-level behaviours are adequate representations of the actors' activity. Often, the mere reproduction of expected macro-level patterns leads modellers to conclude that their model is correct, not realising that many other models could give rise to the same patterns [3]. Although it is necessary to validate at both micro and macro levels, neither is easy.

Macro-level validation is difficult because frequently the patterns of emergent behaviour are power-law, rather than normally distributed (for example, Gallegati *et al.*, this volume). Most simple statistical methods assume a normal distribution and, in particular, a distribution with a constant mean and variance. Power law distributions do not have an asymptopically constant mean and variance, and their moments can be infinite, which means that conventional approaches to random sampling and regression modelling may give misleading results [1]. This in turn means that it is difficult to arrive at meaningful values for the statistical significance of differences between measurements of the actual economy and the results of experiments with the model.

At the micro-level, there are also difficult validation problems to be faced. Agents will often be programmed to have specific goals and motivations. While the researcher may be able to argue that these are plausible, i.e. they have face validity, any stronger corroboration may be impossible to obtain. Does one rely on asking people to verbalise their goals? If so, will they tend to conceal the less reputable ones? Will they even have a conscious knowledge of their goals? What is the effect of asking people about their motivation? The process of seeking information about an individual's goals can bring them to the fore and make them more salient than they would otherwise have been (a problem that sociologists call "reactivity"). In contrast to measuring goals and beliefs, behaviour can usually be observed reliably, but provides little insight into cognitive states.

In some cases, such as financial market trades, the problem is how to deal with the massive volume of data that is collected automatically as a side effect of the activity (e.g. [2]), rather than with its scarcity. However, data from natural settings is created in contexts that are usually either not observable at all, or are too complex to record and analyse. For instance, studies of organisations (e.g. Dal Forno and Merlone in this volume) ideally need to examine detailed data on organisational operations, both "formal" and informal, but mostly have to make do with the official organisation charts and rulebooks.

One approach that economists are beginning to use more frequently to gather data on individuals' behaviour is experimentation, in which subjects are required to play a carefully designed "game" in a laboratory setting. The advantage is that the context can be precisely controlled and the subjects' actions can be directly monitored. A corresponding disadvantage is that the context is inevitably artificial and it needs a leap of faith to believe that the actions of subjects in the laboratory given an artificial and simplified task tell us much about what those people would do in a real world situation.

Another, quite different data problem that agent-based simulation raises comes from its focus on dynamics. While the fact that agent-based models provide the opportunity to study and experiment on social processes is one of the approach's principal strengths, validating such models does require temporally-based data. If, for example, one wants to model the evolution of industrial sectors and then compare the output from the model with empirical data, a historical series is obviously required. However, such data are often very hard or impossible to obtain. We have good long-term historical data only for the grossest of macro indicators, and even these are subject to errors and the effects of changing definitions and methods of measurements. In short, while all modellers would ideally like to validate their model to the fullest extent, it is not surprising, given this list of problems, that not all of the work reported in this issue lives up to the ideal.

2. What criteria should be used to validate models?

Models are most often judged by their correspondence to observed data, but as we have noted, obtaining adequate data to make a reliable judgement about the adequacy of a model is often hard. There are, however, other criteria that are at least as important as a model's empirical "fit" to sometimes dubious data. One is that the model is useful, either for increasing our theoretical understanding of some phenomenon, or because it allows experimentation with policy changes, or both. In some ways, a model is like a map (indeed, maps are models, but that is another story). A map can be a useful guide to show us how to get home, or like the sixteenth century maps of America, can alter our understanding of the world. The map analogy is also helpful in answering the question often posed about how much detail there should be in a model. Often, there is a temptation to build very complicated models, involving many parameters, because these have the potential to be better facsimiles of the social world. But models, like maps, should be as detailed as they need be, no more or less. Just as a large scale map that shows every house is not much use for crossing a city, so a finely detailed model of an industrial district is not the right tool to help to understand the growth of industrial sectors. A second important criterion is that the model tells us something new. Admittedly, it is an achievement to build a model that does represent a good part of what we already know about some phenomenon, but more is desirable. Surely, the ultimate goal of modelling is to gain some new understanding, or, even more precious, to find a previously unsuspected relationship or connection. But in order to see what are the new insights stemming from a model, we need to relate it to other work in the field, and that brings us to the third open problem.

3. How can the conclusions of research on similar topics be integrated?

Science (and social science) works by the gradual accumulation of knowledge, each small stone eventually building a mighty wall. Every new piece of work needs to be related to previous work, both so that its own contribution can be identified, and also as a means of quality assurance - if the latest result is at variance with the current orthodoxy, there is probably a mistake in the new results (or it is time for a paradigm change!). This view of science as gradual accumulation has two methodological implications for modellers. First, it is important that the contribution that is being made should be coherent with existing work that uses more conventional methods. To return to the map analogy, if all the other maps use the Mercator projection, a map drawn using another projection will be, at best, difficult to join to its neighbours. What exactly 'coherent with' means will vary from research area to area. At the very least, researchers need to make some effort to link their work with other, more conventional approaches. This is particularly true of the research described in this volume, which is using new and unfamiliar methods to understand problems that are important but often at a tangent to the concerns of traditional industrial and labour economics. Second, the contribution needs to relate clearly to other agent-based models. This volume is an excellent illustration of the present vigour of agent-based computational economics. It includes many examples of studies of, for instance, innovation and labour markets, and others are to be found in the literature. Yet, it is quite hard to see how these various studies relate to each other and the extent to which they give consistent answers to basic economic questions. There is still a major job of synthesis to be done and it is not yet clear quite how best to do it.

Despite these problems and difficulties, the papers in this issue are evidence of a thriving and growing field that is contributing substantially to our understanding of industry and labour dynamics, using and refining methods that are quite new, but clearly powerful and productive. There are still challenges ahead to demonstrate that our models are empirically valid, valuable in both theoretical and policy contexts and able to be integrated with other studies, but nothing in social science is easy.

References

1. E. F. Fama. Mandelbrot and the stable paretian hypothesis. *The Journal of Business*, 36:420–429, 1963.
2. J. D. Farmer, P. Patelli, and I. Zovko. The predictive power of zero intelligence models in financial markets. Technical report, Los Alamos National Laboratory Condensed Matter archive, 2003.
3. N. Gilbert. Varieties of emergence. In D. Sallach, editor, *Agent 2002 Conference: Social agents: ecology, exchange, and evolution*, Chicago, 2002. University of Chicago and Argonne National Laboratory.

